HE MOON "

the
autobiography
of

Quincy Jones

DOUBLEDAY

NEW YORK   LONDON   TORONTO

SYDNEY   AUCKLAND

PUBLISHED BY DOUBLEDAY
a division of Random House, Inc.
1540 Broadway, New York, New York 10036

DOUBLEDAY and the portrayal of an anchor with a dolphin
are trademarks of Doubleday, a division of Random House, Inc.

BOOK DESIGN BY MARIA CARELLA

Library of Congress Cataloging-in-Publication Data
Jones, Quincy, 1933–
Q : the autobiography of Quincy Jones / Quincy Jones.—1st ed.
p.   cm.
Includes discography, filmography, and index.
1. Jones, Quincy, 1933–   . 2. Jazz musicians—United
States—Biography.   I. Title.
ML419.J7 A3 2001
781.64'092—dc21   2001028151

Photo credits appear on pages 411–12

Printed in the United States of America

October 2001
First Edition
1   3   5   7   9   10   8   6   4   2

To the memories of my beloved
mother and father, Sarah and Quincy, Sr.,
and of my cherished brothers
Lloyd and Waymond.

Contents

Q

the autobiography of

Quincy Jones

CHAPTER 1

The promise

I remember the cold. It was a stinging, backbreaking, bone-chilling Kentucky-winter cold, the kind of cold that makes you feel like you're freezing from the inside out, the kind of cold that makes you feel like you'll never be warm again. I had no music in me then, just sounds, the shrill noise the back door made when it creaked open, the funny grunts my little brother Lloyd made while we slept together, the tight, muffled squeals the rats made when the rat traps snapped them in half. My grandmother did not believe in wasting anything. She had nothing to waste. She cooked whatever she could get her hands on. Mustard greens, okra, possum, chickens, and rats, and me and Lloyd ate them all. We ate the fried rats because we were nine and seven years old and we did what we were told. We ate them because my grandma could cook them well. But most of all, we ate them because that's all there was to eat.

My mother had gone away sick one day and she never came back. That's all we knew. That's all my father told us. "She's gone away sick and she'll be back soon," was what he said, but "soon" turned into months and

QUINCY JONES

2

years, so the two of us had left Chicago and gone to Louisville to stay with Grandma. Laying in bed at night in my grandma's house, I could remember the night before my mother left us. We were downstairs in the living room back home in South Side Chicago during the Depression, Lloyd and Daddy and me, and we heard a crash and the noise of a window breaking, and we ran upstairs and I felt the rush of cold air and saw my mother at the broken window looking out into the street. She was wearing only a housedress, standing in the freezing nighttime air, the snow blowing in on her face, and she was singing, *"Ohh, ohh, ohh, ohh—oh, somebody touched me and it must have been the hand of the Lord."*

As a young boy, I thought it was odd for my mother to sing out the window. She played piano and sang in church, but my mother was a private woman, solid and proper. She never spoke out of turn like that. She did not like loud things or loud people, but her behavior had become more and more strange. She had frequent fainting spells. She would yell at us for no reason. She quoted the Bible and scribbled notes endlessly. The lines around her eyes seemed to grow tighter and tighter every day. Her angry outbursts were crushing affairs, sometimes lasting for days.

My daddy never knew what to do when my mother had spells like this. He was not a complicated man. He was a carpenter for the Jones Boys, the black gangsters who ran the ghetto back in Chicago—the policy rackets, the Jones five-and-dime stores—the V and X, as they were known in the 'hood. When my Aunt Mabel asked him once why he worked for hoods and hustlers, he made a funny face and said, "Gangsters need carpenters too. They're no worse than the gangsters who won't give me jobs." He grew up in Lake City, South Carolina, so I was told, but to be honest I never knew exactly where he was really from. I'd heard his father was a white man—either Irish or Welsh—who had killed somebody, and Daddy had to get out of the South because of this, which made as much sense as anything else in my life, because since my mother left us, nothing seemed solid except the black space in my stomach. Daddy was a quiet man, with smooth straight hair, soft brown eyes, and firm face. His shoulders were broad, his arms were thick and muscled, and his hands were gigantic, huge iron fists with fingers as thick as cigars. He'd been a catcher with the Metropolitan Baptist Church team in the Negro Leagues—he even caught the great Satchel Paige once—and all those years of catching baseballs with a thin mitt had smashed his fingers and made them flat and crooked. He could bend the first knuckle of each hand and hold them out like claws. His fingers were so strong that he could make a circle with his forefinger and thumb and pop you upside the head so hard it felt like a bullet smashing through your skin. My brother and I called that "the Thump Bump," and when he thumped you, it stung for hours.

He tried to talk to my mother as she stood by the window singing. He said, "Get ahold of yourself, Sarah," but she ignored him and kept singing, so he turned away and went downstairs. As he swept past me I heard him mutter something, so I ran to my mother and told her what he said: "Daddy's gonna send you away," I said, but she didn't hear me. She stood with her back to me, staring out the window, and the next morning my daddy came back upstairs with two ambulance attendants in white and one of them said, "Mrs. Jones, you wanna come get your luggage and things?"

She looked over at him without a word, so he said, "Either you come or we'll carry you."

She said, "Can I take my Bible?"

He said, "You can take it."

She slowly picked up her Bible, then suddenly darted for the door to escape, but the two men grabbed her and threw her down on the bed, spread-eagled. She kicked and screamed as they threw a straitjacket on her and carried her out. We followed her downstairs and sat on the steps. Lucy Jackson held Lloyd on her lap and covered his eyes with her hands. I sat next to them, crying, and covered my eyes too, singing the same song, *"Ohh, ohh, ohh, ohh—oh, somebody touched me and it must have been the hand of the*

Lord." And just like that she was gone—for days, weeks, months, who knows how long. Soon after, my daddy packed us up and the three of us headed to St. Louis to stay with relatives, then back to Chicago, then back to St. Louis again, till Daddy finally gave up and took us to Louisville to stay with his mother. Then he left.

We didn't hate it in Louisville. We didn't like it either. My grandma's house was a shotgun shack near the Ohio River with no electricity. We drew our water from a well in her backyard. We got our heat from a black potbellied coal stove. We used kerosene lamps and bathed in a big tin washtub. We slept in the kitchen on a cot next to the back door, which was held closed with a rusty bent nail. When the door was closed in the day-time, you could see daylight all around the doorframe. At night we slept with socks on our hands and feet so the rats wouldn't nibble our fingers and toes. In the wintertime, the floor was frozen and wet in the morning. In summer, it was like fire and the smell of old pee stung my nostrils con-stantly. Breakfast was grits, lunch was nonexistent, and dinner was what-ever my grandmother could find that would fry. The teachers at the Samuel T. Coleridge Colored School wanted to make examples of us as strangers and would march Lloyd and me to the back of the classroom every morning and make us take our shoes off and scrub the dirt off our feet and faces with commercial Lifebuoy soap while the other kids cack-led. We had no hot water for washing. They seemed to have no idea who we were. My grandmother didn't understand the 1940 Jefferson County school system either, only the notion that we had to go there. Grandma was a proud, strong woman, a former slave; she was thin, rangy, coal-black, wise, and old. She had African beliefs, like hanging asafedita, a hor-rid-smelling gumlike bark-and-garlic concoction, on a string around our necks to ward off colds, fever, and bad spirits. She led us to the Baptist church every Sunday and spoke in a tongue that me and Lloyd could barely understand. She had been born a slave and used African words we never heard of, like "mwena" for "kids." She'd say, "Mwena, come over here and lift this tub," or "Mwena, go down yonder to the river and catch me some rats." She told us that the more the rats wiggle their tails, the better they'd taste, so we'd wait by the river, snatch up the biggest ones we could find by the tail, and stuff them in a burlap sack. We were free to roam in Kentucky, that part we liked, but at night it was cold and lonely in that dark shotgun shack and it was too much for me, because I wanted my parents. I was mad at them both, but more mad at my daddy, because he was the one who kept it together. Daddy was the one who was solid. Daddy was the one who said we'd always be together. My brother Lloyd, 16½ months younger than me, would cry at night for his daddy, and one night as we lay in bed, he asked, "Did Daddy go away 'cause he's mad at us?"

"Stop whining," I said. "He'll be back." I had a faint recollection of Daddy promising to come back, but I wasn't sure. He'd been gone a long time. We'd been there a year. Nothing seemed certain.

"I didn't hear him sayin' nothin' about coming back," Lloyd said.

"He'll be back," I said.

"Well, if he's coming back, he oughta come on then."

"Who needs him anyway?" I said. "Stop cryin' like a kindygarden baby." But deep inside I was scared and nervous, and each night I fell asleep with my teeth chattering from cold and my heart buried someplace near my feet, until that winter night in 1941 when I heard the back door creak open and I saw a huge shadow blocking the entrance, the breath coming from his mouth in clouds as he moved inside, lit a kerosene lamp, which Grandma called coal oil, and sat down, sighing. My fear and anger dissipated like water as me and Lloyd scrambled out of the bed and landed in his lap.

"You promise me you won't go away and leave us no more," I sobbed. "Promise."

"I promise," my daddy said. And he kept his word.

CHAPTER 2

Little Lucy

Lucy Jackson, childhood friend

God is in this house. In these
walls, in these halls, in the
light fixtures, everywhere.
That's why I'm never lonely. I'm seventy-three years old and I been in this
bed fourteen months, but I got friends who come look in on me, my son
lives here, my Bible stays open, my wig still fits, and Sixth Grace Presby-
terian Church still thinks I'm the organist—I only been playing there
twenty years—so I'm doing perfect. Only thing is, my legs are bad from
when I was little, running around playing baseball and chasing after
Quincy and his brother Lloyd.

  The first time I met Quincy was on the South Side of Chicago
around 1939. He was a tiny boy then and I didn't pay him too much mind.
How I first got to know him was, I was standing at the back door of my
house and saw him running down the alley behind my house holding a
watermelon almost as big as he was that they'd stolen off Mr. Winningham's watermelon cart, him and Lloyd and some other boys. No need to

lie. That boy was stealing and if it wasn't for his ma and pa he'd be running policy now or living in the boneyard. He was a skinny little something, all head and teeth, and I didn't see him good, just the back of his head, but I recognized those skinny bowlegs and knickers. I lived at 3633 Prairie Avenue. He lived next door at 3631 Prairie. There was no mistaking who it was.

I saw them cut into the vacant lot next door to Mrs. Goldsmith's house at 3617 Prairie, so I came out my front door and went into the lot the front way. That lot was my territory. That was my baseball field, and I didn't want Mr. Winningham coming over there telling my mother that someone from my ball field had stolen his melon. I would do anything for baseball back then. I was the best baseball player on Prairie Avenue. If they had let colored women play in the Negro Leagues you would've seen my name there in bright lights: Little Lucy Jackson. They called me Little Lucy 'cause I was so tall. I was the tallest kid on Prairie Avenue on the Chicago South Side and the biggest tomboy you ever saw.

The boys had gathered near the back of the lot toward the alley, and when they saw me marching at 'em they said, "Lucy's coming! Lucy's coming!" and they backed off. They kind of parted and there was Quincy in the middle, crouched over this half-eaten watermelon.

I got right up on him and said, "Quincy, this is my ball field here and you got to get Mr. Winningham's watermelon off it." I was tall and he was looking up at me. He had a mouth full of watermelon. Then I threw in there, "I oughta tell on you."

He damn near choked to death when I said I was gonna tell. He blinked and twitched and finally held out a piece of melon and said, "You want some?"

Well, those were the magic words and we put a hurtin' on that melon. Since he lived right next door, we became like brother and sister, me, him, and Lloyd. We did everything together, went to school, ate, fought, played baseball. I don't think Quincy liked baseball too much. He liked to cause foolishness, him and Lloyd, playing the dozens, marbles, and a game called Root the Peg played with an ice pick, and running around after the gangs. There was a bunch of gangs at that time, the Scorpions, the Vagabonds, the Giles A.C. gang—the members were called Dukes and Duchesses, senior and junior. Not a soul on the block got left out. One of those gangs caught Lloyd near the back fence of their house once, and when Quincy beat 'em off Lloyd, they pinned Quincy's hand to a tree with a switchblade. But I'd make him play ball when I wanted him to. I'd stick him in the outfield 'cause he was a dreamer. He'd stand out there scratching his head, itching, whistling, hands in his pockets. He had too much on his mind to play the game. Looking back, I think the only reason he played ball with me was because I had the only piano on Prairie Avenue. Our houses were connected, and he heard me playing stride piano through the walls one day and I couldn't keep him off my piano after that, though I tried. He made too much trouble for me. My mother would say, "That boy is seven years old and you're twelve and he marches in here and plays so easy! What am I wastin' my time for?" Even then Quincy had a gift. He didn't know it yet, but music was in his soul. It came natural to him. But I couldn't explain that to my mother. She thought I was practicing too much baseball and not enough piano.

I think he got his music from his mother. She played piano too, but not jazz. Religious music was her style. Sarah Jones was quite a woman before she got sick. She ran the Rosenwald Apartments over on 46th and Michigan Avenue. Back then the Rosenwald was *the* place for the colored in South Side Chicago. It was for the high-and-mighty of the colored race only. There must've been a hundred apartments in that place. Huge places with big bedrooms, stone staircases, a fountain in the plaza, fine wood floors. It would break your heart to see it now. It's like a prison. Metal gates and security guards, all kinds of folks shuffling in and out, it's a mess.

Anyway, his father, Mr. Jones, was the carpenter for the Rosenwald.

He was an excellent carpenter. The railings and ceilings he built in my house on Prairie Avenue you can still see today. But over at the Rosenwald Apartments, his wife ran the show. To get in there you had to deal with her. She was a beautiful woman, Mrs. Jones, I mean physically beautiful, and smart. She went to Boston University. She taught me to type. She could type over a hundred words a minute. She spoke and wrote several languages, she knew stenography, religion, white history, colored folks' history, all kinds of things. She was one of the smartest people I ever met in my life, till she got sick.

I never did understand it, what happened to her, but I was a child then and lots of things went over my head. I heard rumors that she threw Quincy's coconut cake off the porch when he had a birthday party and that she chased some of Elvera Miller's kids around, things like that, but I was a child myself and you never questioned grown-ups. Plus, grown-ups yelled and fought in those days just like they do now, so even though I could stand in my own living room and hear Mrs. Jones yelling through the walls, it didn't seem unusual to me. I remember a neighbor telling my mother, "Mrs. Jones ain't crazy, she's just mean," but my mother said, "No, she's not well, and they're gonna send her away," and sure enough, they sent her to Mantina State Hospital—that's about fifty miles off in Kankakee, Illinois. This was around 1941, I guess, and who knows what went on in there except'n you know that for a colored woman at that time to be in a place like that, well, you know they wasn't servin' 'em pumpkin pie with whip cream every day, I'll tell you that. Be that what it may, that's where she was. Not long after she got sent off, Quincy and Lloyd disappeared to Kentucky and I didn't see them for a long time. They came back for a short time around 1943 and then left again. I remember their daddy was in a hurry that last time. He threw a suitcase and some boxes in the trunk of a car and hustled them into the back seat and they were off. I ran down the street waving goodbye to Quincy and Lloyd when they left. They cried and waved at me through the back window till they were out of sight. I'll never forget that as long as I live. They were the cutest boys you ever saw in your life.

Not long after, there was a knock on my front door and I opened it and Mrs. Jones was standing there. I hardly recognized her. She used to wear beautiful dresses and lovely hats, but now she was wearing a hospital gown and some kind of coat. Her hair wasn't combed, and it was cold outside and I don't remember whether she had shoes on or not. She said, "Have you seen my boys, Lloyd and Quincy?" and I said, "No." Then she asks to see my mother and my mother says, "Come inside," so she comes in and my mother says, "They've moved and they haven't left no address." Then Mrs. Jones says, "You're lyin'!" and my mother says, "No, I'm not lying, Sarah. Mr. Jones didn't tell a soul where they were going." So Mrs. Jones says, "Well, if you see my boys, tell them I'm looking for them," and then she left.

She came back several times after that, dressed oddly, talking strange. She'd wander around the neighborhood sometimes, in the morning, and at night, walking up and down Prairie Avenue, even in the alley behind the house, asking everyone, "Have you seen my boys? Have you seen my boys?" and no one knew where they'd gone. Of course, some people were afraid of her, because they'd heard she'd been in the nuthouse, but I was never afraid of her. She'd come up to me on my baseball field and ask me, "Have you seen my boys?" and I'd say, "No, Mrs. Jones." She'd say, "Don't forget, Little Lucy, if you see my boys, tell them I'm looking for them," and I said I would, but I never saw Quincy and Lloyd after they left that second time. I didn't see them again for forty-seven years.

Lucy Jackson died in May 2000.

CHAPTER 3

You shall have no pie

One Saturday morning after we returned to Chicago from Kentucky, my father woke me up and said, "Get dressed and get your brother up. We're going out."

"Where we gonna go?" I asked. He looked at me for a moment as if trying to decide what to say, then left the room. Daddy didn't believe in wasting breath, not on a ten-year-old. He'd brought us back to our house on Prairie Avenue without explanation and put us back in school, but he was in over his head. There was no one to dress us, cook for us, do our laundry, pick us up from school. Looking back, I see now how overwhelmed he was; his furrowed brow, his fidgety manner, his nervous energy, always smiling as if nothing was wrong, yet slamming the dresser drawers each night as he fished for our socks, grumbling as he went to bed, only to wake up the next morning and find the missing socks in his green toolbox, sandwiched between his saws and chisels. Each evening after work he built us furniture like a madman, rummaging through his toolbox in the living room, yanking out nails, hammers, and his favorite saw—the one he'd had since he was sixteen with his name, Quincy D. Jones, etched on the handle—and creating chairs, tables, beds, but the work didn't calm him. You could see as he sawed and hammered away that something was eating him. My sweet Aunt Mabel, my mother's sister, came by one night and said, "Quincy, let me keep the boys. They need a woman to care for them," and he grunted, "Never. They ain't leaving me no more."

Yet he didn't know how to care for us. Each morning he put on his gray felt cap, grabbed his toolbox, and left for work, leaving two quarters on the table with instructions to eat and go to school and from then on Lloyd and I were on our own. Compared to our lonely life in Kentucky, South Side Chicago was sweet liberty, and we roamed the streets like explorers. Our side of town was called "the Bucket of Blood" because there was always fighting, stabbing, cussing, kicking, and loving going on, and as boys we loved it. We fought. We stole. We ran *with* gangs and *from* gangs, depending on who had the biggest switchblades, the best slingshots—made from clothespins and inner tubes—and the strongest will. Once a rival gang of boys from State Street confronted me, Lloyd, and Little Lucy Jackson on the stairs at Raymond Elementary School and said, "Give us your coats." Little Lucy was so tall, she towered over them. She said, "Come take 'em, you gotta get past me first," and she knocked every one of them down the stairs. We loved her. We joined her baseball team. We pretended to be the Jones Boys, the black gangsters who ran all of black Chicago. If someone robbed a store, if you hurt someone, you had to deal with them. Daddy tried to rein us in by taking us to work with him when he could, but he often worked for the Jones Boys on their suburban homes—he'd work for anyone who paid him—which only brought us closer to the hoods we idolized. He once led Lloyd and me up a big staircase to a room above the Drexel Wine & Liquor Store, not far from our house. Inside, the place was dark and filled with men standing around a table smoking and laughing. Behind the table was a one-way mirror where two guys sat holding tommy guns, watching downstairs and watching the men watching the table. While Daddy talked to a tall, light-skinned man in a suit, Lloyd and I peered through that dark haze of smoke and laughing shadows and saw more money on that table than we'd ever seen in our lives. Piles and piles of dollar bills, tens, and twenties. We came home and fantasized about being the Jones Boys—stabbing the air with our toy knives and later exchanging the fake knives for real ones. Every weekend we watched a legendary black cop named Two-Gun Pete who carried two pearl-handled revolvers shoot black kids in the back in broad daylight, right in front of a Walgreens drugstore—the kids dropped like potato sacks. We fantasized about making Two-Gun Pete pay. The South Side was our own world, an entire universe where the law was nonexistent and white people were a fantasy, a dream, an entity that lived somewhere far away, a land of picket fences and wide lawns that we saw in picture books and only dreamed about. I don't think I ever saw a white person's house until I was eleven and had moved to Bremerton, and by that time I was carrying a knife and doing whatever I thought I had to do to survive. Why not? My world seemed to be senseless, there was no cause and effect. If my mother could go crazy, who couldn't? Anything seemed possible. One morning on the way to Raymond Elementary School, me, Lloyd, and Little Lucy turned the corner of 36th and Prairie and saw a man hanging from an iron rung on a telephone pole with an ice pick plunged into his neck. We stood and watched him a while to see if his blood would drip down, and when it didn't, we headed on to school and told our teacher what we saw. She just yelled, "Wash your hands!" and sent us to class. That typical ghetto aroma of vintage urine that wafted up at us as we walked to school was something we could never wash out, though—it just lingered, like an unwelcome memory.

I knew my mother wouldn't have approved of the way I was behaving, but she was gone, and thinking of her was like peeling back my own skin and poking at the scorched flesh beneath it, so I refused to. For me, Daddy was the only thing that stood between us and the deep blue sea, and he refused to explain the world. He gave orders. He issued announcements. We listened.

So when he told me to get up and wake my brother, I did as I was told. We got dressed and followed Daddy outside to his old struggle-buggy Buick, parked at the curb, and only after we climbed in did he announce, "We're going to see your mama," and, saying nothing else, started the engine.

Fear raced through my insides as the engine roared to life. I loved my mother, but I didn't know who she was and I feared her. I feared the pain she wrought on my soul and hers. I feared the confusion, that feeling that maybe I did something wrong that made her sick, or that maybe Daddy did it, or maybe Lloyd did it, who knew? But as I tried to calm the butterflies that danced inside my stomach, I remembered the dream I had almost every night since she'd gone away two years before: I'd dream I'd be sitting at a piano wearing a powdered white wig and playing classical music, the songs of which seemed to have no notes or melody. As I played, my mother would stand behind me saying, "Don't play for the devil. Play for God. Play for the Holy Ghost. Play for Jesus. Play for the Pope. Make sure, *absolutely sure*, you play for the Pope." It didn't matter that she was a Christian Scientist and that we were raised Baptist. She would exhort me again and again to play for the Pope, and as she did, her voice would suddenly split into two voices, then three, then five, then a hundred, then a thousand voices, angrily dogging me, yelling, coaxing, urging me to play for the Pope. In my dream, I always did the same thing. Lifting my tiny head the size of a green pea from a giant puffy pillow as big as my bed, I'd stand up and shout back at the voices, "Please, stop it! Somebody sing about love. Somebody sing about lovin'. Somebody sing about lovin' me." Then the voices would go silent and my head would fall back down and drown in that huge, overstuffed pillow. It was my own private dream. I could never tell it to anyone.

As Daddy drove down the road, distracted, unaware of me and my brother in the rumble seat, I looked at Lloyd and saw the fear on his face, the confusion, his face a reflection of my own insides, as the reality of where we were going hit him. He said, "Dewey"—he used to call me that 'cause he couldn't pronounce Quincy—"you think they got food where we're going?" and for some reason that made me mad. I loved Lloyd with all my heart. Ever since I can remember, I always felt an obsessive need to protect him, but God knows I gave him a hard time. I said, "Who cares? Look at you, man. Stop being a baby." I razzed him till he finally said, "I ain't talkin' to you no more," and slid over to the other side of the car, sucking his tongue and fingering the stained edges of his blanket, silently watching the treetops spin past as we roared out of the city and down the highway.

We drove for what seemed like hours, and finally arrived at a bunch of white brick buildings surrounded by grass, flowers, and trees. As we walked down the sidewalk and I saw the neatly manicured grass and shrubbery, I thought maybe this wasn't so bad after all. Only when we were inside the two huge wooden double doors did the terrible shock hit. Inside, it seemed cold. There was a smell of Lysol and deck soap in the air, but beneath it was the smell of something else, something putrid, like sheets soiled with urine and sweat. As we followed Daddy down a long hallway, my knees grew weak and I became afraid. There seemed to be slivers of light coming through the high windows, and in the light, shadows moved, and it took me a minute to realize that the shadows were people, in gowns, sprawling about in total disarray everywhere, on the floor, on beds, laying down, on chairs, in wheelchairs, curled into balls. Some were talking, groaning, and laughing hysterically, some were chattering their teeth as if they were cold. They moved like ghosts. We passed one lady in a gray dress who stood on a wooden chair in bare feet pointing at us and laughing. We turned down a couple more hallways into another big room, where a group of people were milling about like walking dead, muttering and making funny noises. They seemed to notice us all at once, and they all stopped and stared. Suddenly and without warning a fat woman with bare feet burst out of the group and ran toward us screaming hysterically, *"You shall have no pie! You shall have no pie!"* She held out her hands. In each hand was a tin plate full of human shit. Daddy backed us away from her and she floated past. The mass of groaning shadows and bodies seemed to part further, and there, standing along the wall with her back to us, was my mother.

She was wearing a hospital gown and tattered slippers, gazing out the high, barred window in silence. Daddy quietly called out, "Sarah," and she turned around and saw us, and for a moment a look of recognition and a smile blew across her face, that beautiful smile I had seen when I was five years old and she combed my hair and washed my face and fixed my knickers. Her hair was uncombed but her face was clean and shiny, as if someone had rubbed fresh oil across it. The smile lasted a moment, then disappeared as anger, then rage settled in on her eyebrows. Her face grew ashen. Inside, I died.

"Say hi to the boys," Daddy said. My mother ignored us. She began to rant at him, quietly at first, then louder. She ranted about a woman he was seeing, about the conspiracy, about Jesus, about the Pope, about whiskey, about Joe Louis and the Germans, and on and on it went as Lloyd and I stood there, too stunned to move. Daddy tried and tried to talk with her but his words seemed to make her angrier. "You took my boys away!" she screamed. "I had a life until your gangster priests dragged me off! I can't sleep here!" On and on it went, as Daddy drew back, confused. "Say hi to your boys," he kept saying. "Say hi to the boys, Sarah." But she refused. She gestured angrily and began to yell louder, almost hysterically, then suddenly she stopped short and froze. Her waving arms grew still, and in what seemed to be a cone of silence, she squatted on her haunches. She placed her hands behind her knees, defecated into one palm, drew the hand out from beneath her, then dipped a finger into her own feces, using it as a fork. She then raised the finger full of shit to her mouth.

It was rare for my father to lose his temper, but when he did, it was no joke. The sound of his muffled cry seemed small compared to the roaring thunder in my own ears as he stepped forward and knocked the feces out of her hand with such force that it spun her around and knocked her to the floor. She got up in fast motion and screamed at him again as he grabbed me and Lloyd by the collar and dragged us out of the room, down the corridors, and out into the hospital parking lot, her high-pitched screams echoing in my ears. When we reached the car, he hurriedly fumbled for his keys, dropped them, then finally stopped to gather himself, panting hard as he leaned on the car fender.

"I'm sorry," he said to me and Lloyd. "I'm sorry I brought y'all here. To see that."

We said it was okay.

"Your mama's not well," he said. "Do you understand that?"

Me and Lloyd said we did.

"Get on in then."

We climbed in the back seat, Daddy started the car, and off we went. As we hit the highway, I opened the window and felt the wind blowing at my face, then I looked over at Lloyd, and he did the strangest thing. He slid over to me, held both his palms out, and whispered, "You shall have no pie," and I started to laugh. And he laughed, and suddenly we couldn't stop laughing. We laughed and laughed, holding each other, the tears rolling down our faces, and what with the wind in our faces and the speed of Daddy's old Buick bouncing down the highway, you couldn't tell whether the tears were from pain or joy, and it was just as well.

His, hers, and theirs

Lloyd Jones, brother

Back in Chicago when I was little, our daddy would go to work and leave us with various babysitters. One was a prostitute who would sit me and Quincy in a room while she disappeared into her bedroom with different men. He got rid of her and found this lady named Mrs. Wolfolk. We used to call her "the Bear Lady." She was your basic country babysitter. She wore slippers with the heels pushed down and had a knot in her stockings just below the knee. She walked around with just a bathrobe on in a drunken haze. She'd say, "Mr. Jones, you have the nicest boys. They're my babies." She'd do that to placate Daddy. Then the moment he left for work, she didn't give a damn. She'd drink and read the newspaper. She used to try to slam a whole teaspoonful of cod-liver oil down my mouth and I was too little and I wouldn't take it. When I wouldn't swallow it, she'd get mad and pull out a torn flyswatter, one of those wire ones with the open metal in it, and whip my ass till it was bloody red. And while she did it Quincy would be trying to kill her, biting her around the ankles to get her off me. He always looked out for me. He had to, because it wasn't like our mother Sarah was around to take care of business. I hardly remember her as a kid. I only remember that whenever she came around, it was trouble.

Daddy never mentioned our mother after he took us to the mental hospital that last time. As far as he was concerned, he was done with Sarah and she was out of the picture. She escaped from there several times—escaped or got out somehow. In the course of one escape she broke thirty windows in the hospital and bloodied her hands badly. Once she came to the back of our house on Prairie Avenue and banged on the back door while the three of us were sitting at the table having dinner. Me and Quincy looked out the window and saw her standing there in a housedress and no shoes, banging on the door with her fist wrapped in a towel. Daddy said, "Go back there and sit down at the table," so me and Quincy sat back down at the table with pounding hearts and listened to the banging until it went away. It was freezing outside too. It was fucked up. The whole thing was bad.

We never knew what to do about it, so after a while you just dropped it, because there was nothing to do. Daddy found out about Mrs. Wolfolk whipping my ass and got us another babysitter through Joe Louis, the boxing champion. They'd become friends when Joe and his wife lived in the Rosenwald Apartments across the hall from us when Quincy and I were toddlers. Joe had a sister-in-law who lived down the street from us on Prairie Avenue and Daddy took us to her. She was real nice to us, but no matter how nice she was, we'd spend the whole day waiting for Daddy to get home. If he got back late, or didn't show up till after dark, man, we were lost. There was nothing worse than that feeling of waiting for him to show up and him not being there. But he never let us down. He always came back.

Daddy was an easygoing man who liked to have fun, and he had a lot of interesting friends in the neighborhood. One was a guy named Yellow. He was a plumber, a light-skinned man who liked to sit on our porch and drink skidoodle with Daddy. He'd say all our favorite bad words as we'd eavesdrop. The other friend was Joe Louis. One day Joe gave Daddy a pair of boxing gloves after one of his fights, and while Daddy was at work one day, Quincy took those gloves and traded them for a BB rifle with a kid who lived down the street named Waymond Miller. When Daddy came home from work I told on him: "Daddy, Dewey's got a pistol." When he learned Quincy had traded his boxing gloves away, he took off his belt and tore Quincy's ass up. Then he marched down the street to Waymond's house to get his gloves back and came back with Waymond's mother, Elvera, instead.

That's how Elvera became our stepmother.

We didn't know who she was at first. She just appeared one day, then disappeared just as quickly. Not long after that, Quincy and I were getting haircuts in the barbershop around the corner from our house on Prairie Avenue when Daddy walked in and said, "Let's go." He loaded us into a car and the next thing I know we were on a Trailways bus to Seattle. Me, Quincy, Daddy, two suitcases, and Daddy's tools in a trunk. Elvera was left behind. We had no idea where we were going, but anywhere with Daddy was an adventure. At one point the bus stopped in Idaho and the white people on the bus went into a restaurant to eat, but they wouldn't serve blacks, so Daddy took me and Quincy to some black people's house near the restaurant and he paid them to feed us. I was eight then and Quincy was ten.

We rode on that bus for what seemed like forever, and finally got to Seattle. When we got off the bus, we took a ferry over to Bremerton, about an hour's ride, and from there we took another bus and got off *that* bus and started walking up a long hill. This hill was about two miles long, and the three of us struggled up it dragging our duffel bags and Daddy's heavy wooden chest with his tools inside. When we got to the top, we saw newly built little wooden houses in the middle of a wooded area. They looked like bungalows. It was wet and muddy and the place was empty except for a couple of bulldozers sitting in the drizzling rain. All around were huge pine trees. We had never seen so many trees before. Behind the bulldozers and trees was a tall fence with barbed wire, and behind the fence was a huge Army base with antiaircraft guns pointing at the sky. You could see the muzzles of all the weapons peeking through the barbed-wire fence and the trees. It was right across a pond of rainwater from our house. That was Sinclair Heights. It was still being built at the time. It seemed like the end of the world.

Daddy took us to a little bungalow at 5453 Linden Place, set our bags down, gave us fifty cents, put on his gray felt cap, and said, "Get something to eat. I got to go to work." Then he grabbed his toolbox and he walked off. When I say walked off, you know that long hill we walked up? Well, he walked down it to catch a bus to his new job in the carpentry shop at the Puget Sound Naval Shipyard.

Quincy and I were all alone in this little house. Inside was a coal stove, running water, no insulation, no phone, no furniture, just a big mud pond out back. No stores, no humans, nothing but that fifty cents.

We played outside a while and we got hungry. We searched our luggage, found nothing, so I went out and picked up a couple of oranges that one of the construction workers had left laying around near the bulldozers. We ate those but were still starving, so Quincy said, "Let's go find a store."

I said, "Heck no, man." It had gotten dark and I was afraid to go outside. It was pitch black out there. There were no streetlights.

Quincy tried to talk me into going, but I wouldn't go, so he left by himself. From the moment his back disappeared out the door, I had every nightmare imaginable. From crowded South Side Chicago to an empty house in the woods in Sinclair Heights, Washington, is a long leap.

It seemed to take him forever, but he finally came back in and pulled out a box of Luden's cough drops. I said, "Cough drops?" We were so hungry those cough drops tasted like mustard greens, sweet potatoes, and fried chicken all at the same time.

After a few days we settled in. Daddy bought us a few things with the little money he had. He built our dining-room table out of one of those big wooden spools used to hold power wire. When you pulled the table-cloth off, you could see the words "Bremerton Power Company" stamped on the table, but we were okay. A few weeks later, Elvera arrived from Chicago with her kids and that changed everything.

Elvera was a light brown buxom woman with thin legs and a large behind. She spoke with an accent and was supposedly from New Orleans or Panama, though I'm damned if I know exactly where she was born or where she was from. She never told anyone. When she beat us, she spoke in broken Spanish, I know that much. She had three children of her own—Waymond, Catherine, and Theresa—and they were close in age to me and Quincy. Whether she loved them or not you have to ask them, but I do know one thing for sure: She didn't give a damn about me and Quincy.

The kids got along all right. Waymond, Quincy, and I slept in a closet off the girls' bedroom on a foldout cot Daddy made from some old wood he'd gotten from the shipyard, and the girls slept in the bedroom on a double bed. We hung our clothes on hooks from the wall. But Elvera divided the kids into three categories: His, Hers, and Theirs. Me and Quincy were "his"—meaning Daddy's—kids. Waymond, Theresa, and Catherine were "her" kids, and Richard, Margie, and Janet, the three who came later, were "their" kids. Even among her own children, Elvera divided them. She treated her light-skinned children differently from her dark-skinned ones. And me and Quincy were completely off her radar screen. If Quincy and I needed a bath, or if we needed clothes, food, anything, we were on our own. If we had a shirt that needed washing, maybe we could throw it into the sink to be washed, or maybe not. The refrigerator was off limits. It was Elvera's refrigerator. You couldn't go in there. You couldn't touch it.

I'm not saying everything that happened in that house was Elvera's fault. She was in over her head. She had to deal with all these kids, she didn't have any money. Daddy was refined, skilled, he was the one with vision, but he worked and left everything up to Elvera, who, for whatever reason, wasn't up to it. Not only that, our mother had terrorized Elvera back in Chicago. During one of the times she was released from the mental hospital, she learned Daddy and Elvera were having an affair and did her best to make Elvera's life miserable. She chased Elvera's daughter Theresa home from school one day and even came into her house and attacked Elvera, who threw her down the stairs. This was in Chicago long before we even got to Bremerton, so Elvera hated Sarah, and she had to look no further than me and Quincy's faces to see Sarah, because we both favor her. She never let us forget who our mother was either. She used to tell us, "Your mother's crazy. If she ever finds out you're here in Seattle, she's gonna come and kill you." That scared the shit out of us. We used to have nightmares about it.

We couldn't go to Daddy about all this. He was up to his neck trying to feed all those kids with that $55 a week plus whatever war bonds the Navy gave him. He depended on me and Quincy. We knew that. He'd say, "Boys, I trust y'all to do the right thing." He was not a complicated man. He was into right and wrong, left and right, no middle ground. If he had been one of those abusive-type fathers, I don't know where we would've ended up, but he was a kind, gentle, old-school dude who hated confrontations, unless you pushed him too far. Provide food, shelter, school, do your best—these were his things. His motto was: "Once a task is just begun, never leave it till it's done. Be the labor great or small, do it well or not at all." Over and over and over again he made me and Quincy memorize this from the time we could walk. Even when we did try to talk to him about Elvera, she would run interference. She'd say, "Jones is asleep now," or "Don't touch that refrigerator. It's got Jones's lunch in it." But I noticed when it was time for her kids to eat, they ate, and when it was time to wash her kids' clothes, they got washed, and when it was time for her kids to get dressed for Catholic church on Sunday, they went. Especially the girls. Me and Quincy—and Waymond too—we were on our own, shining shoes, stealing to eat, shoplifting, whatever we could do to survive.

We were starving, for food, for affection, for love. We didn't know nothing about that. I read once that a child needs twelve hugs a day to be successful in life. Me and Quincy didn't get twelve hugs in twenty years. Quincy's first crush in life was this girl named Sarah Ann. She was a pretty young thing whom all the boys in Bremerton liked, and Quincy was just a raggedy-ass skinny kid with a paper route and no money; but even as a kid, Quincy tried to charm the girls. He talked Sarah Ann into coming by the house to see him one day. He put on his best striped shirt, which he'd washed himself, and he waited for her to come by. When she knocked on the door and asked for Quincy, Elvera was standing in the doorway. She said to Sarah Ann, "Honey, I don't know why you want to see him. That boy still pees the bed." Quincy was standing right behind her when she said it.

It was true that Quincy had done that more than once, but why would she say it? Quincy was eleven years old, and that just killed him. He was so hurt he turned around and walked into the closet where our fold-out bed was. He stayed in the closet all day. He wasn't a violent kid. He was sensitive, he liked to laugh and make people happy, but when he was mad, he was hell to deal with, and that thing with Sarah Ann made him mad. He sat in that closet all day and never said a thing about it, till Elvera took it upon herself to whip him a few weeks later.

I don't know why she whipped him. I'm sure he deserved it. We were always into a million troublesome things and he probably put her over the top, but I'd been whipped by Elvera myself, and getting an ass whipping from her was like getting beat up by a stranger, 'cause she got on top of you and cussed in ghetto Spanish while she tore your ass up, and you knew she didn't give a shit about you even if you couldn't understand what she said. She put that belt to Quincy's ass and he turned around and knocked the shit out of her. She was shocked. She said, "I'll fix you. You just wait till your daddy gets home."

"You can tell him," Quincy said. "Tell him I peed the bed too. But you ain't never gonna whip me again." She never did either.

CHAPTER 5

Jook joint

Lloyd and I were the first kids to arrive in Sinclair Heights. For years we'd been running from and with gangs in Chicago who wouldn't think twice about punching out a stranger, tying a knotted sheet around each ankle, and dragging you face and hands down five blocks from State Street to South Parkway over pulverized glass till your face was ground to pulp. Whiskey and pop bottles that had been thrown in the cobblestone alley were ground down by the steel wheels of wooden wagons whose drivers chanted, "rags and old iron!" The ground glass had an exquisitely torturous texture.

Finally we had graduated to our own turf. Two things you can depend on carrying through life from the 'hood are attitude and antennae. We had the run of the land, and we let everyone who arrived after us know it. We took charge of everything in Sinclair Heights like we saw the gangs do back in Chicago: all the jobs, the territory, the crime—all ours. Bremerton was surrounded by farmland, and the nearby farmers would wake up in the morning to find their apple trees picked, their strawberries stripped and eaten, and chickens missing. Sometimes they'd wait for us with shotguns and fire on us as we helped ourselves to their apples and chickens, but the shots never hit us or scared us away for long.

Lloyd and I had learned to kill chickens from our grandma in Kentucky, and we showed off for our urban-bred new stepbrother Waymond and our "play cousins" Lucian and Earl and Audrey who arrived from New Orleans after us, demonstrating how to first break the neck, then whirl the chicken around until the head was limp. Sinclair Heights was still being built when we moved in. It was meant to be temporary housing for blacks who worked at the nearby shipyard during World War II, and we broke into the construction office and stole the keys to every unoccupied new house. We roasted our stolen chickens in brand-new electric ovens in brand-new houses. We plucked them, washed them, gutted them by pulling the gizzards and innards out, then fried the breasts, thighs, necks, and wings, with not one drop of seasoning. The chickens tasted horrible.

There were no playgrounds, no swing sets, no marbles, no monkey bars: just miles and miles of towering evergreen trees, cougars, and wilderness. We made up our own games. We cut open the bottom lining of the pockets of our knickers to make them flow into the lining of the pants below, then walked into Bremerton stores with legs like toothpicks and walked out with our thighs bulging like football players'. We loaded up on peanut butter, jelly, salami, Twinkies, cinnamon rolls, and soda crackers. We once stole a crate of honey and went into the woods and drank jars and jars of it until we OD'd. It was twenty-five years before I could even look at honey again. I delivered newspapers to the Army base next door, then slipped into the ammo dumps and filled my empty double newspaper bags with ammo belts, gloves, helmets, boots, leggings, and live artillery rounds. We imitated the cool black sailors from the segregated Navy base who marched around with their hats laid to the side, their boots shined, and their pants tight. We stomped around Sinclair Heights with the real Navy and Army stuff, playing war in our own secret territory in the woods, "Camp Victory," dressed like soldiers, carrying stolen .30.06 rifles, 30 mm air-cooled and water-cooled machine guns, with .50 caliber antiaircraft ammunition in our pockets. We hid dozens of belts of live ammo in the coal bin behind our house. We stole a fully loaded 2-inch artillery round and hid that in the coal bin too. It's a huge shell meant to be shot from a battleship cannon. It's about four feet long, packed with gunpowder and coated with a metal jacket. The Army base was missing so much ammo they sent a second lieutenant over to Sinclair Heights to look around, and when he peered into our coal bin and saw that 2-inch battleship shell, he freaked. He said, "You have enough ammo here to blow up the entire town of Bremerton." They sent some soldiers over to cart our ammo off, and when they asked us about it, we shrugged and tried to look ignorant. After that it was not unusual to see a Bremerton police car cruisin' up to our back door every weekend. The funny part about it was that I served on the student safety patrol, with a flag, a belt, a badge, the works.

None of this seemed wrong to me. It didn't matter. What mattered was survival. I knew my mother was sick, I loved her, but I couldn't handle it. I'd learned early on to tune out and forget about whatever was wrong. To wipe out darkness with light was my process for survival. There was no one to talk to about it anyway other than Lloyd, and he knew better than to bring up our mother's name in Elvera's house. Elvera had no use for Sarah, and vice versa. She couldn't stand her. And I confess I was pretty confused about her myself. It was the only thing in my life that made me angry. I didn't want to hear it wasn't Sarah's fault. I didn't want to know that she'd suffered in the mental hospital. I was suffering myself. We weren't old enough to try to understand her pain instead of our own. Later in my life I learned that my grandfather had been running a brothel in Mississippi back in the day for white owners, who wanted him to put my mother and her sisters in there when they came of age. My grandfather snuck them out and drove them to St. Louis. It may have been a key element in why my mother came to be the way she was.

Every time Elvera looked at my face she saw Sarah, and every time I looked in the mirror I saw Sarah too. I'd wonder, "What difference is there between her and me? What did I do wrong? Why did she leave us?" I could never answer the questions. The only way I could deal was to put as much distance between me and her as possible. Even back in Chicago, Lloyd and I were convinced that Sarah would kill us if she found us, and we had horrible nightmares about it. The fear that the woman who nursed me, loved me, cuddled me, dressed me in clean suits on Sundays, and marched me to all-day Baptist church back in Chicago would one day come to Bremerton to us was paralyzing. I blanked it out.

I wanted to talk to Daddy about it, but this kind of thing was off his radar screen. Back in those times the word "nurture" was not in the vocabulary. He provided a roof, a warm place to eat, and food; the rest was up to you. Besides, for as long as I knew him, he seemed to be in water over his head. Our house constantly teetered on the edge of emotional collapse, with one crisis after another. He had all these kids, everything always seemed to be falling apart in our house, no one seemed to know what was going on, everyone was bent on his own survival, yet he smiled and shrugged and went to work every day as if nothing was wrong. "Boy, do your best and keep your nose clean," he'd say, but the best I could do was get up in the morning, scrub my shirt and socks and underwear in the sink so I'd have something clean to wear to school, and watch him dress for work. I'd get up at five-thirty just to be alone with him. I'd stare at him as he dressed and say to myself, "Does he see? Does he understand what we're going through?" But it was the only chance I had to be alone with him and I didn't want to spoil the moment with idle talk about my lonely feelings. He was like clockwork: grab the shirt, the pants, eat breakfast, plop the gray hat on the head, grab the toolbox, and join the long line of black folks marching down that long hill to the bus stop where the green Navy bus took him to carpentry shop 334 at the Puget Sound Naval Shipyard. I'd walk along with him until I reached the box for my paper route.

At the top of the hill I'd gaze at him till his hat disappeared down the hill and out of sight. It was the loneliest feeling in the world, watching him leave for work.

I'd wander around Sinclair Heights with a gaping hole inside, not knowing whether the hunger was in my stomach or my soul, until one day Lloyd and Waymond pulled me aside and said, "They got food in the rec center."

The rec center in Sinclair Heights was called the Armory, after the base next door. One night a gang of us broke into the soda fountain area and found the freezer where they stored lemon meringue pie and ice cream. We were stuffing ourselves with pie when I broke into a small room next door. There was a tiny stage in the room and on it was an old upright piano. I went up there, paused, stared, and then tinkled on it for a moment.

That's where I began to find peace. I was eleven. I knew this was it for me. Forever.

Each note seemed to fill up another empty space I felt inside. Each tone touched a part of me that nothing else ever touched. Before that moment, every musical grade I got in school was poor. At Navy Yard City Elementary School, Lloyd, Waymond, and I pulled switchblades on white kids who didn't even know what they were. Coming from the ghetto in Chicago, we had never seen white kids before. They made racial remarks and laughed at us. I was in a constant state of befuddlement. But suddenly, on that stage, the world made sense. For the first time in my life, I felt no loneliness, no pain, no fear, but rather joy, relief, and even understanding. To other people I was always smiling, energetic, and happy, but inside I was in pain. I felt different, and never knew why, but from the moment I plinked those notes and laid down those first chords, I finally found something real to trust, and began to learn how to hope and to cope.

Lloyd and the other kids departed for basketball and pie fights but I stayed. The search for just the right piano notes soothed me, healed me, killed my fear, so I went back the next day, alone, and the next day and the next. With each visit, my nervousness was calmed and my fear dissipated. I'd found true love and nurturing. I'd found music. I'd found another mother.

The feeling those notes brought to me was so good I couldn't let go of it. It got to the point where I'd climb through the window of the locked rec hall to play, until the kindly black woman superintendent with well-groomed gray hair and glasses who ran it, sweet Mrs. Ayres, unlocked the door to keep me from having to break in.

While Lloyd, Waymond, and the other kids would march off to basketball, I'd slip inside the rec hall and play songs on the piano for hours. I knew church music from going to Baptist church with my mother and grandmother. I remembered the honky-tonk songs Lucy Jackson played on her piano next door to us in Chicago, and I knew the blues from hearing the scratchy 78s on my grandmother's Victrola as well as at my aunt's house in St. Louis. I played boogie-woogie, church music, songs I remembered such as "Down at the Bad Man's Hall," "The Dirty Dozens," and "Earl Hines' Boogie-Woogie on the St. Louis Blues." When I ran out of the ones I remembered, I tried to make up my own.

I was hooked. Anything that had music in it I suddenly had to be a part of. One afternoon as I wandered past the house of the lone barber in Sinclair Heights, Eddie Lewis, he stepped out onto the front steps of his house in his undershirt holding a trumpet, blasted a few notes, then stepped back inside. I was amazed that he could create all those notes using only three valves. I followed him inside and peppered him with questions. I decided I wanted to play trumpet. But getting one was out of the question. Daddy had no money for that, so I took up violin and clarinet for a minute—these weren't for me. Then it was on to percussion, sousaphone, B flat baritone horn, E flat alto peck horn, French horn, and trombone at Coontz Junior High School—those were the only instruments they had available that I could borrow. I had an ulterior motive for my interest in the trombone: because of the long slide, the trombones marched right up front, behind the foxy majorettes. Later, a kid named Junior Griffin, who played the C melody sax, showed up at the rec hall with his horn. We started jamming, with him on sax and me on piano.

A local music teacher named Joseph Powe, a tall, brown-skinned, elegant man with round rimless glasses who led a Navy swing band that occasionally played at the rec center for black soldiers from the base, noticed my interest. Mr. Powe was the former director of a famous black gospel choir called Wings Over Jordan and he asked me to join in an a cappella singing group called the Challengers. It was an all-boy group—Billy Kincaid, Gus Robinson, Clayton Harrell, and myself. We started to sing in Bremerton on the sidewalk for tips, and even did a concert in Seattle at the Cecil B. Moore Theater, my first gig, singing gospel songs like "The Old Ark's a-Moverin' " and "Dry Bones." Mr. Powe had books by Glenn Miller on arranging, and Frank Skinner's book on film scoring at his house. I asked him if I could babysit just so I could study his scores and arrangements. He agreed. I couldn't get enough: I was in heaven. I don't know how his babies survived it, snot pouring out their noses as I awkwardly changed diapers and absently heated up their milk bottles while I buried myself in Mr. Powe's books, trying to figure out why a B flat trumpet had to play a whole tone above the concert note, and what a G clef was. Daddy saw my interest in music and he encouraged it, but he issued one ultimatum. "Boy, I'll help you as much as I can," he said, "but don't let me catch you down at that jook joint hanging out with any of those low-life jigaboo musicians."

Well, why did he say that?

There were two jook joints in Sinclair Heights, and both were popular. Dick Green's Cafe was the best; he was from New Orleans. We're talkin' "sho nuff country" now. It was in an old wooden structure next door to a storefront, jam-packed with every black preacher, wino, cement mixer, hustler, and worker within twenty miles of Sinclair Heights, not to mention the young black sailors from the segregated naval base downtown who also hung out there. In a dirt-floor basement beneath Dick Green's jook joint a guy named Roscoe, a good brother and a good hustler, ran a dry cleaners.

I crept around the edges of the jook joint every day, listening to the musicians jamming inside, trying to figure out a way to get in and keep my skin at the same time. I thought, Daddy said to keep out of the jook joint, but he didn't say anything about working underneath it. Roscoe hired me, at eleven years old, to dry-clean and steam-press clothes, put them on hangers and in paper bags—there was no plastic back then—make out the bills and deliver them to his customers on my raggedy bike. I also took care of the rooms for the prostitutes who worked for Rick, a mack man and a shore patrol officer. Rick had four or five women who worked in a wooden shack up the street, and my job was to make beds, change sheets, clean the glasses, arrange the wine and whiskey bottles on the shelves, take their clothes to the cleaners, and generally tidy up the rooms. I thought it was odd that the women, some of whom I'd see on Sunday mornings going to church, would sleep all day. Back then I wouldn't know poontang if it came up to me and shook my hand. We were just at the threshold of the "post office," "doctor and nurse," and "hide and go get it" phase. The women were like mothers and were protective of me. They didn't allow cussing or yelling or rudeness. If I was impolite, they'd say, "Keep your narrow little ass outta trouble, and don't be puttin' our bidness in the street." For tidying up their rooms I got fifty cents extra.

After a while I started to shine shoes for the pimps and high rollers who came over from Seattle. They were cool, suave, smart, hard, and always funny. They wore brand-new Stacy Adams shoes with white silk stockings, and with a razor blade they'd cut two slits across the top outside part of the brand-new shoe for a little bunion relief. You had to polish that shoe with an applicator and leave just enough black polish on the tip of the sponge so that when you got to the part where the two slits were, you could gently swab it and not get their socks wet with black polish. First you had to bleach the strings white with Clorox on a toothbrush, though. My technique got so tight with never wetting the socks that the pimps wouldn't let anybody shine their shoes but me.

I made five dollars a week from shoe shining alone, and with my money I'd buy the kind of meals I never got at home: bologna, a sweet roll, a carton of milk. I'd sit underneath the jook joint with a homemade doo-rag on my head eating my delicious meal and listening to blues bands from Seattle and California busting loose with sounds that put a smile on my soul. I had never broken Daddy's rules up to that point, but one day there was a little group upstairs funkin' so hard, I couldn't help myself. I talked Waymond into helping me get a ladder so we could sneak a peek through the back window. Back in the day Waymond was my prime partner in crime and almost anything else you could name. We loved some adventure and danger, and I loved me some Waymond.

We got the ladder, climbed up, and peered inside. I don't remember what I saw, nor do I remember what the band was playing. I only remember the feeling that came out that window. It hit my heart so hard, washed over me with such beautiful force, that I'd spend the next fifty-five years trying to get back to it: the darkness, the women, the laughter, the gambling, the dancing, the drinking, the joy, the funky blues that splashed across my face like rose water. There was a family in there. A family gettin' down. I knew I belonged there.

As Waymond and I peered in, hypnotized, we felt the ladder shake underneath us. I looked down and saw Daddy standing at the bottom of the ladder with a two-by-four in his hand. "Get your narrow behinds down here now," he said.

We climbed down, ready to take our beatings like men. When I tried to explain, Daddy didn't want to hear it. "I told you, you ain't got no business at no jook joint," he said, and he wore our asses out. We took our whippings like men but we felt in our hearts that he was wrong. We'd seen him there ourselves with our own eyes on Saturday nights, "creepin'," as he called it, holding a gin bottle, laughing with the rest of the jook joint-ers as he climbed the stairs to Dick Green's dressed to the nines, his gray felt cap tipped to the side. Only he didn't see me. It didn't seem fair.

I stayed away from the joint for a few weeks after that, so I couldn't make any money shining shoes or pressing clothes. I worked at a country club as a locker boy for a while and then in a bowling alley setting up pins. They used to take twenty of us in the back of a truck at 6:30 A.M. to pick strawberries all day at a nearby farm for thirty cents a basket, plus all you could eat. I took up the trumpet in the school band led by Harold Jeans, who was our young, good-looking musical director at Coontz, and I hung out with Mr. Powe, who gave me music lessons. One day Mr. Powe rec-ommended that I get a certain music instruction book, which cost about a dollar. I went home and asked Daddy for the money. "Naw, boy," he grunted. "I just can't get next to that kind of money right now." I noticed Elvera looking on grimly. I said nothing. I knew he was still angry about seeing me at the jook joint.

Several days passed, and one evening when Elvera was out and the house was empty, he came home from work and said, "C'mere, boy." He sat down and opened up his green toolbox and pulled out the music book I wanted. He slipped the music book inside my shirt with a dollar bill tucked inside it so none of the other kids could see it. Then he hugged me, wordlessly, silently, and the sweet smell of the sweat on his strong chest stayed in my nostrils for weeks afterward. It's damned near impossible to describe my love for my daddy, and for my brothers Lloyd and Waymond.

CHAPTER 6

Rugrat

Clark Terry, trumpeter

I was in Count Basie's small group when I met Quincy. This was in 1947. He was a kid. The way I came to know him, Basie had lost his ass playing horses and his band had broken up. He'd blown so much bread on these ponies that he was working his behind out of debt. While doing so, the cats whom he owed said, "You can run your band for salary, and we'll take so much every week out of your bread to get you back up to par." He had problems like that all his life. Teddy Reig, who worked as a liaison between Basie and the record man Morris Levy, he had practically taken everything, he almost owned Basie's band.

So Basie's big band just went kaput—shrunk from eighteen musicians to eight. I went home to St. Louis, and one day Basie called me from his house on Long Island. He said, "Who do you know that's playing real good saxophone in St. Louis?" I said, "There's two cats around here. An established cat named Jimmy Forrest and another young Caucasian kid named Bob Graff." Basie said, "Get the kid and come to Chicago." When

Basie left New York for Chicago, he was at the train station and looked up and there was Freddie Green with his guitar and his bags. Freddie had played with Basie for ten years. Basie says, "Where you goin'?" Freddie says, "I gave you the best years of my life. Where the hell you think I'm goin'? Move over." He stayed with Basie another forty years. So anyway, we met in Chicago: Me, Freddie Green, Buddy de Franco, Bob Graff, Gus Johnson, Jimmy Lewis, and Basie, of course. There was a club in Chicago named the Brass Rail. We worked there for a while. Then Woody Herman came through town and absconded with our tenor player, Bob Graff. We replaced him with Wardell Gray and left Chicago and played several places around the country, including a place in St. Paul. Then we went up to Seattle.

We were playing a joint there called the Palomar Theater for about a month. Basie's trying to make that money back, you know, and we were working our asses off. There was this kid hanging around backstage every night, all night long. One night he comes up to me before the gig and says, "Mr. Terry, my name is Quincy Jones and I'm learning how to play trumpet and write music. I'd sure like to take some lessons from you."

I guess he was about thirteen then. He was a little skinny dude. I loved his little skinny ass from the first day I saw him. He was a conscientious little cat, you know.

I said, "You're in school while I'm sleeping. And you're sleeping when I'm working. How we gonna solve that?"

He said, "Well, I could get up early and come before I go to school for a couple of hours."

That put me on the spot. I had to play till two or three in the morning, then have to teach him? But there was something about him. Plus that's what music is all about. Giving back. Tradition. Life. Love—conscientiously staying involved in the perpetuation of our craft. So I said, "You come on by before school."

I'd go to bed at two or three and here he'd come at five, six o'clock in the morning. We'd work a couple of hours and then he'd go to school. He had a beautiful embouchure. I had to straighten out his upper embouchure a little for high notes and power because his lips used to bleed, but he had great potential. He had a nice little sound. St. Louis was a town that produced many good trumpeters, so I was always sound-conscious. Miles Davis was from East St. Louis. A bunch of other great trumpeters came from there, cats like Charles Creath, they called him the King of Cornet; Levy Madison—he supposedly had the most beautiful trumpet sound ever heard; Crack Stanley, Baby James, Dewey Jackson—Dewey Jackson was supposedly the loudest trumpet player in the world. They called him Squirrel. He used to play on the riverboats that floated down the Mississippi and you could hear Squirrel for ten miles up and down the river.

Quincy had exceptional potential. I don't know how diligent he was with his practicing, but he's the type of cat, anything he wanted to do he could've done. If he wanted to be President of the United States, he could've done that. That's just how resourceful and intent he was with his goals. You can see in a person whether they're really intent on becoming successful at whatever they do. He had that about him.

So he'd come every day and finally the last week when I was getting ready to cut out of town with Basie, he says, "Mr. Terry, I've learned to write too, and I would appreciate it if you'd listen to my first arrangement here." I said, "I'm leaving but give it to me and I'll look at it when we get to San Francisco." That was our next stop.

When we got to San Francisco I passed it around to Basie's band. This was just his small group. We were working a little club and we had an afternoon rehearsal. I said, "Holy"—we called Basie "Holy" because in the context of the Basie band jargon, "Holy" was something very special—I said, "Holy, remember that little kid in Seattle that was hanging around the bandstand? I got a chart he wrote." Basie said he remembered the kid and let's try it.

We played it, and to be honest, it was a little tired. I don't remember exactly what it was, but it wasn't great. But I knew damn well he was going to be a success. The kid was only thirteen or so.

We did our date in San Francisco and came back to Seattle and as soon as we hit town here comes the kid. I gave his music back to him and said, "Kid, you made a couple of mistakes, but I can tell you're really on the right track. You're gonna be a major talent someday."

He said, "You really think so?"

I said, "I know so."

You know, I can't help but think, What if I'd said, "Kid, put that stuff up on a shelf, forget it, be a plumber, do something else . . ."? What would've happened? I don't even like to think about it. You know what? Twelve years later, me and Quentin Jackson, one of Duke Ellington's star trombone players, quit Duke's band just to play with Q's band, that's how bad that skinny little dude was, and he was only twenty-five then. He's a prince, a prince of black music, if you ask me, and I love him now as much as I did when he was a little rugrat shaking me outta bed at six in the morning.

CHAPTER 7

Bumps

Daddy's work dried up in Bremerton in 1947. Once World War II was over, the Navy was done with black folks and Sinclair Heights basically fell apart. It was only built as a temporary housing project anyway—that's why they didn't put phones in the homes; there was just one booth on each corner. Blacks weren't that welcome in Bremerton after the war. So Daddy found us a little house at 410 22nd Avenue in the Central District section of Seattle. Waymond, Lloyd, and I set up shop in the attic while the girls, Daddy, and Elvera had the two bedrooms downstairs. It was cold in that tiny attic, and in winter you caught what little heat you could from the coal furnace downstairs. At night you could stand in the backyard and watch rats run out from under the house into the yard, but it didn't matter. I'd found a home—outside with the music.

The internal journey had begun back in Bremerton. One thing I'll always remember is sitting on a little bench in that raggedy-ass closet before we moved to Seattle. It contained Daddy's workbench and four barrels, two on top of the other two, with a board in between. That's what

we'd packed our clothes in when we'd moved from Chicago originally—
the barrels. As I sat on the bench with my back against the wall and my
knees pressed against the barrels, the room was full. It was so small that I'd
have to go back into the living room to change my mind. I'd sit there with
the light on or off. I preferred it off, because then you relied more on your
ears. This was where I'd dream up another reality—I'd see colors and hear
sounds. I had to get out. Radio helped me do this, to conjure up an imag-
inary world. Sometimes when I listened to *The Lone Ranger* I used to wonder if Tonto's voice might also be that of the Sheriff—I could sense the
same sort of fiber in the voice. One person played three or four parts. Back
in Chicago Lloyd and I loved to play cowboys with a posse of four or five
other boys in the neighborhood, riding broomstick horses on concrete
sidewalks, patting the rhythms of hooves on our corduroy knickers, and
whinnying in full imitation of what we'd heard on the radio or seen at the
movies.

Where was I in all this? Who was I? Despite our cowboy games, I
wasn't sure. There was no one to tell me. The books just said, "See Jane
run. See Spot." The records were it. I knew they were black, from the
world that included me. The music was the substance, but it was also
the metaphor for getting out of the place I was in. You can't even imagine
the impact that the jazz musicians had back then.

Seattle was a music mecca at that time. I was ready to explore all that
it offered. From 1947 till I left town in 1951, up and down Jackson Street
from 1st to 14th Street and along Madison Street between 21st and 23rd,
you could find almost any style of music you wanted: bebop, blues, R&B,
even Dixieland. Musicians came from everywhere to hang. Clint Eastwood told me that while bummin' around Portland and Seattle he used to
come in regularly to hear our band and check out the babes back then. At
the Trianon Ballroom, we'd hang with Sammy Davis, who was with the
Will Mastin Trio. We'd worry him to death all day long. He had all the hip
records: early Dizzy, Bird, Monk, all the bebop, Woody Herman's "Lemon

Drop," "Early Autumn." It had a tremendous influence: he was the first guy we knew who had earphones and a record player that held four to six records. We used to play hooky and go to see him at the Palomar Theater. Count Basie, Jimmie Lunceford, Cab Calloway, Duke Ellington, Louis Jordan, T-Bone Walker, Bull Moose Jackson, Joe "Honeydripper" Liggins—they roared through town almost every week to play at the Trianon Ballroom, the Civic Center, the Eagle Auditorium, and the Washington Social and Educational Club. I tailed the big bands like a puppy. More often than not Count Basie and his musicians would be playing at some joint and look down into the audience and wonder who this skinny kid was who was staring at them through the footlights. The kid wanted to be just like them: independent, talented, proud, fun-loving, and lady-loving, with a 360-degree attitude about life. I hung out at rehearsals of the New York Philharmonic when they came to town under Toscanini, and Harry Lookofsky, the wonderful violinist and concertmaster, who told me that more than anything he wanted to get into playing modern jazz on violin himself. It was jazz that I loved, but anything musical would do: choirs, orchestras, school bands, blues bands, anything. I met a lot of them before I was fifteen: Basie, Duke, Woody Herman, Milt Hinton. I would hound them for lessons, information, pumping them on music. Clark Terry from the Basie eight-piece band gave me trumpet lessons with so much grace— I used to wake him up at 6 A.M. for my lessons before school. He went to bed at 4 A.M. You can imagine how that went over.

Shortly after we arrived in Seattle, I heard a rumor about a blind dude who showed up at the Elks Club on Madison Street one night and tore the place up with his playing and singing. The rumor was this cat had appeared in Seattle out of nowhere and was incredible, so I hustled down there one night to check him out. He was a thin dude, brown-skinned, and he played his ass off. He played piano and sang like Nat King Cole and Charles Brown, and also played bebop alto sax like Charlie Parker. He had a little Bud Powell in his piano playing too. I sat through a set and afterward introduced myself. He said his name was Ray Charles and it was love at first instinct for both of us.

I was fourteen when I first met RC, and he was sixteen, and what I liked about him as much as his music was that he was on his own. At sixteen years old, Ray Charles was a man. He had his own apartment, his own record player, his own older girlfriend, three suits, his own life. That's something I wanted more than anything else.

I had no home. That's how I felt. Everything—all my growth, all my changes, all my music—was geared to getting out of Elvera's house. That's one reason Ray and I struck a chord immediately. I admired the way he shopped on his own, cooked on his own, did his own laundry. I'd watch him cross the street without cane or dog, dodging traffic, shopping, counting his change, scuffing his shoes as he climbed the curb, never missing a step, and I'd say to myself, "Damn, if he can do it, I can do it." I would go by his little apartment and find him on the couch taking a radio apart, shocking himself. He'd say, "Where you been, Quince? I ain't seen you in a while, man." I'd say to myself, *"Seen?"*

It was like somebody forgot to tell Ray he was blind. In fact, Ray never acted blind unless there was a pretty girl around, then he'd get all helpless and sightless, bumping into walls and doors, trying to get laid. I'd often go by his place just to eat—he'd cook chicken in his kitchen with all the lights off and the shades down. We'd eat and he'd sit at the piano and show me what he knew, and I ate it all up, everything, his fried chicken, his knowledge, his friendship. He even taught me Braille. Ray was a role model at a time when I had few. He understood the world in ways I didn't. He'd say, "Every music has its own soul, Quincy. It doesn't matter what style it is, be true to it." He refused to put limits on himself. We both loved bebop—Ray was so good he used to trade fours at the Jackson Street Elks Club with the great saxophonist Wardell Gray, and that was on sax—but Ray liked the blues, he liked country and western, he liked classical. He bought a Wurlitzer piano and stuck it in his living room. It sounded tinny and thin. At first folks laughed at Ray's stupid little electric piano, but when he wrote a hit on it called "What'd I Say," no one laughed anymore.

Ray typified what Seattle meant to me: the big time. Moving there from Bremerton was like moving to Paris. Three unusual, life-changing things happened to me before I met Ray. The first was meeting my music teacher, school bandleader Harold Jeans, at Coontz Junior High. It was in his band room I finally got my hands on a trumpet after trying all those other brass instruments, starting with French horn. The second was meeting a kid back in Bremerton named Dennis Washington, who was a tall, good-looking white kid, but poor and raggedy like me. When I set up my shoeshine stand at the Bremerton YMCA right next to the ferry dock to hustle cash, Dennis would set up on the other end of the building and this sucker could shine shoes as good as me! We both had a *Bremerton Sun* paper route. He was a tough, fun-loving kid, and he grew up to become the largest copper and railroad magnate in America. We're still close friends; fifty-five years later, we hang out together every chance we get. That opened my eyes some, to see a white kid hustling as hard as I was. The third was another kid, named Robin Fields, at Coontz Junior High School buggin' me to run for boys' club president. My first response was "Hey, man, forget it!" I thought he was crazy. These kids at a school that was almost 98 percent white were gonna vote for me as president? It didn't seem likely. It was white kids who had the money, the power, the homes, the prestige. This was 1946 and blacks were still colored and Negroes. Plus I was only a couple of years removed from South Side Chicago and I still carried my rusty switchblade in my back pocket and occasionally a snubnosed .32 that I still have, just to remind me. But after meeting Dennis and Robin, I began to understand that, whether it be black, brown, white, or yellow, "all" of anything ain't gonna work, positive or negative. This was when I started to roll with one on one, and it's never let me down; neither has my "redneck-detecting" antennae. On a day-to-day basis, a lot of these kids didn't seem to have the same prejudice as adults. You have to be taught bigotry. I ran for boys' club president at Coontz and was shocked when I won. That meant a lot to me. It helped me learn about trust a little bit. So instead of spending my last year of junior high in Seattle with Waymond and Lloyd, I got up at 5:30 A.M. every day and took two buses and the legendary Puget Sound ferry, the *Kalakala*, to Bremerton. It was an hour-and-a-half commute each way, and I often slept or tried to write music on the ferry, but it was better than being at home anyway. By the time I graduated Coontz and entered James A. Garfield High School in Seattle in 1947, I had something I didn't have before: confidence.

The music teacher at Garfield, Parker Cook, let me have free rein in his band room, and I met a kid there named Charlie Taylor, "C.T.," who became one of my best friends. Charlie lived just a few blocks from me—he was at 153 18th Avenue and I lived at 410 22nd Avenue—but Charlie had a nice home with his own father and a mother—aka Evelyn Bundy—who was a legendary pianist and who cared for him. I often spent more nights at his house than I did at my own. Charlie was a little older, with one of the brightest, most inquisitive minds I've ever encountered. When we met he was just getting started on tenor sax, and I was just beginning trumpet. We practiced together for three, four hours a day in Charlie's house after school, then we'd go see a movie for eleven cents. We'd play out our dreams in the movies too. I'd say, "C.T., I'm gonna write music for the movies one day," and he thought that was fine. I was already familiar with the house sounds of the major studios: the work of Al Newman at Fox, Victor Young at Paramount, Stanley Wilson at R.K.O. C.T. and I were as far away from that as you can imagine, though. We were naive and ignorant, and, in a strange way, completely pure.

Charlie and I decided to start a band under his name. We got a kid named Oscar Holden, Jr., to play sax. Oscar talked his sister Grace into playing piano. We got Billy Johnson to play bass, Major Pigford on trombone, and Buddy Catlett to eventually replace Oscar. I got my stepbrother Waymond to be our drummer, but we had to fire him. I loved him to death, but Waymond did not have the soul of a true musician. Right in the middle of a fast song he'd stop playing. Chewing gum, he'd say, "Shit, I'm tired." So we got Howard Redmond to replace him. We liked to tease and call Howard "Clubfoot" because he had a heavy, four-four foot on the bass drum. That was the original Charlie Taylor Band. We elected a president, a vice president, a secretary/treasurer (me!) who took minutes, we had fines for drinking, fines for being late to rehearsal, fines for not looking cool. Everything was aimed at being cool. That was the point. You had to look cool. You paid a huge fine—twenty-five cents—if you didn't look cool. Charlie and I started taking lessons with a teacher named Frank Waldron, a formally dressed, rotund man who seemed to have stepped out of the Harlem Renaissance. We improved steadily and before long we played our first gig at the YMCA on 23rd and Madison. We made seven dollars apiece.

Soon after, a local bandleader named Bumps Blackwell approached us and said he wanted to front us. That's how the Charlie Taylor Band became the Bumps Blackwell Junior Band. Bumps—his real name was Robert—was a light-skinned black man who played the vibes and conducted us, but he wasn't primarily a musician. He knew how to read music and had a little theory, but Bumps was more of a front man and promoter with a great ear for talent. He had a senior band, a junior band, a taxicab business, a jewelry business, he worked off-nights at the nearby Boeing aircraft plant, plus he ran a butcher shop at 23rd and Madison, where we'd hang all day. We did everything under Bumps's tutelage: rehearsed, played, listened to records, chased girls, brought them by his house which was our headquarters. Bumps was a funny guy. He didn't let any member of his junior band drink and had a rule against dope, but he had a special room in his house where we could have sex with all the girls we met. By then I had seriously discovered girls. I loved me some thirty-five- and forty-year-old ladies too when I was young. I discovered the ladies not in the same way I discovered music, but enough to win the heart of a beautiful girl named Jeri Caldwell from my high school. Bumps used to make all his band members contribute to clean sheets for our dating room—the Penthouse, we called it. He'd have the girls taking hot baths, which he knew would jump-start their monthlies when they were even a little bit late. Luckily, my girlfriend Jeri never needed those services.

Bumps got us uniforms. We had two types: a light green suit from the sharpest store in town, and white cardigan jackets without any collar and black pants. We looked good, sang, danced, did comedy, and played tight, so we were always busy. Buddy Catlett was the great player in the band: he played with authority beyond his years. We had a regular routine on weekends: from 7 to 10 we'd work places like the Seattle Tennis Club playing schottisches and pop tunes like "Room Full of Roses" and "To Each His Own" using cup mutes in our horns. Then from ten to one in the morning we got loose at black joints like the Rocking Chair or the Washington Social and Educational Club or the Black and Tan playing R&B tunes like Eddie "Cleanhead" Vinson's "Kidney Stew Blues" and "Good Rockin' Tonight" and "Harlem Nocturne" and "Red Light" for the strippers. Then we'd play bebop jam sessions for free at the Elks Club in the red-light district down on Jackson Street with Ray Charles and Buddy Catlett and Floyd Standifer and Cecil Young and Gerald Brashear and a bunch of other in-and-out-of-town cats, until the break of dawn.

The Washington Social and Educational Club was run by none other than the Reverend Silas Groves. I never did figure out where the Reverend Groves's church was, nor did I know how his club got the "education" part in that title, unless you consider the act of lifting a peach jar full of VAT 69 whiskey to your lips and sliding it down your throat educational, but the Reverend's club was definitely social. People brought whiskey and wine in paper bags, paid a dollar or two for a "setup" from the club—a bucket of ice, four water glasses, and maybe some soda pop— and then partied all night long drinking whiskey and eating home-cooked barbecue while watching us play. Occasionally there were police busts, fistfights, even gunfire, and we'd have to haul ass out the back door. There were thickets in the backyard that ripped your clothes and eyes as you ran.

Bumps made us into a show band. He added a shake dancer named August Mae, a tap dancer, and a dance team called Chicken 'n' Giblets, and had trombonist Major Pigford and me work up a comedy routine using the names Dexedrine and Benzedrine, where we put on fedoras and had empty wine bottles and panties in our coat pockets and used raggedy "country" one-liners like this one:

Me: *Say, Major, is that a diamond in your nose?*

Major: *No, it's snot!*

He added a beautiful young singer named Ernestine Anderson to the band who later became the greatest jazz singer to come out of Seattle. Later on, she was tagged as the heir apparent to Sassy and Ella. He replaced Grace Holden with a piano player who could read well but didn't have much soul. He was so stiff we tried to get him involved with one of the shake dancers to loosen him up. We asked her to seduce him. It worked a little bit, but he was so stiff and introverted that even juicy-loosey couldn't shake a smile out of him. I think he became an accountant.

Night after night, as I wandered in and out of clubs, bars, and jook joints with my trumpet beneath my arm and my scores tucked beneath my shirt, a tiny glint of something new began to emerge in my life, something I'd never had before. I had no control over where I lived, no control over my sick mother, no control over my hard-hearted stepmother and my overwrought father. I couldn't change the attic where I slept, or stop the anguished tears of my little brother Lloyd, who sometimes cried himself to sleep at night; I couldn't control the angry whites who still called me nigger when they caught me alone on the street, or the bourgeois, high yella blacks who considered me too poor, too dark, and too uneducated to be a part of their lives. But nobody could tell me how many substitute chord changes I could stick into the bridge of "Cherokee." Nobody could tell me which tempo to play "Bebop" or "A Night in Tunisia" in. Nobody could tell me how long I could stay up at night with earphones to check out Dizzy or Bird or Miles solo at the Sherman and Clay Record Store booths. Music was one thing I could control. It was the one world that offered me my freedom.

When I played music, my nightmares ended. My family problems disappeared. I didn't have to search for answers. The answers lay no further than in the bell of my trumpet and my scrawled, penciled scores. Music made me full, strong, popular, self-reliant, and cool. The men who played it were proud, funny, worldly, and dap dressers. The New York cats and kittens who came through town were like kings and queens. Jazz gave black men and women dignity. Even Bumps, hustler that he was, typified that. It wasn't till I was grown that I realized how clever Bumps was, and how complicated things must have been for him. Bumps's junior band was one of the first black bands in Seattle to play white fraternity and sorority parties, cotillions in the exclusive neighborhoods like Broadmoor, and at the all-white Seattle Tennis Club. In those days, it was rare for a black to stand toe to toe and look a white man in the eye, and Bumps was not so confident when dealing with white people. He was sure of himself when dealing with blacks, but he had a tad more "yes, sir" and "no, sir" to him when dealing with whites. So he got taken advantage of, and while we thought he never paid us enough, he never exploited us. He never booked us and stole our money like a lot of people did. He later moved to LA and helped launch the careers of Little Richard and Sam Cooke, but he never got the credit he deserved for doing those things.

Bumps's motto was: Get the gig, forget the rest. He'd book us anywhere. He once booked us at a provincial carnival in Canada where they made Ernestine Anderson dress up like a shake dancer and advertised us with posters over our tent that showed little black kids eating watermelon with a sign that said, "Bumps Blackwell and His All-Colored Harlem Review." We did eight shows a day and had to ballyhoo outside the tent to bring people in. We were so tired that sometimes we slept on the ground in our white cardigan jackets. Between shows Bumps even had us join the National Guard band out at nearby Camp Murray—which was a mistake.

This was no one-night gig. We were sworn in as part of the all-black Washington National Guard 41st Infantry Division band. They gave us uniforms and brand-new instruments and had us drill at the armory in Seattle weekends and go on active duty for two or three months in the summer at the for-real Army at Camp Murray. Bumps became our commanding officer. I was a staff sergeant and company typist. Charlie Taylor became a master sergeant. The rest became privates and corporals. We had a real first sergeant, Ish Dotson, a tenor player, but we could barely make a right turn on command, let alone handle live ammo on the rifle range. We got our uniforms tailored, though—we were always trying to look cool—and we marched kind of hip, but we didn't quite know or care what we were doing yet. The music was sounding good.

One time we played a gig in Tacoma with Bumps's band, partied all night, and the next day came back to camp late. We all got busted—including Bumps. I couldn't believe it. They were really pissed. They said, "Good to see you, Sergeant, we hope you have an explanation for this." I said, "No." As we got off the truck, the real Army officers said, "Well then, Corporal, stand over there." We'd been demoted.

I was also the company bugler and was supposed to play reveille at 6 A.M. for a 7 A.M. bivouac. Because we stayed out all night and didn't get back until 11 A.M., the whole base overslept. The officers were so pissed with me that they made me sleep in the MPs' quarters after that, so I'd get up with them. Finally they ended our misery by transferring us out and making us telephone operators and cooks for the officers' mess.

It was just as well, because we were focused on jazz. We lived for the latest gossip from New York. Word traveled slow in those days. There was no MTV: in fact there was no television, period. Radio was one jazz station with Jimmy Lyons from San Francisco, plus Hattie McDaniel playing

Beulah the maid, Jack Benny's henchman Rochester, and Amos 'n' Andy, who were white men playing black roles. You lived for word of mouth. *Bird, Dizzy, Prez, Miles, New York,* those were the code words. We knew this music called bebop was being created in New York at a joint called Minton's by a genius named Charlie Parker, who they called "Bird," and we were dying to get closer to it. Anything that came out of New York was like gold. That's why when Bumps marched into a rehearsal one day in 1948 and announced, "Billie Holiday is coming to town and we're gonna back her up," we freaked in disbelief.

We said, "Why us? Why the junior band? Why not the senior band?"

He said, "Because y'all can sight-read better than anybody else around here." Like most singers in those days, Billie traveled with just a pianist who served as musical director and hired local musicians in the various cities.

We were so excited we couldn't stand it. Lady Day was like Michael Jackson back then: People talked about her upcoming concert for weeks. Five minutes before show time, standing there in my cardigan jacket at the age of fifteen, in front of a packed house of 900 people at the Eagle Auditorium, the biggest singer in the world standing in the wings, I was scared to death.

Billie's musical director who traveled with her was the great arranger and pianist Bobby Tucker, who later became Billy Eckstine's musical director for forty years. Bobby was not much older than us, maybe twenty-three or so. As Lady Day stepped onto the wings, Bobby gathered us around him and looked us over like a war-weary sergeant looks at green troops who step onto the battlefield for the first time. We were bug-eyed. He was cool and suave. "Just be cool," he said. "Just read the charts and don't miss the repeat signs. Have fun with it." He pointed out a few things in the music, a few entrances and exits, then sat down and got ready to play.

Billie was standing offstage in the wings in a long sequined dress. She looked just like she looked in the pictures, elegant, beautiful, with the gardenia in her hair. The MC announced, "Miss Billie Holiday!" Bobby counted off the intro and we started in. Billie didn't come onstage. She stood in the wings, completely stoned. She was numbed out, totally unconscious from dope. Then this guy next to her, it must've been her manager, he almost kicked her out of the wings. She swayed unsteadily, then walked onstage and wandered right past the microphone. Then she came back to it and just stood there. By then we'd already played the intro and were well past her entrance.

Bobby stopped us and counted the intro off a second time. We hit it tight and she came in right on the money. She sounded like the legend she was once she started—just beautiful. We, on the other hand, began to sound like a truck trying to crank on a cold October morning, except for Buddy Catlett on alto, who always sounded smooth and mellow like Johnny Hodges. We lurched through the first couple of numbers and were staggering through the third when Bobby got pissed off. He leaned over his piano and hissed, "If you motherfuckers are gonna stand there gawking at Billie instead of reading the music, get off the bandstand and go buy a ticket." That straightened us out. We buried our faces in those charts and got it together again, quick.

The concert was a success, but afterward Bumps said, "You see what bad shape she was in? That's a perfect example of what not to do," and I silently agreed. It seemed too much of a price to pay. Also, the last thing I wanted to deal with was getting busted, because I'd already gotten busted twice the year before, and both times I wasn't sure who would bail me out. The first time was with Bumps when we were returning from a gig in Port Orchard. The guy who was driving lit a joint and got so mellow he drove like a snail. We got stopped—if you can believe it—for driving too slow. The cops put us in a cell and interviewed us separately. When it was my turn, just as I stepped into the room a cop reached into my pocket and pulled out a joint and asked, "How'd this get here?"

I said, "It's not mine."

He said, "Sure it's not."

I said, "I know it's not mine." I knew he was trying to set me up. They kept all of us in jail over the weekend. The headline in the *Bremerton Sun* the next day said, "Teenage dope fiend Negro musicians arrested for reefer in Port Orchard." A few years earlier, in 1943, when Gene Krupa got busted, the headlines nationwide emphasized jazz instead of race.

The second time was more serious. My stepbrother Waymond and a guy named Eddie Mitchell broke into the basement of a black business-man's house in broad daylight and stole a cigar box full of money, some jewelry, plus two guns. They asked me to run interference. I was the decoy who sweet-talked his daughter, distracting her while Waymond and Eddie climbed through a basement window and got the box of cash that be-longed to her daddy. We got away clean, too. We bought meals and cardi-gan sweaters and new shoes, and had a pocketful of money until the next day, when Eddie showed up at school in a taxicab. He lived five blocks from Garfield High and the dude took a taxicab to school, drunk, wearing a brand-new pair of shoes, a wide-brimmed pimp hat, a rust-colored cardigan jacket with a pint of wine in one pocket and cash in the other, and shades. That tipped off the cops, and they picked up the three of us and carted us off to jail. Waymond and I were stashing money in the ceil-ing of the attic as the cops arrived at our house to pick us up. We thought it was funny till we got down to the juvenile house and realized we weren't getting out. When the police called Elvera and told her me and Waymond were locked up, she told them, "I hope you keep 'em in there forever!" As for Daddy, he couldn't believe I'd violated his trust by screwing up. I didn't expect him to do anything for me.

Waymond and I sat in the joint for five days while Lloyd, who shared our attic bedroom, helped himself to our stolen loot and bought himself a new jacket, ate some good food, and used our money to buy front-row seats for himself and his guest Buddy Catlett to see Nat King Cole with the Woody Herman Band at the Civic Auditorium. The joint wasn't pleasant—the guard put saltpetre in our saltshakers. Waymond and I always slept with one eye open. A huge brother named Tiny with a big part in the center of his do took a liking to us, so no one messed with us. Maybe he was saving us for himself, who knows, but there was no peace in our house after we got out. Elvera wouldn't let Waymond and I hear the end of it. It embittered me even more toward her. I never wanted to hear it and stayed clear of her as much as possible, because her cold attitude and ranting disapproval hurt me. It pained me, but the truth was, a lot of my pain had nothing to do with Elvera. In fact, an event happened some months before I got locked up that made Elvera's rantings seem tame by comparison.

Lloyd and I were sitting on the steps of Elvera's house one afternoon when we heard yelling down the street. In the distance, we saw a woman marching toward us, yelling and gesturing. When she got closer I realized, to my horror, that it was my mother. She was screaming. "My boys! My boys! I've come for my boys!" Lloyd and I were stunned. All those nights, four years' worth, of hearing about how crazy she was, how she was going to find us one day and kill us; all those anguished nights of wondering where she was and why. My brother and I did the only thing we could do. Instinctively we jumped to our feet, turned on our heels, and ran, the sound of our pounding feet echoing through our hearts like bricks.

Six-nine

Ray Charles

I became blind at the age of six, and my mother died back in Greenville, Florida, when I was fifteen. My only brother had died as a child, and I had no father to speak of, so when my mother died a lot of folks felt I wasn't gonna make it. But before she died, my mother taught me to live. Everything I am today is because of her. She sent me to the Florida State School for the Blind when I was seven. At home she made me cook meals, dress myself, haul water, even chop wood with an ax. The neighbors would say, "A wood chip could fly off and hit him!" but my mother would say, "A wood chip can fly off and hit me and I can see." So chop wood I did. She used to tell me, "I may not live to see what you do in this life, but there is one thing I know you will never do: You will never hold a tin cup and beg." She was only thirty-two when she died and it broke my heart so much I can't put words to it, but her words always stayed with me. I have done many things in this life, but if you can find anybody who ever says they saw Ray Charles begging for a penny, you're a better man than me.

I hung around Florida for a couple of years. I played in Tampa, I toured the South with a couple of different bands, but those were hard times. I was living off biscuits and soup. I had a friend named Gosady McKee who played guitar, and one day in '47, I told Gosady to pull out a map of the United States and I told him, "Point to the farthest city on that map from here." His finger came down on Seattle, Washington, and that's how I came there. I came by bus. Alone.

I hit town hustling. I got a gig playing at a black joint called the Rocking Chair and at another black joint called the Black and Tan Club. I had a group called the Maxim Trio; I used to sing like Nat King Cole and Charles Brown in those days—it was the only way to get paid. I had my little trio at the Rocking Chair one night and this fourteen-year-old cat comes up to me talking about music, about jazz, about Dizzy Gillespie and Charlie Parker. He said, "I'm Quincy Jones and I play trumpet and I want to write music," or something like that. That's how we met.

When you're blind, you become a soul reader. Everything a person says is a soul note. It comes straight outta their soul, so you read a person immediately. Quincy had a loving style about him. He was genuine. He didn't have a single evil strand of hair on his head. He was smart. He liked to have fun. He wasn't afraid to touch you and laugh. He was infectious, man. We hit it off right away.

He seemed fascinated that I had my own life. I had an apartment, a hi-fi, three suits, a girlfriend, a piano. He said, "I can't understand how you can have all this stuff being only sixteen." We spent hours in my apartment talkin' about music. Back then we had no money. We were into sounds. Textures. Who was playing what. We didn't read *Down Beat* or *Metronome*. Nobody gave a shit about that. There was no politicizing. We listened to a lot of radio. Radio was the pipeline for music in those days. We used to hear a DJ named Jimmy Lyons out of Oakland on one of those fifty-thousand-watt stations playing Slam Stewart, Bird, Lee Konitz, and Dizzy Gillespie. We loved Dizzy's big band. We were trying to learn to write figures, and Dizzy had this tune "Emanon"—that's "no name" spelled backwards. One morning I was in bed and Quincy came banging at the door getting me out of bed talking about that tune. I used to go to work at the Rocking Chair at one in the morning—Seattle was live in those days—and I'd get home at 5 in the A.M. At 9 A.M. here comes Quincy banging at my door.

I let him in and said, "What the fuck you want, man?"

He said, "Ray, how come that cat Jimmy Valentine, when he arranges for Mr. B's band, can get four trumpets and four trombones to play at the same time but using eight different notes?"

I already knew how to arrange. I was arranging when I was twelve years old back in Florida. I was playing bebop down there before I even came to Seattle. I went over to the piano and played this chord for Quincy, a B flat seven with a C seven over top. That's the eight-note brass voicing for the Eckstine band sound.

He said, "Man, that opens up a whole brand-new world for me." He understood it right away. He's always had that focus. You find your great musicians have that: a great focus and usually a great memory. This is what allows them to learn the language of music. Quincy's got a great memory. He can remember your middle name, your girlfriend's name, the chords you like, the color of your shoes, what you played two weeks ago. He'd wear me out with that. He'd say, "When we played 'Cherokee' last week, what were those substitute chord changes you played in the bridge?" I'd say, "Quincy, you know I can't remember, man. We were just stretchin' out at the time. I guess that's why they call it jazz."

We both worked for Bumps Blackwell, who was like a father to us. Or sometimes we'd work at clubs for the kitty, which was tips that people would throw into a tin can or wooden box shaped like a cat's face with its mouth wide open and a light inside; we'd do songs like "Big Fat Butterfly," the black version of "Poor Butterfly," which was a white hit back then and that brought a lot of tips; or we'd hang at Bumps's butcher shop with

Buddy Catlett, Floyd Standifer, Ernestine Anderson, a lot of the dynamite young jazz musicians out of Seattle. In fact I was walking past Bumps's meat market on my way to a gig one day when I heard somebody holler, "Ray!" so I crossed the street and came on in. I knew who it was.

I said, "Man, don't be hollerin' my name out loud in the street like that. It ain't cool."

He said, "Okay, what if I call you Six-Nine from now on? That way you'll know it's me."

That sounded cool enough, so I said, "Okay. I'll call you Seven-O." That's how I became Six-Nine and he became Seven-O. He still calls me Six-Nine to this day. When I was in the White House receiving my Kennedy Center Award in 1986, they brought some people onstage to give tributes to me and I was sitting next to Nancy Reagan when I heard him holler from the stage, "Six-Nine!" I went to the producer and said, "Has he got any notes? 'Cause I don't want him up there talking without notes. Give him some notes, because I don't want him rambling. He knows too much about me."

We split up after '51. He got on with the Lionel Hampton band in New York and I went to LA. The first thing Quincy did when he got in Hamp's band was to pull Hamp aside and tell him to hire me. Hampton came through Seattle looking for me the next time his band went West, but I was on the road with Lowell Fulson by then. Lowell had put out a record called "Every Day I Have the Blues," and I put out "Baby, Let Me Hold Your Hand." So I was on my way, and I didn't see Quincy for a while.

We used to talk about the day when we'd be able to sit in a restaurant and order any food we wanted, and get on planes and fly anyplace we wanted to go to, and do records and symphonies and movies together and meet lots of women, and all those things happened. We lived out a lot of our dreams together and we're still doing it. Do you know that in all the years we've worked together, we've never had a contract—ever? All the records, the movie scores we did, never had one. He's the only person in the world I'd ever do that with. Course, if I've got a dime, he's got a nickel of it anyway, that's how I feel about him.

He hasn't changed a bit in all the years I've known him. He's still the same. He still likes to laugh. He's just a goddamned kid. I love him to pieces, and you can print that any way you want to. And say Ray Charles said it.

CHAPTER 9

The four winds

When I was fifteen, I began to dream I would fly off to the four winds. It was a fitful dream. Living in Elvera's house in Seattle, I never slept well unless it was on my stomach. I snored heavily, like a monster. I had sleep apnea, a breathing condition I would take into adulthood, and I always felt cold, no matter how warm the house was. I was never comfortable there. I loved Elvera's children like brothers and sisters, but their mother I could not handle. Neither could I handle my own mother, who had moved to an apartment just blocks from us. I just wanted to get away.

Sarah never left Seattle until 1952 after she appeared out of nowhere that day in 1948. She proceeded to follow me and Lloyd—literally follow us—around to different towns and through our lives for the next fifty years. She was desperate for us to live with her, but that was out of the question. She'd searched for us for years before finding us in Seattle—God knows how she did it—but she was smart, skilled as a typist and secretary, and she could always get a job. She was coherent enough to work, but beneath her coherence her illness lurked. We were afraid to trust her. She was too far gone. Her rare moments of kindness were followed by torrents of irrational meanness and criticisms. I'd mention music and she'd say, "Do you know Jesus?" or "God doesn't like sinners, Quincy Junior. Make music for God only or you'll be redeemed in hell." Lloyd and I visited her only when driven by hunger, because sometimes she would cook for us and she knew Elvera never fed us well, but we often left her with full stomachs and starving hearts, resolving never to return. She kicked your ass. There just wasn't any peace to be made. She went through religions like most people drink soda pop—Jewish, Baptist, Methodist, Christian Scientist. Daddy said, "Boy, leave her alone and g'wan about your business," but you can't ignore your mother. There was never any resolution. All I needed to hear was "I love you. I approve of what you're doing," and I could've handled it; but she wasn't capable of that. She was a schizophrenic. Dementia praecox, they call it. I didn't know a name for it back then. I just knew something wasn't right and I couldn't deal with it. I just closed down. At fifteen, I wanted to cut, split, leave.

I hung in every club, in every ballroom, in every rehearsal hall in Seattle with a purpose, and when I wasn't in a club playing a gig or practicing my horn, I was writing music. I'd write in my attic bedroom by flashlight at night, a habit I'd picked up in Bremerton when we slept in the closet. Back in Bremerton, I used to write music before I even knew what key signatures meant. If I were writing in the key of F, which has one flat— B flat—I would write a footnote across the bottom of the page saying, "Play all Bs a half step lower on this tune because if you play B naturals they sound funny." But by the age of sixteen, I knew key signatures and technique, and more important, I knew how the act of writing music made me feel. I was a nervous, fidgety kid. Writing music calmed my nerves, literally. It gave me comfort, peace, hope, love. It gave me what nothing else could.

One night as I lay in bed at Elvera's house, I composed a piece about my dream of flying away. I wrote it in my mind first, then dropped by Ray Charles's house and started working it out on his piano. Then I went to Charlie Taylor's piano, then the piano at Bumps's house, then over to the band-room piano at Garfield High, then up to the Washington Social and Educational Club after hours, where they also had a piano. Up and down the streets I went, in and out of clubs, upstairs into jook joints, downstairs into empty clubs, working it out bit by bit on every piano I could find. That piece was the most valuable thing I owned. I carried it around with me every day like money, scrawling on it, fixing it, changing it, carrying it under my sweater with a Black Wing No. 2 pencil in my pocket to make continual fixes. I wasn't sure if it was good enough to show to the big boys who came through town or not, so I tried it out with the Garfield High band. It was too hard for them to play, so I got ringers from Bumps Blackwell's stable to play it for me: Floyd Standifer, Billy Towles, Buddy Catlett, Billy Johnson, Ray Charles. Later, Gus Mankertz's band at Seattle University performed it with me on trumpet, with members of Bumps' junior band. My mother and Jeri were in the audience: I still have the photo.

I still wasn't sure about it. I had to test it out first. I'd already given an arrangement to Clark Terry of Basie's band when I was thirteen and Clark encouraged me, but inside I knew I wasn't ready yet. I had to be sure. Only after Billy Eckstine came through Seattle in '49 did I begin to believe in the piece. Billy's musical director was Bobby Tucker, the same Bobby Tucker who hired us to fumble through the Billie Holiday gig the year earlier. Bobby hired us again to accompany the great Mr. B, and as we played through Billy Eckstine's reduced charts of arrangements by the greats Nelson Riddle, Bobby Tucker, and Hugo Winterhalter, I said to myself, "My piece is getting close enough to this. It's getting closer."

That experience gave me the confidence to stand backstage at the Palomar Theater in 1949 holding my "Suite to the Four Winds" as Lionel Hampton and his mighty band marched off their tour bus. Hampton was like a god in those days. He had the rockingest band in America, with a rhythm section socking that backbeat so hard your shoes flew off, and he had groovin' and honkin' sax players who walked on the tops of the audience's seats with soft-soled shoes. When it came to stomping, jammin', rockin' and groovin', Hampton was a great jazz player and the entertainment king. Every time he showed up in Seattle, I was like Dracula at the blood bank.

Janet Thurlow was a local jazz singer who had joined Hamp's band the year before. We'd played with her around Seattle, and it was she who kept my name on Hamp's mind. She told me that saxophonist Bobby Plater was his straw boss, the guy responsible for hiring players and buying arrangements, so I approached Bobby as he walked off the bus and showed him my music. He was kind but noncommittal. He promised to show it to Hamp, but I didn't think he would.

Later that night, about two in the morning, Hamp and some of his band walked into the Elks Club, where I was onstage playing in the nightly jam session. In those days, it was common for bands that came through Seattle to come to our jam sessions.

Bobby Plater motioned me to come offstage and brought me over to Hamp. He said, "Gates, this is the li'l cat I was tellin' you about," and disappeared. Hamp had picked this up from Benny Goodman, who called everyone "Gates" because he never remembered names. It was contagious.

Hamp was holding my score in his hand. He told me to sit down. I sat, my heart pounding. He said, "You wrote this arrangement, Youngblood?"

It was the closest I'd ever been to a star, which Hamp was in those days. He was dressed to the nines: a crisp blue suit, the band uniform, white teeth, gold ring on his hand. He carried a leather-bound Bible with a zipper. He had a wide smile; his hair was cropped close. People floated around his table like he was royalty. It was like talking to God. I could barely speak. The words caught in my throat as I said, "Yes, sir."

He smiled and looked at the music again. Back then I didn't know that Hamp did not read music, or even need to. Without looking up from it, he said, "Why'd you name it this?" I had to bite back the nervousness in my mouth. I could barely get the words out. I said, "Each part of the music represents one wind. The wind to the north blows fierce and cold, the wind to the south is warm, the wind to the east is moist and wet, and the wind to the west is dry." I didn't tell him about my dream of flying off to the four winds. Later for the dream. We'd get to the dreams later. I wanted a job.

He asked me my age.

"Fifteen," I said. "I play too," I added. I had my trumpet in my lap and showed it to him. Man, I was ready like Freddy.

"I know, Gates, I already heard you," he said. He wasn't smiling anymore. He was looking at me closely.

Then and there I knew it was an audition, right there at the table. Not a note was played. Sometimes you wait all your life for a moment, and I knew that this was my time. God bless Janet Thurlow, Bobby Plater, and Hamp, because they felt it. The average age of Hamp's band was thirty years old. There were some serious cats in there, dynamite players: Jerome Richardson, Benny Bailey, Jimmy Cleveland, and Milt Buckner. I was fifteen. I felt like if Ray Charles could do it, so could I. Ray was always talking about leaving Seattle. He wasn't gonna leave me behind. If Hamp had asked me to jump out the window at that moment to join his band, I would have. I sat up straight and tried my best to look thirty years old. I wanted it. I willed it. I visualized it with every inch, every pound of me, c'mon, man . . .

Then he said it: "Young huss, you wanna join my band?"

I said, "Yes, sir."

He said, "Okay, Gates, the bus leaves from behind the Palomar tomorrow afternoon. Gladys'll talk details with you."

Just like that. I was free. I couldn't believe it. I stood there stunned as he got up and walked away, laughing and joking with the other musicians in the club, his head disappearing from sight as every eye in the club followed him to the back bar. That's how Hamp did things. You joined his band with no ceremony, and I later found out you left the same way. But who cared. I was in the band! Lionel Hampton's band!

I didn't even pack a bag. I went home and sat up all night packin' up my music and practicing my horn. I said not a word to anyone; no one was going to pee on my leg at a moment like this. The next day I went to the Palomar with my trumpet and my score and got on the bus. I took a seat in the back and waited. After a while, Hamp's musicians piled on, sweaty, tired, and loud, ritualistically tossing their instruments in the overhead racks, lighting cigarettes, laughing and joking. They seemed huge, glistening, secure. A few looked at me in surprise as they piled on. I said nothing. Not a peep. I was ready. I felt like I belonged. I would say hello to them later. I wanted the bus to get rolling before Hamp changed his mind.

But he didn't. He got on the bus, saw me in the back seat, and said, "Hey, whassap'nin', young huss," then sat down at the front behind the driver. We were ready to go. Just as the bus was about to pull off, a tall, elegant, Indian-looking woman got on. She was the last to board. I later found out she was Hamp's wife, Gladys, the band's manager.

She looked over the musicians seated on the bus as the road manager counted to make sure everyone was there. When they got to me sitting in the back, the counting stopped. She turned to Hamp and said, "Lionel, what's that boy doin' back there?"

Hamp said, "He's in the band."

She said, "That's not a man, that's a boy. What's the matter with you? We can't take a child on the road."

I waited a moment, hoping Hamp would argue. He said nothing.

She said to me, "C'mon up here, son."

That walk down the aisle to the front of the bus was the longest walk in the world.

She said, "You get back in school. Get your education. When you're finished, call us. Maybe we'll find a place for you then."

My heart crashed. I climbed down off the bus and looked up from the curb as she stood in the bus doorway watching me.

"You go back to school," she said. The door closed and they were gone. Standing there with my score and my trumpet in the leather bebop case in my hand, I watched the bus till its taillights were out of sight.

Finish school, she had said.

"Fuck school," I said. Then I went home.

I took her advice and did finish school. I had to. My girlfriend Jeri was comforting. She said, "You'll get your chance at the big time," but I didn't know when it would come again. Jeri was my heart and soul then. She knew how badly I wanted to leave. She'd promised to marry me and come with me to New York, which was my dream, but that seemed far away now. I graduated Garfield High without ceremony. As always, our band played at the prom dance. I lived right across the street from the school and Elvera never even bothered to attend my graduation. My mother came, but Elvera did not. It was like we were total strangers. To keep peace in our household, Daddy did not come either.

A few weeks after I graduated Garfield, I got a music scholarship to study at Seattle University, but the music courses were too dry, and no challenge for me. Shortly after the semester began, I read in *Down Beat* that a school in Boston named the Schillinger House, later renamed the Berklee College of Music after its founders, Larry Berk and Lee Daniels, was offering scholarships. I sent them "The Four Winds" and got a letter from them saying I was accepted. This time my out was solid.

I had the letter in my hand when I went to speak to Daddy about getting train fare to Boston, and as soon as I walked into Elvera's tiny house I realized there was nothing I could ask him. By then he had eight kids. Janet and Richard, the littlest, were just toddlers crawling across the living-room floor, and Daddy was still making $55 a week. He was still growing vegetables in his garden and canning peaches and pears that he grew in the backyard to feed everyone. In desperation, I approached my mother, and after giving me a solid hour of rhetoric and "tight jaws," she finally gave it up. God bless her. Despite her objections to "pagan" music—she once even gave me a 1943 U.S. Armed Forces manual on music appreciation she'd found that said jazz was created by "an inferior race of people from feeble stock"—she saw how much I wanted it and did a temporary about-face. She called her sister Mabel, who ran a soul-food restaurant with my uncle in Chicago. Aunt Mabel, who was the closest thing I'd ever had to a mother, sent me the money, and I took the next thing smoking. Everybody in the family saw me off at the train station: Lloyd, Elvera, Daddy, Theresa, Waymond, Richard, Janet, Margie, and Catherine. Someone packed me a little lunch in a white shoebox: some greasy fried chicken, boiled eggs, potato salad, a tomato, an apple, and I was gone. I didn't think twice about leaving, but on the station platform when I saw Lloyd's face, I knew he felt betrayed. He said, "Dewey, I want to come too." He made that long face he makes when he's sad.

I said, "Don't worry. We don't have any money now. When I get it together, you know I'll send for you." I knew he was miserable in Elvera's house. Lloyd was a year behind me in school, but he had no out. He loved music too. He hung out at all the spots, worked full-time at Bumps Blackwell's meat market, he even played a little bass, but Lloyd's gift was electronic and mechanical. He inherited my father's skills. I couldn't drive a nail if my life depended on it, but Lloyd could conquer anything with his hands—radios, electric trains, cabinets. He could wire a whole house when he was nine. He used to rig the phones in Bremerton so the coins would spit out into his fingers. He had a regular route collecting money from the phones. But Lloyd was no thief. He never stole for fun. He stole to eat. We often ate and showered at Garfield High. Dinner was at Father Divine's. You gave them fifteen cents and said, "Peace, Brother," and they gave you as much veal stew, rice, and tapioca pudding as you could stomach. Years later, when he got married, his wife, Gloria, had to break him of the habit of standing in front of his own refrigerator and asking if he could go inside it for a glass of juice. He never had the privilege of living in a house where he could go into the refrigerator anytime he wanted. I still remember him hovering around Elvera's refrigerator wanting to get inside it, too afraid to ask, too hungry to walk away, yet preferring to starve rather than walk down the street and face our mother's wrath. Damn, memories kill me.

Standing there watching him, I knew the tight space he was living in. We had never been apart. Yet there was nothing I could do for him. He was just out there, floating. I had to get out. I had to run. I had to survive. There was no other way.

He said, "Don't forget to send for me, man." I promised him I wouldn't forget. But even as I watched him and Daddy waving at me as the train rolled away, tears welling up in my eyes as I smiled and waved, I was already trying to forget him. I was trying my hardest. I'd felt since I was eleven that I was on my own, but this time it was for real. This train was leaving.

The first stop was Chicago, to see Aunt Mabel and Uncle John, who couldn't have been more welcoming. We celebrated my eighteenth birthday with my cousin Mildred and her new baby, Darice, and many others. As a gift from Mildred I received a warm coat to prepare for the Boston winters; no one had warned me in advance. I was a kid when I'd left Chicago before, but those days were behind me now. I was completely on my own for the first time in my life, in a northern city, with no job and no place to stay. To this day I can still remember the terror I felt the night I arrived. Boston was dark and scary. Finally I found a room in a rooming house run by a lady named Jones, on Columbus and Massachusetts Avenue across the street from a club called the Hi Hat. Along with the scholarship came the chore of copying the music parts for my teacher Dick Bobbitt's radio show, anything to live. The school was a house at 284 Newbury

Street, where me and guys like Charlie Mariano and Herb Pomeroy studied arranging, big-band ensembles, the Schillinger system of musical theory, and jazz solo analysis during the day. One night I lucked out and found
a gig at a club called Izzy Ort's next to the Paramount Theater in Boston's
Combat Zone with a group of old-school Boston cats. Bunny Campbell
was the bandleader and alto sax player. The pianist and seasoned arranger
was Preston "Sandy" Sandiford. After weeks of work I'd bring the score of
my arrangement on "All the Things You Are," every single note carefully
written out for piano, bass, drums, a brass section, and saxes. Downstairs,
during breaks, Sandy would check it out, then blow me away by tearing up
the whole score and saying, "To hell with a score. Learn how to do it up
here in your mind. First write out the chords and rhythm parts, then do the
top line for the lead horn parts. Then finish writing out the transposed parts
for the whole band and forget the rest of this shit."

Izzy Ort's was a hellhole, complete with drunk sailors, strippers,
fights—you name it. The drummer, Floyd "Floogie" Johnson, had a technique that could make women take their clothes off. He could spot the potential strippers from the bandstand, which seemed miles away. Once he
started his tom-tom spell he'd bring it home every time, with women
sometimes even getting buck naked. Shortly after I arrived at Schillinger,
the famous bebop bassist Oscar Pettiford came through with his band at
the Hi Hat. Oscar Pettiford was regal, real, and handsome, half black, half
Indian, and three-quarters bald. He'd played the first jazz cello solo ever
on a record of "Perdido" and was considered one of the best bass players
ever. I showed him some of my arrangements and he said, "Man, I dig it.
I'm sending for you when I do my next record." A couple of months later
he was as good as his word and I was off to New York to do two arrangements for him. He promised me ten dollars an arrangement, plus a bus
ticket. It might as well have been a million dollars. I was off to New York
to do a Pettiford session supervised by Leonard Feather, the jazz critic, on
Mercer Records, Duke's son's label. My classmates were impressed. I was

going to the Big Apple to do a recording session and stay there three days. I was going to get a full taste of it.

I'd been waiting for this moment since 1945. When I got off the train in New York it was like arriving at Disneyland, the lights, the people, the sounds, everything seemed huge and bright. Oscar paid me for my arrangements, then showed me around. He took me to all the clubs: the Embers, and Snookie's, where the bell of Dizzy Gillespie's horn was accidentally sat on and bent upright. There was Basie's band and Duke's band with Al Hibbler and Sarah Vaughan and Billy Eckstine, George Kirby, Coles and Atkins, Jimmie Rogers, Erskine Hawkins, the Nicholas Brothers, Lady Day, Moms Mabley and her protégés Redd Foxx, Slappy White, and Willie Lewis, the Berry Brothers, Butterbeans and Susie, Pearl Bailey, Louis Jordan. I thought I'd gone to heaven, just knowing that so many of my idols were in one spot on the planet. It was dazzling. Birdland, the Capitol Theater, the Paramount Theater—these were the holy venues. Oscar introduced me to everyone, telling them how bad I was supposed to be for my age: Kenny Dorham, Art Tatum, Howard McGhee, Art Blakey, Billy Taylor, Miles Davis, Charlie Mingus. Standing at the bar, eighteen years old, watching Dizzy sipping whatever, it was like a dream. These were the baddest cats on the planet. These were the gods that me and Ray Charles and Charlie Taylor and Buddy Catlett and all the guys back in Seattle used to talk about and never dreamed we would see. I stood at the bar and didn't speak to a soul. I was afraid. I spoke only when spoken to, but I was in heaven. Oscar stayed close and constantly reminded me, "This is the Apple, bruz. Be cool, watch your back," but with the money he'd paid me for my arrangements burning a hole in my pocket, I went to clubs every night on my own and was fresh meat, waiting to be hustled.

One night I went up to Minton's with Howard McGhee and Earl Coleman, the club on 117th Street at the Cecil Hotel in Harlem where bebop was born and where Bird and the other beboppers hung out. Sure enough, there was Bird at the bar. Bird was the originator of bebop, the king of them all. Charlie Parker, the greatest musician of the twentieth century, was standing at the bar alone, drinking. It was like watching God.

Howard and Earl introduced me to Bird. I was nearly paralyzed with awe. He said, "Yeah, OP hipped me to you. You wrote some shit for him, and the cool thing is, you got paid." He slapped me a chilly five. "We're gettin' ready to go cop some vonce. Are you down with it?" I said, "Shit, yeah!" When you're eighteen and hangin' with Bird, you've gotta be down. The four of us took a cab to 139th Street. Bird was sweating a lot. He had a white shirt on and a big belly. One button was off his shirt and I could see some of his meat. We got out of the cab in front of a beat-up tenement and I felt like a million dollars. I was hangin' with Bird. I couldn't believe it. Bird and me.

He asked me, "How much bread you got?" I said I had about seventeen dollars left from two arrangements I'd done for Oscar. I asked if he wanted to see my arrangements.

Bird ignored that. He said, "Youngblood, why doncha let me hold on to that li'l piece of chump change you got there." I gave it to him. He said, "Cool out here for a minute. We'll be back in a few." I thought he was talking about coppin' some reefer. Pleeze!

I waited and waited in the downstairs doorway in my seersucker jacket and Stacy Adams shoes, but he never came down. After about forty minutes of standing there tryin' to be cool in my little Seattle threads, watching junkies wander in and out, I was starting to get the message. I waited a little longer, hoping one of them would come down and at least give me a token so I could ride the subway back downtown to Howard McGhee's room at the America Hotel on 44th Street, where I was sleeping on the couch. But they never showed. Finally I wiped a tear from my face, turned around, and started walking. A young and green turkey from Seattle, first time in New York—the city so nice, they had to name it twice. It started to rain.

CHAPTER 10

Rock 'n' roll

Jerome Richardson, saxophonist, flutist

I was playing with Hamp's band in Boston in '51 when he brought in this kid. I didn't know him. Nobody introduced you in those days. You just got in Hamp's band and after a while everybody knew who you were, if you stuck. Sometimes you didn't stick. There were a lot of reasons for that. The money was bad, the travel was hard. There were eighteen or twenty horn players in that band, and in those days it was survival of the fittest. Nobody stroked you. You got on the bus with your horn and your drawers and if you couldn't play or didn't want to, see you later—and sometimes see you later anyway. You didn't make any money. Everybody in Hamp's band was broker than the Ten Commandments. Hamp only paid seventeen dollars a night, and he did a lot of things I didn't agree with, but one thing he could do was put together a band that could rock. Hamp's band could fire like Peck's hardwood.

What Hampton did then, they call it rock and roll now. He'd criss-cross America playing barns with sawdust on the floor, concert halls, clubs, jook joints—whatever it was—and he'd kill 'em. He'd pound that back-beat on two and four and I don't give a shit who you were, he rocked your ass until you got up on that floor and did the jigaboo. It was almost like jungle music. Pound that beat on two and four, just pound the natives into submission, till every single one of them hollered. He'd hit it till he saw pimps standing on oil drums dancing, people flipping each other doing the jitterbug, and every single person hollering, all that kind of stuff. Hamp was wild. He wanted that every night. He lived for that.

Hamp's single purpose was to entertain, and if you were in that band, that's what you had to do. I sang "Bali Hai" and played sax in the band. He had two or three singers, a comedian, a dancer or two, Janet Thurlow, who was the first white singer to ever sing jazz with a black band. Janet was the one who got Quincy into the band. Apparently Hamp had tried to hire Quincy the year before when we were in Seattle, but he was too young and Gladys—that was Hamp's wife—threw Quincy off the bus. Hamp didn't care about age. He tried to take me on the road when I was fifteen back in Oakland, but my father wouldn't let him. If you could play and would take that seventeen dollars a night, Hamp would take you.

Quincy was just an overgrown kid. He was seventeen and I was thirty when he came into the band, and a lot of older cats didn't take to him because he was so young, but I always liked him. He was such an enthusiastic kid, and he was a pretty good little jazz trumpet player, second or third trumpet. His writing, that's what made him stand out. Quincy could write. He was a quick study. What he didn't know, he would go learn. He absorbed every bit of music around him. He used to write in the kitchens of the hotels where we stayed, or in the halls before the gig, writing all the time. In my mind's eye, I can see him sitting there, little skinny dude sitting backstage, scoring something out. He wasn't shy about asking questions. He learned by doing. You could see he wasn't going to be in that band long.

One of the first things Quincy did when he got in the band was pull

Hamp aside and say, "I got a friend back in Seattle that you have to hear. He plays sax and piano, plus he sings."

Hamp said, "What's his name?"

"Ray Charles."

Hamp went looking for Ray Charles when we came back through Seattle that year, but Ray wasn't around there. He'd left by then.

From the time Quincy joined the band in '51 till the time I left the band about a year later, we did hard road. Traveled through thirty states straight. At one point we did seventeen straight one-nighters. We went all across America, did twenty-seven cities in California alone, then went back across America again: Phoenix, Albuquerque, Wichita, Kansas, Oklahoma City, Tulsa, St. Louis, and all through the South, which I'll never forget as long as I live. As long as I'm sucking air, I'll never go back there. We'd drive by churches in Texas and see black dummies hanging from the steeples. In Miami, they had signs up that said, "No niggers and no dogs after nine P.M." It was like jail. There was no place to stay, no place to eat. You stayed in fleabag black hotels or in people's homes. In Alabama, they'd run ropes down the middle of the room to keep whites and blacks from dancing together; in Memphis we played the Three-Day Theater: two days for whites and one day for blacks. We were there one night and a local piano player wanted to sit in. Our piano player was Milt Buckner, a great player—Milt invented block chords—but he didn't want to let the guy play. Finally, as we were walking out, the guy sat down and played. He was incredible.

His name was Phineas Newborn. One of the finest jazz pianists to ever walk this earth.

There were lots of treasures we came across down there. Even when they'd make us play where white folks paid a dollar and a half to stand on the upstairs balcony and watch the niggas dance, there were still treasures down South. It wasn't all bad. I wasn't frightened down there. I'm from Oakland. When I was a kid, any white person bothered me, I'd hit them in the mouth and be done with it. But it was demeaning to know that every time you got to a city, you had to head across the tracks to Naptown, U.S.A., to find a meal and a place to sleep. In Norfolk, Virginia, Quincy and the singer Jimmy Scott had to sleep in a funeral home in a room full of caskets—caskets with bodies inside them. One time we played a job out in Oklahoma City and had no place to eat. We were sitting on the bus starving, with two hundred miles to our next stop. Finally a trumpet player, a Southerner from New Orleans, he said, "I'm sick of this shit. I know how to get us some food." He stopped the bus in front of the biggest, fanciest restaurant in Oklahoma City. He went in there—walked in the front door—and stayed a while.

The bus driver kept the motor running just in case the Klan was in there to run his ass out.

He came out a few minutes later and said, "C'mon inside."

Who knows what he said, but we filed in there and the white lady inside set up a great big table in the kitchen and fed us like kings. We were so grateful we pitched in and tipped her a hundred dollars. She couldn't believe it. She went around the whole restaurant telling people, "Look at all the money these Negroes gave me." But we were grateful to eat.

That band had some of the funniest cats in the world in it. Little Jimmy Scott. He could gain a hundred pounds and he'd still be small. It seemed like every city we went to, he'd say, "One of my ex-wives lives here." He'd face up to cats six feet tall and the singer Ernestine Anderson would have to talk the guy out of fighting Jimmy. Monk Montgomery, the first guy to ever play a Fender bass, was in that band; Billy Williams, a sax player whose job it was to honk and walk the tables, he was in that band. That was Billy's job, to get up in the middle of the show and walk the tables and back of the seats at theaters. Sometimes he'd stand at the edge of the stage with his back to the audience, still playing, and let himself fall into the audience, and they'd catch him. Hamp tried that one night in Oakland and damn near killed himself. Sometimes Billy and another sax player would do a routine where they'd have a sax battle onstage till one of them fell out like he was dead. Hamp would fan the dead guy, throw water on him, but nothing could wake him until Hamp took off his shoe and stuck it in the guy's nose; then he'd leap to life and start dueling again. It was a wild band.

Some of the greatest jazz musicians in the world came through Hamp's band: Al Grey, Jimmy Cleveland, Clifford Brown, Wes Montgomery, Fats Navarro, Quincy, Gigi Gryce, Charlie Mingus. A lot of them wrote for the band. I heard Mingus once wrote a suite called "Death" in four parts and Hamp passed it out to the band and made the drummer put a backbeat on it. Hamp was obsessed with backbeat. They say Mingus got so mad he threw the drummer off the back of the stage. But see, Hamp wanted his arrangements hot, he wanted excitement. He told his arrangers, "I want those last two pages dark." Meaning full of notes. That's how Quincy cut his teeth, writing those arrangements for Hamp. Those were thunder-and-lightning arrangements.

Quincy learned a lesson from Hamp. He was a kid and he was on the road with men, and he saw how important it was to entertain and enlighten audiences at the same time. That's what Hamp did. Music was very segregated back then. Benny Goodman was called the King of Swing. Paul Whiteman was the King of Jazz, while blacks got to be Dukes (Ellington) and Counts (Basie) and Earls (Hines), but in reality, the blacks were making the music. Hamp and Basie and Louis Jordan, they were kicking ass. Hamp's band was a swing-ass, enlightened band. You had to really play to be in it. It wasn't bullshitting. It was pure and raw, and even though it was rock 'n' roll to make people dance, a lot of it was great jazz.

There was a lot of competition between bands in those days, and Hamp refused to be put down by any band. It didn't matter if it was Duke, or Louis Armstrong, or Benny Goodman, Hamp wanted to be the best. One time, we played the Brooklyn Armory, there were maybe five hundred people out there. We set up and hit them with everything we had—

eighteen men strong—blasting, and not a soul moved. They were dead. We played all the hits, "Air Mail Special" and "Flying Home" with all those big hits in it, da-da-da-di-di-ba-boom! We did this for two hours, which was our usual set, and nobody moved. They just stood there and listened. Finally Hamp said, "Okay, forget it." We took a break, and I noticed Hamp walking all around the hall, mingling with the crowd. The next band that played after us was a little seven-piece band. They counted off a number and kicked our asses. They wore us out. People were going wild.

We said, "Who is that?"

Hamp said, "Some guy named Tito Puente."

I'd never heard of Tito until that moment. He was killing it.

When Tito's band was done and it was our turn to play again, Hamp got in front of the band and said to me, "Jerome, can you play 'Begin the Beguine'? That's a Latin thing. I got up and played it on flute. Hamp hollered, "Play Latin!" The whole band jumped in and played Latin. We played all Hampton's arrangements, every one of them, in Latin style, and wore it out, and got the crowd dancing. See, Hamp had walked through the audience and figured out they were all Latin people, so he gave them that. There wasn't nothing that would stop him from trying to be better than the other guy.

Quincy watched all this. He took it all in and put it in his writing. He had purpose. He didn't announce, "I'm gonna do this or I'm gonna do that," because some of those old cats, they were hard as nails and didn't speak to him for a year. He was too young for them. But he'd work by himself, on a piano someplace, writing out these arrangements eight bars at a time, and he'd get a few of us together to play them for him. That's how his first recording, "Kingfish," was done. He was eighteen when he wrote it.

He was experimenting with that "birth of the cool sound" that Tadd Dameron and Gil Evans were writing. He wrote this thing and we were setting up to practice it, just a few of us, and just as we started to play, someone said, "Jerome, your wife is on the phone from California." I got up and told Bobby Plater, the other alto player, "Bobby, play my part." I came back and they were already playing and Bobby was playing my part, so I stood next to Quincy, who was playing the trumpet part, and took my flute out and played the lead up an octave with him. Quincy said, "I like that sound, I like that blend of trumpet and flute." He asked me to play flute on the recording. They say I was the first person to ever record a jazz flute solo. I wasn't the first to play jazz flute, but there's an argument about who recorded the first flute solo. There was Frank Wess doing the same thing a bit after me, and there was Herbie Mann, who also plays flute and says he put his record out first with a flute solo on it.

Who knows who was first? That's not the point. The point is that no one remembers what the truth is and isn't when it comes to jazz. The history is lost. Even black kids call Kenny G a "jazz" player. I'm seventy-nine. I've done hundreds of sessions in my lifetime. I knew Bird. He was a genius. He could memorize ten pages of music instantly. I played rhythm and blues with King Curtis, I knew rock 'n' roll when it was black music.

I did a workshop a couple of years back with some high school students out in Missouri. It was an all-star jazz band, all white kids except for one. I asked them what they wanted to do with music. Some said teach, others said play.

I said, "Who knows who Louis Armstrong is? Who knows Charlie Parker?"

Not one kid raised their hand.

I said, "If you don't know who they are, you better find out. Class dismissed." I had to leave there quick. I imagine they won't have me back.

At my age, it's the truth you want, that's all. Jazz got its name from sex, thus the term "jazz me." That's why we always played whorehouses and clubs. It's been that way till today. A lot of jazz cats say, "Quincy sold out. He's a businessman. He opted for the swimming pool." Shit, I've had to bless these cats out. I worked with him for years after we left Hamp—with Dinah Washington, with his big band in Europe, most of his records. He and Thad Jones are the best arrangers I've ever played for. I learned more music from those two than from anyone else in my life, and neither was related to the other. When he moved to LA in the sixties, he called me and said, "Jerome, c'mon out here. I'm scoring films. I'm doing records. I got all the work in the world for you."

I said, "Quincy, I'm just an old bebopper. I was honkin' and rockin' and rollin' with King Curtis back in the fifties. I can't go back to that."

He said, "I can't stand to see someone I love starve to death."

I said, "I ain't starving."

He said, "Well, I'll keep calling till you come."

He did that too. He always did that. He was good for it. That's why I love him.

Note: Jerome Richardson died on June 23, 2000.

CHAPTER 11

Pogo

I was officially in the Hampton band now. George "Kingfish" Hart, the road manager, contacted me in Boston from New York. Janet Thurlow had reminded Hamp to hire me before, and she stayed on his case. Finally someone left and I was in. In heaven.

On the bus, the musicians sat in four groups: the Nod Squad, or junkie mainliners; the potheads; the juicers; and the heavenly-bound high rollers. Hamp, who always traveled with a Bible in his lap, sat up front with the church people. Behind them sat the potheads—that was our group. On the other side sat the drinkers. In the back sat the mainliners.

Each time we arrived at a city, the four groups would scatter in all directions to bone up on our various needs. Most times the dope dealers would be waiting for us at the hotels when we arrived. There were several at the Majestic Hotel in Detroit who were like that, and there was another character among them who caught my eye, though as far as I know he was no drug dealer. He was a tall, thin, light-skinned, handsome cat, with red hair, dark amber-tinted shades, a stingy-brimmed hat, shiny shoes, a well-fitted Italian-style suit, and a tie. A cool customer. Always polite and calm. He'd watch as our bus pulled up at 4 A.M., then step out from the shadows and watch the dope dealers do business, saying nothing. No dope dealer fucked with him. He dug the band and I was curious about him, so I asked him his name. He said, "They used to call me Detroit Red, but my true name is Malcolm X." He became one of the greatest leaders and symbols of pride to ever emerge from black America. Even then, there was a certain sureness about him, and dare I say it, a sense of peace. Malcolm X was a peaceful, proud man, and a great one, whose unyielding, warriorlike stance balanced the nonviolent passive resistance of Dr. Martin Luther King.

Hamp liked Malcolm X. He used to tell Malcolm to find the Lord. Malcolm would laugh and say, "I've already met Him."

Malcolm respected Hamp. He used to say Hamp had a lot of racial pride, and he was right. Hamp's wife, Gladys, a black woman, was his manager and she made a ton of money for him, which was unheard of in the forties and fifties. Hamp was a groundbreaker on a lot of levels. He and his wife dealt with some of the toughest, smartest cats in the business, including Joe Glazer, who got his start running concessions for Al Capone and whose Associated Booking Corporation managed Louis Armstrong and represented Duke Ellington. All those people respected Gladys. She and Hamp owned their band. They owned every single music stand and every single musician in the Lionel Hampton Orchestra, including me.

I loved them, but by 1953 I was thinking of leaving. Three years was enough. I'd done my first recording with Hamp when I was eighteen, "Kingfish," my first composition, solo, and arrangement. I learned a lot in Hamp's band, writing arrangements eight bars at a time, bit by bit, under any piano I could find, or in kitchens and in hotel rooms, trying them out on his band. It was the best school in the world and I loved Hamp, but I'd grown out of it. I'd gotten married to my high school sweetheart, Jeri. Our first-born daughter Jolie was born while I was touring Europe and I didn't see her for the first three months of her life. I had a family. I had a wife. I needed money and that seventeen dollars a night wasn't enough. If I could pick up an extra arrangement for Hamp for $31.50, I felt rich. Big bands never made money back then. Count Basie offered Jimmy Cleveland, Jerome Richardson, Benny Bailey, and me gigs constantly, but we stayed with Hamp because he worked more. Basie worked three months and was off six weeks. Hamp worked three hundred and sixty-five days a year. Still, at seventeen dollars a night, there was no way Hamp could've kept that killer band together. Nearly half that band became solo artists: Ernestine Anderson, Art Farmer, Jimmy Cleveland, Jimmy Scott. Then, of course, there was Clifford Brown.

I loved Clifford. Some people called him Brownie, but I called him Pogo after a cartoon character from a newspaper comic strip, because he was little and cool, and he wore this funny Pogo hat. He was the sweetest, humblest, most intelligent cat in the world and the greatest trumpet player I've ever known. Miles Davis, as bad as he was, had bigtime respect for Clifford Brown. On many occasions Clifford would give Miles the mumps down at the jam sessions at Birdland. He'd come down there with his trumpet and light Miles's butt up. He was a genius. No one could touch him.

I first heard Clifford at the Club Harlem in Atlantic City, New Jersey, with Tadd Dameron's band, playing for the Larry Steele Harlem Revue, along with Gigi Gryce and Benny Golson, while we were playing nearby in Wildwood. We were always sniffing around for great young beboppers. One night after we played the Earl Theater in Philly, I was dragged out to a joint in Atlantic City to check out a rhythm and blues band fronted by a singer named Tiny Bradshaw. The tenor player in the band was kicking ass. I said, "Who the fuck is that?" Jimmy Cleveland said, "I think his name is John Coltrane."

We begged Hamp to hire Clifford, Gigi, and Benny, and after hearing them once, he didn't need convincing. Clifford and I were near in age—he was about twenty-two when he came into the band and I was twenty—so we became close. We had a lot in common: ambition, youth, trumpet, arranging, and being too naive to be afraid. When we played the Band Box next door to Birdland, Hamp made the band dress up in purple jackets, Bermuda shorts, and Tyrolean hats and play like bandoliers. We'd march up the steps to the street behind Hamp, who beat his drumsticks on any available surface. Hamp didn't give a hoot about looking cool. He was a showman and he'd do anything to bring people into clubs to catch his band. While the rest of the band marched out, Clifford and I hung back, tying our shoes, pretending to be busy, terrified that Mingus, Miles, Thelonious Monk, and Bird would see us. We went to our first bordello in Europe together. Clifford didn't do drugs or smoke or drink, but just like me, he loved women. When we traveled to Amsterdam in 1953 and walked down that famous Canal Street in the Red Light district, it was like walking through the Saks Fifth Avenue of love—gorgeous women sitting in every window with exquisite sensual lighting. Clifford pointed at the first doorway and said, "Quincy, this one is hip." I said, "Wait, Pogo. Take your time and shop around a little," but he was gone. He ducked into a storefront, burned his money up, came out, ducked into the next, burned up some more money, then borrowed some of mine, then burned that up. When we toured Morocco, Clifford hit those sin dens in Casablanca so hard they threw him out after five o'clock in the afternoon. In those joints, the bouncers would wait behind the walls of the next room, and the minute you did your thang, the girls would knock on the wall with their fists and the bouncer outside would knock on the door, appear, and escort your ass out. They threw Pogo outta every joint down there. Milt Buckner too. Milt got so drunk in one of the joints down in Mexico that he ejected his false teeth out the window of the bus.

Clifford wasn't a womanizer. This was long before he had met and married his beautiful wife, Larue. He was a guy experimenting as young guys do. When we first hit Europe, we were in culture shock. Me, him, and

Art Farmer were walking down the street after our first gig in Oslo, Norway, on our way to a party. Snow was falling, and five sweet young things approached us and said, "We're going to the same party. We'll show you the way." They fell in with us. We walked. A car pulled up driven by a white man. He drove slowly, his old jalopy idling, creaking along. He rolled down the window. We reached for our switchblades. He said, "*Jorgen snorgen . . .*" and some other gobbledygook. We asked the girls, "What did he say?"

The girls said, "He asked you if you would like a ride to the party."

Clifford and I loved Europe, loved the tradition of it. He fit right in because he wasn't your partying type. He was more like a professor, an innocent, sweet guy. We came out of a club in Morocco at 2 A.M. one morning and saw a five-year-old girl begging in the streets in the rain with one hand amputated. Somebody told us her uncle cut off her hand so she could beg, and Clifford gave her every dime he had, and so did I. When he met Toots Thielemans, the great Belgian harmonica and guitar player with George Shearing, who back in the fifties was relatively unknown, Clifford pulled Toots aside and said, "Toots, man, the way you play your ax, *Down Beat* shouldn't even think about calling it miscellaneous." That's the type of man he was, a thoughtful, kind, intelligent, highly skilled man, nothing like the stereotypical jazz musician, who drank and smoked and did drugs. But by and large beboppers were artists, proud, sensitive, intelligent people who practiced for hours and didn't want to shuffle and entertain white folks anymore. They said, "We're artists and want to be treated that way." You can imagine how that kind of attitude came off in the forties and fifties—black men and women talking that way. Forget it. That's why so many turned to drugs. These were the days when managers would sign an artist, record him, take out a million-dollar life insurance policy, record him, let the artist tour Vegas, record him again, then smoke him and collect the insurance. At the first sign of Charlie Parker's jones coming down at a recording session, they'd have him sign away all his composing, publishing, and artist's royalties before they'd let in the dealer so that Bird could shoot up. Monk, Bird, Miles, Basie, nobody knew the business. Most of us sold our songs and publishing rights for peanuts to people who didn't give a shit about anything but money. There was an old joke that if you saw somebody being held by his heels outside a thirty-story window, that was the singer Jackie Wilson renegotiating his contract. The record business was cruel in the fifties; I was there.

Clifford was not only a jazz genius. He was a genius at numbers. He'd studied math at Delaware State University, which makes a lot of sense, because music and math are both absolutes and closely related. I can't stand math. I used to ask Clifford about soloing across thirty-two bars because he and Benny Bailey would have contests to see who could play the longest single melodic line for the umpteenth time during their solo on "Air Mail Special." Jesus. Talk about focused improvisation! They took it to another level. It was composing, is what it was. Clifford would tear that shit up and when I'd ask about it, he'd say, "It's all math." Well, just count me out, then. Clifford was so good at numbers that when the band went to Europe, he'd go around to each member of the band and ask what they'd paid for hotels and meals in the local currency. We'd do three days in a Swedish hotel, four in Belgium, three nights at a hotel in Germany, four nights in France, and he'd find out the exchange rate and do the numbers in his head for the whole band instantly from francs to marks to kronor. His mind was like a computer.

He put my song "Wailbait" on his first record, and when we got to Stockholm in 1953 and Borje Eckberg of Swedish Metronome asked us to do a record. Gigi Gryce asked me to arrange and conduct. We got Clifford and Art Farmer to do it, as well as the Swedish All-Stars: Åke Persson, Arne Domnerus, and two other great players, Lars Gullin and Bengt Hallberg. It was risky business because Gladys Hampton refused to allow anyone in the band to make a record without her permission. She promised to fire anyone who was caught and not give them the money to go home.

That's the exact thing we were afraid of. In fact, a few days before we left for Europe, a rep from the musicians' union in New York called a bunch of us into his office and said he'd heard a lot of bandleaders were taking guys to Europe and stranding them there. He said the union had no jurisdiction once we left U.S. soil and we'd be on our own. That made me nervous. Europe wasn't a six-hour jet ride in those days. It was twenty-seven hours on a prop plane, with two stops for fueling. You were far from home and totally dependent on your bandleader. I knew how Hamp worked back in the States. If we were in a town and a horn player sat in with the band and played better than you, Hamp would fire you, hire that guy, then pay your carfare home out of that guy's seventeen-dollars-a-night salary. Well, seventeen dollars a night wasn't enough to ship a *package* home, much less a person.

A few of the musicians went to a lawyer in New York, who drew up a simple agreement that said Hamp would have to guarantee us passage back to the States if the European tour didn't work out. The contract also guaranteed half the pay up front so they could leave their families a little money. When they brought that letter to Gladys she said, "Nobody in this orchestra is indispensable," and refused to sign it. Moon Mullins, Bobby Plater, Ernestine Anderson, and Elmer Gill quit three days before we left for Europe. Cats in New York were getting their asses kicked. Howard McGhee, the great trumpet player who worked with Charlie Parker and who let me sleep on the couch in his room at the America Hotel, paid so many dues that he borrowed my trumpet for a gig and pawned it! He gave me the pawn ticket slip and said, "Sorry, little homeboy." The great arranger and composer Tadd Dameron, an idol of mine, pulled me aside on 52nd Street one day. "Y'know, li'l bro, just between you 'n' me, ain't nobody out here writing shit but us."

I said, "Yeah?"

As he pointed toward a marquee, he said, "I can see it now, in big, bright lights on Broadway. Music by Tadd Dameron and Quincy Jones.

No, no, no—make that music by Quincy Jones and Tadd Dameron. Are
you diggin' me diggin' you?"

"Cool," I said.

"Now lemme hold two till I see, Lou," he said. I gave him the two
and he was gone. Wilbur Ware, the great bassist, saw me on the street and
said, "Young blood, I'm trying to kick my habit. Lemme hold four dollars
to get back to Brooklyn." I gave him the bread.

These cats had been out there a while, and they were struggling, and
there was no way I wanted to do that. Not with a wife and expecting a
child. I didn't have the luxury of calling somebody up and saying, "Send
me some money." I couldn't call Daddy or Lloyd. I had to go with it. I
hung on and went to Europe with Hamp, so when the opportunity to
record came up, I said, "I'm in," despite the risk.

We decided to do the sessions from midnight to 7 A.M. That way we
could still do Hamp's gigs and no one would miss us, but somebody dimed
on us, for Gladys posted the road manager George Hart in the lobby of
the hotel so no one could leave. Me, Art, and Clifford climbed out the hotel window and down the fire escape each night to get to the studio to do
the sessions. We began at midnight, played till 6 or 7 A.M., then climbed
back up the fire escape and through the hotel window. The subterfuge was
worth it, though more than once we were caught out in the midnight sun,
which appeared at 1 A.M. The record was released in Europe almost immediately as "Clifford Brown, Art Farmer, and the Swedish American All-
Stars," and by the time we got to Brussels a few weeks later, word was out
that we were kinda hot for bebop. A famous Belgian jazz critic named
Carlos De Radinsky came by our hotel to interview me, Clifford, and
Monk Montgomery, the bass player. It was our first-ever European interview, so Clifford said, "Let's get cool." First the three of us took our jackets off, put on the hotel's terry-cloth robes—which we thought had been
left behind—and our new Tyrolean hats, and poured tea into finger bowls
normally used to clean and soak fingernails. Clifford walked into the bath-

room and spotted a tiny sink next to the toilet. It was low to the ground. It had two faucets on it. He said, "What's that fountain for?"

I said, "I don't know."

He said, "Let's soak our feet in it. That's really chilly."

"Okay."

We ran hot water into it and stuck our bare feet in it. It was a bidet. A bidet looks like a toilet bowl except women use it to wash their privates. You see it only in top European hotels. To a guy from the South Side of Chicago, it still looked like a footbath. In the same large bathroom, we found three tall stools, which we immediately mounted.

In this position, we greeted our interviewer.

When De Radinsky walked into the hotel room and saw the three of us sitting in that bathroom in bathrobes and Tyrolean hats, soaking our feet in the bidet, and sipping tea out of finger bowls, he almost backed out of the room. Who cared? We were cool, and ready for whatever came.

Clifford, myself, and some others from Hamp's band did several more underground sessions in Europe, some in Sweden, some in Paris, and Gladys was furious about it. It caused a lot of tension that eventually erupted in Algiers when George Hart confronted Clifford in a street behind the hotel and started to rough him up. Clifford fought to defend himself and dislocated his shoulder. We took him up to the hotel room, where I had to put his shoulder back in. He was screaming in pain, crying, as I did it, but that night he still played the gig.

That was it for me, Clifford, and a lot of the others—all this subterfuge, all this hiding, the infighting, and making that seventeen dollars a night. When we got back to New York in December 1953 after nearly four months in Europe, eleven of us, including Walter Williams, Anthony Ortega, Gigi Gryce, Jimmy Cleveland, Buster Cooper, Art Farmer, Clifford, and myself, quit. For the first time in his life, Hamp nearly didn't have a band. And me, I didn't have a nickel.

We made a lot of promises to each other while we were together, me and Clifford. Two years on the road and the people you're with become more family to you than your own. He said, "Quincy, you write good, man, we're gonna do a lot more records together." I agreed. He didn't have to convince me. It was just a matter of finding the right opportunity and record company. We both hit New York broke and had to hustle. I wrote for everyone who would pay. Clifford recorded whenever he had the chance. We survived and got together when we could. I arranged and produced an album with Clifford and Helen Merrill in 1954. I saw him in Washington, D.C., when he was working together with the great drummer Max Roach. We went to see Nat Cole, then sat up in my hotel room all night talking about music until we fell asleep across the bed with our clothes on. Clifford slept with his Pogo hat on. When we got up the next day I said, "Brownie, lemme hold your lid till I see you back in the Apple."

He said, "You got it!" and took it off his head. That's the kind of cat he was. He loved that hat.

I said, "Naw, Pogo, I'm just kidding."

A few months later, in June 1956, I was in the studio with Gil Evans and Helen Merrill when Gil walked into the control booth with his face white as a sheet. He said Clifford had just been killed in a car wreck on the Pennsylvania Turnpike with Bud Powell's brother Richie and his wife, Nancy, who was driving. Clifford was sleeping in the back seat when the car lost control on a rain-slicked road, hit a bridge abutment, and rolled down a seventy-five-foot embankment. I couldn't believe it. I was twenty-three and he was twenty-five. It was the first time a close friend of mine had died. The next day I went out and bought every newspaper in New York, hoping to save the clippings that would talk about Clifford and what a great artist he was. I wanted to save them to show to my daughter Jolie when she got grown. It was a waste of time. His death hardly made the paper.

CHAPTER 12

A sip of water

Jeri Caldwell-Jones

I remember the day I first saw him. I was in the chorus of a school production called "The Funfest" at Garfield High in Seattle in 1947. We were rehearsing with the orchestra, and during a break in rehearsal I was sitting on the edge of the stage with my girlfriend and I looked down into the orchestra pit and I saw this beautiful little face. Quincy was sitting on the edge of a piano stool holding his trumpet. He looked up from the pit and saw me onstage and he said, "What's hapnin', huss?" or something like that. That was the hip talk in those days. Huss. I turned to my girlfriend and said, "I'm in love."

I was a sophomore at the time and he was a junior. I'd never seen him before, but after that day I started to look for him in the hallways and I'd find ways to bump into him. Every day he came down some stairs from a chorus class and there was a water fountain at the bottom. I knew he'd pass the water fountain after his class, so I hung around there and sipped water, hoping he'd notice me. I stood there a few days drinking myself silly while he passed by; finally he figured out I was trying to get his attention. Then he came to the water fountain and he took a sip himself. Then I took a sip. Then he took a sip. So for a while we had this thing about going to the water fountain and sipping water. Finally he spoke up and asked for my phone number. I was so excited.

We talked a little, then he called me at home, and we started dating. He was the kindest, sweetest soul I'd ever met. He was my first love. It hadn't sunk in that him being black and me being white wasn't okay. Garfield, our school, was the most integrated high school in America. Jimi Hendrix and Bruce Lee both went there later. It was right out Quincy's back door, and the kids were black, Filipino, Asian, Jewish, poor whites, rich whites from Broadmoor and Montlake. It was very progressive, with an awful lot of students, so it didn't seem unusual. I was completely naive about the race thing because of the way I was raised. It was never a problem in my house—till then.

One night I was sitting at the dining-room table doing my homework and my mother was in the kitchen. If I talked to her, she could hear me from the kitchen where she was cooking. I said, "Oh, Mother, I met this wonderful guy." I was telling her all about him and then I threw in the part about . . . we did not use the expression "black" back then. I guess I said Negro. Now it sounds so funny. Negro. Quincy the Negro. God, that's funny. But that's the word we used. So I mentioned he was a Negro, and that I had a crush on him, and my mother came out of the kitchen holding a frying pan, and she nearly dropped it. She said, "Jeri, don't say that!" I was shocked she reacted so vehemently over my expressing an interest in this black guy. I didn't know what to say. My parents were always so liberal. I was always taught that everybody is as good as everybody else, and this was the first realization that this was true until it was about me. So I became a little bit leery about being too open at home about the situation. I knew I had to be secretive about it. I could never tell my father about it. He definitely would not have approved.

I was a member of four high school sororities, two local and two city-wide. When they found out I was dating Quincy, all hell broke loose. One mother called the sorority president and said, "If Jeri Caldwell is going to stay in this group then I want my daughter out, because Jeri's dating a Negro." They asked me to resign, which I did. My sister Gay was then attending the University of Washington and had pledged Tri Delta. My mother had been a Tri Delt twenty-five years earlier, and I was on their legacy list. They called my sister in and said, "It has come to our attention that your sister Jeri is dating a Negro. This is not behavior we can condone. Tell your sister to stop or she will be dropped from the legacy list." This is how my sister Gay learned of my relationship with Quincy. My days as a sorority girl were over.

It didn't end there. The principal of Garfield High and the girls' guidance counselor both called me into their office on separate occasions and told me I was ruining my life by dating Quincy. I wasn't defiant. I listened and left. It was ironic to me that years later Garfield High named an auditorium after Quincy. They said, "He's one of our most famous graduates." That gave me a lot of satisfaction.

Quincy wasn't surprised by any of this. He understood it in a better way than I did because he had experienced prejudice. He always thinks the best of people. He's warm to everyone; he's always concerned about everyone. It doesn't matter whether it's the garbageman or the President of the United States; he has the same amount of love for them. That's just his personality. That's just him. It's his gift, so he ignored these things, and I did too.

We did everything low-key. We didn't go to movies or restaurants. We went to drive-ins or Bumps Blackwell's house or talked on the phone. My mother figured out that I was dating him and insisted she had to meet him, so I arranged for them to meet at a restaurant. Quincy got all dressed up in a suit and tie and went down to this restaurant on Queen Anne Hill and told my mother he loved me and he was going to marry me. He told her he would always take care of me and he knew she was not happy about it, but that's the way it was.

Mother came home and said, "Oh, he's got the prettiest eyes. He is so sweet. I understand why you love him." That's just like Quincy to turn her around. Here she went down there to tell him, "Stay away from my daughter," and she came back in love with him. It's hard not to love Quincy. She said, "Okay, maybe someday you guys can get together, but not now. Promise me you won't see him anymore until you're out of high school." So I promised her, but I didn't keep that promise. We dated till he graduated, and then he went to Seattle University on a scholarship for a few months until he got a scholarship to go to music school in Boston. I was supposed to move there after I graduated from high school and we would get married, but before I could get there, he joined the Lionel Hampton band and went on the road. He wrote me and said, "Come to New York, because that's where we'll eventually settle and that's where all the musicians are anyway." I made plans to come to New York after high school with a girlfriend who wanted to be a singer. After I arrived in the city we went ahead with our plans to get married.

I was eighteen and he was nineteen at the time. Women could marry at eighteen, but men had to be twenty-one. Quincy had to get a notarized form from his father granting him permission to get married. We got blood tests, did all the paperwork, and went down to City Hall to get married. We planned to go to Philadelphia afterward on our so-called honeymoon where I'd meet the Lionel Hampton band and they'd throw us a party as newlyweds. This was supposed to be our big moment. We were all excited about it.

When we got to City Hall, they refused to accept our papers. The day before, when I'd gone down there, everything had gone smoothly. But when I showed up with Quincy, they said, "These forms are no good."

We were devastated. We didn't know what to do. I started to cry. Quincy said, "Who cares, Jeri? I love you and we're married. No piece of paper says you're not my wife." We went to Philadelphia anyway and told everyone we were married, even though we weren't. We actually didn't marry until 1957, well after Jolie was born. That one hurt me a lot, more so than a lot of other things, because I wanted to be married. I didn't care about civil rights. I didn't know what that meant. I just wanted to marry Quincy. But the way Quincy is, he forgets anything negative immediately. It doesn't register with him. He blots it out or goes around it or over it and it's done. It took longer for me to get over that one.

He was on the road in Europe with Hampton when I discovered I was pregnant with our daughter Jolie in early 1953. When I'd arrived in New York, I'd stayed at the YMCA with a girlfriend. When I found out about the pregnancy I moved in with Oscar Pettiford's wife, Harriet, in a tenement apartment on the Lower East Side. It was a fourth-floor walk-up with no doors between the rooms, a bathtub in the kitchen with a door on top for a table, and the toilet in a hall shared with four other apartments. When Quincy was in town we slept on a mattress on the floor of the "living room." But we were grateful because it gave us the chance to save for our own place. God bless the Pettifords for what they did for us when we came to New York. Them and Harry Lookofsky, who bought Jolie her first crib when we couldn't afford to buy her one. Quincy was only making seventeen dollars a night with Hampton, but I was working and we managed to save what we needed. Then I got swindled out of every dime of it.

I found a nice apartment. The woman living there told me I could sublease the place from her if I bought her furniture, which came to just about all the money Quincy and I had saved. She seemed so nice, I gave her all our money, and she disappeared. Come to find out that the furniture was not paid for, and she'd run out on the apartment lease. So I had no lease, no apartment, and all our money was gone. I searched out the real landlord of the apartment and told him what happened and he said, "That's okay. I'll still rent the place to you." I filled out an application. But when I went back to him to sign the lease he said, "I did a background check on your husband. You didn't tell me he was Negro."

I said, "He's got a good, steady job."

He told me, "No Negroes."

They didn't say black people back then, but everybody knew the Lionel Hampton band was a black band. So just like that I was out of an apartment and the money we'd saved. And I was seven months pregnant, big as a house, climbing up four flights of stairs at Harriet Pettiford's walk-up. It was horrible. I wanted to die. I had to call Quincy long-distance and tell him that I had lost all our money in this stupid deal.

He wasn't angry at all. He said, "Don't worry, Jeri. We'll get more money. We'll figure out a way." We did find an apartment before Jolie was born, on the Upper West Side. Quincy had this attitude about money, that if you live as though you have it and you are doing the right thing and utilizing yourself to the best of yourself, the money will come. You have to find your divine inheritance, he used to say. When Jolie was born he left the band. Then he came home and we got our own place, but we were broke. The musicians' union in New York wouldn't let him play trumpet when he came back from Europe because you had to be in New York six months before you got your union card, so the only way he could make money was to write arrangements. After he wrote them, I'd take the scores to the copyist Bunny Bardach on the other side of town so he could copy out the parts. Quincy used to take two subway tokens and go down to Birdland at 52nd and Broadway and hang out trying to find work. He couldn't even afford a glass of wine down there. James Moody hired him under the table as a standby trumpet player and paid him twenty dollars an arrangement. And Basie hired him. Dinah, Moody, and Basie's arrangements saved us.

Even though we were poor, we were happy. In those days, we were still young enough to dream. On New Year's Eve in 1953, Oscar and Harriet Pettiford came to our fourth-floor walk-up apartment to celebrate. Quincy and Oscar weren't working. For a musician, if you're not working on New Year's Eve, that's bad news, because everybody's playing a party or something for twice the usual money, but we had fun. We had meat loaf, Wonder bread, a bottle of cheap red wine, and two grapefruits split four ways for dessert. We watched the new year come in on our little fifteen-dollar black-and-white TV set. Quincy was all excited about the records he'd done in Europe with Clifford Brown. He kept saying, "This album is going to do it for us, Jeri. Things are really looking up. We're big in Europe."

I said, "I'll be glad when you're big here." Oscar and Harriet thought that was funny.

Quincy said, "Don't worry, Jeri. If I keep getting better, I'll be big— I promise you." He was right too, but our marriage didn't survive his career. We were both just too young to handle it. I'm glad now that I saved all his letters. Our life together gave me my greatest blessings, our incredible daughter, Jolie, and two wonderful grandsons, Donovan and Sunny. The older I get, the more I appreciate Quincy and value our continuing friendship. I think he has evolved into a truly admirable human being. I took that sip of water a long time ago, but I can still taste it—and it's still sweet.

CHAPTER 13

Dinah

Me and my wife, Jeri, were sleeping on a mattress on the floor of Oscar Pettiford's apartment in 1952 when I woke up to find her father pacing the floor. I had no idea how he'd gotten in: I almost had a heart attack when I saw him.

Her father didn't know me and he damn sure didn't want to. He never did approve of our marriage because of the racial thing. He had his own problems, including the fact that he'd lost all his money during the Depression. He paced the floor wordlessly while I jumped out of bed in my Fruit Of The Looms, got dressed, and took off. When I came back later that day he was gone.

Her parents had come to visit from Seattle to see our new baby, Jolie. They were delighted about the baby, but her dad was not delighted about us. I don't remember whether he was around long enough to see that I messed that marriage up, because Jeri's parents divorced not long after. But her mother was right about one thing: we were too young.

I did love Jeri. She was special: passionate, beautiful, kind, and supportive. She listened to every single one of my dreams and encouraged them all. She seemed to have none of the problems I had. All she did was do her best to make our marriage work. But from 1954 to 1957 the work started to flow: I did hundreds of arrangements, jingles, and recordings with James Moody, Harry Lookofsky, Dizzy Gillespie, Ray Anthony, King Pleasure, Count Basie, Sonny Stitt, Tommy Dorsey, Cannonball Adderley, Gene Krupa, Betty Carter, and Dinah Washington, and with the work came money, and with the money came temptations. Women and money and work came together and I embraced them all.

It wasn't hard. All of my life I met women, even when I was broke. Believe me, groupies didn't start with rock 'n' roll. Young, in the prime of my life, and some of the finest women in the world, women that most men dream about, were available. I couldn't stop even if I wanted to. When we arrived in Stockholm with Hamp in '53, some of the guys still held to the conventional ghetto wisdom that European women couldn't make love. They found out that this was inaccurate. The Swedish women had never seen black men from the States before. The women in Oslo would run their hands across our faces to see if we were real. The women thought we were made of chocolate. The children loved us, the women loved us more, and there was no racism hanging over our heads to hold us back. Brothers, mothers, even fathers were giving up their beds for us. For the first time, we felt free and we embraced that, as our jazz expatriate predecessors had. When I got back to the States in '53, I kept going like I was in Europe, dogging it. I slept with women I was working with and those on the outside—black, white, Asian. Some turned me down. One woman, a Broadway star, told me, "You're too short," and another one said, "No, baby, you ain't got enough money for me—I can't go there." But most were game.

I did my best to keep it from Jeri at first. The late nights of hanging at bars and clubs and studios, these were all things she knew I needed to do to get work. None of the work I got came while I was sitting home. I was eligible for unemployment, and I once tried standing in line to collect it. I was desperate and it was degrading. I stood there from 8 A.M. till noon, and when I got to the head of the line, the guy put up a "Closed for lunch" sign and said, "Go get some coffee and come back in an hour." I said, "Up yours, your momma's, and your dog's too, I'd rather starve." I left and never went back. It was either starve or get out on the scene, hang out, get work, let people know I was in town and available. I'd hang at Birdland or at 1619 Broadway, the Brill Building, or at Sam Herman's or Emile Charlap's copying places with the rest of the arrangers.

The songwriters and arrangers hung out in front of the Brill Building doorway like Mafia hit men, hands in pockets, collars up, freezing their asses off, broke, hungry, always looking for the next job. Broadway shows, television and film scores, records, nightclub acts, commercials, industrial shows—we did it all. These were some of the finest arrangers on the planet: Johnny Mandel, Billy Byers, Don Sedesky, Tadd Dameron, Don Costa, Marion Evans, Ernie Wilkins, Thad Jones, Jimmy Mundy. Whoever happened to be working would invite us to Charlie's Tavern and we'd gather there, sip coffee and whiskey, and have rap sessions that could last for days. Cats would walk to Sam Herman's and Emile Charlap's copying places at 4 A.M. like it was noon, talking arranging. Arranging is difficult work, but at its best it's like painting. The final product is a beautiful thing to hear, a tapestry of different colors and textures and densities, but the meat and guts of arranging is sweatshop work, a blend of experience, architecture, soul, and science. You're literally tearing fears, observations, harmonies, and rhythms down to their essence and building them back up to support and re-create the song. We'd work out arranging problems for days, not hours. It always began with one of us asking the same question: "Why?"

Why did Duke and Billy Strayhorn put the Harry Carney baritone sax part above the second tenor sax? Why do brass in buckets and four unison C flutes doubling a melodic top line accompaniment give the aural illusion of strings? Why does Coleman

Hawkins playing "There Will Never Be Another You" at 33¹/₃ rpm sound like Bird when you speed it up to 45 rpm? Why did Benny Carter and Fletcher Henderson and Don Redman use three, four, or five saxes when they created a sax section rather than six or two? Why does the combination of four alto flutes, four French horns, four flügelhorns, four trombones, and a tuba blend so naturally, especially for arrangers who understand the value of good voice leading? Why, why, why . . .

We'd attack each "why" like mechanics working on a broken car, disassembling it, laying the pieces out, reassembling them, and before you knew it the night had passed and the sun was coming up over the horizon. On Monday afternoons we'd gather at Birdland, each of us holding our arrangements nervously as Count Basie, his mighty band in tow, would have his straw boss and lead alto, Marshall Royal, look over our arrangements by Ernie Wilkins or Frank Foster or Neal Hefti or Johnny Mandel or Thad Jones and casually pick out a few to try during his weekly Monday rehearsals. We'd wait with bated breath as he looked them over, hoping he'd choose ours, knowing that the next meal sometimes depended on it. Basie had a keen eye for a groove. One afternoon Neal Hefti, an exceptional arranger with a high-energy, gum-chewing manner, pulled out an arrangement for a tune he'd written called "Li'l Darlin'." He stood before the Basie band, cigarette dangling from his lips, and counted it off in fast motion: "1-2-3-4" bang! Away they went, off to the races.

Basie stood up, waved his hand, and stopped the band immediately. "Uh-uh—hold it! I think it's too fast. I wanna hear more of those big fat juicy horn voicings. So try it right about here. Let's put it in the pocket— y'all know what I'm talkin' about," he said with that typical Basie smile.

He counted off the tempo in ½ time, slower, stomping his foot: "A-one, a-two . . . 3 . . . 4." Ray Charles's version of "Drown in My Own Tears" on the *Live in Georgia* LP was the only song that came close in terms of tempo: you could shave between the beats. The band launched into Hefti's piece again and created the most beautiful portrait you could imagine. The song sounded like billowing puffs of transparent clouds floating through a clear blue sky. "Li'l Darlin' " became a classic. Basie made it that way. He'd just delivered a master class in the power of the perfect-in-the-pocket tempo, a lesson that has stayed with me all my life.

I kept it in mind when I presented my first serious arrangement to Basie, an arrangement of "Somewhere Over the Rainbow" featuring Marshall Royal on alto sax. I made it tight, mellow, and with delicious chord substitutions, and he bought it the first time he heard it. I loved him. I met him at the age of thirteen in Seattle and we became tight for the rest of his life. He was the most gracious, kindest, gentlest, most fun person you'd ever want to meet. In contrast, Duke Ellington was urban and regal. I admired and loved Duke, but I was much closer to Basie, who was country and down-home. Basie was family to me, an idol, a father, a brother, a mentor, a manager, whatever he had to be. He taught me to survive in the music business. "Learn to deal with the valleys, the hills will take care of themselves," he advised. "And always be fair." Back in those days, black entertainers were like a close family: they supported each other, cared about one another. They all knew one thing for sure—no one ever stayed on top. When I started my own big band and was struggling to get started in the early sixties, Basie signed a loan for me to get a $5,500 advance from a bank. One time he got me a gig in Hartford, Connecticut, subbing for his band to play for the Black Shriners up there. I got there with my kick-ass New York band, eighteen musicians strong, and only 700 people showed up. They were expecting 1,800. I collected the money for the gig and was about to split town when Basie showed up unannounced and said, "Give the man half his money back."

I said, "Are you serious?"

Basie said, "Your name was on the poster. You didn't draw. That ain't his fault. You may have to meet this promoter down the road again. Give him half the money back."

I gave it back.

The lessons you learned from Basie couldn't be learned at home writing arrangements at the piano. Jeri knew this, but it was what she didn't know that killed us. The hanging out with Sidney Poitier, who used to drop by Birdland while working on the elimination of his Bahamian accent, the nights of laughin' and low-lifin' with young Marlon Brando in a red fedora hat, who was hanging at Small's Paradise in Harlem late nights after doing *A Streetcar Named Desire* on Broadway. Sidney, Marlon, myself— we were all hungry then, eager to find out who we were. We had a mutual respect, common interests, the same kinds of goals. And we'd all had raggedy childhoods. But it was the women I couldn't figure out. Jeri would field calls from women at all hours of the day, and I would tell her, "Such and such needs me to do a song for her," or "Such and such is Basie's secretary." But she knew the truth. The woman who loves you always knows.

I got caught flat, red-handed, several times, one of the most notable times being with Dinah Washington, which was ironic because Dinah and I never had a real thang thing. It was just a big friendship and a series of small affairs, but my tryst with Dinah Washington was the beginning of the end of my marriage, which lingered on for the next five years but began to fizzle and fall apart at that point.

Dinah was a star. She was established and I was not. She had a voice that was like the pipes of life. She could also do something a lot of singers then and now could not do: She could take the melody in her hand, hold it like an egg, crack it open, fry it, let it sizzle, reconstruct it, put the egg back in the box and back in the refrigerator, and you would've still understood every single syllable of every single word she sang. Every single melody she sang she made hers. Once she put her soulful trademark on a song, she owned it and it was never the same. She was complete, original, and magnificent.

I met her at the Apollo Theater and she became a great friend to me. She was innately kind and generous. She had heard of the four-horn arrangements I was writing for James Moody, so she hired me to write arrangements with the same instrumentation for her road band. We went to Chicago for our first session to record songs that had lyrics like "I love my trombone-playing Daddy with his big, long, sliding thing." In that period all her songs, like "TV's the Thing" and "Long John," had risqué double meanings. When we got back to New York, she said, "I want you to write the arrangements for my next record." Her label, Mercury Records, said, "No, we want a name." Dinah said, "Here's a name, for your ass: Dinah Washington, and Quincy Jones is my arranger." Dinah didn't play. She could give you the mumps if she had to. They capitulated. The record, *For Those in Love,* was a big success and we became good friends. We ended up doing ten albums together.

Dinah was something else. She was married four or five or nine times, who knows? I'd seen her take an ex-lover's clothes she'd bought, brand-new clothes, and put all of them—shoes, hats, overcoats, everything—in the bathtub, pour kerosene on them, and set them on fire. I'd seen her in the middle of a show at the Douglas Showbar in Philly introducing one of her current husbands this way: "Ladies and gentlemen, in one month this man you're looking at up here tonight will have been gone three and a half weeks." Yes, she was tough, but she had to be. Some of those dudes weren't the type you'd see sneaking off to the library to read Ellison's *Invisible Man.* Two notable exceptions were Jimmy Cobb and Night Train Lane, the defensive back for the Detroit Lions—always were, and still are, two classy brothers.

Dinah was always in my corner. One closing night at Pep's in Philly, after fussing all night she came down to the basement on a ladder to help me with the bookkeeping for my big band. She was a true, kind, sweet, generous sister-friend who wanted what all good women want: true love. But let's be clear here: she could get black belt ghetto on your ass in a New York minute. Make no mistake about that.

I seemed to amuse Dinah because of my age. She used to call me "grasshopper kid" because I was young and green, and because we used to drink grasshoppers together. She cooked chitterlings for me and my brother Lloyd when he came to New York to visit me—Lloyd never touched chitterlings after that unless Dinah made them. I took her to my Aunt Mabel's restaurant in Chicago when we toured there. People treated her—and me—like royalty. She took me in, adopted me, showed me the ropes in New York. One night she took me out to the Apollo Theater and afterward we drank the green off of those grasshoppers and got paralyzed together. We laughed and partied all night, ended up at her place, and I came home at 11 A.M. after hanging my head out the cab window on the way home to breeze the booze and perfume smell off me.

When I walked in the apartment Jeri was justifiably furious, but said and showed nothing. Normally she would have been taking Jolie to school at that time and I was hoping she'd already left that morning, but she hadn't. So I sat up till noon, afraid Dinah would call. I knew she would. This wasn't some sweet little barmaid you could sweet-talk with "You need space, I need space, let's have our space." Shit. This was Dinah Washington. She was the Queen, but I was so tired I fell asleep.

The ringing phone woke me up. I dove for it, but too late. As I picked up, I heard Jeri pick up the line in the other room. Before I could get a word out, Dinah said, "You know what, Mr. Green-ass Grasshopper? In case you forgot, I got your li'l ass drunk last night and we did the doogie three times."

There was nothing to say.

I heard the click as Jeri hung up the phone extension in the other room.

CHAPTER 14

The meaning of mother

Lloyd Jones

When I came to New York in 1955, the first thing Quincy made me do was change clothes. I walked into his apartment on 92nd Street wearing alligator shoes, a big ole pimp hat, purple silk shirt, and a huge tie in a Billy Eckstine knot. He said, "Little bro, I think you need a little help." He gave me a few things from his closet and the next day went out and bought me some new clothes.

He said he didn't know how "country" he looked when he first got to New York until he saw me that day. Looking at me was like looking at himself when he first hit the city four years before. Three years with Hampton across the United States and Europe changed him. He'd seen a lot of the world and he wanted me to know all about it.

I was a bit disappointed because he'd never sent for me earlier. Seattle had been rough once he left. Daddy and Elvera's marriage was breaking up. There'd been a lot of fights at home between me and Elvera. I got a work-study track scholarship to Washington State University in Pullman.

The day I left for college, Elvera told me, "I don't know why you want to go to college, nobody else in this house is going to college, but I'll tell you what: You won't get a dime out of me." That was my send-off. There were four black students in the whole school. I was miserable and came home after a year. When I got back to Seattle, I was trying to get my life together when Elvera threw me out of the house. I was nineteen. I spent Thanksgiving eating hot dogs and soda pop on a park bench at Garfield High School, just around the corner from where we lived.

When I told Quincy this, he said, "Why the hell didn't you write and tell me what was going on?"

Then I said something that really fucked him up. I said, "I did."

He was going three thousand miles a minute and never stopped. He's a master at shrugging off bad news, but he took that one in the chest. He really felt bad about it, and he tried to make it up to me. He took me with him to recording sessions all over New York. We went to a Lurlean Hunter recording session, then to an Oscar Peterson session. We traveled to Philadelphia, where he did a Dinah Washington gig. Dinah was crazy about him and cooked chitterlings for us. Toots Thielemans (just in from Belgium) told me she cooked him the best spinach he'd ever tasted in his life after being served a plate of her collard greens. He introduced me to everyone. I felt good being around him. He's the only family I've ever felt close to. He always made me feel safe.

We had fun. One afternoon he brought home this little girl who was maybe four. She was beautiful. She had copper-toned skin and light eyes. He stood her in the middle of the living room with a twinkle in his eye and said, "Lloyd, watch this."

He put on a Dinah Washington record and the kid sang every note, every nuance of Dinah. She was incredible. I said, "Who's she?"

He said, "Her name's Patti Austin." Patti was Dinah's goddaughter. She would sing with Quincy for the next forty years. Then somehow Quincy became a midget magnet and got to know a bunch of twelve-year-old kids: Aretha Franklin, Stevie Wonder, Michael Jackson, Tevin Campbell. He has always been blessed by being in the right place at the right time when it came to hearing major singers. I was there when Dinah Washington told him about Aretha Franklin. She said, "Rev. C. L. Franklin has a twelve-year-old daughter up in Detroit named Aretha. She's the next one. You watch."

Sometimes we'd wander around New York all day, hanging out, smoking hemp, getting the munchies, just laughing. Sometimes Ray Charles would come by. Quincy had a new stereo once and Ray walked in, headed straight to the stereo and started messing with it like crazy, twisting them and experimenting with the sounds they made on an analog glass tube, shocks and all. Quincy would come back to the apartment all excited at night and tell me about what he'd seen that day. He loved to tell stories. One night when he was doing arrangements for Jackie Gleason's summer replacement show with the Tommy and Jimmy Dorsey Orchestra, he said, "Lloyd, they brought this kid in from Memphis. He was shaking his ass all over the place. He couldn't quite sing in tempo with this band, so a man named Sam Phillips asked CBS to fly in some guys from Memphis just to play with him. Tommy said, 'Let's get through this so we won't ever have to listen to this shit again.' The next day they got 8,000 letters." The kid was Elvis Presley. This was the beginning of the end of big band, swing, and bebop. Young white America's emotional revolution and mainstream rock and roll were on the way.

Quincy could see right where he was in history. He understood it, man. By that I mean he saw the great American musicians and what they did and where they were taking American music. The arrangements he wrote, he would've done them for free. He was getting ripped off all the time. He was arranging and conducting records you never heard of and he didn't give a shit. He'd get forty or fifty dollars and do full arrangements, thirteen horns and a rhythm section and sometimes getting no credit on the records at all. Other guys were getting two or three times that amount and they weren't nearly as good as him. I collected a lot of those records for years. Pop records, jazz, all his old arrangements, everything. A lot of them don't even have his name on them. I have records where he's singing background with Milt Jackson, the vibes player, and Ernestine Anderson on Russell Jacquet's record. He played trumpet with Louis Jordan, James Moody, Dinah Washington at the Apollo. Shit, he was struggling back then. He took whatever he could get. Even he didn't remember all the sessions he did, there was so many. Then I dropped a bomb on him.

I said, "Sarah's in New York."

Sarah. Our mother. I'd seen her around. How she got there or where she stayed I never knew, but Sarah could always hold a job. She was smart.

It always hurt him to talk about our mother. Even as we got older, we never had any idea how to handle it. Sarah wouldn't let go; she'd follow you around. She did that to me in Seattle after I got out of high school. She'd appear at any time, just pop up, and follow me everywhere, harass and criticize me till I paid attention to her. She used to fight with Elvera, call the power company and get Elvera's lights shut off, send the police to her house by calling them and telling them her boys were kidnapped and being held hostage. She could raise hell and there was no stopping her. It was a complete mess for us, because despite all that we loved her, but we never knew what to do about it. So me telling Quincy that she was in New York was bad news for him, I know, but it was a warning, our own secret code: *Sarah's around. You know what to do. Better lay low.*

Quincy said, "I know," and he thanked me and didn't say anything else, so we drank in silence for a while. Finally I said, "This is half the family I got, right here. You and Daddy."

Quincy said, "You shouldn't feel that way. Elvera's kids are our family too. We ain't the first group of kids raised by two messed-up women who don't typify normality."

"That's easy for you to say," I said. "You been out of Elvera's house a long time."

"You don't have to stay there," he said.

I said, "I ain't. I'm joining the Air Force."

He was shocked. He said, "What would you want to do that for, man? Stay here with me."

"Man, you got your own life, you got your own family. I gotta get mine. For once, I'd like to sit around a table with a family and a wife and hear her say, 'Merry Christmas, honey. I love you.' "

He got so mad I thought he was going to get up and walk out of the room. I felt sorry about bringing it up then, but I was always fighting to reconcile myself with it, always fighting to try to come to grips with Sarah. Quincy could never do that.

He said, "I don't know what that word 'mother' means. What does the word 'mother' mean to you, Lloyd? Tell me."

I thought about it and thought about it, but I couldn't answer him in any way that made sense, so finally I said, "Forget it," and told him I was sorry. He told me he was sorry too, and he raised his glass and we toasted Merry Christmas.

I left New York a few days later, joined the Air Force, and didn't set eyes on him for eight years. Every time I reached out to him, wrote him, he wouldn't reach back, and I knew why. It was my fault, really, for taking him to a place where he didn't need to be, going into that whole deal about our mother. But who else could I ask about it? He was the only one who had the same hole in his soul that I had. There was no one else who understood. There was no one else to ask.

CHAPTER 15

Dizzy

The 1954 Supreme Court decision *Brown v. Board of Education* outlawed racial segregation in public schools and set a tone for the country at that time. In 1955, the famous congressman from Harlem, Adam Clayton Powell, Jr., went up to Dizzy Gillespie, who was playing a concert down in Washington, D.C., and said, "Birks, if you put together a big band, I'll have the State Department sponsor it and send it abroad. It'll be a first." Dizzy agreed, but he was about to go to Europe for a tour with Jazz at the Philharmonic when it came time to organize the band, so he called me and said, "Young catter, I want you to play trumpet, arrange, and be musical director of that band. Put it together for me."

Just a month before, George Avakian at Columbia Records had called and asked me to work with and arrange for a uniquely gifted seventeen-year-old unknown jazz singer and track star from San Francisco who was doing his first recording, and I'd accepted. So I had a dilemma.

It took me about a minute to decide. I went to George's office and said, "George, I really love your new singer and I'm sorry, but I gotta serve my country," and I was off. Bebop was my god, I idolized Dizzy. They moved on and the arranging chores were then reassigned to Gil Evans, John Lewis, and Johnny Carisi. That's as good as it gets. The subsequent jazz album was released to less than stellar sales. The singer was then summoned by the pop director Mitch Miller to record "Chances Are" and "The Twelfth of Never." Johnny Mathis has never looked back since.

I handpicked the musicians. Dizzy told me, "Pick cats that are good, but also pick cats that can get along," so I picked a few of his and a few of mine. Some of the older cats that Dizzy picked didn't want a twenty-three-year-old leading them. Saxophonist Billy Mitchell told me, "I'm sorry, man, I love you, and I know Birks put you in charge and all that, but I just can't handle a young muthafucka like you telling me what to play." I'd been there before. When I first joined Hamp's band, some of the older cats like trumpeter and arranger Moon Mullins didn't speak to me for months. Other cats like one of my first idols, Sy Oliver, the arranger, when I approached him in New York at the Brill Building and asked to study his scores, he said, "I can't do that, young man. I'm the biggest Negro arranger in the music business." That was exactly what I did not want to be. By this time I was almost able to write anything I could hear on score paper anyway. Later I got along with Moon Mullins and Billy Mitchell just fine. We played to be good and to eat, and not always in that order, and no thirty- or forty-year-old musician wanted a kid taking his gig or his pride.

So when Billy Mitchell said, "I can't handle you telling me how or what to play," I didn't say a word. I just did my gig, continued the rehearsals, and as time passed, when he saw me do what I had to do, he never complained about it again and we became friends. In fact, once the cats in Dizzy's band saw I could handle the music, they didn't see my age as a factor. They appreciated my desire to see that the music was right.

I rehearsed Dizzy's band hard for about two months. It was a burnin' band: Ernie Wilkins, Melba Liston, Phil Woods, Herb Lance, Charlie Persip, Nelson Boyd, and Frank Rehak, a serious crew, and each of us understood what was happening. This was a chance to take jazz to places in the world where it had never been heard before and to represent our country. The State Department was apprehensive about a bunch of black musicians going overseas to represent the United States. In Beirut the U.S. Information Service thought Dizzy was Dizzy Dean, the old baseball pitcher. Before we left New York they sent over a guy from the American National Theatre and Academy to brief us. He was arrogant and condescending. He came to rehearsal and stood in front of the band in a preppy wool suit and bow tie, and gave us advice in a flat, patronizing voice, saying, "I have nothing to tell you except that when you're abroad, you're representing our country. So please indulge in your various idiosyncrasies discreetly."

We couldn't believe it. If the New York Philharmonic were about to tour Europe for the State Department, would he feel obliged to say the same thing? You have to remember, the jazz musicians he was talking to were highly educated, skilled, dignified. Some had been around the world several times to Europe, North Africa, and South America. This kind of talk got our jaws tight. We were good and pissed off, but like the black soldiers in World War II, we kept on keepin' on. The irony was that when we got overseas, the people who were doing the freaky-deaky were the State Department emissaries themselves. They partied harder than all of us. Some of the embassy posts in the Middle East, Pakistan, Greece, Turkey, Syria, Iran, at that time were called hardship posts. They attracted the C and D list emissaries, the Foreign Legion of the U.S. diplomatic corps, the guys the State Department wanted to sweep under the rug. They were the alcoholics and the ones who were issued oversized diplomatic privileges plus, who rode around in air-conditioned limousines which were almost too big for the dirt roads, with the young local boys wearing tunics, sandals, exotic musk, and little else.

Still, we left New York for Rome to pick up Dizzy, who welcomed his wife playing "Sweet Lorraine" on his upright trumpet. We thought we were high-minded diplomats 'til we hit our fourth city, Beirut, which was

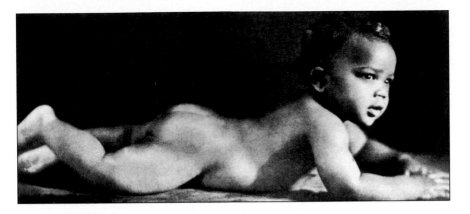

Me at age one—the infamous "booty shot."

My mother, Sarah, my brother
Lloyd, and me in Chicago in 1936.

Looking out
for my little brother,
Lloyd, 1937.

My mother, Sarah Jones.

Daddy dressed to play for the
Metropolitan Baptist Church
baseball team in Chicago.

On the porch in Bremerton. From left: Catherine, Lloyd, Earl Smith with baby Margie, and me.

Waiting for my first crush, Sarah Ann, in Bremerton, 1944.

Playing trumpet with the Charlie Taylor Band in 1947 at the YMCA, with Oscar Holden, Jr., on sax and his sister Grace on piano. Charlie is on sax, too, and next to me on trombone is Major Pigford. My brother Waymond is on drums. We made seven dollars each at our first gig.

My brother Waymond and his wife, Audrey, in 1952.

In Seattle at age fourteen, adopting the pose of the world-weary musician. The cigarette is a prop that I used to get into nightclubs—I didn't even smoke at the time!

From the *Arrow*, the yearbook of Garfield High School, 1950: my girlfriend, Jeri Caldwell—later my wife—and me.

The Bumps Blackwell Junior Band performing at the Washington Social and Educational Club in Seattle. I'm on the trumpet, second from left.

Bumps Junior's band performing with Billy Eckstine at the Trianon Ballroom in Seattle, 1949. Bumps is far right; I'm to his immediate left.

A note from Lady Day's musical director, Bobby Tucker, a month after we played behind her with Bumps' band at a Seattle appearance in 1948.

(*Below*) Finally, a place in Lionel Hampton's band, at age eighteen. Art Farmer is to the left in this photo, Walter Williams on the right. Hamp is behind us.

Carrying my
daughter Jolie on
my back at a pool
in Paris, 1957.

In the mid-1950s with my high school sweetheart and first wife, Jeri Caldwell-Jones, at the Café St. Germain in Paris.

Clifford Brown, me, and Art Farmer with the Swedish American All-Stars: Arne Domnerus, Lars Gullin, Ake Persson, Bengt Hallberg, Gunnar Johnson, and Jack Noren.

With the queen, Dinah Washington.

Dizzy Gillespie and the band arriving straight from Turkey in 1956. I'm at the top of the stairs with a pipe.

Touring for the State Department with Dizzy. To my right at the Parthenon is the jazz critic and scholar Marshall Stearns, who accompanied us. To my left are Billy Mitchell, Ernie Wilkins, and Rod Levitt, and an unidentified man.

My composition teacher, "Mademoiselle," the legendary Nadia Boulanger.

Nicole Barclay in Paris with my daughter Jolie and Pascal Barclay, one of her first beaus. Nicole hired me in 1957 to be musical director of Barclay Records.

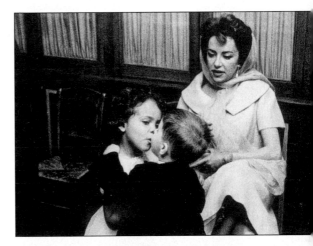

(Below) My band members from the *Free and Easy* show in Paris in 1959. I'm in the bottom row, second from right.

(Above) **W**ith Eddie Barclay
and Frank Sinatra at the
Sporting Club in Monaco
in 1958. This is our first
meeting.

Getting the pose just right
at a New York session—a
classic shot by Milt Hinton.

Recording with Sassy in 1961 in Copenhagen. Arranger and conductor Robert Farnon is in back with the cigarette.

(Below) **N**orman Granz hired my band for three weeks to open for Nat King Cole. Here we are backstage in Zurich, Switzerland, in 1960.

At a Mercury Records reception with Irving Steinberg to my right, and Andy Stroud, Nina Simone, Irving Green, and Hal Mooney to my left. Irving Steinberg was Executive Vice President of Mercury Records. Irving Green was president.

With my protégée Lesley Gore, her dog Buffy, and her #1 hit single, "It's My Party."

Winning my first Grammy for my arrangement of "I Can't Stop Loving You" with the Count Basie Orchestra in 1963, the same year a young twenty-one-year-old singer named Barbra Streisand won her first Grammy, too. With other Grammy winners Jack Jones, Steve Lawrence, Barbra, Eydie Gormé, Tony Bennett, and Count Basie.

At the Capitol Records studios recording "Fly Me to the Moon" with Count Basie and Frank Sinatra in 1964.

My daughter Jolie, one of the first black models
on the cover of *Mademoiselle* magazine in 1969.

a shock. We arrived at the airport and 3,000 people were waiting. We saw an Air Force One plane en route to Israel swoop in and watched John Foster Dulles get out and stretch his legs. We thought this was his crowd, but they had come to greet us. Still, it was hot, funky, and tense. There was civil unrest going on and no one could really guarantee our safety. We were a long way from home, a world away from what we knew, with folks fighting over matters we knew nothing about. When it came time to play the concert, there was no one who could outright say we'd be safe onstage, but Dizzy wouldn't hear of canceling it. He said, "Fuck it, we're here to play," and we did.

Everywhere we went, there was tremendous love. The foreigners treated us better than our own. In Turkey, local cultural and religious customs made a good party hard to come by. Turkish police would bust us in our hotel rooms before we could even get started. If you even tried to flirt with a Muslim woman, you stood a good chance of having a knife pulled on you in the street.

Finally I met an adorable girl in Karachi, Pakistan, a Catholic who took me home to her parents. Her family lived in a small house. They graciously served me dinner, which was cooked on a small stove. We had some shandy and a few other local items. It was fine, but I smelled something weird the whole time I was there. I kept smelling something odd. I saw some burlap sacks along a wall that had been cut open and sewn together to form a curtain. I asked my hosts what was behind the curtain. They said, "We'll show you." They pulled back those sacks to reveal thin pieces of dried cow dung, matted flat with straw like patties. They were using that as firewood for the stove, handling the cow dung—and my food— with their hands. My stomach went "blip" and I knew it was over. I had dysentery and diarrhea for weeks. Most of the band did. We called it "Karachi Tummy" and did the "green apple two-step" for the rest of the tour, running from the stage to the toilet.

The State Department was stunned by the response the band got.

For three months, they sent us to every post where there were problems and got nothing but raves: we were the black kamikaze band. The American embassy in Athens was getting its ass kicked, being stoned by the Cypriot students, so they rushed us over there from Ankara, Turkey, and the Greek people loved it. At the concert there a huge crowd rushed the stage when we finished. We panicked, but there was nowhere to run. Before anyone could stop them, the mob swarmed the stage and picked up Dizzy, put him on their shoulders, and carried him around like a rock star, chanting, "Diz-zy! Diz-zy!" We were amazed and relieved.

Washington was so happy with the response they sent $4,000 to the U.S. embassy in Greece to throw us a party. Some party. The cultural attaché there advised his staff not to mingle with us. He told the Greek women to steer clear and informed his female staff that in the United States respectable girls did not mix with black jazz musicians. We learned this firsthand from my Greek lady friend, Katy, the attaché's executive assistant. When we arrived at the party thrown in our honor, the American staff, with their Greek elitist friends, totally ignored us as we wandered to the back of the upstairs dining room while the attaché, his wife, and the rest of the staff sat up front drinking our champagne with the elite and continued to ignore us. We just sat there and watched our American emissaries get drunk, throwing and breaking plates on the floor in the Greek tradition, while the Greeks who were brave enough to defy the attaché's orders came over and sat and drank wine with us. We were furious. Three months of 110 degree heat, crappy food, swarming with flies, no showers, no baths, dysentery, constant traveling, and this was the thank-you we got. To add insult to injury, at the end of the night the attaché's wife came over, juiced out of her mind. She leaned over the table where we were sitting and said, "It's getting late. You boys gonna jive a little bit for us tonight or what?"

She didn't know who she was talking to. If Dizzy's reputation hadn't been on the line, we would've turned that joint out: boys, my ass. But some people are so out of touch nothing you say can change their attitudes. She reminded me of the people at Dwight Eisenhower's 1953 inaugural, which we played with Hampton's band. They came over and said, "Guess what, boys! Miles Davis is playing tonight." We couldn't believe it. Miles coming to the White House? I said, "This I gotta see." I'd met Miles Davis at the Downbeat Club that same year when I was eighteen. He drifted behind me and whispered to a friend in a way he knew I would overhear, "I was getting down last night with three of my freaks and heard some young muthafucka with Hamp on the radio trying to sound like me." Oh, Lord—he was talking about a trumpet solo I'd taken on my first recorded song with Hamp's band, "Kingfish," which was getting a little airtime on the radio. I was paralyzed; I had no idea how to respond to Miles. That was his way of acknowledging me and that was fine, because Miles was our god, totally untouchable and unapproachable. Miles truly did not give a shit, even when he was young and broke. Everyone knew that Miles always spoke his mind.

So we sat back and waited for Miles to show up at the White House that night, and after a while the *Meyer* Davis band showed up. It was a white society cocktail band.

The guys were upset by the way the embassy in Greece treated us. In fact, Professor Marshall Stearns from Columbia University, the excellent jazz critic and writer, was livid. The State Department had sent him along as the great white father to make sure the brothers didn't get out of control. He was a great dude, though, and he bonded with us immediately; we had big fun together. Dizzy nicknamed him "the boss catter." He said, "I can't stand this jive mollytrotter. I know exactly who he is and I'm gonna file a report and bust his alcoholic ass in D.C." He did, and we had to testify at a hearing. I was told they threw the rude attaché out of that embassy. But this same State Department staffer showed up with his wife three years later in India when I tried to book a tour for my own band, and unfortunately for me, he'd have the upper hand again, and I'd be on my ass.

Still, the tour was a success for me because of who it brought me in contact with. We were in Ankara, Turkey, one night when this elegant young gentleman in a white silk scarf and black tuxedo came up to me with a score in his back pocket. I looked it over and it was good work, so when I got back to the States I conducted an all-star band on the Voice of America (supervised by his friend Tahir Sur), with one of his arrangements and wrote a recommendation for him to attend the Berklee College of Music. His name was Arif Mardin and he attended Berklee on a scholarship named after me. Later he taught there. Arif later co-produced (with Jerry Wexler) and arranged for the Young Rascals, for Aretha Franklin's most famous records, like "Natural Woman" and "Respect," for the *Saturday Night Fever* soundtrack with the Bee Gees, for Bette Midler, and many others. He was a brilliant cat, a true gentleman, and he wasn't even supposed to be in the music game. His father wanted him to become an ambassador rather than coming to America. His family had been prominent industrialists and diplomats in Turkey for years and was friendly with Nesuhi and Ahmet Ertegun's family in Istanbul, also diplomats. He later became a VP at Atlantic Records. Arif broke the mold. Turkey's diplomatic loss was American music's gain. Who would have guessed that my friend would become part of the Turkish music mafia? What a classy human being.

The tour was so successful that the State Department brought us back to play at the White House Correspondents Association's annual shindig and then sent us out again, to South America. In Buenos Aires, Dizzy and I were in a club after a gig and heard this young dude playing some fine jazz piano with a small combo. He introduced himself as Lalo Schifrin and hooked us up with Astor Piazzola, a visionary composer and bandoneon player who created the modern city tango and later did a record with Dizzy. Lalo also told us about the new bossa nova movement in Brazil, which was our next stop. One afternoon at the Gloria Hotel on the Copacabana beach in Rio, Dizzy sat in with the house samba combo. In the audience that afternoon were teenagers João and Astrud Gilberto,

and Antônio Carlos Jobim—the creators of bossa nova. When the Brazilian rhythm section kicked off a samba rhythm, Dizzy threw his bebop
trumpet into the mix and that was the first time any of us had ever heard
the fusion of jazz 'n' samba. In fact the song "Desafinado" by Jobim feels
just like a Dizzy solo. Dizzy had a great hand in cooking the jazz 'n' samba
gumbo. He put his fingerprints all over it. Eight months later all the great
Brazilian musicians were invited to play a midnight concert at Carnegie
Hall—Sergio Mendes, Luis Bonfa, Vinicius de Moraes, the poet laureate
of Brazil, Jobim, and dozens of others. But awareness of the music wasn't
really heightened until the release of Stan Getz and Charlie Byrd's hit
"Desafinado." Ironically, the flip side of this breakthrough record was the
theme from "Medic," composed and arranged by Lalo Schifrin. The press
forgot to mention that Dizzy, more than any other American musician,
had a hand in influencing the sound, as he also had in the 1940s with
Afro-Cuban music.

I had loved Dizzy ever since I was twelve years old. He had style,
soul, technique, substance. He was like a leprechaun, with the thick
glasses, the cheeks and neck that bloated like a frog's face when he played,
the bent bell of his trumpet, the suspenders and hats he wore. He was one
of the funniest, most generous men I've ever known. After we did our last
date in South America, we flew home in a prop plane that ran into a hurricane, Hurricane Connie. A flight attendant was standing next to me with
a tray of oranges and the plane suddenly dropped down about 10,000 feet
with a loud, menacing drone, out of control. She dropped the whole tray
on my head. Oranges, suitcases, jackets, bags were flying everywhere. The
flight attendant's white knuckles were hanging on to my seat for dear life.
All of her "cool school" training quickly disappeared. We all hung on
tight, paralyzed, silently praying, gritting our teeth, imagining impact at
any moment. In the silence, someone yelled out, "Shit!" Dizzy shouted,
"Don't be cussin' at a time like this, you dumb asshole! You tryin' to get us
all fucked up?" As the plane regained control, he realized what he'd just

said, and silence settled over us until we landed in the Dominican Republic hours later.

When we got back from South America, I signed as an artist with Mercury Records, got busy with a lot of arranging work, and reluctantly had to quit the band. I loved that band. Dizzy wired some money to Lee Morgan, the talented young trumpeter from Philly, to have him come to New York and take my place. When I left the band, I was dying to hold on to that special Dizzy trumpet with the upright bell that they'd given to the trumpet players, but Dizzy told me, "Naw, we need it for Lee." I thought he was pissed at me for leaving the band. We let it go, and I moved on.

Not long after I quit his band, there was a ring at the front door of my New York apartment on 92nd Street. I opened the door and there was no one there. Just next to the door there was a little plaid tote bag. I picked it up and opened it. Inside was Dizzy Gillespie's original Martin trumpet in two separate pieces with "Diz" engraved on the bell bent to the sky, and a tiny note that said, "Q, one lick from the back, love, Birks." That was our running joke from the tour. We'd meet so many fine women that all you wanted to do was dream about giving them one lick on the back of the neck because sometimes in the Middle East, that's as close as you could ever get.

I ran down into the street to thank that crazy, talented, soulful, Geechie sapsucker, but just like a leprechaun, he was gone.

Nadia

Bobby Tucker, arranger, conductor

I was Billy Eckstine's arranger and musical director for forty years, from 1949 till he died in 1989. Back in '57 he went to Paris to work for a woman named Nicole Barclay. Nicole was a business genius who owned Barclay Records with her husband, Eddie. She started her label with $180 and some Don Byas tapes. She loved jazz. She had Billy Eckstine on her label, and Jacques Brel, and Charles Aznavour. She had Don Byas, of course, and she wanted an American musical director. So Billy said, "I know somebody. Call Quincy Jones. He's one of the best arrangers in New York." So she called Quincy.

Billy and I had known Quincy since he was about fifteen. I met him in Seattle in 1949 when I was with Billie Holiday. We'd gone to Seattle and hired a bunch of kids to back her up and Quincy was one of those kids. He played pretty good. He played good enough so that when I came back with Billy Eckstine later that year, I hired him again. He'd ask me after every gig. "How'd I do, Tuck?" but I learned long ago that whatever happens on the bandstand, you leave it there. Maybe that's why I've worked for fifty years.

By 1957, though, Quincy didn't need to ask me how he was doing. He was doing just fine. He was one of the top arrangers in the world and he was only twenty-five. I read once where Benny Carter, one of the greatest arrangers ever, said, "Quincy's a guy whose success actually overshadows his talent," and he's right. I know arrangers. Arrangers are funny people. They use the same twelve notes when they work, but they're all different. They're like stonemasons. Stonemasons build houses one rock at a time, but if you give five different stonemasons the same exact pile of rocks from God's green earth, they'll each build a house that's a little bit different.

Now, my top five arrangers, if I had to name them, would be Robert Farnon, Sy Oliver, Duke Ellington, Nelson Riddle, and Don Redman. And every one of them got stuck. I don't give a fuck who they are, they all got stuck. That's part of the job. You're writing for eight or twenty or fifty instruments and you hit a wall. You come upon a bar or two, a chorus, or a chord that just won't work, and you got to find something that fits. What separates the good arrangers from the great arrangers is how you get unstuck, and how fast you do it, because there's always a time element involved. The time element is what kills you. You can be the greatest arranger in the world, but the record company wants the shit yesterday, and if you can't do it, shame on you, 'cause you've lost the job. Myself, I prefer an arranger who comes in at the last minute with coffee stains and ketchup all over the score. I never trust an arranger who shows up with a suit and tie on two weeks early, with his score neatly copied out and collated. The guy with the ketchup and coffee stains all over his score, who's been rolling under the piano all night trying to work it out, he's the guy I want.

Now what separates Quincy from other arrangers is his speed and

technical ability to get unstuck quick, and his first eight bars, which is often the most important part of a song because that pulls you in. If you
want a surefire kick-ass first eight bars, call Quincy Jones. That's what set
him apart, that and one other thing: If Quincy were writing Dante's *In-
ferno,* he'd have Satan's telephone number. He knew how to get the job
done. He'd call any cat at any time: Cannonball Adderley or Little
Richard or Little Richard's mama or Jesus himself, if he knew Jesus was
in town and played E flat baritone sax and could read. And if Jesus
couldn't read, Quincy would call him anyway and talk him through the
part. He's good at that. He's been writing "Put some grease on bar thirty-
seven" and "A little garlic salt and butter at bar twenty-three" on Toots
Thielemans' harmonica parts for thirty-five years. Ask Toots about that.
For all I know Toots can't read music. Only he and Quincy know what
that grease and garlic butter shit means. Maybe it's a recipe.

When Nicole called Quincy and asked him to come to France to
write for Barclay, the first thing Quincy asked her was "Can I write for
strings over there?" because he wanted to write for strings. Back in the
fifties, the easiest way to starve in America was to be a black arranger writing for strings. You could've been Mozart, Stravinsky, Wagner, and
Beethoven all rolled into one, but if you came from Harlem, U.S.A., and
had nappy hair and black skin, your ass went to the blues and jazz department of every record company and I don't give a hoot if you were
God. Strings were considered sophisticated and for whites only. Quincy
was burned about that. So he asked Nicole about it first thing, and she
said, "My dahling you can write for whatever you want in France." So he
went to France for three months to work for Barclay Records and ended
up staying in Europe almost five years.

He wrote arrangements for a couple hundred dates at least for the
55-piece resident orchestra, including prominent American and French
musicians—Kenny Clarke, Lucky Thompson, Don Byas, Stéphane
Grappelli, and Pierre Michelot—and worked with some big French stars

like Henri Salvador, Charles Aznavour, and the Eddie Barclay Orchestra. He played a key role in helping to launch Double Six, which was one of the first major jazz vocal groups in France, and included Mimi Perrin, Ward Swingle, and Christianne Legrand, who I believe is Michel Legrand's sister. Quincy helped put Barclay Records on the map if you ask me, but one of the main reasons he'd come to France was to work on his string writing, because when he'd been in Argentina with Dizzy's band, Lalo Schifrin had told him there was a teacher in Paris named Nadia Boulanger, and he wanted to study composition, counterpoint, and orchestration with her.

Nadia was one of the greatest teachers of twentieth-century composition. She was the first woman to conduct the New York Philharmonic and had a lot of influence on American classical music. Some of the greatest composers of the twentieth century studied with her, guys like Aaron Copland, Michel Legrand, Philip Glass, Virgil Thomson. People like Igor Stravinsky, Maurice Ravel, Leonard Bernstein, Francis Poulenc, Darius Milhaud, Olivier Messiaen, these were her friends. They were the baddest cats around when it came to *that* kind of music. This was the fifties, remember, and classical was still considered *that* kind of music and jazz was considered *this* kind of music, and we were still Negroes and colored, so this was all part of that too, if you get my drift.

Nadia wouldn't just take anyone as a student. You had to audition more or less, go visit her at her home at 36 rue Ballou upstairs, talk to her, show her what you knew, tell her what you wanted to learn, and then she'd decide whether to teach you. She turned down George Gershwin. I heard Ravel brought Gershwin to her, but she said he made too much money and he'd already perfected his style in the short song form and she didn't want to mess him up with long-form studies. Well, here comes this li'l corn-bread-eating nigga Quincy Jones. He went out there with his scores and his little pens and told her what he wanted to learn and showed her what he knew and she accepted him. I read someplace that she said two of the most influential musicians she ever knew were Quincy and Igor Stravinsky.

Quincy was studying with her when I was over there doing the *Mr. B in Paris* record, and when I found out he was studying with Nadia Boulanger, I said, "Show me what she's showing you" because arrangers are like that. They're like bloodhounds when it comes to musical knowledge. So we got into it. We were supposed to be writing arrangements for Billy Eckstine's record and instead we'd sit up all night and analyze Ravel's *Daphnis and Chloe* and Stravinsky's *Firebird Suite*. In fact, one day we were at his house analyzing one of those pieces and Quincy said, "I have to go down to Fontainebleau later today for my lesson with Nadia. You want to come?" I said, "Hell yeah."

We took the train down to this palace in Fontainebleau, just outside Paris, for her summer class. When we got there, we were standing in this courtyard, we had our little suits and porkpie hats on, you know, two young brothers from the U.S.A., and Quincy yells up to the window, "Bonjour, Mademoiselle Boulanger!"

The window opens and this old lady puts her head out. She says, "Ahhh, Quincy!" like he's her long-lost son. I'm saying to myself, "Goddamn . . ."

So she comes down the stairs to the courtyard. She was about seventy then, spry as a kid. She hugged him and joked with him and asked him about his wife and his daughter, and he joked with her and teased her. Then he introduced her to me and she shook my hand, and they started upstairs to her classroom.

As they left, I sat down in the courtyard to wait for him. Quincy turned to me and said, "Bobby, c'mon up." I wanted to go up. As an arranger and orchestrator, you're ten feet from one of the greatest composition teachers in the world, you want to go. But I didn't know if it was cool or not, because Nadia hadn't said anything to me other than hello. So I said, "Naw, man, I'll wait in the courtyard."

I sat outside in the courtyard and watched maybe ten students walk upstairs to Nadia's class. A few minutes later, the door to the courtyard opens and Nadia herself comes over to me and says, "Come on in here." So I hustled inside and followed her upstairs.

Inside her class, the students had the score to Stravinsky's *Firebird Suite* open on their desks. I took a seat in the back next to Quincy.

Nadia sat down at the piano and played a few bars of the *Firebird.* She was sharp as a razor. She played energetic, like a teenager, just zipped through the piece. Then she turned to the class and said, "Now, clap the rhythms of the second violin." We started clapping the part and she stopped us right away. She said, "No, no. *No retard!* Stravinsky told me himself!"

That just flipped me out. I'm just a little raggedy-ass motherfucker from Morristown, New Jersey, ain't I? What am I doing here?

I peeked at Quincy and I saw he got it too. He was thinking the same thing I was thinking. I leaned over to him and whispered, "Stravinsky told me so himself!" And Quincy whispered back, "Damn right, mademoiselle."

CHAPTER 17

Nicole

I moved to Paris by myself in August 1957 after Nicole Barclay hired me to work for Barclay Records as musical director, arranger, and conductor. I was twenty-four years old. I wanted to set things up before sending back to New York for Jolie and Jeri. When I called Nicole to tell her when I was arriving, she said, "Darling, Paris is shut down in August. We'll be in the South of France. You should come too, darling."

I said, "No, I need to get set up, get my things ready for the fall. I need to buy some score paper and find a piano for my apartment."

She said, "Okay, suit yourself, darling."

When I arrived in Paris, I set out to find copyists, locate recording studios, and check out the musicians I'd be working with. One day when I went to the dry cleaners to have my clothes cleaned there was a note on the door that said, "Closed—back in September." I said no problem, and hurried to the South of France to join Nicole and her husband Eddie down in Cannes.

Nicole was a true original. She was a short, dark-haired woman, with large breasts, long eyelashes, a narrow behind, thin legs, a classic Bourbon nose; not super beautiful, but a charismatic and attractive woman, and what a woman she was. She built an empire from nothing. She told me she got started when her husband Eddie, a pianist, was playing cocktail piano at a club called the Lido. She came around to the club to see him play one night and he said to her, "What are you doing here? Stop following me around and get a job." She went out and got a job all right. She scraped together $180 and used it to sign saxophonist Don Byas. Then she went out and got some Charlie Parker tapes, made some licensing deals with Irving Green of Mercury Records and Norman Granz, who had a jazz label there. Eventually she and Eddie built a $44 million record company.

She was incredible. Her mind was like a computer. She'd wake up, drink a full glass of Bacardi white rum, swallow a full container of Preludin, and go meet with thirteen top European record company executives without pen or paper. She had everything in her head—the sales figures in each territory, licensing agreements, contract commitments and expiration dates, the marketing plans, the distribution strategy. She was truly a genius. That's one reason I never thought twice about hiring women in any capacity, in my band or in my business, because women like Nicole, Gladys Hampton, the Fender bass player Carol Kaye, the trombonist and arranger Melba Liston—these were women who could do anything and leave men in the dust.

Her husband Eddie was a handsome orchestra leader and composer who loved life and women: I've had the experience of being best man at Eddie's weddings five times in my life. Eddie was my friend and gustatory guru. He taught me all about wine, food, and dining. He gave fabulous dinners where we'd dine with the literary and entertainment elite of France: Charles Aznavour, Henri Salvador, Line Renauld, Jeanne Moreau, Sasha Distel, Catherine Deneuve, Jacques Brel, even the great writer Boris Vian. Eddie's meals weren't dinners, they were events, fabulous twenty-course affairs where he always planned something crazy. Sometimes he'd serve the dinner courses backward: coffee, dessert, wine, salad, main course, appetizer, bread, then an aperitif. Or a late guest would arrive at Eddie's sumptuous apartment to find clothing—jackets and dresses and body stockings—strewn on the floor of the entryway and Eddie's note saying, "We've all decided to dine nude tonight. Please join us." The guest would undress in the hallway, say, "Okay, what the hell," and walk into the room nude where ten people would be seated around the table dressed in tuxes and evening gowns. It was decadence at its best as only the French know how to do it.

Though I had toured Europe with the Hampton band, nothing I'd seen or experienced so far in my young life had prepared me for the surrealistic world of the real jet set. There's nothing, even today, that can compare with the South of France or Italy. When I joined Nicole and Eddie at their beautiful villa in Cannes, they said, "Make yourself at home." I cooled out in a way I never had before. The sea, the food, the topless women, the sun—it was like a dream, one miracle after another, Villefranche, St. Paul de Vence, Monte Carlo, St. Tropez. I tried not to miss anything: most of what I missed was a good night's sleep. Early one morning I looked out the window and saw a beautiful braless young French woman herding ducks and goats down the steps of the villa next door, her breasts bouncing up and down. Nicole told me, "That's Picasso's wife, Jacqueline." They lived next door in the Villa La Californie. A few days later I was sitting in a restaurant when Picasso, his wife, and a friend walked in. They joined us. He ordered sole meunière, ate the fish carefully, arranged his silverware neatly when he was done, and gently inched the plate with the fish bones into the sunlight, where it became parched enough to serve as the master's canvas. Then he took marker pens and turned the bones into a multicolored Picasso design. When Nicole said, "Check, please," Picasso pushed his plate forward: that was his way of paying. The next day those bones would be on the wall. I said to Nicole, "That's who I want to be when I grow up."

Nicole knew Picasso well. In fact, she knew just about everyone in France. Her vices were as well known as her generosity and her sexual exploits were legendary. Nicole was an innovator, in that most of the French record companies at the time were formal and stodgy. Nicole partied like American music executives: at the Eden Roc or the Colombe d'Or, at Chez Tetou or Le Moulin de Mougins, or the Palm Beach Casino or the Whiskey à Go-Go—which was *the* place to go—we'd run into Aristotle Onassis, Maria Callas, Doris Duke, Brigitte Bardot, Grace Kelly, Prince Rainier, Marlene Dietrich, Jack Warner, Simone Signoret and Yves Montand, Sasha Distel, James Baldwin, Darryl Zanuck, and then-Senator Jack Kennedy. At the Carlton Beach on The Croisette Edith Piaf told me, gesturing to the male stars strolling by, "At one time or another all these men have used me as their staircase—on their way up or down." For a sucker from the South Side of Chicago, it was all completely dazzling.

Drugs eventually got the best of Nicole, God bless her. Her husband Eddie took control of the record company after she died and he ran it well. He treated me like a king. I worked with artists over there the likes of which I would've never had the chance to work with in the United States, like Charles Aznavour, Michel Legrand, Stéphane Grappelli, Henri Salvador, the Double Six, plus artists from America like Sarah Vaughan and Andy Williams and Billy Eckstine. In fact, *Vaughan with Violins* included the very first version of "Misty." Erroll Garner had given me the lead sheet with brand-new lyrics by Johnny Burke before I got on the plane. Sassy called from Stockholm about a song she wanted to include called "The Midnight Sun Will Never Set," which I'd written with Henri Salvador and which was a huge hit then in Sweden in an instrumental version by Arne Domnerus with the Harry Arnold band. I set to work on lyrics with Dorcas Cochran.

Sarah was like royalty to the French. Her earthier side surfaced years later in New York when we were all riding in a car to the Armory for a recording date I'd arranged for her with Count Basie. Sarah and the French composer Michel Legrand, whom I had just introduced, were in front; I was in the back. After a while, Sassy—who was a very introverted lady—lit up a joint and offered to share it with Michel—a gesture of the highest honor in the jazz world. Having just arrived, and not yet streetwise, Michel rolled down the cab's window and threw the joint out. Sassy yelled, "What's the matter with you, muthafucka? That's my shit!" All the French-American congeniality went out the window too. What Michel couldn't have known was that after all those years on the road with the eighteen men of the Eckstine band, Sassy had learned to be one of the boys: she had to, like all the girl singers on the road, or her ass would have been grass.

I'll always be grateful to Nicole, to Eddie, and to France. In France, the yoke of black and white was off my shoulders. There I saw that the Armenians were fighting with the Turks, the Irish with the British, the Swedes with the Finns, the Greeks with the Cypriots: America was not the only place where people didn't always get along. In France I was able to envision my past, present, and future as an artist and as a black man; I took a wider view of the human condition that extended to both art and life, and later helped me to take stock of global markets in business dealings. I became comfortable as a citizen of the world. France treated me like an artist. Years later, in 1991, France inducted me into the Legion of Honor, an award that began in 1802 with Napoleon. France made me feel free, and glad to be who I was.

I was in Paris at Eddie Barclay's when we got a call from the office of Princess Grace of Monaco. They told Eddie, "Frank Sinatra is coming here to sing for the premiere of his movie *Kings Go Forth*, and he wants you and Quincy to bring an orchestra to the Sporting Club in Monaco." We agreed right away. Even though I was far from home, I wasn't that far. If you didn't know who Frank Sinatra was in 1958, you needed to trade in your ears for some lovin'-cup handles. The man was bigger than life.

We caught the train with fifty-five musicians from Eddie Barclay's stable, including drummer Kenny Clarke, Stéphane Grappelli, Lucky

Thompson, and the Double Six, and we headed south to play behind Sinatra. We set up onstage to rehearse with Frank, and I was ecstatic to meet him so I could learn what he wanted in terms of band, arrangement, and feeling. Even though I was only twenty-five years old, by then I'd learned that every great singer is different; each has different nuances, and you have to know what makes them comfortable so they can let loose. In a way a conductor and arranger has to put an emotional X ray on the singer, and to explore their creative psyche. You have to understand their ranges and registers, the place where they break between natural voice and falsetto. As Toots Thielemans once put it: "You have to know how to crumble my cookie," which involves everything from truly loving the soul of the singer to understanding density in the music in their individual terms—where they need it airy or thick, where they should be pushed. That's why Nelson Riddle and Sinatra enjoyed such a long and successful collaboration: Nelson knew Sinatra's soul. He gave him his space, never putting instruments in his register so that he felt crowded.

Dinah Washington liked a tightly prerehearsed band so she could come into the studio, keep it real, and get out quick. Ella Fitzgerald was a shy, almost withdrawn person, so she liked arrangements that allowed her to cut loose and be free. When I arranged "I'm Beginning to See the Light" for Ella with Basie's band, I put a tag repeat on the end of the song that allowed Ella to do her thang. Before we started the song I said to Basie, "Let's take Fitz to church when we hit the vamp at the end," which got a laugh out of Basie because he knew how timid Ella was. Sure enough, when we hit the vamp Ella was testifying. She was dead in the pocket and was wailing so hard that she didn't want to give it up. She wailed on and on; she didn't want to give up a drop. Each chorus was better than the last, until she and the band were getting musically drunk on each other. She was groovin' and shakin' booty so hard that I couldn't stop the band. I just kept conducting them through the coda until she had had her say. Sarah Vaughan, on the other hand, preferred a different kind of sophistication and hipper chord changes. But like Ella, she thought like a horn and sang like a horn. Lyrics were almost secondary to both of them. This was the secret of the longevity and success of the great big-band singers: Sassy, Ella, Frank Sinatra, Billy Eckstine, Peggy Lee. They were all influenced by great musicians, who were the superstars of the day.

I was curious to see how Frank liked his music cooked up. He was straight ahead about it. He walked into the rehearsal at the Monaco Sporting Club with his "Swinging Lovers" hat on, hit me with those steely blues, and said, "You've heard the records, you know what to do. You know where I'm coming from."

We rehearsed the show with that fifty-five-piece orchestra for four hours until it couldn't get any tighter. When we were done he said, "Koo-koo," shook my hand, and walked out. He didn't say more than ten sentences to me the whole time. He was all business.

The night of the show, as they dimmed the houselights, I wasn't sure which side of the stage Frank was going to enter from. When the MC announced him, I was still mouthing the words "Where is he?" to the stage manager, who kept looking around and shrugging. When I heard the words "Frank Sinatra!" and heard the audience applauding, I cued the orchestra into "The Man with the Golden Arm" theme and conducted while keeping an eye on both sides of the stage so that I could lead them into "Come Fly with Me" as soon as Frank hit the stage. I was conducting the orchestra, following the score, and searching left and right for Frank, trying to spot him. Three minutes into the number, I still couldn't see him. It felt like an eternity.

The applause grew louder. I still didn't see him.

Finally I glanced over my shoulder and said, "Oh, shit."

He was coming from the back of the room.

The Sporting Club in Monaco is shaped like a long bowling alley, and Frank was taking his time. He stopped by a table to shake hands with Noël Coward, stopped at another table to greet Cary Grant and Grace

Kelly, and stopped at yet another table, taking his own sweet time. Then after a few more steps toward the stage, he stopped altogether, stood right in the middle of the floor, reached into his pocket, pulled out his gold cigarette case, opened it, took out a cigarette, tapped it on the case, and lit the cigarette. I was dying. Three minutes of clapping and that's long. Four minutes of clapping, five minutes . . . finally he reached the stage and they were *still* clapping. I steered the orchestra into "Come Fly with Me." He turned, faced the audience, and hit them with that signature voice, and I knew then why the applause had held up so long.

Some singers like to work in front of the beat. Some lag a little behind it. Frank did it all: in front, dead center, and slightly behind, as though it were inevitable. Just like Billie Holiday and Louis Armstrong, whom he adored, Frank had grown up singing with the big bands and learning how to sound like a horn, so he knew exactly where the beat was at all times. He swung so hard, you could've turned him upside down and shaken every piece of change out of his pocket, and he would have never missed a beat. He grooved through the first sixteen bars of "Come Fly with Me," then took a long drag on his cigarette just before the bridge. When he hit the bridge and sang, "When I get you up there, where the air is rare . . . ," he turned his head so that a pinspot of blue light onstage would catch his profile, and finally blew a stream of smoke out of his mouth. It was incredible. He had every delicate nuance down. He wasted nothing—not words, not emotions, not notes. He was about pure economy, power, style, and skill.

He lit up the Sporting Club for an hour and a half, I mean tore that muthafucka down to the ground. When the concert was over, he shook my hand and said, "Yeah, nice job, Q," and was gone. Poof. I never heard another word from him until 1962.

That was the first time anyone ever called me Q. I didn't even have time to say thank you. I went back to Paris with my head tripping for weeks. In fact, during one of my private lessons with Nadia Boulanger, I talked to her about my experiences with Frank, about his style and musicality, wasting nothing, using every available hip instrumental nuance and melodic approach in vocals, and his conversational approach to lyrics.

Nadia confessed that she didn't know anything about Frank, but she wholeheartedly approved of what I told her about his approach to music. "Sensation, feeling, belief, attachment, and knowledge," she said. "That's what every artist strives for. This type of music is immaterial when you are aiming for those five qualities."

I loved talking about music with her. We'd sit in the warm living room of Fontainebleau, her summer residence at the American School of Music, and she'd talk for hours about music. No pencil. No paper. No lesson. Just knowledge. She admired jazz. I wanted to learn to write symphonies, but Nadia wouldn't hear of it. She said, "Learn your skills but forget about great American symphonies. You already have something unique and important. Go mine the ore you already have." This was years before most universities in my own country, including many black universities, even thought of teaching jazz. In America they taught Beethoven and Bach as if they had a direct line to God. Stravinsky himself admired jazz. Nadia introduced me to him one day and he asked me, "What are you doing in Paris now?" I told him the truth, that I was doing some arrangements for the singer Henri Salvador. He nodded, a bit puzzled, but respectful. But when he left, Nadia asked, "What's wrong with you? I've never seen you like this before."

I said, "I just told Mr. Stravinsky I was arranging 'Blues du Dentiste' for Henri Salvador. I'm intimidated when I meet a genius." Nadia said, "That's a stupid word. If you must use it, it should be to describe someone who has achieved something that reaches the pinnacle of the five qualities I keep telling you about: feeling, sensation, belief, attachment, and knowledge. Again, the type of music is immaterial."

I adored her: she was a beautiful, passionate combination of Russian, French, and elegant Euro-ghetto. I used to bring her a nice bottle of

Beaujolais and canned peaches from the American Army base PX, which she loved. Mezz Mezzrow, the jazz musician, was my connection. Privately I loved to tease Nadia about her and Stravinsky doing the iggly-wiggly, which was a sacrilegious thing to say about the first female conductor of the New York Philharmonic.

Not that I was in a position to tease anyone. In France I had a serious thing with a beautiful actress/singer from Harlem named Marpessa "Gypsy" Dawn, and even while we were together I was seeing one or two others. One night Marpessa had made plans for dinner and I said, "Let's make it next week, baby. I might have to work with Eddie Barclay in the studio tonight." Later that night I walked into a Chinese restaurant with a Moroccan lady friend and Marpessa happened to be sitting there. Busted again! I liked her even more because she let it go: later I discovered she was also dating my friend the arranger and conductor Ian Fraser in London. There is balance in the universe.

A few weeks later she called me all excited about an offer from Marcel Camus, a filmmaker, who wanted her to go to Brazil to star in a movie.

I asked, "Does the picture have a decent budget?"

She said it wasn't a lot. Plus she would have to travel passenger berth on a freighter from France to Brazil to get there. I asked her, "Are you sure you want to do this?"

She made her own decision. I went all the way to Le Havre by train to escort her to the dock when she departed. As we stood on the dock I told her, "We can figure out better things to do than hopping a freighter and going to South America to make a movie with somebody you don't even know."

She said, "When you think of something, call me."

She got on the freighter and the next time I saw her she was on a seven-foot screen, bigger than life. The movie she made was *Black Orpheus,* and it became a film classic. Just goes to show you how much I had to learn.

CHAPTER 18

Free and Easy

While living in Paris I paid a flying visit to New York, and the legendary talent scout and record executive John Hammond, the black sheep of the Vanderbilt clan, fixed me up with Stanley Chase, the producer of a Harold Arlen/Johnny Mercer show that was slated to open in Utrecht, Amsterdam, Paris, and Brussels, with Harold Nicholas, called *Free and Easy*. The plan was that I'd assemble a dream big band, take them to Europe for a few months, and work the kinks out of the show there; then it would be on to London, where Sammy Davis would replace Harold Nicholas. Finally we'd take it to Broadway—as if anyone could really predict a plan like this!

I always wanted to try a Broadway show and I agreed. In New York I immediately called every person I ever dreamed about playing with— Jerome Richardson, Jimmy Cleveland, Phil Woods, Benny Bailey. I got some of my homeys from Seattle: Floyd Standifer on trumpet and bassist Buddy Catlett, who'd played alto sax in Bumps Blackwell's band when we were kids. I called pianist Patti Bown, who was a child prodigy back in

Seattle, Swedish trombonist Åke Persson, and Billy Byers, the brilliant trombonist and arranger. Soon the buzz got around New York that this dynamite band was going to Europe and several cats were interested. Clark Terry and Quentin Jackson left Duke Ellington's band to join me in Europe, one of the highest tributes I will ever receive; but I promised myself that I wouldn't go after anyone in Basie's band. I'd never do that to Basie—he'd been too good to me.

The show, a remake of a piece called *St. Louis Woman*, starring Pearl Bailey and Harold Nicholas, was a lot of fun. The band was in costume and was actually part of the show. Our unprecedented participation was pre-*No Strings*, the Richard Rodgers musical. The musicians memorized the music, and some even had major speaking lines. The other performers included Patti Austin, who was seven, and singer Robert Guillaume, who later became a famous television and stage actor. We rehearsed in Utrecht, Holland, for two months; then the cast and crew of nearly seventy people went on to Amsterdam, Brussels, and then Paris, where we met disaster head-on.

We opened at the Alhambra Theater in Paris just as the Algerian crisis hit. We could hear machine-gun fire in the street during our rehearsals. Police and soldiers roamed the streets around the clock every day. There was a boxed notice on the front page of the *Herald Tribune* that said, "Any swarthy-complexioned person is advised to stay off the street after six o'clock in the evening." It was 1959 and several of us, going to and from the theater, were stopped by police with cocked machine guns. People were afraid to leave their homes at night to get a carton of milk, let alone to see a show, and the show started hemorrhaging money right away. All we needed was to survive two months in Paris; then we'd follow our game plan to go to London and subsequently to New York with Sammy Davis. We made it to about six weeks. We needed two more weeks to get to London and meet up with Sammy—two more weeks. We didn't make it. The show closed.

The producer had a meeting at the Alhambra on a Thursday and gathered everyone together. He said, "The plane's leaving Saturday. If you miss that flight you're stuck here." I couldn't stand it. It was the best band I'd ever had. It was like the United Nations. Two beautiful and gifted women, Melba Liston on trombone and Patti Bown on piano; a "skol" brother, Åke Persson; Billy Byers, Jimmy Cleveland, Clark Terry, and Quentin Jackson from Duke's band; Benny Bailey, who was an ex-Hampton band member and an expatriate American living in Germany and Italy; Julius "Phantom" Watkins, the first ever jazz French horn player; and saxophonists Phil Woods, Jerome Richardson, Budd Johnson, Porter Kilbert, and Sahib Shihab. This was a super band: it doesn't get any better. They sounded so good that when Basie dropped by our rehearsal in Paris he graciously pulled me aside and, kidding on the square, he said, "Quincy, don't you even think about bringing this band back to the States; you're fixin' to mess up my thing, you hear?" He always wanted to make me feel good. The band had gotten tighter and tighter over those four months of performances. Our record, *Birth of a Band,* was drawing rave reviews. I felt we were as good as any band in the world, so when I heard the producer give us marching orders home, I stood up and told the band, "Wait. Give me a day to think on this. There's got to be a way for us to stay together."

That was a Thursday. Fortunately, we were already booked for a concert that Saturday at midnight at the Olympia Theater with Daniel Filipacchi and Frank Tenot producing for Europe 1, a radio station. I called Willard Alexander, my agent in New York, who said, "I'll get back to you momentarily." Pleeze! Momentarily was three days later. The plane had long gone back to New York, with everyone from that show on it except for us. In the meantime I had thirty people sitting on their thumbs: eighteen musicians; wives, kids, my own wife, Jeri, and daughter, Jolie; Phil Woods's wife, Chan Parker, who later became our press lady, and was Charlie Parker's ex-wife; Chan and Phil's two kids; Bird's son Baird, who had a flirtation with my four-year-old Jolie, and daughter Kim; and two dogs. I even had Phil Woods's mother-in-law. They needed hotels, food, and salary. I scrambled like a madman finding places for them to stay and money to pay them. I had to come up with $4,800 a week—that was like a mountain of money. I got on the phone and began to line up dates.

I only had one more concert in Stockholm after the Olympia gig, but the next morning, a Friday, I gathered the band together and said, "We all know this is a great band. Let's stay here and try to work it out. I'm gonna line up a tour." Every single one of them agreed. That's the difference between musicians then and now. It wasn't about wealth, or fame, or limousines.

I had no manager, no booking agent, no secretary. After hiring a classical opera singer from the show named Elijah Hodges to act as road manager, I met a young French promoter, who lined up sixteen dates for us in France and got advances on them. Knowing I had those dates in my pocket, I chartered a raggedy prop plane to take us to Stockholm, Sweden, where we did two dates. When we got back to Paris, the French promoter had skipped town—with the advances for the sixteen dates. He was gone, with all the money, and I was stuck.

We traveled through Europe for ten months like vagabonds. No plan. No agent, no manager, no set itinerary. Just gigging on pure ass. We did Holland, Belgium, Italy, Yugoslavia, Finland, Austria, Germany, Sweden, back to Germany, back to France, Switzerland, over to Portugal again, jammin', doing the best we could. We went from town to town like gypsies, traveling by bus, train, car—we even traveled on foot at one point in Yugoslavia. The bus came to a bridge that couldn't support the weight of all those people. The bus driver made us get off, and men, women, children, and dogs walked over the bridge carrying their luggage and instruments.

At one point I put the band on a slow train from Spain to Yugoslavia, then flew from Spain to Paris with Billy Byers to meet Dave Grusin, both of whom bailed out my ass with help on arrangements so many times I can't even count them. At that time Dave was Andy Williams's musical director. When we'd all worked together on "The Steve Allen Show," Andy had expressed an interest in doing an album with us. It was time to take him up on his offer, so we did a recording session to help me hustle up some money. I flew to Yugoslavia to meet the band in time to pay their salaries.

Norman Granz called me to offer three weeks opening for Nat King Cole's first European tour. That's when I really got to know Nat well. In a beer hall in Germany he said to me, "I remember the moment I stopped being just a pianist and a singing star and became an industry back home. I had to make a choice between moving up fast and burning out in five years, or taking my time and building it slowly so I make it for the long haul." The first time we played Zurich, Switzerland, they booed him for singing. The European jazz fans didn't care about his American reputation as a singer. His first exposure had been with *Jazz at the Philharmonic*, and they only wanted to hear him play jazz piano. That's all they would accept from him. He came offstage, ruffled, and said, "Quincy, call the cats back on and let the band play a few more tunes." I said, "With all due respect, Nat—go back out and try 'Sweet Lorraine.' On piano with just the rhythm section." He turned around, walked back onstage, and played the shit out of "Sweet Lorraine" and tore it up. Then he sang again, and this time they loved it. He was one of the best who ever did it, a talented, highly intelligent man, with perfect pitch on top of it all.

I was grateful for those three weeks with Nat and Norman Granz, but after we did the dates, I burned the money on payroll and found myself broke again. In fact, with the little salary I paid them, the entire band was always broke. We became a family. Our lack of money and gigs became a source of laughter and derision among us. We spent long hours riding buses overnight from country to country, arguing, fighting, laughing, drinking. I'd look in the back of the bus and hear cursing, laughter, woofing, the dozens in two or three languages. One night, sitting in the front of the bus, I heard Budd "Old Dude" Johnson and somebody else arguing over something. I peered back into the dark haze of sleeping bodies and saw Old Dude asking Julius Watkins to pass him his knife from his bag so that he could cut him. Like many brothers, Budd had a lot of Indian blood, and could not handle drinking that "ignuit oil." I didn't want to see any more. At twenty-six years old, I sometimes felt like Budd's daddy: he was in his late sixties.

We'd pull into towns and sit around train stations looking like a bunch of war refugees, exhausted, broke, with no place to stay and no gig while I got on the phone trying to line up both. I spent hours on the phone, contacting everyone I knew, calling in favors, drumming up work. We slept on the bus for two days in Nice, France, just sitting there, snoring, hawking, spitting, looking like a bunch of bums, while I called everyone I knew. I was constantly in a state of waiting for money to be wired from Irving Green or someone else so I could pay the guys and buy some uniforms, and so that we could sleep in a hotel. The women would cry for a bath.

Still, we had a ball. Brice Somers, a very talented inventor and the chief executive of the Swiss office of Mercury Records International, and his wife, Clare-Lise, bailed us out at one point by reaching into their own pockets and paying for an entire train car that got us out of Yugoslavia like a band of Eastern European refugees. He paid for it out of his own pocket. I'll never forget Brice and his lady as long as I live. Sometimes the train would pull off and half the band would be gone and I had no idea where they were or if I'd ever see them again. Pianist Patti Bown missed the train once, took a cab, and ended up beating us to the gig in the next town. There were so many drinkers in the band that I put two of my musicians who had been known to have an "occasional sherry before dinner," Phil Woods and Budd Johnson, in charge of them. They would hold mock court sessions on the bus, where they tried offenders in court sessions that always began like this:

Budd: Hear ye, hear ye, the court's in session! And these are the rules. Are you ready, Mr. Prosecutor?

Phil: Anytime, Old Dude, I mean your honor.

Budd: This is the first rule.

Phil: Will you please state the rules, your honor?

Budd: Are you ready for the rules of the road?

Phil: We are ready, goddammit, your honor.

Budd: The first rule is . . . You can fuck up, by gettin' fucked up! Now would you read that back to me, my main man.

Phil: You can fuck up, by gettin' fucked up!

Budd: Hear ye, hear ye—amendment sustained.

We cut down on problems with drinking on the job.

We laughed at one silly predicament after another. This one lost his coat. That one stole this one's knife. This one lost a passport and still got through three countries. Somebody's wine bottle was missing. Julius Watkins, the French horn player we called "Phantom" because he was so quiet and performed backstage during the *Free 'n' Greasy* show, as Clark Terry dubbed it, left his mouthpiece at the top of the Eiffel Tower in Paris before we played a concert there. Our road manager had to climb up there and find it. In Yugoslavia, we did thirteen straight one-nighters, and after paying the band I had $62,000 in Yugoslavian money, which was worthless outside that Communist country, so I took a chance and spent the entire amount on train tickets to whatever cities I could think of. I had no gigs in these places but I was gambling on the ones we might get, hoping to recoup the Yugoslavian money. Now that's a bitch—having a big band and buying tickets to a town hoping for a gig. I guessed right about 90 percent of the time: Berlin, Stuttgart, Baden-Baden, and Cologne in Germany. In Sweden we played thirty-two one-nighters in folk parks all over

the country thanks to the concerned intervention of musician and composer Bengt Arne Wallin and journalist Hans Fredlund, my true friends to
this day, who persuaded Seymour Osterwall, the director of the folk parks,
to save our butts. The folk parks were government-sponsored places like
the Tivoli in Copenhagen—the original inspiration for Disneyland—that
provided everything from big bands to opera and symphonies to jazz to
folk music for the local community, everyone from eight to eighty. Entire
families of mothers, fathers, kids, grandparents—sometimes 600 or 700
people overall, including outrageously beautiful young Swedish women—
would gather to dance. The finest taxi dancers would come in and throw
their pocketbooks up on the bandstand so that they could go off with the
men who paid twenty cents a dance for the honor of their company.
Sometimes band members attempted comedy routines from the stage. My
feeble attempt at a joke got over hilariously night after night when instead
of asking "Are your feet cold tonight?" my fractured Swedish yielded an
inquiry about a private part of the female anatomy.

If I guessed right about a potential destination, we had work. If not,
we'd sleep on the bus or train, or I'd hole them up in a hotel until I could
get something else.

The guys were always so broke, they were constantly coming up to
me to borrow against their salary. From Lionel Hampton I'd learned both
sides of the coin about the finances of running a band, but I had no cal-
culator. I'd advance five different guys in five different currencies, then do
the math and pay them off in a sixth currency. I'd write what they owed
me on the back of matchbooks and napkins and menus. I'd say: "OK,
Sahib Shihab needed $200 in Swiss francs—or was it Belgian, or French?
Phil Woods hit me up for $50 in Spanish pesetas. Jerome Richardson owed
$100 in French francs. Phil gave me $30 back and Jerome gave me $25
against his next loan. Melba Liston and Buddy Catlett each got $125 in
Italian lira, then paid me back in escudos when we got to Portugal. And
who was it that asked for Swedish kronor? Maybe Julius Watkins? Benny

Bailey wanted $75 in German marks, plus a raise; Porter Kilbert needed francs to pay for his hotel room in Belgium. Then I'd tell Benny I didn't have any money for raises, so I'd offer him another solo. Sometimes that worked.

Despite the headaches, I loved them all, I really did. They were my family, the greatest musicians and most colorful human beings in the world. It was the greatest band I could ever dream of, but after ten months of hauling thirty people across Europe and coming up with that $4,800 a week, I started to break down. I was twenty-six years old and felt like I was fifty. I felt responsible for them. I would never let them down. They were also starting to crack, one by one. We took a charter flight through the Alps, and the plane was so loaded we couldn't go over the mountains but had to fly through them. During this hair-raising flight, Budd Johnson and trombonist Åke Persson, with his black American wife, Gerri Gray, got into a fight about Hannibal crossing the Alps. Then, in Milan, Budd lost his wallet, called the Italian police to his hotel room, and blamed the hotel maids for stealing it, then showed up late, drunk and uncontrollable, in the middle of the Nat Cole set. So I had to send him back to the States. It was the hardest thing in the world for me to do, because I loved and respected the shit out of Old Dude, but I sent him home. I softened up later and brought him back to Europe with me the next year on a sixteen-city tour of Switzerland sponsored by the Migros Corporation.

When we got to Turku, Finland, I sat in my hotel room, exhausted, and tried to figure out my next move. I'd begged and borrowed from everyone I knew, called everyone I could call, tapped out everyone for every last favor. Most didn't even want to hear about it: a big band stranded in Europe did not exactly seem like a good investment. We were stuck over there. There was no way for me to get them home. I had no money. I didn't know what to do. Earlier that week, I'd gotten a letter from my dad, pleading with me to write to him. He hadn't heard from me in months. It hit me like a sledgehammer. He was all I had. He sounded sad.

To make matters worse, his birthday had just passed, and I was sitting in the middle of Turku, Finland, without even a fucking birthday card to send him and someone was knocking at the door saying that this one didn't get a hotel room, that one lost his hotel key, this one needed money to wire his wife back home, one of the dogs had shit on something and the hotel was pissed, so I had to pay. I wanted to shut them all out and send Daddy a card. That's all I wanted to do, get up and go out and send him a birthday card; but I knew the moment I walked into the lobby of the hotel, fifteen crises awaited me because I had all these people dependent on me. I was completely distraught and overwhelmed. For the first and only time in my life, I contemplated suicide. I wanted to be outta there. I just wanted fifteen or twenty minutes of peace.

I picked up the phone and called Irving Green in New York. Irving was an old friend and the record maverick who founded Mercury Records and had always been there for me. I said, "Rip, this is it! I'm stuck. I got thirty people here and two dogs. I don't know what the fuck to do next." He sent me $1,700. A friend in need finds out who his friends are in a hurry. Then I called my wife, Jeri, to contact the co-owner of my music publishing company in New York, Charlie Hansen, who'd been introduced to me by Billy Taylor, to try to get an advance of $14,000 against my half of all my songs. This was everything I owned. But it was time to go home. When they used that famous phrase on the Statue of Liberty—send me your tired, your poor, and your raggedy-ass homeless—they were talking about us. Jeri didn't read all the fine print, though. Later I had to buy back the songs for $105,000. Between the sale of my music publishing and the loan from Irving and help from Brice, I had enough to get us home on the USS *United States,* a slow boat from Le Havre, and pay the guys one more time.

When we hit shore in New York, the FBI was waiting for us. They had a tip from the dealers who sold some sweet wheat to my band that some jazz musicians were smuggling grass from Europe. They searched every bit of luggage we had, then took Melba Liston, Chan Parker, and Les Spann into separate rooms and searched every inch of them bodily. They found a few seeds of sweet wheat in Les Spann's things and confiscated them. Chan Parker had sewn an ounce of pot into her jacket and managed to flush it down the toilet before they could search her. I took care of someone to the tune of $5,000 to handle the FBI charges and bad press so we could work in the United States and all stay out of jail. Then for the first time in my adult life, I went out and got me a real job.

CHAPTER 19

Living it

Buddy Catlett, bassist,
Free and Easy tour

When we got to New York everyone in Quincy's band lost momentum and our lives more or less fell apart. My marriage was on the rocks and failed. Julius Watkins, the French horn player, played for the New York City Ballet and later died. Porter Kilbert, the alto player, died within a year. Les Spann, a fantastic guitarist and flutist, hit the bottle and ended up on the Bowery and died. Åke Persson, the great Swedish trombonist, killed himself. He took some pills and drove himself into a lake or something in the seventies. And Quincy came back dead broke and deeply in debt.

I think the tour changed him in that he'd never been so disappointed before. I'd known him since we were both fourteen back in Seattle. We played together in Charlie Taylor's band, and Bumps Blackwell's, and in the National Guard band. We started taking lessons on the same day. I was playing alto sax until I got tuberculosis when I was fifteen and they put me in Firland Sanitarium at 145th and Lake City, way up at the northern city limits. Quincy and his brother Lloyd used to walk up there every other day to see me around dinnertime, just so they could eat. I was so happy that he'd pulled me from Denver, where I was playing bass with Horace Henderson, Fletcher Henderson's brother, and Cal Tjader, among others, to do this tour with him.

But he had so many people depending on him. He had at least thirty people with him on that tour: kids, wives, dogs, plus Phil Woods's mother-in-law. He had a good sense of humor about it. One time when we were at a train station and he went to buy our tickets, he pulled out a wad of money and told the ticket clerk, "I want a ticket for Phil Woods, a ticket for Jen Woods, a ticket for Chan Woods and Baird Parker [Charlie Parker's ex-wife and son], and a ticket for Dog Woods." Then he turned around and said, "I oughta eat that dog." But it got to him at the end. At one point he got into a fight with Jimmy Cleveland, the trombone player. He was standing in front ready to conduct the band before a show and he walked right through the sax section to get at Jimmy, who was nobody to fuck with, by the way. Jerome Richardson grabbed Quincy before he could get there. Who knows what it was about. Quincy actually loved Cleve like a brother. They were roommates in Hamp's band, but by then we were all so road-weary it was pitiful.

We sat in train stations like bums, man, tired, broke, drinking, always laughing at some silly shit. It was the experience of a lifetime. Not one person in that band would've traded it for the world. If you listen to the records we made, like *Birth of a Band*, you'll see why. That band was one of the greatest big bands you'll ever hear, in my opinion. Look at the personnel: Phil Woods, Jimmy Cleveland, Clark Terry, Jerome Richardson, Quentin "Butter" Jackson, Benny Bailey, Sahib Shihab, this band was ridiculous. I played with Basie for five years after that, and in terms of tightness, Quincy's band was as tight as Basie's. In fact, our first date for that crazy-ass tour was at the Olympia Theater in Paris, and just before the curtain opened, the sax player, Jerome Richardson, was sitting up front and pointed offstage and said, "Hey, is that Marshall Royal over there?" And sure enough, there was Basie's legendary alto player Marshall standing there. And behind him, and all around him—all around the back stage—was Basie's band, Sweets Edison, Frank Wess, Sonny Payne, and Basie himself. They came just to watch us. That was our indoctrination. We played that night like there was no tomorrow, and from then on the experience of struggling all those months in Europe made us even tighter. We were one big, fuckin' note.

Quincy had tears in his eyes when he bought our boat tickets home from Paris, and that was something I'd never seen before. He refused to believe that a band that good couldn't survive. It was a dream come true for him, to have a band like that with all those super players in it and to roll through Europe the way we did. He used to call me Bumblebee and sometimes when we'd be rolling on the bus through some beautiful town in Europe, he'd come to the back of the bus where I sat and say, "Whad'ya think, Bumblebee, is this a dream or what?" He saw every step. He realized every step of what he was doing. And so did I.

When we got back to New York, he did his best to keep the band together. He got trombonist Curtis Fuller to take Quentin Jackson's place, and he got trumpeter Freddie Hubbard to take Floyd Standifer's place. Oliver Nelson joined the band, and we did a few dates around the United States and a tour of Switzerland, which the Swiss company Migros sponsored, but it was never the same. The band was changing, the times had changed, and Quincy got a job as an A&R man at Mercury Records. That's what began his change from hard-core bebop to pop music. He didn't run to pop music to sell out on jazz. He did it because he was broke. Bebop was dying anyway. When I say that, I mean Birdland in New York was over, Bird had died, and a lot of bop musicians were starving. Quincy took the big band up to the Newport Jazz Festival in '61 and he told the audience, "Just because Bird is dead doesn't mean this music is dead. There'll be somebody else." He signed Cannonball Adderley, Dizzy, Gerry

Mulligan, Rahsaan Roland Kirk, and Julius Watkins to Mercury Records, but the great era of bebop was gone and it wasn't coming back. Quincy told me the record company used to complain about him signing all those jazz players. He told me, "Buddy, the guys at the label say I'm a budget buster. I make great records that don't sell."

A lot of jazz critics began calling Quincy a sellout when he started making pop records. They wanted him to be the next Duke or Basie, but he wanted something different for himself. Why is it that Leonard Bernstein can conduct the New York Philharmonic one day and do a Broadway show like *West Side Story* the next day, and no one calls him a sellout? To a lot of white critics, the only time a black musician is authentic as if he's toothless and wearing overalls and concrete boots, playing blues harmonica on a porch in the Mississippi Delta someplace, scratching his ass and dying with a bottle of wine in his lap. Fuck them. They only wish they could've done what Quincy did. Now I'm reading stories in the papers saying, "Guess what. White people haven't been given their due for their contribution to jazz."

Quincy took jazz as far as it could go for him. The best part of his life, he gave to jazz. Think about it. What was he supposed to do after Europe, spend his life playing jazz so he could apply for a lot of grants and shit? So some middle-aged college professor and some nerdy bunch of dudes can sit around and give him a grant to play the music he helped make? No way. Dig, how far can jazz go anyway? Think about it. How different is the shit that the young cats are playing now from what we played fifty years ago? They play it better. They sound fresher, newer, they add a lot to it, but it's the same shit. It's coming from the same place. The difference now is that they're playing it as history, and back then it wasn't history. It was our lives. It was real, and we lived it.

CHAPTER 20

My life as a dog

In 1961, I was onstage at Birdland in New York, the jazz mecca, anxiously preparing to start the last set of my first appearance with a big band in my own name. The moment was golden. All of a sudden I heard a commotion on the stairs. Pee Wee Marquette, the midget MC, hollered, "Lady, you can't come down here," and I heard a woman say, "Get out of my way!" My heart sank. There she was, alive and well—my mother.

I knew right away she was going to turn the joint out, and she did. She stood at the doorway of the club with her hands on her hips wearing an elegant Salvation Army–style outfit, glaring at me and ready to praise the Lord. I'd known she was around New York. She'd turned me in to the IRS a few weeks before. I owed them $60,000 for the salaries I paid on my *Free and Easy* tour. She wrote the IRS a letter and told them she wanted me to get busted by the government so I'd stop writing sinful devil's music and turn to religious music. The IRS put an agent on my tail, who caught up to me and summoned me to his office on Madison Avenue, but he had a sense of humor about it. He said, "You know, I was looking all over the country for you and couldn't find you till one day I had my legs propped up on my desk, and I just peered through the blinds on the windows of my office." The IRS office was on Madison Avenue just across the street from Basin Street East. He said, "I saw on the marquee there: 'Peggy Lee, orchestra conducted by Quincy Jones.' "

I told him, "I just paid my taxes two weeks ago," which I had done. I'm sure he checked. I left and never heard from him again.

Sarah stomped onstage at Birdland and chewed me out in the name of the Lord while the musicians on the bandstand stared. I was keenly embarrassed and we argued quietly before I gave up. No sense trying to rein her in now. I'd learned that you didn't rein Sarah in. You kept quiet, rode out the storm, and hoped she'd leave when she was done. How she got to New York and where she stayed when she was there, I never knew. Fortunately for me, Sarah spotted an even greater nemesis that night in the form of Father O'Connor, the jazz priest of New York. Father Norman O'Connor helped jazz musicians when they were down and out, had a congregation full of jazz players, and was a fixture at several clubs. He was also a major supporter of the Duke Ellington religious concerts. When she spotted him in his priest's collar, sitting in a booth up front with Morris Levy, drinking a glass of scotch and holding a cigarette, she stomped over to him and said, "Father, you oughta be ashamed of yourself! Look at you. You got the nerve to call yourself a man of the cloth." Pee Wee the MC interjected, "Come on now, lady!" She told him, "Shut up, mister! If you didn't drink so much, you wouldn't be so short." She wore their asses out for about twenty minutes before finally leaving. From the bandstand, I watched her climb the stairs and leave, my pride splattered all over the floor.

Buddy Catlett, my bassist and my childhood friend from Seattle, had a visit that night from his wife, who was sitting near the stage. As Sarah left, Buddy's wife said, "Quincy, how could you treat your mother like that?" Before I could utter a word, Buddy, one of the kindest, gentlest people I've ever known, said, "Woman, shut up and mind your own business!" I had never heard him talk that way in all the years I'd known him. Buddy knew Sarah all the way back to our days in Seattle. He was so mad at his wife that he got up and walked back to the bandstand, and not once did he even look my way. He's never mentioned that incident to me in all the years I've known him. That's the sign of a true friend. Thanks to him, I got it together and made it through the gig that night. I even got up enough nerve to ask Sarah Vaughan, who was in the audience, to come up and sing. Ella was there too, but I didn't know her. Years later I had the once-in-a-lifetime thrill of recording an album with her and Count Basie for Norman Granz. When we went out to lunch and on the way back to the studio she told me shyly that she'd heard on the grapevine that I didn't invite her onstage that evening because I didn't think she could even shine Sarah's shoes. Pleeze!

That was one huge difference between Europe and the United States. In Europe, my mother couldn't just appear out of nowhere. But in the United States, my life with women was just one big mess and it wasn't limited to my mother. My marriage was falling apart. There was no excuse for it. I could say that as a kid I never had the opportunity to control what happened to me. As a kid I'd been at the mercy of adults who made un-reasonable choices and left me and my brother to our own devices. That was true. And now that I think on it, I could also say that my issues with my mother manifested themselves in my relationships with women. That was true too. But the fact is, I was twenty-two, twenty-three, twenty-four years old, in the prime of my life. What was I supposed to do? As far as I'm concerned, celibacy is a highly overrated virtue. For whatever emo-tional and psychological reasons, I always loved the idea of being in love, full bloom, all the time. I went through several stages, the first being the discovery that we are hormonal animals. The second was the most neu-rotic: on the road, pulling ladies in, then pulling back. Then there was the obvious trait of dogdom, conquest. After a while my emotions started to short-circuit and I began to worry about losing my sensitivity to the things that mattered most to me. That scared me more than anything, because it could affect my soul and my music and my karma. It wasn't until years later that I realized that unconsciously I may have been emulating my father's relationships with dysfunctional women.

At a certain point after separating from Jeri I was living in the apartment of the legendary music mogul Morris Levy, who had generously loaned me his place at 25 Central Park West. Some friends and I had partied all night and fallen asleep sprawled all over the tiny bachelor apartment—three guys and five Playboy bunnies. We'd forgotten to pull the shades down, and the next morning when that sun blares brightest for those with a hangover woke us, we looked up and saw that the lights on the third floor of the building across the way were still on: all these guys were looking down at us. Hurriedly I grabbed the drapes to conceal our nudity. My efforts at concealment had been in vain—it was a school for the blind!

The fact is, I love women—every touch, every whisper, every glance, every scent, every drop of them. To me, loving a woman is one of the most natural, blissful, life-enhancing—and dare I say it, religious—acts in the world. I grew up in Seattle and Chicago, and not having a mother, it gives you a perspective on life and women that others simply don't have. I understand what it's like to live in an emotional vortex: giving love, using love, finding and losing love, and yearning to feel real love. I lost my cherry to an older girl in Sinclair Heights in the blackberry bushes when I was eleven. I weighed ninety pounds and by the time I figured out what to do, she was grinding on me like a rolling pin on a piece of dough while I hung on for dear life. That was the beginning of the game, the introduction to one of life's most primal and exquisite pleasures. I never denied myself. At Garfield High when I was a teenager playing trumpet at the prom dances in Bumps Blackwell's band, the girls would dance cheek to cheek with the star jocks and wink at me over their boyfriends' shoulders, indicating with a raised index finger that we were to meet later at one o'clock at the usual place, Bumps's lair. By then my lady would have gone out with the football player for a banana split, ditched him afterward, and changed from her virginity socks and Sunday school pumps into sheer black hose and a pair of high heels for her rendezvous with me at the witching hour. The appeal of "bad boys" is nothing that started with rock 'n' rollers or rappers. As jazz musicians in the late '40's we clearly owned the territory.

One of Bumps's many girlfriends, a seriously healthy redhead who was about thirty-five when I was fifteen, kept saying, "Cutie pie, I bet you're afraid to come over here and get what I got for you." I said, "I bet I ain't." One night she led me to the back seat of Bumps's car and left me comatose. Forty-two years later, in 1988, my mother called and said, "I met an old friend of yours who would love to call you. Can I give her your number?" I agreed. Later that day, I got a call from a woman who spoke in a tiny, quivery voice. "Quincy, remember me?" It was Bumps's girlfriend from forty-two years ago. God bless her, she was seventy-seven and still trolling.

My first real love was Gloria Jenkins, who went to another local high school. I met her at one of the dances at the Y. She was an "older woman" who had two years on me. Gloria had beauty, class, and style; she was a real lady. Her parents—a Filipino mother and a black father—welcomed me warmly. I used to walk down an eight-block hill to her house dressed in my Stacy Adams suede-and-alligator shoes and my zoot suit, looking like a gangster. One day when I got down the hill, lo and behold, there was my nemesis, Don Phelps, who was also older, hanging out in his raggedy-ass old car with the antenna with a fur tail on it. I had to sweat it out a long time before Gloria decided that I was the one she loved. Don had always been a friend, and remained so. Later he became the head of the Board of Education in Seattle.

But puppy love ended with Hamp's band. That's where my life as a dog really began. During twenty-two consecutive one-nighters, with pretty women in every small town, I'd watch how the old cats did it. They had a ritual because the striking time was short. On a typical tour of forty-two consecutive one-nighters in the Carolinas, we'd travel seven hundred miles a night on the bus, arrive in a town at 5 P.M., check into the fleabag hotel, then eat and/or shoot pool. After the gig we'd go back to the room, wash the shirt, fold and slip the pants under the mattress to press them, hang the shirt and jacket on hangers in the bathroom, and run hot water in the shower to let the steam flatten out the wrinkles. Then wash the handkerchief and stick it to the mirror to let it dry overnight. Then the hair: First you slap on a dab of Murray's from the famous orange tin container, an industrial-strength, hurricane-proof ghetto hair pomade guaranteed to hold your do in place for a week—that shit was like Super Glue; then you gently slide a little Black Beauty on your hair for coloring—that could potentially get dark stains all over your pillow; finally topping it off with a taste of Three Flowers to bring out the sheen, and a finesse to give it that sweet aroma. The last step of the process was the delicate application of the "doorag." By this time I was an expert at doing my do. I had negotiated my way out of gym in high school with Coach Lindquist in return for playing four of his choice dances a year. I didn't want to shower after gym and go through the whole hair routine again: I preferred to practice my boogie-woogie licks on the piano in the choir room.

After this elaborate preparation we'd hit the stage clean. Hamp, wearing Italian suits, and the entire band wearing glow-in-the-dark white gloves for exquisite pre-Temptations hand choreography, would rock our audiences till the rural workers in red suits were dancing on top of oil spills in warehouses in North and South Carolina while the crowd would jitterbug holes into the sawdust floor. I'd spot my prospective pretty young thing from the bandstand. The big-time dogs in the band had all the music memorized because we knew we needed to have our eyes free for trolling. The new guys, in contrast, had their eyes buried in the music stand.

The band usually took a twenty-minute intermission: it was now or never. I'd come down, say something funny or stupid to gauge a girl's responsiveness, to make sure this wasn't a one-handed clap. There was no time for wining and dining. Romance for musicians was, by the necessities of time and circumstance, less than glamorous. With three years of being on the road in the United States behind me, by the time we toured Europe in 1953, I felt pretty comfortable with women, having been trained by the best in the business. I'd gone from the American South, where I met pretty country sisters who tried to fatten us up with sweet potato pie and pig ears and rice; to Los Angeles and Washington, D.C., to Harlem, where the sweet young debutantes from "Sugar Hill" would bring me home and try to sneak me past their parents, who would inevitably announce, "He's too dark," and in some cases slam the door in my face; to Oslo, Norway, where the women followed the band around in snowstorms in their cars saying, "We'll keep you warm." No one could ever accuse me of leaving some sweet "skol" sister out in the cold. I did the best I could at all times. By '64, I was so confused and mixed up in relationships that I didn't even know what I felt anymore. There was Annick from Paris, Little Red from Sweden, DeeDee the Norma Miller dancer from New York, Doreen from Karachi, an ex-Miss Sweden and stewardess from TWA, "Skataki" from Athens, Sister "Stop!" from Tokyo, Ernestine the ex-Miss Ohio from Cincinnati.

It got so out of control that at one point I was in love with and dating Marpessa Dawn, the leading lovely from *Black Orpheus;* a Chinese beauty; a French actress; Hazel Scott, the gifted, cosmopolitan ex-wife of Adam Clayton Powell, Jr.; and Juliette Greco, the Queen of French Existentialism, all at the same time. Juliette was also dating Miles Davis then. She was wonderful. She had $35,000 miniature lifelike dolls she'd received as a gift from Darryl Zanuck. You wound them up and they moved in slow motion, curtsying to each other in silhouette against the flames of the huge stone fireplace. She was brilliant and sweet and would imitate a kitten purring when we made love. Miles was irritated with me for years about it, though it was some time before each of us figured out what the other had been up to. He was also pissed when he found out that I was attracted to Frances Taylor, a breathtakingly beautiful female, inside and out. This was before they married. We would rendezvous at the Oliver Cromwell Hotel on 72nd Street in New York when I was scoring my first film in 1964. Frances and I used to meet for a little afternoon tea and empathy. After she moved in with Miles she made the mistake of mentioning my name around him. Little did he know that my brother Lloyd and I had known her at the Rosenwald Apartments in Chicago when she was two and was on our A list of "special friends" who'd receive a wad of used gum collected from various places, including underneath the benches in a nearby park. I heard Miles locked her out of the house without her clothes in the winter. He even wrote in his book that Brando and I were both in love with her, and that I even gave her an engagement ring. I told him, "Miles, man, you know I never gave Frances no engagement ring." He said, in that raspy voice of his, "I know, Quincy, but the shit sounds good." I loved Miles, man. He was a giant in every way. I wasn't competing with him when it came to women. We were fellow pound puppies, that's all, just trolling and rolling. Everything about Frances was something to adore; neither of us deserved her. To top it all off, she was a wonderful dancer with the Katherine Dunham troupe and was responsible for Marlon Brando's prowess on the dance floor.

It was fun, but it got too crazy. I'd have six different women in six different countries, and after a while I'd get a call and someone would tell me, "So-and-so in France is heartbroken. She's threatening suicide because you're playing her." After trying to calm her down, I'd have to look in the mirror and confront my conscience and my arrogance and say, "Okay, I'm gonna get back with Jeri right now and make it work." That was an effective stopgap temporarily, but I didn't really know how to deal, because, between me and Jeri, only one of us was really married. We were childhood sweethearts. We outgrew each other. Jeri was the best and she deserved the best, and she was tolerant to a fault.

She busted me several times while we were in France. At one point I was having a matinee in a hotel near Neuilly with a lady from the *Free and Easy* show. By this point I was living on the edge, and I knew it. My excessive instincts were beginning to betray me and to lead me down a self-defeating path. I knew it, yet I couldn't stop myself. The lady and I were exploring an afternoon plié one day while Jeri was in Amsterdam—where we'd just performed—getting her teeth fixed. Then the next day a French lady I'll call Jasmine came by the apartment: our mutual attraction was the true aphrodisiac. Afternoon delight and all through the night—have mercy!

The next morning Jasmine and I had been oblivious to the world for about an hour when I heard a ring on the buzzer. I knew then that I should have asked Jasmine to leave much earlier. I tiptoed over to the door. This was one of those old French apartments, where the floors go "creak, creak, creak." I creaked over and looked through the crack under the door and saw Jeri's shoes. She was still supposed to be in Amsterdam. She said, "Quincy?" I uttered an internalized "Holy shit!"

I didn't answer. When you take chances like this, it's like having a picnic at the end of the Concorde runway. She tried her key but I'd double-bolted the door. I heard the elevator go down and ran back into the bedroom to tell Jasmine to put on her clothes quickly.

She dressed and I put her in the small kitchen, which was just off the front door. When I released the latch to open the front door I peeked through the keyhole just to make sure the coast was clear. I came face to face with a cold stare from Jeri, dead-on. As she tried to push open the kitchen door, she said, "Renée, I know you're in there." Renée was the name of the lady from *Free and Easy.*

Now Jasmine was mad. She hissed, *"Who the hell is Renée?"*

Oh, boy. It ain't easy being sleazy.

When we got back to the States, Jeri had had enough, and I can't blame her. In 1962 we decided to separate. I moved out of our apartment and into Morris Levy's place. On my first night as a single man, I went to my office, finished some work, and made a call to a gorgeous honey with not a brick out of place named Freda Payne, who at the time was just nineteen. I'd met this pound cake at Danny Simms's club in New York, and we'd fallen in love. Little did I know until a year later, when she jumped onstage in Chicago with my big band after drinking almost a bottle of champagne and killed it on "If I Were a Bell," that she was a really talented singer. We put her in my band on the Eckstine tour of the chitlin circuit along with Nipsey Russell and the Coles and Atkins dance team—the Apollo in New York, the Howard in Washington, D.C., the Royal in Baltimore, and the Regal in Chicago. Freda went on to have a major career and a huge hit, "Band of Gold." We were at Morris's and I was in the shower when she said, "Somebody's at the door."

I said, "Answer it." Morris' apartment wasn't the safest place in the world. Reputedly he had mob connections, and the last time I'd opened his door, a dude named Big Sneeze dressed in a black suit and dark shades was looking down at me asking for Moishe. The doorbell rang again.

She said, "I think you better answer it."

Morris had a big cedar closet in his apartment, so I made her climb in it just to be safe, and opened the apartment door. It was worse than I thought. Instead of a thug waiting there to break my knees, it was Jeri. She said, "I just wanted to see how lonely you were on our first night apart."

Like a jerk, I stood at the door and couldn't even get a word out. She looked at my face and she knew. She walked into the apartment, into the kitchen, straight up to the closet where the woman was, and said, "I felt it when I saw you two at the Apollo. Honey, you can come on out now." Then Freda sheepishly emerged.

Jeri turned to go, and left without saying another word.

Many women would have given up on the relationship years earlier. Jeri had hung in, for way too long. There's only one first time, and we were both reluctant to let go.

Right around the time my marriage was winding down I had lunch daily at the Playboy Club two blocks from my office at Mercury in the Scripps Building at 745 Fifth Avenue. I had a friend who worked at the club, Chuck Childers, who was the manager in charge of 129 bunnies, if you can imagine it. A "reluctant" Clarence "Sweet Potato" "Bump" Avant and I would go over there regularly for lunch and a little light window-shopping. Chuck was my main man and our guide, because Playboy Clubs had a lot of serious rules. You cannot hit on a bunny on the premises of the club—no notes to the girls, no dog talk, no target practices, no nothing. Ritualistically we'd pick out four or five and Chuck would run down the status—available or not—and let them know that we were interested. We had our own choreography. Then we'd meet the girls at a place two blocks away called the Pussycat, where anything went.

We got to be real friendly with most of the bunnies. We wanted to hit on all 129—okay, I'm exaggerating, but it was a serious challenge for any serious dog. There was one mixed girl there named Devon, from Minneapolis, who was nineteen at the time, who was Chuck's girlfriend, and later lived with Jimi Hendrix. I had in fact met her earlier in Vegas, when she was fifteen. She was with Jimi when he died.

My most vulnerable point as a dog—and one of the most bizarre in retrospect—involved an incident that would take place in the wake of a numbing marital breakup. On September 6, 1986, I got a call at the Bel Air Hotel from a woman who called herself Ariana and said she was a friend of a friend of mine in the record business. When I phone him to check her out, he raved on and couldn't say enough good things about her: she's fantastic, the real thing. Later it came out in *Vanity Fair* magazine in an article titled "The Obsession with Miranda" that Ariana had gotten through the phone defenses of no fewer than thirty-seven guys, including such serial black-belt golden retrievers as Robert De Niro, Warren Beatty, Billy Joel, and Tony Curtis. Tony agreed with me that we couldn't bust her because in her own way she was a genius. I'll always be grateful to her for making me risk love again after my nervous breakdown, even if it was only "phone jones" in the beginning. At the time I met her, I was totally shut down emotionally.

She knew how to reach people, when to strike, and exactly what to say and how to say it. She'd leave a message—always when you were out—saying "hi" in the most enchanting and seductive voice I've ever heard in my life, clinching it with a snippet of an appropriate soulful song. I still have the tapes. "I'm nineteen years old, a student at Tulane, and a member of the Whitney family, as in the Whitney Museum. Most guys tell me I'm the most beautiful girl they've ever seen. I'm in town shooting a cover for *Elle* and would like to know if we could meet for a drink." There is not a dog on the planet who can resist an invitation like this.

Who let the dogs out? She'd snared all these guys, even though they didn't want to admit it. They had literally never even seen her. "I've been in love with you since the first time I saw you. I will make you happier than any woman you've ever met in your life, or ever will." Any man wants to see such a woman right here and now. The first time I called her back, we talked for five hours. She knew exactly which buttons to push. By FedEx she sent me my favorite cookies, a bottle of 1961 Château Pétrus, and cashmere sweaters in all my favorite colors. She wrote me beautiful letters in calligraphy, quoting any known poet on any subject, then getting down and dirty. She'd even send cryptic photos of isolated body parts—hips, eyes only, or the top of a head—to keep the mystique going. But I soon noticed that they weren't all from the same woman! Well, no one's perfect. Ariana knew how to play the players.

When I suggested a get-together, she said, "I want you to get to know my soul and mind first; then my fine body will be gravy." Only two guys ever met her in person, Richard Perry and myself. The others fell madly in love with the spellbinding sound of her voice and were insanely addicted. She was masterful. One time I was staying in New York at the

Westbury, and she called to say that she'd been looking for me while she'd slipped in and out of town for the day on her girlfriend's father's corporate jet. She urged me to check with the concierge. The manager and the concierge agreed that there had been a stunning young woman in a chinchilla coat who looked like Grace Kelly who'd been asking for me. It turned out she was a hired model! Ariana didn't miss a trick.

She played all of us like a Stradivarius—a pound of world-weary dogs who'd heard and seen it all. She never asked me for a cent: she was just having fun, and demonstrating her prowess and control. The showdown came three or four months later in Los Angeles when I was recording *Bad* with Michael Jackson. Supposedly she was calling from "Mumsy's penthouse" across from the Stanhope in New York, where I often stayed. She was asking for Bobby Shriver's number. My secretary trapped her, though, when she called from "New York." Ariana made the mistake of putting her on hold, enabling my secretary to identify the Los Angeles hotel on the "hold" message. One of our staff members had a housekeeper friend at the hotel, and when they gained access to Ariana's room, there were some CDs I'd given her, not to mention my photograph!

I was working in the studio with Michael Jackson when my secretary and Clarence marched in and asked to see me alone. They confronted me with the accumulated evidence. Tears in his eyes, Clarence like a true friend furiously asked, "Where's Ariana?" When I said that she was in New York with her mother, he retorted, "She's right here in L.A. Dammit, you're so blinded by all this love shit. Someone's trying to mess you up big time, and you're too stupid to see it." Clueless as I was, the pieces were falling into place quickly.

Busted! When Ariana called the studio at around six o'clock I tried to set her up by telling her I couldn't take it any longer and wanted to fly to New York right away to meet her for the first time. There was a long dramatic pause before she said, "You bastard! I was trying to make a nice surprise for you, and now you've spoiled it. You probably want me to do something low and cheap, like meet you at the bar at the Bel Air Hotel."

"You got that right, baby—meet me there at eight o'clock," I said as I slammed down the phone. At the hotel as I waited, she called again: "Baby, let's be good to each other. Why don't you come down here." She suggested I meet her at the Regency and ask for the key to the penthouse. She also asked me to bring a scarf. At this point Clarence freaked and told me I was out of my mind.

After eluding my bodyguards and ignoring the advice of my best friend, I took a limo downtown with champagne and a hamper of smoked salmon sandwiches in a box, all excited. It had been seven months now, and I was finally starting to be able to feel love again. Showdown time! At last I'd get to see this mystery woman in the flesh. At the penthouse the door was cracked open. "Don't come in till I tell you," she said. By the time I went in it was pitch black. I was beginning to think Clarence had been right about my sanity—what a gamble! It didn't matter. My curiosity had reached the point of obsession. I felt a very strong presence. She took the scarf and blindfolded me. Then she took the box of sandwiches, removed my coat, led me over to the bed, and took off my shoes as I stretched out. "Don't touch me until I touch you, OK?" I had a glass, into which she poured champagne. I felt her hand on my leg. This was the moment I'd been waiting for—my turn! I started tenderly with her hand and worked my way up, my reach widening as it ascended, until I hit the neck. Ray Charles had taught me how to read Braille, so reading a woman was child's play. This was a big woman: I could tell, even as pitch black as it was. I decided to remember an urgent business appointment, and got the hell out of there without ever actually seeing her. Later, when I checked with various other members of the dog pound who'd hired private detectives, I found out that in reality she was forty-five, a social worker in Baton Rouge, and weighed 250 pounds. Her name was Ariana Walton.

I admired Ariana. She really knew how to dance graciously on your head with velvet spiked heels and make you love every minute of it. If she ever writes a book, ladies, run, don't walk, to get a copy. What Ariana taught me was the power of the imagination, and the thrill of seduction by implication. The most powerful part of seduction is already in your own soul waiting for someone at the other end of the line to discover it and release it. The beauty of it is that I never saw her.

You never know who you're going to fall in love with—my choices were never made on account of color. Love is like ice cream, and I don't care if it's French vanilla or chocolate chip or maple walnut or lemon sorbet. When I look at a woman, race is the last thing I'm looking at: I'm checking out her legs, her pretty eyes, her whatevers, how she expresses herself, how she relates to me. It all started in the Pacific Northwest, where if there were three or four fine sisters, they were nailed down already. I expanded my criteria quickly.

My kids are all of mixed blood and proud of it. They relate deeply to the rich heritage of black culture, with all the heartache and joy that goes along with it. My current relationship is with a dream lady who is African, Portuguese, and Belgian.

It's God's sense of humor and sweet revenge to give a dog six beautiful daughters and leave him alone with his imagination. What I've learned from them is that guys have a long way to go. Most men think their conquests with women happen because the female of the species just can't resist the power of their persuasive rap. They think they're in the driver's seat because they're making the moves. Bullshit! Most of the time men are walking into traps that were set long before they drove up—they just don't get it. From the international master hound of them all, Porfirio Rubirosa, from the Dominican Republic, who knew how to kiss a woman's hand in thirty-two different situations, I learned that to be equal to a woman, a guy has to be thirteen years' smarter, just to catch up. I also learned innumerable lessons from my longtime pound partner, Richard, "the Hound of Baskinville."

What took me even longer to figure out is that even if you're always out there looking for Miss Right, you won't find her until you look inside yourself and become Mr. Right. If you don't love yourself, you're not capable of loving someone else. It's a lesson I wouldn't really absorb until much later in my life, when I finally established not only real friendships with a variety of extraordinary women but a happy relationship with someone who is not only a friend but a loving person from a large and very happy family.

At heart I suppose I'm an incurable romantic. My favorite intimate gift to a woman could involve all five of the senses in simultaneous enjoyment: I'd send butter cookies from Pont-Aven, to be eaten to the accompaniment of a Moscato d'Asti dessert wine; a container of J. F. Lazartique orchid shampoo; *The Captain's Verses* by Pablo Neruda, the Nobel poet laureate in poetry; a Natori nightgown that drapes and clings in all the right places; and a CD of Miles's "Kind of Blue," or my own long CD version of "The Secret Garden," played softly in a room lit by scented candlelight. I can only hope my lady would be the sort of sensuous, intelligent woman who could receive the gift in the spirit in which it was sent.

Despite the dramas I've managed to live and love through, my feelings concur with the immortal chanteuse Edith Piaf: *"Je ne regrette rien."* Above all, a man must embrace the feminine side of himself, especially if he is an artist. You can't let your machoness mess up your good "thang."

CHAPTER 21

It ain't necessarily so

Clarence Avant, record executive	"Where am I from? You don't need to know where I'm from. Who the hell

cares where I'm from as long as I pay taxes. Why do you ask? It's none of your goddamned business where I'm from. I'm from Bloomfield, Illinois. No, Wisconsin. No, no, Mississippi. Yeah, I'm from Clarkstown, Mississippi, sounds better. No, wait . . . I'm from Climax, North Carolina. That's right. Climax. Just write down "Clarence from Climax." No, I'm not a Tarheel neither, muthafucka. Just Clarence. Clarence from Climax. Go check a phone directory out there, you'll see me. Look under the letter "I" for "I haven't told you shit yet and won't, neither."

I grew up in the record business—over forty years I been in it—and one thing I've learned in all that time is that you don't say nothing. Say nothing. My mentor was Joe Glazer. He was an ex-concession man for Al Capone. He managed Louis Armstrong and booked Dizzy, Duke Ellington, Sarah Vaughan, Lionel Hampton, Billie Holiday, and a seventeen-year-old that I met with Joe at the Blue Angel named Barbra Streisand, a class act. He used to say, "Keep your mouth quiet about what you know, and when you make a deal ask for as much money as you can without stuttering," so when I first met Quincy in 1963, that's what I did. He was working at Mercury Records as a vice president under Irving Green, who was forty years ahead of his time. Irving made Quincy the first black vice president of an American record label. Not VP in charge of black music, just VP in charge, period. Check the executive roster of any major label today and tell me how many black vice presidents there are who deal with anything other than so-called black music. Call me when you can count past two.

I was managing the composer Lalo Schifrin and the organist Jimmy Smith at the time. I'd heard Quincy had given Dizzy Gillespie and Gerry Mulligan $100,000 on their record deals, which was an unheard-of sum for a jazz artist in those days. I went to see him about signing Jimmy. He said, "I'd love to sign him. How can we make it happen?"

I said, "I need four hundred and fifty thousand—in dollars, jelly beans, or coins, take your pick."

He exploded. "What? You must be out of your freakin' mind! Forget it."

I went to Verve Records, which was a division of MGM, and got a huge deal from them, and we became friends after that. Quincy respected me for pulling off that deal. We celebrated by going to the Copa to see the Supremes together. We got drunk, me a lot more than Quincy. He carried me up to my room. Then I passed out. I apologized, and we've been best friends ever since. That was more than thirty-five years ago.

Though we're best friends, we don't always agree. I love Duke. He loves Duke, but he'd kill for Basie. I don't hug no-motherfuckin-body not related to me by blood or business. Quincy, on the other hand, he's a guy who . . . let me put it this way: If God came down to Earth tomorrow on a motorcycle and had to talk to you, before He left He'd say, "Tell me, have you hugged Quincy lately? Where is he?" And I guarantee you before He left, Quincy would have spoken with Him and they would have hugged and cut a deal. And food. He screams at me when I put a bottle of red wine in the fridge, because I don't know a good bottle of wine from a bottle of Mad Dog 2020. He knows what a bottle of 1922 blah-blah is, and whose grandma made it, and why they sit on the grapes or whatever the fuck they do. I have no idea why he cares for all that dumb shit, but I love him. Only in heaven will I find a better friend.

The man is a musical genius, there's no question about that, but he's too kind. As long as I've known him, he's been surrounded by people who always want a piece of him and never talk to him straight. When he wants a straight answer, he comes to me. When he wants the truth, he comes to me. When he has questions about a record, he'll ask me. Sometimes he doesn't want to hear the answer, but so what. That's what friends are for. We talk three, four times a day on the phone. There's not much conscience in the record business today. It's all bottom line: Takeovers. Getovers. Fast money. In the Morris Levy days, you shook hands, backed out the door, watched your back, and if a guy said, "I'll deliver Sarah Vaughan in Paris by Thursday," she showed. Nowadays they say, "Our star isn't showing up in Paris unless you let her sing her crappy new song. Plus have three million bucks ready. Plus have three limos for her dogs, and make sure she has yellow towels in the dressing room." It's all limos, power, beepers, cell phones. There were three thousand managers and five record labels in the old days. Now there are five hundred labels and three thousand managers. One day you're talking to a guy who's a photographer for the star. The next day he's her manager. The next day, he's her husband and is running her label. The next day he's a photographer again. I've been in the business a long time. I've seen a lot.

Quincy survived in the record business because he's like that Duke Ellington song "New World a-Coming." He knows what's coming and going before anyone else. He knows about Bill Gates and eBay and music on the Internet and all that shit, and he shares that with whoever he knows.

That's part of his problem. A lot of these young executives come to Quincy's record company, cut their teeth on his dime, then split. Yet he still gives them the benefit of the doubt. I tell him, "How come you're gonna work with such-and-so? He hasn't done shit in ten years."

He says, "Belly button, Clarence. I got a feeling about him in my belly button."

I'll say, "What if your belly button is wrong?"

Because he's one of the greatest talent scouts the business has ever seen, he doesn't listen and I can't argue with that. The thing is, if Quincy has twenty-seven cents he'll give away twenty-five. He's generous to a fault with friends and strangers. I've never met anyone who can walk into a room and have grown men—seasoned, grizzled businessmen—hugging each other. If I hugged as many motherfuckers as he did in a day, my arms would be banana peels. He's so personable. Shit, I couldn't be that personable with my mother.

I worry about him all the time, because he gives nothing but heart and soul, and he gives it freely, especially with women. I've never known anyone who's had so many wives and girlfriends and can get them all to sit down at the same table to eat, which is what he's done. Because they still love him, and he loves them back. That's his Achilles' heel, women. He and women are like . . . let me put it this way: Love is a dangerous word. It's all through the Bible, but like Gershwin said, "It ain't necessarily so, what you read in the Bible." When love is good, it's fine, but when it's used wrong, it can be deadly. He's fallen in love so many times in his life, and he means it each time, but when it hurts him . . . Goddammit, I've seen him go through some decimating times with his marriages, especially with his divorce from Peggy Lipton. That took a horrible toll on him. What he's been through with love would drive a normal man insane. I tell him all the time, "Why can't you just fall in love with one woman and make it last forever?"

He told me, "Clarence, you're right. But sometimes, maybe the only thing worse than being alone is wishing you were."

CHAPTER 22

Frank

I was working with Frank Sinatra at the Sands Hotel in 1964 when I called my brother Lloyd in Seattle and said, "You gotta come down here and be with me for this."

He didn't want to come. He said, "Why didn't you ever call me back?"

I didn't know what to say. My marriage to Jeri had come undone two years before, though it ended officially in 1966. To compound it, I did a gig in 1962 composing an original show and conducting an orchestra for the AMA Auto Show in Detroit and had a brief affair with a female dancer there. My second lovely daughter, Rachel, was born as a result. So I had two kids, my marriage was breaking up, and I had to pay alimony and child support. Rachel's mother got a cash settlement of $11,000, which was all I had at the time. I was working as an exec at Mercury Records, trying to get from under $145,000 in debt from the *Free and Easy* tour. I wanted to move out of New York and get into LA film scoring, something I'd wanted to do since I was nine and Lloyd and I stole fourteen dollars out of Grandma's apron pocket and sat in a movie theater for three days, eating candy and watching Lena Horne in *Cabin in the Sky.* Yet getting into scoring was proving to be difficult. I didn't have the space to look back and see what Lloyd was doing. Look back to what? Our childhood? Give me a break. Lloyd, on the other hand, refused to rid himself of it. That's probably why I'd avoided him.

I said, "Awww, Lloyd. Just come on, man. We've been through a lot of hills and valleys, and this is definitely a hill. Who else am I gonna share it with?"

He agreed.

When he showed up in Vegas and saw me conducting Basie's band at the Sands with Frank Sinatra singing up front, it knocked his socks off. Frank was at the height of his powers then, and I was steering his musical ship, the greatest band in the world. In the words of "Sweets" Edison, who was also in the band: "It don't get no better than this!"

I'd come to Frank while working as a vice president of A&R at Mercury Records. I was in charge of the big orchestras and the sweet divas, Sarah Vaughan, Dinah Washington, Shirley Horn, Nana Mouskouri, Damita Jo, and Nina Simone. I paired the "King of Strings" arranger Robert Farnon with Sarah Vaughan, a string section, and the sixteen-voice Sven Saaby Choir in Copenhagen; worked with French horn virtuoso Julius Watkins on an album arranged by Billy Byers titled *French Horns for My Lady;* and wrote an arrangement of "I Can't Stop Loving You" for Basie that won my first Grammy, the same year a twenty-one-year-old singer named Barbra Streisand won her first Grammy too. I did sessions by the dozen with Billy Eckstine, Dinah Washington, Sarah Vaughan, Bette Davis, Louis Jordan (one of my childhood idols), Louis Armstrong, Charles Aznavour, Bobby Scott, and Josh White. They were great records all, but they were great records that made no money. Irving Green, my boss and founder of Mercury, came by my office one day and said, "Quincy, we need to talk."

Irving was a big man, six feet four. My nickname for him was "Rip" because he would growl if you stepped on his tail, but he was more bark than bite. He was hip old school. Brilliant. Visionary. Strong. Loyal to a fault. And at the time, a hard-core party animal on top of it all. He grew up in the business when gangsters had their fingers in everything. He'd helped me out when I was in trouble with my European big band tour and let me have free rein at Mercury, and I loved him for that. He and his daughter Kelli, who used to run my publishing company, were like family, and always will be. He made me a vice president after only a few months, the first black VP ever at any record label, and taught me the "business" side of the music business worldwide from A to Z. We did 250,000 miles a year all over Europe to meet with Philips' executives worldwide, as well as managers and international artists. We used to go to Philly and put on our smocks and work anonymously retail behind the counter at record stores to understand the customer's point of view, asking for a record by song, artist, tempo, lyrics, or hook. We went to pressing plants in Greece to work out problems between distributors. Irving was tall, smart, smooth, and laid-back; he always played his cards close to the vest and never let anyone—or anything personal—get in the way of a deal. I remember once during an executive meeting at Philips in Holland he mentioned to the execs in an off-hand way, "I just bought the Chappell catalogue for $42 million. It may look like just some dusty file cabinets. Don't worry about it." Dusty file cabinets full of Gershwin, Cole Porter, and Rodgers and Hart songs, and many other treasures. Twelve years later the catalogue was sold to Hill and Range Publishing for $110 million, and subsequently Steve Ross purchased it for Warner Brothers for over $300 million and combined it with Warner Brothers–owned Chappel music. I couldn't resist a smile when Steve called me with news of the acquisition. Irving was a brilliant man. He, Steve Ross, Clarence Avant, and Dr. Billy Taylor taught me most of what I know about business. They were also great human beings.

One day in 1963 Irving said, "Quincy, your records are all great musically, but we could sure use some help with our bottom line."

I said, "Rip, cutting a pop hit is not that big a deal."

"Well, Q, if it ain't that big a deal, then lemme see you do it, pal. Behind your back, your A&R buddies are calling you a budget buster!"

I took him up on it, but it turned out to be harder than I thought, plowing through piles of demo tapes, listening to bad singers do awful songs, trolling my way through all of this garbage. I understood the basics of communicating but musically there seemed to be a line I could not cross just to make a hit. One afternoon in Chicago at one of Mercury's monthly A&R meetings, Irving tossed a tape down on the table. "Joe Glazer gave me this," he said. "A friend of his is a fight manager or something, and this girl is his niece. He wants a reaction from us on it. Whatever you guys decide is okay with me."

The other executives played it and then slid the tape back to Irving across the table, but I caught it on the way and said "I'll take a shot." The tape was made by a sixteen-year-old kid from Long Island named Lesley Gore. She had a mellow, distinctive voice and sang in tune, which a lot of grown-up rock 'n' roll singers couldn't do, so I signed her. One day Joe Glazer came up to my office with her mother, Ronnie, and said, "I want you to make this girl a star, Quincy, and blah blah blah. Do this and do that." I said, "Don't worry, Joe, I'm on top of it." But I didn't really know what it meant, to make someone a star, or to make a hit. I just wanted to make a good record.

I started looking for songs for Lesley. I culled through a few—just flavor-of-the-week stuff—but with the help of publisher Aaron Schroeder and Claus and Shelby Singleton, we finally decided to cut a single called "It's My Party," with a very energetic twenty-year-old singer-songwriter named Paul Anka writing the B side, a song called "Danny." The crowning touch was a hot commercial horn-and-rhythm arrangement by a major 360-degree musician named Claus Ogerman, and we had the two songs in the can by 3 P.M. on a Saturday. After the session I went to Carnegie Hall to see the French singer Charles Aznavour, whom I'd worked with in Europe, and with whom I was doing an English-language record. As I walked into Carnegie, a car pulled up. Out pops a young producer I'd recently met named Phil Spector. He was heading to the concert dressed in his usual cool sixties garb, purple shirt, cape, and shades. I said, "What's up, Phil?" He said, "I just cut a smash with the Crystals. It's called 'It's My Party.' "

I freaked out silently and didn't say a word. I walked backstage, said *bonsoir* to Charles, and hauled ass back to Bell Sounds, where the engineer Phil Macy and I cut 100 acetates that night. Acetates were the records you sent to radio stations. That was the way it was done back in those days.

That was Saturday night. Along with fellow Mercury exec Shelby Singleton, I licked stamps all weekend and shipped all 100 acetates to radio stations and program directors across the country by Monday. I had to leave for Japan the following day to score and act in a one hour Japanese television drama called "Blues for Trumpet and Koto," with soap actor Anthony George, and music composed by a brilliant sixteen-year-old songwriter named Marvin Hamlisch. I called Lesley before leaving and told her "All we need now is to change your last name. It still bothers me. We'll figure it out when I get back."

I was in Japan three weeks when Irving called. He said, "We didn't have time to change Lesley's name."

I said, "Aren't we gonna have a problem with a last name like Gore?"

There was a long silence. He said, "Didn't anybody call you?"

"No."

He said, "Quince, the record's number one. Do you really give a damn what her last name is?" I can still hear us laughing together.

I rushed back to the United States and we did an album. We had eighteen hits with Lesley, including "Judy's Turn to Cry" and "Sunshine, Lollipops and Rainbows," the first song written by Marvin Hamlisch, and "You Don't Own Me," with another brilliant sixteen-year-old, a piano player named Leon Huff, which was number two behind the Beatles' "I Want to Hold Your Hand." In the following four months the charts were dominated by the Beatles on four different labels. All the arrangements on Lesley's records were again by Claus Ogerman. The records sold millions, and I didn't get an extra dime. I'd signed a contract with Mercury that clearly stated that "in *no* event"—and the word *no* was underlined—"will you make over $40,000 a year." As VP, it had seemed okay to me at the time. Before then, I never knew what a producer was or did. I remember back in the fifties when Cannonball and Nat Adderley had shown up at my basement apartment on 92nd Street with a blue-labeled homemade acetate recording of a blues jam backed with "Frankie and Johnny." I called up Bobby Shad, the producer and head of jazz A&R for MRC, a Mercury-owned jazz label. I said, "Bobby, I heard these incredible brothers from Florida. We gotta record 'em, trust me, you've gotta hear 'em."

Bob said, "Great. I want to hear 'em. Book the studio and the engineer, call the musicians, write the arrangements and songs if you have to, and I'll see you there on Tuesday." I did all that and he showed up and said, "Take one" and "Take two." For that, he was producer and got percentage points based on record sales, which could be in the thousands. Me, I got my salary and the arranging fee, which came to hundreds. I didn't know producers got percentages back then, but after Lesley's records sold millions, I learned quick. I'd done so many sessions I was seeing double. Let's get real. Number 1 is euphoric and addictive; numbers 2, 6, and 11 are my least favorite chart positions.

Rip and I knew each other well enough not to waste words. Two years earlier Irving had done a stock merger with his label and Philips, a huge Dutch Westinghouse–type conglomerate manufacturer that made everything from TV sets to vacuum cleaners. He said, "This business is all marketing now. It's not a ma and pa business anymore. It's rack jobbers now. No more eyeballing the inventory. They want quarterly projections, bottom line, sales figures. Do what's best for you." Philips made me an offer of a million dollars—more zeros than I had ever seen in my life—for a twenty-year contract. I thought it over. That's fifty grand a year for the next twenty years; it felt like a lifetime. I couldn't see it. I said to myself, "Is my life worth only fifty grand a year?" I don't think so.

Despite the financial security I'd been offered, I knew I had to follow my dream and go to California. I'd always wanted to get into movie scoring. I'd scored a small Swedish film by 1949 Oscar winner Arne Sucksdorff, the Swedish Disney, in 1961, *The Boy in the Tree.* Arne's daughter, a fan of my band, had tracked me down in a Swedish restaurant. The film starred Tomas Bolme and Birgitta Petersson, best known as the young girl in Bergman's *The Virgin Spring.*

I had blown another opportunity to score another film in Paris two years before. In 1959 a director named Jacques Demy asked me to score his first movie, *Lola,* introducing the young French actress Anouk Aimée. When I went to Nantes to screen the film, I knew something was wrong with what I was seeing, but I was too inexperienced about film scoring to know what it was. Jacques had filmed Anouk mouthing lyrics on-screen to an unwritten song—just mouthing lyrics, pretending to sing, no music, no melody. Normally in filmmaking, you've got to prerecord vocals with musical backing tracks. Even today, with all the technology available, it's almost impossible to add a missing melody to someone's lyrics-only performance already on film—and she wasn't even singing. At the time, I didn't get it, but I was so anxious to be a film composer that I agreed to score it anyway.

Three days later, back in Paris, after discovering that I had been ripped off by our French promoter, I called Jacques and said, "I've been waiting for this opportunity all my life, but I can't do your film because we're stranded and I gotta keep my band alive." I suggested a friend who was studying with Nadia Boulanger named Michel Legrand, who was a friend and one of my all-time favorite composers. Michel did the film and it bombed, but that same team did a second musical film, a pop-opera musical called *The Umbrellas of Cherbourg,* which won an Oscar nomination and put Michel, Jacques, and a nineteen-year-old Catherine Deneuve on the international map.

The actors in this unique film never uttered a word. The vocals were all prerecorded by professional singers, standing in for the actors.

I wasn't going to let an opportunity like that pass me by again. When Sidney Lumet asked me to score a film called *The Pawnbroker*, I said yes quickly. This was my first scoring assignment for an American film. I went by A&R Studios, co-owned by Phil Ramone, who was one of my best friends (he and his wife, Karen, still are today). Phil's little A&R Studios was a tiny box on 48th Street right above the musicians' favorite watering hole, Jim and Andy's. The big record companies were hit-making machines in those days. They had industrial-strength recording machinery, big, powerful studios with state-of-the-art equipment (two tracks) and all the latest gadgetry, but Phil's tiny A&R Studios was the little engine that could. The music that came out of that little shitbox was incredible—hits by the dozen. Phil was like the Wizard of Oz, pulling knobs, fixing machines with Scotch tape, glue, wrenches, screwdrivers, paper clips, bagpipes, whatever he could find. He was brilliant. We did hundreds of recordings together. We once walked into the control booth after a take of Ray Charles doing "Let the Good Times Roll" with half of Duke's band and half of Basie's band. I'd been hired as the conductor and arranger. He said, "Quincy, listen to this." He had the sound coming out of the right speaker, then he hit a few knobs, and the sound came out of the left speaker. I said, "What the hell is that?" As a kid in the Northwest in 1948, I had been lucky enough to hear binaural sound on earphones in Oregon with the inventor, Emory Brooks. Phil said, "It's called stereophonic sound, man. You'll be hearing about it." In those days you'd find Nesuhi Ertegun and Jerry Wexler in the studio with their ties on, because there was no "we'll come back tomorrow and fix it in the mix." What you heard there was what you got on a two-track tape, and there was no changing it.

When I told Phil I wanted him to record the score of *The Pawnbroker* with me, he laughed and said, "Quincy, I know nothing about movie scoring."

I said, "Me neither, but I got some tips on it from Henry Mancini in London and Armando Travioli in Rome, and I've been checking it out since I was thirteen."

"Oh yeah? What did they teach you?"

"Well, Mancini sat me down in the Mayfair Hotel and explained the process of synchronization to me."

"Synchronization." There was a long pause. "Okay. Let's do it."

I got the best players I knew—trumpeter Freddie Hubbard, drummer Elvin Jones, Dizzy Gillespie, Oliver Nelson, Bobby Scott, a harpist, a woodwind and string section, percussionists—including Don Elliott on mouth percussion—everyone I could find. I wrote the score for *The Pawnbroker* in two months and recorded it in two days. I wrote the last cue with fifty musicians sitting around yawning as orchestrator Billy Byers and I scratched out pages furiously, but we got it done and the picture really worked on all levels. I have major respect and love for Sidney Lumet as a pioneering film director who gave me a leg up when I was just a young dreamer. He was also a great technical guru and one of the first to use subliminal flashbacks as a story-telling device. Rod Steiger won an Oscar nomination for best actor, and the score received wide recognition as an original "jazz-influenced" score, and would open up doors for me in Hollywood, or so I thought. My agent then, Peter Faith, the son of composer-arranger Percy Faith, was ecstatic. He said, "We're not taking any jobs from B list directors and producers. A list people only!" I agreed.

We waited, but no calls came. No A list calls. No B list calls. A couple of C list calls. We passed.

Then a year passed.

Two years.

Finally a call came from Hollywood, but it wasn't from a producer. I was sitting in my office one day in New York in '64 and the phone rang. I picked up. I heard him say, "This is Frank Sinatra. I'm directing a film in Kauai, Hawaii, then I'm doing an album with the Basie band in LA. I like what you and Basie did together, and I'd like you to arrange and conduct. Can you get over here next week?"

I hadn't heard from Frank in six years, since the gig in the South of France. I had no way of knowing if I'd stuck in his mind or just evaporated. I nearly fell out of my chair. *Can I get over there next week? Man—is pig booty pork? Pleeze!*

"Okay, yeah."

"Koo-koo. My office will handle the details, see you in Kauai next week." Click. He hung up.

I learned from Frank that he wanted me to arrange and conduct Basie's band, plus add a string section for his next album, *It Might As Well Be Swing,* which included the original version of "Fly Me to the Moon."

Looking back, that call from Frank was a major turning point in my career and my life. His work with the great arrangers Nelson Riddle, Billy May, and Gordon Jenkins were some of the great musical collaborations of the twentieth century. If you worked for him, your ass was out front with him. That's how he played everything—up front. Race wasn't a chasm that he had to cross.

Frank was my style. He was hip, straight up and straight ahead, and, above all, a monster musician. I loved him, man, I admit it, I loved him as much as anyone else I ever worked with, because there was no gray to the man. It was either black or white: If he loved you, there was nothing in the world he wouldn't do for you. If he didn't like you, shame on your ass. I know he loved me too. In all the years of working together, we never once had a contract—just a handshake. The Sinatras always made me feel like part of their family, children, grandchildren, and all.

I went over to Hawaii where Frank was directing *None But the Brave,* his first such assignment. He had a Jack Daniel's flag flying from a tall pole outside his cottage. He sat me down in his office to explain to me what we needed to do. In the middle of our conversation, he got on the phone and called a military friend at the Pentagon. He said, "I'm shooting a picture over here. It would be great if you could arrange to have the Pacific fleet ease by here tomorrow so we could film them in the background." The next day, the Pacific fleet just eased on by. They didn't call him Chairman of the Board for nothing.

Two days later, the picture wrapped, and the Chairman led us aboard a 707 to head out to Honolulu to take over the top floor of his favorite hotel and bop till we dropped. It started out with seven of us, plus Francis, but after a call to some local ladies and starlets, within forty-five minutes there were nineteen. For three days we did significant damage to some mai-tais and as usual put up a noble fight against sin: with bloodied but unbowed heads, we lost. On the plane home, Frank asked if we could go into the cockpit to call his daughter, Nancy, and Tommy Sands, newlyweds who were cruising 35,000 feet below us on a ship.

After landing, we went to the Warner Brothers lot, where I was supposed to write the arrangements for the album he'd called about originally. There was no office space for me there, so Frank put me up in Dean Martin's bungalow, which was upstairs right next to his. I got to work right away and got so involved writing arrangements I lost track of time and got locked in the quarters. They locked the bungalows at night and I couldn't leave, so I wrote all night and fell asleep at 4 A.M.

At around 6:30 A.M. I heard a knock on the door. I opened it. Frank was standing there wearing fatigues, his costume for the war film he was directing. He looked me dead in the eye and said, "How do you like your eggs, Q?"

I mumbled, "Scrambled."

He scrambled them up, we ate breakfast, and from that day on, we were tight. He was a brother in disguise. He knew that about himself. He was crazy about the big-band culture, his roots. One late night in Palm Springs, he told me about a crush he'd had on Billie Holiday when he was young, but you couldn't follow it through because of the times. "Q, you couldn't get away with that back in those days, no matter who you were," he said.

Frank was so buzzed about Basie's band that he took the entire band to Las Vegas in 1964 and hired a bodyguard for each member. Vegas was mob territory back then. No black musician in their right mind would wander around those casino hotels alone for long. Harry Belafonte, Fats Domino, Sammy Davis, and Lena Horne, they performed in the casinos, but ate in the kitchen and slept in black hotels across the tracks as recently as a few years before. Frank wasn't havin' that shit. He assembled the bodyguards backstage at the Sands and told them, "If anybody even looks funny at any member of this band, break both of their fuckin' legs." He assigned to me a big, bald-headed, buff Yugoslavian who taught me to speak in Serbo-Croatian. The guy was trained in about three different martial arts and looked like he could swallow a brick. I walked around Vegas like I was Kirk Kerkorian *and* Steve Wynn!

My first night in Vegas, Frank introduced me to Lucille Ball and Loretta Young. We had drinks at the roulette table and those two led me around, one on each arm, maternally making sure I didn't do anything stupid with my money. I sat down at a blackjack table and won at everything. Each time my chips piled up, they'd mysteriously disappear. When I finally got up to leave, Lucy and Loretta opened their purses and handed me all the chips I'd won. They'd slipped them off the table, stashed them in their purses, and saved them for me so I wouldn't lose it all back in my state of ignorance. I won about $4,000 with their help that first night, but after that I never won again. Little did I know it could be worse—much worse.

Basie was the sweetest cat in the world, but a serial, black-belt gambling junkie. He'd go to the roulette table and put $100 on every number—zero, double zero, one through eighteen, nineteen through thirty-six, black and red, odd and even, and while they spun the wheel, Frank, who was a 10 percent owner of the Sands, would slip over and sweeten some of the bets with a $500 chip on top of the pile. With one hand at the roulette wheel, Basie was simultaneously placing his bets with the other hand at the closest blackjack table; from there he'd segue to the telephone to call his bookie. He also loved to play the ponies. He'd lay money on horse races in California, Ireland, and Florida at the same time. I'd finish a show at midnight, gamble with him for four hours, go to bed, or whatever, and wake up to find Basie downstairs still in the casino, gambling at noon, still wearing his tux from the night before. They had slot machines in the Vegas airport, and after losing everything, Basie would still be dropping quarters into them until I dragged him aboard the plane. One night Basie and I stayed out all night at the Flamingo with Sarah Vaughan and Billy Eckstine. When we got back to the hotel Frank shouted, "Hey, Q, where'd you guys go all night?"

"Me and Basie were out hanging with Sassy and Mr. B."

Frank looked at me with those eyes.

"How come you didn't come get me?"

These were the days when he and his buddy Jilly were into practical jokes, throwing cherry bombs around all night. I said, "We saw you hangin' with the cats. We didn't know you wanted to come, Francis."

"You and Basie are my cats, too. Come get me next time, okay?"

Frank led me into a new world. A land of dreams, high living—anything you felt like doin', whatever, with whomever, whenever you felt like doin' it—and making the music we both loved. Jack Entratter, who ran the Sands, pulled me aside one night and said, "He's never like this except when he works with you and Basie." When he worked with Dean or Sammy, he'd arrive late, having gotten a head start with "five o'clock cocktails" in the steam room with his fellow Rat Packers.

Frank would come to the gig forty-five minutes before I did. I'd arrive at my dressing room and hear him singing in the next room, warming up. *"Amanda, won't you walk with me . . . Amanda, won't you walk with me . . ."* up a half step on each phrase. Since his days with Tommy Dorsey and Harry James in bands where the instrumentalists were the stars and the singers the relief team, Sinatra had approached working with a big band as an almost religious experience, and treated it with profound respect.

Our level of communication was such that when there was a problem, I'd discuss it with him privately—never in public.

It was all unbelievable, and I needed Lloyd to be with me to see it. More than anyone in the world, he'd know what all this meant. This was as good as it gets—that's why I wanted to share it with him. When he showed up, we hung out at the casinos all week while I worked with Sinatra. Lloyd, shy and quiet guy that he was, danced around Vegas like he was king of Emerald City, hanging with Frank, Leo Durocher, Yul Brynner, Orson Welles, and Cary Grant. He had the time of his life. Nothing in life could touch me more deeply than seeing my little brother happy. One night after a set we were sitting around my room and he said, "Dewey, I thought I was mad at you, but I realize it's not you I'm mad at."

"I know it," I said. As usual, I didn't want to talk about it, but at that moment I couldn't bear it. I had to know. "Where is she?" I asked. He knew the *she* I was talking about.

"I don't know," he said. "But wherever she is, I know she's doin' okay. She always takes care of herself. But I haven't seen her in a while."

I said, "Well, when she shows up, we oughta start thinking about what we need to do. She's gonna be sixty soon."

"I know it, man."

Even when she wasn't there, my mother was still kicking ass. I knew the time was coming when we'd need to take care of her. We didn't know how. We just knew it was what we had to do.

The next night Lloyd went into the casino on his own while I did the show, and afterward introduced me to a stunningly beautiful Korean woman named Cynthia Myung Wha Kim, who was also visiting Las Vegas that week. Lloyd was grinnin' like a fox eatin' sauerkraut. For the first time in my life, I could see the light of hope on my little brother's face. I could feel his joy. He went back to Seattle and two years later sent me a note saying he had married Cynthia. I called him, furious, and said, "How come you didn't call me for the wedding? I'm your *brother*, man!"

He said, "This thing's so good I couldn't take a chance on it slippin' away, Dewey. I wasn't waiting for nobody."

I couldn't stay mad. I was happy for him. I knew how long he'd waited for love to enter his life, after all those years of waiting for Mama to show up. He was thirty-one. That's how long he waited to hear a woman say she loved him. Three decades and a year he waited. That's a long time.

CHAPTER 23

Helter skelter

I met Ulla in 1966 in Queens, New York, while playing Forest Hills with Frank Sinatra. Basie opened the show, Oscar Peterson followed, then Frank would knock their socks off. The women were throwing their bloomers at Frank—fifty-year-olds and twenty-year-olds. One night after the show Frank said, "TWA is throwing me a party at the tennis club next door. Wanna do it, Q?"

I said, "Can't handle it, Francis, I'm wasted from hangin' with you last night in Detroit."

"C'mon, we'll do a little gripping and grinning and be outta there in fifteen minutes, okay?"

Ten minutes later I was in love. Halfway through the crowd I saw a young woman—a tall fox, just drop-dead beautiful. She was about nineteen, with big eyes you could swim in, and lashes as long as her legs. She was dressed in a short Pucci dress and long white Courreges hip boots and looked like the cream of Swedish aristocracy. Her name was Ulla Andersson. She was a top Ford model. Eileen Ford discovered her in Stockholm at age fifteen, then groomed her in France at the Paris Planning Agency.

Her mother, Lily, and her brother Tomas were just in from Stockholm visiting with her. The three of them were staying at her Fifth Avenue apartment, which she leased from Bob Evans just after he left the clothing business and went to Paramount Pictures. Phil Ramone, Irving Green, and I went there with them after Frank's party, and the place was a mess—stuff everywhere, fingernail polish all over the tub, clothing and empty food plates. It was surrealistic. It didn't matter. She was a free spirit and breathtakingly beautiful and sweet. She was also a great yodeler—I was impressed. I wasn't looking for a housekeeper. I was looking for love and I felt I'd found it. Very early the next morning after staying up the rest of the night talking, Ulla then did the strangest thing and took me to a public indoor swimming pool in Manhattan. She was an expert swimmer and had been a trainer for the Swedish Olympic swimming team. I just barely swim. It didn't matter. I like to drown when I'm in love, and I was drowning in this one for sure.

I went to Florida to finish up Frank's tour at the Fontainebleau Hotel in Miami—finally, a three-week gig with Basie after ten one-nighters. I told Frank about my new affair. He was so excited about it that while Ulla was in Russia to do a *Vogue* magazine shoot with the noted Japanese photographer Hiro, he surprised me and instigated bringing her back to join me in Miami. After the tour, Ulla and I returned to New York long enough to gather our things and head on out to LA, where I went to compose film scores. My next assignment was *The Slender Thread* with Sidney Poitier and Anne Bancroft, which was also Sydney Pollack's first film. We moved into the Sunset Towers. Built in the heyday of Hollywood by the producers as a place to stash their mistresses, the Towers was an Art Deco building with a beautiful entrance, but the main feature was the rear, almost invisible, entrance. You could bring an elephant up on that elevator. The year before, Michael Caine had come into town after making *Alfie*, and the two of us had that elevator running overtime. Michael and I were born the same year, the same month, the same day and hour—"celestial twins," as they say. California was on fire then, and we were definitely qualified, willing, and active members of the fire department.

Hollywood swept me off my feet. Most of my life, I'd lived with my back against the wall, my past, my history, absorbed in the essence of my music. But I had no history in LA. I distinctly remember Sidney Poitier coming into my room at the Sunset Towers. His career was red-hot, too; he'd just made *In the Heat of the Night, To Sir, With Love,* and *Guess Who's Coming to Dinner,* back to back. He told me, "Q, I think our time has finally come. This is the big one. Every little goody we ever dreamed of will be walking our way. Like never before, a lot of goodies will be all ours. Now the thing we have to remember out here is to exercise moderation." Sidney was always there for me, wise and brotherly: he truly cared for me as much as I did for him. But back then I was ballistic and all I could think was: Moderation, my ass. My problem was that God gave me two heads but only enough blood to operate one at a time. Don't pour cold water on me—just let me burn. I had just done the music for *In the Heat of the Night* and *In Cold Blood.* I was ready to jiggle some molecules, as Brando used to tell me. The first time I'd gone to LA was in 1951 with Hamp, when I had three dollars in my pocket. I stayed in the heart of the ghetto at the Central Hotel in South Central. The Central Hotel made the nearby and slightly upscale Watkins Hotel look like the Bel Air Hotel. Now I was living in the prestigious Sunset Towers with my career going full blast, facing wall-to-wall temptation nightly, fighting sin, losing, and loving it.

It didn't happen right away. I couldn't find film-scoring work at first, so my agent, Peter Faith, hustled and got me a bread-and-butter gig scoring a TV show produced by Lee Rich called *Hey Landlord,* starring Will Hutchins and Sandy Baron. Garry Marshall, who later created *Happy Days* and *Laverne & Shirley,* and Jim Brooks, who later wrote and directed *Terms of Endearment* and *As Good As It Gets,* were among the writers. I spent a lot of time learning the craft on the run and making just enough to support myself and Ulla, my ex-wife Jeri, and my children.

Finally, after months of my agent beating the pavement, Universal called me in to talk about scoring a movie called *Mirage* starring Gregory Peck and Walter Matthau. I was ecstatic, but when I walked into the meeting at Universal, the producer froze, looked at me in shock, and stuttered, "Just a minute. We'll be right back."

As they filed out of the room, I waited pensively, knowing exactly what was going down. In those days, some of the guys at Universal walked around Stepford Wife style in charcoal-gray suits, white shirts, black ties, and brown wing-tip shoes. The running joke there was that a junior executive at Universal got on the elevator to the black towers wearing a gray suit with a tiny red dot in his gray tie. His boss asked, "You going to a party or something, son?" I don't think they even had blacks in the kitchen back then.

The producer came back into the room and said, "I'll get back to you." Then he called Henry Mancini, an old and close friend, and asked him, "Can Quincy Jones handle a score for Gregory Peck and Walter Matthau? This is not a black film." Mancini said, "C'mon, guys! He just did *The Pawnbroker* and he was a student of Nadia Boulanger. This is the twentieth century—you think the guy's gonna write the blues for Greg Peck? Hire him!" Way before and after *Mirage*, Mancini was a friend till the day he died, God bless him forever.

Benny Carter was the pioneer when it came to opening doors for black composers in Hollywood. Benny, my friend and hero and one of the most urbane, world-class, groundbreaking band leaders, composers, arrangers, conductors, and instrumentalists who ever lived, took me in to meet Stanley Wilson and Joe Gershenson, the head of the Universal music department, personally. There were others too: Jonie Tapps, music supervisor at Columbia Pictures, who gave me twelve films to score there; Sidney Lumet, who was the first to call and nurture me; and Richard Brooks, one of the original Rat Pack members with Bogart, who kicked ass for me when Columbia Pictures and Truman Capote wanted to hire Leonard Bernstein over me to score the film *In Cold Blood,* which was a 100 percent white film based on Capote's Pulitzer Prize–winning book. Brooks was furious about it. He told Columbia Pictures, "Up yours, Quincy Jones is doing my score." I'll never forget that. After the New York premiere of the film, Capote called me, speaking slowly in a low voice and crying apologetically.

Even after all the drama, I nearly lost the *Mirage* gig. Just after I began work on it, Universal received a threatening letter from "Mrs. Quincy Jones, Sr." It informed them, in the most explicit terms, that the mother of Quincy Jones had been under the delusion that her son had been kidnapped by Universal to write the devil's music and that she would do everything in her power, including sue the shit out of them, to prevent that from happening. Sarah was rough. But Gregory Peck saved the day. He sat down and wrote my mother a letter, patiently explaining that I wouldn't be writing devil's music. Sarah wrote him back, and those two established an unlikely friendship and bond that lasted literally till she died. Once she even told him that if he flew up to Seattle to meet with her, she might let him star in the film of her life story.

Not long after we arrived in California in 1966, Ginny and Hank Mancini had thrown a baby shower for Ulla, and surprised me by inviting Alfred Newman and Benny Carter, two of my idols. Leo Shuken and Jack Hayes were brilliant orchestrators for all three of us. A few months later I got a call from Alfred, singer/songwriter Randy Newman's uncle and composer of over 40 film scores going back to Charlie Chaplin's *City Lights,* who graciously invited me to his famous five-thirty post-time cocktail parties in his Frank Lloyd Wright–designed house on Sunset, where his young sons (Thomas and David Newman, now composers) reportedly used to bowl with his eight Oscars. He had heard I was in a group Johnny Mandel had so aptly dubbed "the Roller's Club," composed of me and Johnny and Dave Grusin, because, while desperately searching for fresh material, we could imagine ourselves resorting to rolling around under the piano. Al was one of the few musicians who'd made it who still acknowledged that scoring films was no walk in the park. For years later he'd make friendly calls when I was on various assignments. When I was doing *In Cold Blood* he called and counseled, "If strong dramatic values are already on the screen, don't try to match them with the music." For Cary Grant's last film, *Walk, Don't Run,* he said, "Remember, for comedies don't tell the same joke twice"—that is, no funny music for funny scenes. We also tried to avoid representative scoring, or "mousing" as we called it, where the music precisely followed the action on the screen, as in a Mickey Mouse cartoon. It was hipper and sometimes more interesting to leave a chasm between the ear and the eye so that the viewer could fill in something with his imagination, somewhat in the style of Fellini and Nino Rota or Morricone's score from *Battle of Algiers,* for example.

I first met Cary Grant at Basin Street East in New York, where I was conducting and arranging for Peggy Lee. My second and most humorous encounter with him was from a laundry truck. I'd just gotten started in the movie business, and I was scheduled to meet Cary and the producer Sol Siegel at Columbia Pictures to discuss scoring Cary's last picture. Ulla went straight to the studio and forgot to pick me up at home first, so in order to be on time I decided to hitch a ride with a laundry truck that was at our house: I told the driver I'd give him twenty dollars if he could get me down there in fifteen minutes. I was standing in the truck in my Italian suit and tie, as clean as a pot of greens, with my briefcase in hand; when we got to Sunset, I asked the driver to drop me at the corner newsstand three doors down from the entrance to Columbia, so I could stroll up to the entrance casually. He said no, no, no. I'll take you right there, and promptly headed up the street and skidded into a U-turn. Cary and Sol were just starting up the steps to the studio, and of course they could hardly ignore the screech of a sharp, country-ass U-turn. When they turned around, there I was, trying to look cool exiting a laundry truck.

I made another lasting friend in an unexpected way when I was scoring *For Love of Ivy*, whose title song with lyrics by Bob Russell was nominated
for an Oscar. With lyrics by a young, regal, beautiful dancer and poet and
writer named Maya Angelou I wrote a tune called "You Put It In On Me,"
recorded by B.B. King, which was a hit when it was later released as a single. The talent assembled for that film was awesome: Abbey Lincoln, Beau
Bridges, Sidney Poitier, and Carroll O'Connor.

Just as my career began to move forward, my relationship with Ulla
was starting to show cracks. Ulla was a beautiful person, but like me, she
was hurting, which is what happens when a father or mother leaves a five-
year-old behind. I self-righteously thought that because I'd made a commitment to one woman after spending several years as a dog, everything
would be fine. It took years before I could accept that the damage from my
mother's emotional and psychological problems made me constantly attracted to women whose dysfunctional childhoods could more than match
my own. In the beginning, in a way I enjoyed and was familiar with Ulla's
eccentricities. After all, my own mother could be described as eccentric.
But as the months passed, it was clear we couldn't understand or meet
each other's needs. She had a hair-trigger, volcanic temper and I confess I
was no rock of Gibraltar myself. She was a great mother, a good cook, a
charming hostess, and overall a very creative person. When Ulla wasn't
angry, she was sweet and kind and tried to be helpful. She truly believed
she was going to fix my life and make everything right, but she was too
emotionally fragile and damaged to do that. Besides, no one else could fix
my life. I had to. And I wasn't ready.

We had horrible fights over things like how much I worked, how she
thought my music should sound, why I didn't drive, why she got way too
many tickets for traffic violations, why she didn't like to wear shoes to
dressy outings. I've never learned to drive. I tried, but my mind always
jumped in too many directions to focus. I took lessons several times. When
I was concentrating I even got as far as driving from my house to the

MGM studio in Culver City—but when my mind wandered, I'd try to stop at lights on the downbeat, and drive over the curb turning corners. Forget about parking. Finally the instructor gave me my money back and said, "Give it up—it's one less maniac on the freeway." So I did. Ulla could drive but most of the time she had no driver's license—she'd drive with no shoes and one leg on the dashboard. We kind of stumbled forward; it was the sixties, everything was wild, footloose, though not quite fancy-free for us. We moved out of the Sunset Towers Hotel and leased film director David Miller's house on Lloydcrest Drive. Our daughter Martina was born and neither of us knew what to do other than to raise Tina, the happiest baby ever born. We literally just rushed forward, not daring to objectively face each other's emotional problems.

I had no prescription on how to handle a family. Like my daddy before me, I focused on the work. There was no turning back to just jazz in New York at that point. It was do or die. I had no alternative. There was no one to turn to. Lloyd would call me from time to time to see if I was alive. He phoned me around that time and said, "Guess what—I got a degree as an electrician and built the transmission tower for this black Seattle radio station, KYAC, so they promoted me. I got a radio license. One day the real DJ didn't show up, so I'm a DJ now. I do Soulful Sunday, Moody Monday, a Tearful Tuesday." He had a show for every day of the week.

I asked, "Who does the news?"

He said, "Me. I read 'em the paper."

"Who does the weather?"

"I look out the window and say, 'It's raining.' "

"Who's the engineer?"

"Me. I fix everything here."

Shit, if Lloyd wouldn't complain about how tough his life was, neither would I. My agent Peter called up excited and told me, "Let's hit it," and got me a ton of work. I took on a new TV show called *Ironside*, scored the two-hour pilot plus eight one-hour episodes. I was going crazy, but I needed the money, because when I'd gone back to Vegas, I'd lost big time. After I'd been turned over to Count Basie, my serial gambling guru, I'd lost $128,000 in three weeks. I had to do something about it. Stanley Wilson from Universal called and said I could take my choice of scoring a two-hour pilot for either *Dr. Kildare,* another one featuring Les Crane and Ida Lupino, or *Ironside.* I chose *Ironside* because of the script. I took a chance, even knowing Frank's cardinal rule about always being near the Sands Hotel two hours before the gig every night. I had to commute to Los Angeles daily, and there was a very thin window after I finished scoring at five or five-thirty. One session, we went into overtime and the commercial flight to Vegas was gone. I called Frank's office and told his assistant Dorothy that I was in trouble. Fortunately, he was in town for the day and was still there. "Q," he said, "you've got ten minutes to get here." His office on the Warner lot was just a few blocks away, but it felt like it was forty minutes. I had my driver screaming past fire hydrants, through back alleys and shortcuts, to get there. I made it just in time to get on his Learjet with him. Once we were up, it was like nothing had ever happened. From the sky, Las Vegas never looked so good.

Scoring the episodes of *Ironside* was so demanding that when I passed the mantle on to Oliver Nelson, the superb composer and saxophonist, it literally did kill him. He died two hours after coming home from a scoring session. Television scoring can be one of the most stressful and demanding jobs in the musical profession, and *Ironside* was especially tough, with car chases, love scenes, and all sorts of last-minute changes. When I first began scoring it for a forty-four-piece orchestra, I'd fill my score paper with sixteenth and thirty-second notes, whatever came to mind. Henry Mancini and/or Benny Carter would sometimes drop by and look over my scores and say, "Are you crazy? You're writing forty-four minutes of music weekly, like it's for a feature film. This is TV, Q, use whole notes, long-sustained passages with your strings and horns. Let a solo instrument, your rhythm section, or your bass player do the dancing on top. Don't try to write

Stravinsky's *Firebird Suite* for every episode, or you'll never live through the year." I finally got the message, but it was still a crushing workload.

I must express my eternal gratitude to the talented orchestrators and arrangers who generously bailed out my butt time after time when I faced devastating deadlines, especially Billy Byers, Benny Carter, Jack Hayes, Dick Hazard, Dave Grusin, and Bob James. At one time or another, every composer has hit that wall. The rule of thumb for scoring a weekly hour-long show was to write an average of about thirty-five to forty minutes of music a week. It doesn't sound like a lot, but it is. You write a detailed, six-line, condensed sketch score for the full orchestra, then you may have to change everything at the last minute to reduce or heighten the intensity according to editing cuts. The film editor could kill you by cutting just thirty or forty seconds out of a car chase at the last minute. You had to make it work, and quickly. Nobody gave a damn about what you went through to make it happen either. It's all part of the job.

I'd write all week to record the entire episode on Thursday, then on Friday at noon we would spot the music and start the whole process over again for the next week's episode. We all busted our asses keeping up. The usual rule was to compose two minutes of music a day, or maybe three minutes. Some guys could do four or five. But a healthy dose of deadline fear and adrenaline can motivate you even further, to ten or twelve minutes, because there is nothing more terrifying than facing a forty-four- or hundred-piece orchestra, with the producers, directors, and editors looking over your shoulder and having no music to play.

As I juggled like crazy to keep it all together, Frank became a real friend and mentor. On a flight to Vegas before an opening night once, he said to me, "Q, wouldn't it be kooky"—he liked that word "kooky"—"wouldn't it be kooky if we added Johnny Mandel's new song, 'The Shadow of Your Smile,' to the show? Can you do a chart by tomorrow?"

I said, "No problem. Can you learn the lyrics by then?"

"Q, by the time you get the music, I'll have the lyrics."

He pulled out a yellow legal pad and started writing the words, over and over, page after page for eighteen pages, in order to force-feed the subconscious mind. I was so tired I nodded off, and when I woke up a few minutes later, he was still writing. He said, "Q, I went down once and I ain't going down ever again. Remember: If you don't give a damn in negotiations, you can ask for anything you want and get it. If and when you get your own company, remember that it's only as strong as its weakest link."

I never knew what he meant that day till years later when I did have my own company, but I also understand now why we became increasingly close over the years. I look at pictures of Frank's face now and I see my own, the smile, the easiness of the eyes; yet tucked behind the smile is a complex mixture of pain and joy. It's a feeling I sometimes feel in myself. That's what attracted us. It's transcending whatever pain you came from to live and to live to the max. He'd always tell me, "Q, you gotta live every day like it's your last, and one day you'll be right." He recognized that in me and urged me to live it. That was his love.

As my relationship with Ulla fell apart, I confided in Frank. He understood the pain of divorce and tried his best to help my marriage, but he didn't understand relationships any better than I did. One Thanksgiving in 1964, before I'd met Ulla, I was at the Beverly Hills Hotel feeling a bit down and Frank called and said, "Come eat with us." I had dinner with him and his family at Nancy Sinatra's house at 700 Nimes Road. After dinner Frank said, "Are you up for goin' to Vegas tonight, since we get into the ring with Basie tomorrow night? How quickly can you pack?"

I nodded yes and he drove me in his station wagon back to my hotel so I could pick up a few things. Frank waited in the station wagon in front of the hotel. As I came into the lobby, the valet grabbed my bags and asked, "Is your driver coming in to help load your bags into the car?"

I said, "I don't think so."

When he walked around to the driver's side and saw Frank Sinatra sitting behind the wheel wearing his "Swinging Lovers" porkpie hat, he nearly fainted. Frank laughed, jokingly called him a bum, and tipped him fifty dollars. When we got to Vegas and sat down at a table in the lounge, the waiter said, "Mr. Sinatra, would you like some water?" Frank said, "Hell, no. I want a drink. I don't need a bath."

His bluntness was a killer, but no one mentions the five-hundred-dollar tips, the unbridled generosity, the mortgages and funeral bills he paid off for down-and-out performers, the loan of his plane to take a very sick Joe Louis to his heart specialist's in Texas. That's the essence of him. At the Sinatra family Christmas dinner, he'd bounce my daughter Tina on his knees for hours. When I told him I was thinking of divorce, he said, "Your kids are gonna suffer, so you gotta try and make it up to them." I told him I would. While we were recording "LA Is My Lady," on the last bar of the very last take Francis looked me dead in the eye and with a smirk he ad-libbed, "Well, I guess I'll have to unpack my bags and stick around a little longer." He'll always be around.

When Ulla and I came back from London in 1969, where I'd gone to score a film and where Snoopy was born prematurely in 1968, the first piece of mail we opened was a letter with a bond in it for five thousand dollars with a note inside saying, "Dear Quincy Delight Jones III, WEL-COME! And let Uncle Frank start your college fund with the hope that you will find friendship, knowledge, and happiness in what will no doubt be a far better world. Love, Francis."

Two years earlier we'd loved a forty-year-old house built by the French actress Michele Morgan at 10050 Cielo Drive off Benedict Canyon Road. We wanted to rent it with an option to buy, but the owner, Rudy Altobelli, a manager for film stars, didn't want that, so instead he rented it to Candice Bergen and her boyfriend, Terry Melcher, the son of Doris Day, who was a record executive and the producer of the Beach Boys. Ulla and I set our sights on a different house. In 1968, while we were living on Lake Glen Drive, our marriage continued to fall apart. We had moved there two years earlier, leasing from John Raitt; young Bonnie was still living at home. The marital situation was bad. At one point Ulla and I got into a screaming match and I began to feel a sharp pain in my lower abdomen. I walked outside and afterward I staggered to the house of Alan and Marilyn Bergman, who lived down the street. Marilyn wasn't home. Alan saved my life. Despite my objections, Alan took me to their doctor, who diagnosed appendicitis and told me that I was risking peritonitis. He gave me a pill and I felt okay. After endless denial, because I wanted to get back to work on my movie score, I woke up at Cedars-Sinai with a bandage on my abdomen and the doctor holding my enlarged appendix in a stainless steel pan.

This whole period in my life, and that of Hollywood in general, was loaded with portents. I think I had my first taste of it in 1967 while I was scoring *In Cold Blood*, one of the best film scores I've ever done. The Bergmans were responsible for introducing me to the director, Richard Brooks. Working on the film was a unique experience: I was hired even before the actors. I listened to the interrogation tapes of the two punks who committed the murders, who were shockingly similar in appearance to the actors hired to play them. One of the actors, Scott Wilson, had also been in *In the Heat of the Night* and was recommended to Brooks by me and by Sidney Poitier.

Richard Brooks and I went to the Menninger Clinic to look at the psychological profiles of the two killers; they were only dangerous together. The eerie thing was that the film was shot in Kansas in the very house where the murders had taken place. To establish the right mood, I used tons of electronic percussion, cellos and basses, and mixed jazz with 12-tone compositions. The jazz bassists Ray Brown and Andy Simpkins represented the personalities of the two killers, portrayed by Robert Blake and Scott Wilson. The score was ahead of its time, I think, because we lost the Oscar that year to the score for *Thoroughly Modern Millie,* a comedy.

Because of my appendectomy, I couldn't score the movie *Bullitt* for director Peter Yates, but when Steve McQueen asked me to take Jay Sebring to see the rough cut, I did. Together the three of us had done our fair share of hangin' and partying together at the Whiskey a Go-Go on Sunset and at Steve's home in Brentwood. Jay was also my hairstylist. In Hollywood, when you pay over fifty dollars for a haircut, the cutter is not a barber but a stylist. Afterward, Jay said, "There's a party going on at Sharon Tate's house tonight. Roman's still in London, but Sharon will be there, and a lot of fun folks, a lot of industry people. And I found something for your 'chintz' patch, the little bald spot on the back of your head that you can't and don't want to see until it blinds you when you come in contact with two mirrors that give you an aerial view." Anyway, Jay and I discussed a hair-growth ointment he wanted me to try. He said he'd bring it that night to Sharon's or he'd see me tomorrow at the salon. I didn't think too much about it.

I said I would come, because I knew the house—I'd almost bought it. Instead, Terry Melcher and Candice Bergen leased it; then Sharon and Roman Polanski had moved in. I knew Sharon Tate pretty well. I had just seen her and Roman Polanski in London at a New Year's Eve party at Michael Caine's house. But when I got home that night, I changed my mind and went to bed.

Early the next morning a call from Bill Cosby in London woke me up. "Did you hear about Jay? He's dead."

I said, "Bullshit. I was just with him yesterday." I couldn't believe it. I got on the phone and called Sebring International. I said, "Is Jay Sebring there?"

The woman demanded, "Who is this?"

I said, "Quincy Jones."

She said, "Jay Sebring is dead." Blam! Hung up the phone.

I turned on the TV set and saw bodies on the lawn, covered with sheets, being brought out of Roman Polanski's house on Cielo Drive. I got chills: someone had cut the phone lines, gone into Polanski's house, and committed five of the most hideous murders LA had ever seen. They stabbed, shot, brutally killed everyone in the house, including Jay, who was wearing the same jacket and boots he'd worn to the screening of *Bullitt*. Peter Hurkos, the psychic who was invited to the murder scene by the LAPD, told me Jay had been tied up and hung upside down on a beam right next to Sharon. The police found semen on the rug. The murderers had scrawled on the living room walls and refrigerator, with the blood of one of their victims, the words "Rise" and "Death to the Pigs" and the misspelled "Healther Skelter," because they wanted people to think the Black Panthers were responsible. Manson's designs involved becoming the self-proclaimed leader of "rahowa," the racial holy war.

People walked around Hollywood in shock for months, deeply frightened, suspecting each other at first. Guards were posted. Security was beefed up. Everyone was looking over his or her shoulder at each other. No one knew who did it until Sharon Tate's father, who was in military intelligence, led investigators to a guy named Charles Manson who had dispatched his followers to the Cielo Drive house with orders to "kill the pigs on the hill." They targeted Terry Melcher because he had refused to support Manson's efforts to do a record. If we had moved in there, Terry Melcher and Candy wouldn't have, and the whole thing never would have happened. It was one creepy, bizarre twist of fate. Ironically, the TV movie on the saga was filmed at the house next door to mine on Deep Canyon Drive, off Benedict.

Ulla and I wished to God that we had taken the house when we came back from London, but a couple of years later, after we all went to Seattle to visit my family, Ulla announced she was going to visit her mother, Lily, in Sweden. I let her go. I didn't want her to take the kids along, but there was no arguing. She left Seattle and took the kids with her. I can still see the expressions on their faces when they left; Tina at six, her sweet little mouth shaped into a smile, her pretty eyes, so gentle; Snoopy at four, his long, golden, curly hair, his tiny handsome face, so quiet, bewildered, standing in the middle of the floor with his little knapsack and suitcase all packed up. Looking at him was like looking at a reflection of my own face back in Bremerton when Daddy left for work and I had to face another day fending for myself in my stepmother's house. I couldn't handle it. I couldn't stand to look at his little face. I turned away. I thought they'd be all right. A week later Ulla called from Sweden and adamantly proclaimed that she wasn't coming back, period, that she'd missed her country more than she'd ever realized. In other words, the marriage was over. She was staying there and keeping the kids with her. Maybe the kids didn't need me—they were with their mother, after all.

Still, for months afterward, I'd wake up at four in the morning, having flashbacks to my childhood in Chicago, where Lloyd and I had been left alone in the house in our cribs during a thunder-and-lightning storm with the windows open, shades flapping in the wind. We cried and cried, but there was no one home.

Now I was feeling my own kind of Helter Skelter, staring out the window for hours, wondering why I couldn't sleep.

CHAPTER 24

Daddy

Hon. Richard Jones, Superior Court judge, Seattle, brother

My daddy was a man full of joy. That's where Quincy got his spirit from, our daddy. Daddy was fun-loving. He wore Vitalis, rose water, glycerin lotion, and Old Spice. He liked to sip Old Crow, which he called "skidoodle," and get clean and skip out to jazz clubs with his little Stetson hat. He loved baseball, boxing, and women, and not necessarily in that order. He'd spot a woman with gray hair walking down the street and he'd smile and wink and say, "Boy, just because there's snow on the roof don't mean there ain't no fire in the furnace!" His joy and spirit bonded a family together that was patchwork. Quincy and Lloyd had one mother. Margie, Janet, and myself had a different mother. Theresa and Catherine and Waymond had a different father. The mothers never got along. But us kids always got along. We considered each other family. Daddy had everything to do with that.

I was the youngest child. I'm sixteen years younger than Quincy.

Quincy changed and washed my diapers when I had a truckload of mustard in them, that was his first experience with me. Over the years, he and Lloyd were like surrogate fathers to me. Kids all around my neighborhood were into dope and crime, but my older brothers gave me something to aim for. Lloyd bought me my first electric blanket so I wouldn't freeze to death in the cold attic. Quincy flew me all over the world with him, to Acapulco, to France, to Switzerland. Waymond always looked out for me. Daddy appreciated that. He expected a lot of you. He expected us to look out for one another—half brother, stepsister, whatever—because he saw us as a family. As fucked up as we seemed from the outside, no matter what you did, no matter how insignificant, he was always proud of you. One time when I was a kid, one of my sisters was in a play at school. She was leaving for the show and I leaned out the window and said, "Break a leg," and Daddy got so mad, he reached over and popped me with his thumb and forefinger. He thought I was ragging her. He didn't understand that I was wishing her luck. Gossiping, ragging on someone—he wouldn't have that in his house.

By the time I was in high school, Daddy was an old man. Exactly how old you didn't know, because he never talked about his age, but he was close to seventy. He was strong as an ox, but he got sick. He got a double hernia which eventually hung down to his knees and needed an operation. But he was old school. He wouldn't go into a hospital if you melted him down and poured him into one. He wore a truss to keep the hernia in place and walked around with it for years, working like a dog. His attitude was "I can't not do something the whole way." It's a sickness he gave to each of us. When Welch's fuel company would dump a half ton of coal in the front yard, he'd work all night long, he wouldn't even change his clothes, to load that coal into the basement. Complaining wasn't in his vocabulary. He didn't believe in negative thinking. He was always talking positively about the Negro and what the Negro had done. He was more than proud of his friend Paul Williams, whom he visited once a year in

California. Williams was the legendary black architect who designed some of the most famous structures in Hollywood, including the Beverly Hills Hotel.

He worked for S. S. Mullens, a big contractor in Seattle, but after a while his hernia and age forced him to retire. After he retired, he began to lose his memory. I was in the eighth or ninth grade and I'd come home from school and the front door would be open. I'd search the neighborhood and find him sitting in the park at Garfield High School, watching the baseball games there. He loved baseball. That was something he lived for. He loved Satchel Paige, whom he'd played with long ago. When he talked about playing ball in the old days, at my age, being a teenager, I didn't know if what he was talking about was real or the murmuring of an old man, but he started slowing down tremendously after he retired. He just stopped moving. He spent a lot of time sitting in the chair in the living room, sometimes he'd be bent over in pain from his hernias. He didn't go out much. Basically, he withered away.

Quincy was not oblivious to what was going on. He came up from LA when Daddy was sick, but he didn't know how to deal with it. Daddy developed bowel and control problems at one point, and Quincy came to the house and sat in the living room as Lloyd and I dealt with Daddy in the bedroom. He couldn't handle it. It was breaking his heart.

I left at the age of thirteen to go to a private high school on a scholarship. Daddy was still fully functional when I left, but he suffered a series of small strokes when I was away and by the time I came back to live at home and attend college in Seattle, his hand started to curl a little bit, and his leg started getting bad. I came home from the university one day and heard Mommy screaming and freaking out and ran into the living room to find Daddy in his chair, slumped over. I picked him up and took him to the bedroom. I started pumping his chest doing CPR. I could hear the sirens as the ambulance was coming. They came in and put a defibrillator on his chest. I thought he was dead.

He stayed in the hospital a long time, several weeks. We had to feed and bathe him. Then he went to a nursing home. I was working at Seattle University in July 1971 when the hospital called me and said he'd suffered a major stroke and passed away. I rushed up to the hospital. He was still warm, but he was gone.

Quincy was crushed by it. He and Lloyd sat up with Daddy's body in the funeral home all day and night—eighteen hours. At the funeral service, he kneeled over Daddy's coffin and kissed him and his tears fell all over Daddy's face. He held Daddy's face in his hands and kissed him again and again, over and over.

CHAPTER 25

Going down

Daddy was all I had. I had to keep him in my mind as a myth. If anything real or human started to happen to him, I had to keep it away from me. I knew he was in trouble with his marriage. I knew his health was slipping. I knew that he and Elvera had gotten divorced but still lived in the same house.

I never wanted to see his frailties. He was bigger than life to me in every way: handsome, gregarious, compassionate, intelligent, skilled. I didn't want anything to get in the way of that. I desperately needed Daddy to be invincible. Elvera cut him out. She was sleeping with the mailman or milkman or whomever, and that's not even the point, because Daddy played the field too. I knew what was going on. When I came home, I talked to Lloyd and he told me everything, but I couldn't hear it. You don't want to hear about anything destroying the only bit of precious past you have. "Daddy's fine," I told myself. "He's just fine."

He never complained to me, but he did reach out to me around 1970, and that's when I knew he wasn't doing well. I took Snoopy up there to see him. Snoopy was just a tiny kid. Daddy and I walked over to Garfield High, which was right across the street from our house. A high school baseball game was being played there. We stood and watched the game through the chain-link fence. Daddy's hernia was down to his knees. He could barely walk because of the pain. He had to lean against the fence to watch the game. I told him, "Daddy, you need to see a doctor."

He shook his head and said unh-unh. Daddy had never believed in doctors.

I said, "Why don't you come to LA to live with me." The dream was always that I'd be independent enough so Daddy could come down and live with me someday, but that "someday" was now, and my life was a mess.

He peered through the chain-link fence at the baseball game, his brown eyes squinting, his beautiful, withered face pressed close against the fence, which pushed back the favorite hat he'd been wearing for thirty years. He said, "Boy, I can't go to California."

I said, "Why not?"

"The mailman knows where my house is now."

"What's that mean?"

He looked at me and smiled. He said, "Quincy Junior, I'm too old."

So I left Seattle and let him go. I let him slip away. And as he got sicker, I ran the other way as fast as I could. When he died I was in a CBS studio scoring a Bill Cosby sitcom about a gym teacher named Chet Kincaid. The news dropped on me like a bomb. No one at the studio was aware of the kind of loss I'd suffered and I didn't say. I simply went up to Seattle and buried him. There was lots of weeping and eulogies said at his funeral, nice things said by nice people, but there was one thing that wasn't said that I kept in my heart, that only Daddy and I and my brother Lloyd knew about. It played itself out in my mind over and over again as I helped lower his coffin into the ground, tears falling off my face: He'd promised me he'd never leave me when I was a boy, and he'd kept his promise. His word was always good. It was the only thing Lloyd and I could ever count on.

After we buried Daddy in Seattle, I tore forward at the speed of light. Work has always been my therapy, and in lieu of work there's always been being in love, and in lieu of being in love there's always more work. I wanted to let Daddy go, but I didn't know how, so I literally began to work myself to death. I ripped forward with blinding speed. I was conductor and musical director and did comedy skits for twenty-seven episodes of the Cosby variety show; co-produced with Aretha Franklin an album called *Hey Now Hey*, from which "Angel"—written by her sister Carolyn—was a hit, and a track called *Master of Eyes*, which won a Grammy; supervised the scoring and co-wrote the lyric for the title song and produced the soundtrack album for Donny Hathaway's first and only movie score, *Come Back, Charleston Blue;* and in twenty minutes wrote the theme song for a series starring Redd Foxx called *Sanford and Son*. I'm a master at diversion when there's pain involved, and there's no better place to deceive yourself than in the dream capital of the world. Besides, I was up to my neck in drama. I had one wife, Ulla, on the way out and a new relationship, Peggy Lipton, on the way in.

I met Peggy in 1968 on a trip with Sidney Poitier and his girlfriend Joanna, who'd met on the set of the film *The Lost Man*, which I had just scored. They invited me, Ulla, Sidney's friend Terry McNeely and his lady, Prez, and Sammy Davis, Jr., for a vacation on his yacht in the Bahamas. Sammy usually traveled with everything he owned, so Sidney told him, "Sammy, you can bring your fifty suits, your thirty cameras, all your records, your film clippings showing you and James Arnett practicing your quick draws, and everything else, but no entourage. Just you and a lady." Sammy agreed. It was the first vacation he'd ever taken in his life. He showed up with Peggy, whom he knew only slightly from her appearance on his television show and over champagne at the Copa the night before he was performing. She was a beautiful twenty-one-year-old star of a hot TV series, *The Mod Squad,* the first young, hip drama on TV. At that time she was not at all on my radar screen. I was totally in love with my wife, Ulla.

We flew from New York to Nassau to meet the boat, and by the time we got there it was clear to everyone that Peggy was in over her head and wasn't having fun. At the time, she had just broken up with Lou Adler. The boat was just leaving the dock when Peggy upped and split with baggage and all: at 7 A.M., Lou was waiting at the end of the dock. She left Sammy high and dry, and he was devastated. All the women were pissed that Sammy's first vacation ever was in jeopardy. Joanna came to the rescue. She told Sammy, "Let's call Shirley Rhodes and Altovese." Altovese was the lead dancer in one of Sammy's shows, and they'd long had a crush on each other. Shirley ran all of Sammy's affairs. Altovese immediately flew down from New York and met us at sea by plane. Sammy later married Altovese, and strangely enough, four years later I married Peggy.

I had no intention of marrying anybody. After my marriage to Ulla broke up, I was determined not to hook up seriously with anyone. I was loving being single. But four years after we met on Sidney's yacht, Peggy approached my eldest daughter, Jolie, who was then a top model at the Ford agency and had been the first black model on the cover of *Mademoiselle* magazine, where she appeared at the age of sixteen. Peggy met Jolie at a party and asked, "What do you think my chances are with your dad?" Jolie felt me out and called her back to tell her, "You know how my dad is, but you're definitely in the top ten." Peggy asked Jolie to see what she could do. Jolie arranged for me to join her and Peggy for a previously planned Sunday-night dinner.

Falling in love with Peggy was like a breath of fresh air. She was independent, smart, charming, musical, beautiful, and understanding; she had her own career and appeared to be from a normal family. Her mother

(Above)
Backstage at the Greek Theater
in Los Angeles after one night
of a weeklong series of
performances with Roberta Flack:
from left, Flip Wilson, my son
Snoopy, my former wife Ulla,
Cannonball Adderly, my daughter
Tina, and Roberta.

Daddy looking dapper
in Seattle.

Recording "Our Shining Hour" with Sammy Davis, Jr., and the Count Basie Band in Detroit in 1964.

Henry Mancini was a true friend and helped me break racial barriers in film scoring when I came to California in the mid-1960s.

With Cary Grant in 1966. I wrote the score to his last film, *Walk, Don't Run*.

Bill Cosby and me on the cover of *Down Beat* magazine in 1969, during our days of hair and 34-inch waistlines.

My "seventies" look.

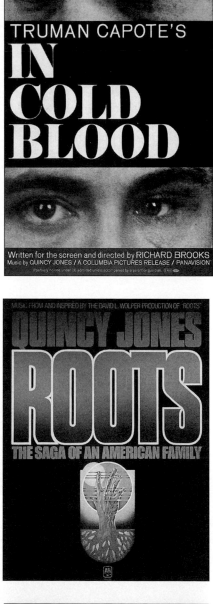

Posters for some of the movies and TV productions I scored.

The Jones brothers on the couch. From left to right: Richard, Lloyd, me, and Waymond.

With George Benson, my good friend Alex Haley, whom I had met fourteen years earlier, and Sidney Poitier.

With Peggy Lipton and Michael Jackson on my birthday in 1978.

Conferring with Duke Ellington on the CBS television special *Duke, We Love You Madly*, my first television co-production, with Yorkin and Lear. Luther Henderson and Dave Grusin are in back.

Lena Horne the divine,
after she won two Grammys
for *The Lady and Her Music.*

Michael Jackson and I accepting
our Grammy for *Thriller*
in 1983. It's the bestselling
pop album of all time.

An outing at Universal Studios
in 1982 after the recording of
"The Girl Is Mine," with Michael
Jackson and Paul and Linda
McCartney and our families.

and father were still together, which was a first for me. After Ulla snuck back to LA, I moved out of Deep Canyon and into the beautiful home of Broadway producer *(Hair)* Michael Butler at the very top of Sunset Plaza Drive overlooking Hollywood. He told me it was all mine until the Stones hit town. When Mick Jagger and Keith Richards showed up too, Peggy wanted me out of party central. So I moved into her house in Beverly Hills. We never even talked of marriage. We said, "We'll do this as long as we feel good." We didn't feel that a piece of paper was necessary to keep us together. Eventually she'd have enough of show business and would devote herself to raising our two daughters, Kidada and Rashida, away from the ravages of Hollywood. All her desires, her focus, she gave to her family and to me so that I could get on with my career.

By the late sixties, I was getting burned out by doing movie scores. I did thirty-five in all. Besides *The Pawnbroker* and *In Cold Blood* and *In the Heat of the Night,* for which Rod Steiger won his first Oscar, I did *The Getaway, The New Centurions,* and *A Dandy in Aspic,* each in eleven days, replacing the original scores. I scored Cary Grant's last film, *Walk, Don't Run,* and Goldie Hawn's *Cactus Flower,* her first Oscar-winning appearance, as well as Sydney Pollack's first film, *The Slender Thread,* and Coppola's first film, *Finian's Rainbow,* for which I conducted and arranged "How Are Things in Glocca Mora?" for Petula Clark's screen test; Fred Astaire came to the session to show his support for her.

I did hits and flops, some of which I can't remember and some of which shouldn't be remembered, scoring films at a maniacal pace—three at a time. Most composers do one or two a year. One year I did eight. Sometimes out of the eight the second film would be ready for me on time, the first would get to me late, and the third would be ready ahead of schedule. Like my friend Steven Spielberg, I focus best when I have a lot on my plate. We both like to specialize in artistic triage. I'd sleep three hours a day, then keep myself awake all night while working at home by lying on the floor, putting my legs on the couch, and running cold water from the faucet onto my wrists. My youngest daughter, Rashida, would often curl up on the floor beside me sleeping as I'd work till midnight, fall asleep, then wake up at 1 A.M. knowing I had 108 musicians coming in for a recording session the next day and no main title yet. I'd put Rashida to bed and plow on, keeping the television on to occupy my conscious mind and letting my subconscious mind work, scoring with or without piano, in ink. That's where the subconscious mind kicks in, when you push the conscious mind aside. You're getting out of your own way and letting God do the work—God and Nadia Boulanger. She used to tell me back in France—and it took me years to accept it—that you only have real freedom when you set boundaries and parameters. When you have total freedom, you automatically create chaos. As a jazz artist, this was hard to swallow until I had to score films on deadline.

Scoring is a multifaceted process, an abstract combination of science and soul: the psychology of scoring is totally subjective, reactive, and highly personal. The science is the technical process of synchronization. The soul is the process of painting the psyche with musical "emotion lotion," of finding the appropriate voice and tone for a film. Above all, the music has to sound organic to the subject matter or even sometimes in direct contrast to the subject matter while accommodating a sequence of scenes that may be interiors, exteriors, medium shots, close-ups, quick seven-second shots à la *Star Wars,* and so forth. Different composers will invariably see or hear a scene in different ways.

As complicated as scoring is, in many cases film scorers back then were at the bottom of the Hollywood food chain. On the Universal lot there is a legendary building called Sprinkler Drain, where the fire sprinklers were once located, which is actually the space shared by music and film editors and TV and film composers. It was lined with offices where excellent composers like Dave Grusin, Johnny Williams, Lynn Murray, Benny Carter, Pete Rugolo, Sidney Fine, and Bernard Hermann worked like zombies in the night. This facility served as a spawning ground for

Henry Mancini and for myself as well. Mancini worked on over ninety-three scores here, including such "classics" as *Creature from the Black Lagoon*, *Francis Joins the Wacs*, Abbott and Costello movies, and eventually the groundbreaking jazz score for the hit television series *Peter Gunn*.

Twenty minutes into the first scoring session, Alfred Hitchcock fired Bernie Hermann, the masterful composer who'd worked with him for years and who had scored classic films like *Psycho* as well as *Citizen Kane*. This time, though, the director wanted a more "contemporary" score for *Torn Curtain*, so Hermann was immediately replaced by composer John Addison. This capricious behavior induced in me a hovering paranoia, because hardly ever is the original composer asked to rewrite his score. A screenwriter might get a second shot at a screenplay, but if you compose a score that doesn't work, you're history and they call someone else, especially if the director has led you down the wrong path. I didn't see that kind of future for myself. I'd done all I could do in the medium anyway. I felt that Henry Mancini, Johnny Mandel, Benny Carter, and Duke Ellington were all pioneers of jazz-influenced film scores. I'd tried to bring the sensibility of modern R&B into scoring. At least I'd done all that I could stand with optical sound, which was so sonically limited at the time. Then in the 1970s three films changed all that: *Star Wars*, *The Turning Point*, and *Saturday Night Fever* demonstrated the emotional power of Dolby's full range of high and low frequencies.

After all the films and tons of TV, I was more than ready to return to the record business. I wanted to throw away the clock and just stretch out in the studio with my favorite musicians. Right on time my agent, Peter Faith, signed me with Creed Taylor of CTI Records, distributed by A&M, in 1969. I did *Walking in Space*, one of the first jazz fusion records and the beginning of black FM radio, with players like Rahsaan Roland Kirk, Toots Thielemans, Hubert Laws, and Freddie Hubbard. With the first-time pairing of Ray Brown on bass playing his trademark "hoong-giddy-ding" and Grady Tate doing his "spang-a-lang" in the rhythm section, the groove was so hot that I almost had to pour cold water on the two of them. It was like total freedom again. I'd been inspired by a chance meeting with Buzz Aldrin, one of the first astronauts on the moon, who told me that while he was up in space, he'd played the recording of my arrangement of Frank Sinatra cookin' on "Fly Me to the Moon" with the Count Basie Band. It was a kick to have arranged the first song played in outer space.

The sixties affected me deeply. It was almost a delayed reaction. I was so busy trying to build a financial platform to stand on I could never look back. The black experience had come with the territory since I was a kid, and as an adult I never had to look farther than my own face to see how things were in Hollywood. When I first started scoring films in the early '60's there was only one black person involved, my hero Benny Carter. It only took me a minute to realize that the phrase "here comes the shvartze" didn't mean "here comes the composer"—"shvartze" being the Yiddish form of "nigga." Contractors in LA very rarely went out of their way to hire black musicians for any kind of work—film, television, or jingles— with the possible exception of "personality solos," such as those by Harry "Sweets" Edison on trumpet or Plas Johnson on tenor sax. On a visit to my home, producers Robert Wise and Saul Chaplin graciously requested me to be the first black musical director and conductor of the Academy Awards in 1971. I remember telling the contractor to include Hubert Laws. He said in a snide voice, "I'm sorry, but I'm not quite sure I know who this Mr. Hubert Laws is." I said, "Well, he's one of the finest flute players in the world—jazz or classical—and I'll bet he's never heard of you either." I got Hubert and everybody else I requested—we had seventeen black musicians in all—and on the night of the Oscars the entire orchestra burned. It was a baptism of fire. The Oscar staff had done the show a million times be- fore; it felt like doing business with an old, established firm. Few reached out to me. I could smell the difference between who was for real and who was not. An hour before show time, one of them goaded me, "You know, Johnny Green and Alfred Newman used to throw up before the show from the pressure of doing this." Pleeze! I had no intention of doing that, nor did I believe for one minute that these two distinguished and experienced gentlemen had behaved this way. Nor did I have the time. You spend ten weeks pulling it all together—completely gratis. Then it's three, three and a half hours nonstop conducting, live on television, and you have an orchestra, a pile of scores, and a pile of stars to rehearse for a three-hour show, including an awards sheet in front of you that lists the films for each category. On a large conductor's score, short musical excerpts for all entries are listed separately and are identified by the numbers one through five. There's the title of the film, the category of the award, the studio, and the names of the stars and/or creators. You take a deep breath, pause, and let the applause give you a second or two to scan the score, identifying the play-on music for the award. Most are in different time signatures. Then you signal the orchestra with the number of fingers and give the downbeat, all in split-second timing. Goldie gets to the microphone and gets emotional and forgets her lines and screams, "Oh my God, it's George C. Scott," and you have to be cool long enough to identify the cue and give a downbeat for the play-on. Not five or six seconds later. That's an eternity in television. Right now. Everybody in that orchestra was on it like a hornet. They were as alert and intuitive as I knew they would be.

Despite this breakthrough the racial climate made me feel like I was knocking my head against a wall, inducing social vertigo. In 1972 producer Bud Yorkin, Ray Brown (who was at that time not only my favorite musician but also my manager), and I went to Vegas to confer with Duke Ellington on the CBS special, *Duke, We Love You Madly,* that I was producing. It was my first producing job for television. There he was, seventy-five and exhausted, one of the twentieth century's greatest musicians and composers, sitting at his piano in front of his legendary orchestra playing in a casino lounge, maintaining his dignity throughout. His famed tenor saxophonist, the great Paul Gonsalves, was strolling around the lounge in a semi-sober state, going from table to table playing to customers like a one-man mariachi band. Unlike Basie, Duke very rarely let anyone get too close to him, but I loved and admired him as the greatest. I'd been lucky enough to play trumpet in his band a couple of times back in New York in the fifties. In 1966 we did four jazz seminars organized by Mary Jane Hewitt, who was one of Angela Davis's professors at UCLA, traveling with Duke's full band and a panel of jazz critics, including Leonard Feather, at state universities in California. At one point Duke turned to me and said, "Quincy, you need to get away from movies and records. You should be writing symphonies for the New York Philharmonic." I said, "Duke, nobody's ever asked me." He understood. He was a giant, the king, and the gifted black intellectuals in his circle—like Billy Strayhorn and Luther Henderson— were kings too. Back in the fifties, I'd sit up all night in composer-arranger Billy Strayhorn's Harlem apartment drinking and eating red beans and ham hocks cooked in beer over rice with writer Langston Hughes and Billy. These were intellectual and artistic giants, and it was a privilege to sit there and listen to these men mine their souls, and feed my own.

I had approached a couple of network executives several years before and said, "We need to do a television special honoring Duke Ellington while he's still here with us." No one was interested. They'd fall over themselves to do an Irving Berlin or Cole Porter special, but wouldn't touch Duke. This started me on a mission. As usual, I called my best friend, Clarence Avant, whose mind is like a human Internet. He knows where every skeleton on the planet is buried and he was on the case after one phone call. He had a friend at the White House, the attorney and one-time jazz saxophonist Leonard Garment, who smuggled out a tape of Duke receiving the Medal of Freedom from Richard Nixon, who was President at the time. We used that tape to sell our idea to the networks and sponsors. We tried several agencies and were turned down. Finally we got one of the biggest agencies in New York to commit to the show, but they flipped on us. They said, "We'll sponsor the show only if we can have it on the air before election time, because we want to use the footage of

Duke with Nixon at the White House to help Nixon's reelection campaign." I said, "We'll get back to you," and walked. We went through holy hell finding someone else who was interested.

I finally found an executive at CBS Specials named Phil Capice, who said, "I'm very interested, because the concept really works, but you've got to work with an established TV production unit, because your television experience is zero." He gave me five choices of the top production companies and I chose the first on the list, with Bud Yorkin and Norman Lear. Norman graciously turned over his office to me, and Bud stayed on to be co-executive producer. This was to be the first show ever televised out of the new Shubert Theater across the street from the office in Century City. We were on our way. I called in every favor. Not one of the people I asked needed convincing. Sammy Davis, Jr., Billy Eckstine, Joe Williams, Ray Charles, Aretha Franklin, Roberta Flack, Sarah Vaughan, and Peggy Lee showed up, as did the Count Basie Band, Paula Kelly, Rev. James Cleveland and his choir, and the Chicago Transit Authority, aka Chicago (red hot at the time), accepting this as their first television appearance out of respect for Duke. Phil Ramone flew out from New York to engineer the show, which was a godsend because the show was a technical nightmare. The director, who had a hearing-aid problem, didn't hear Phil say that the sound equipment wasn't ready to run: we had pictures, but no sound. The opening number involving the entire cast was one of those moments where everything that can go wrong did. Phil spent the entire night running from the sound truck to the director's booth putting out fires. It was a long night, with complex camera setups, and the artists were getting edgier by the hour. We were sensing that Roberta Flack, Sarah Vaughan, and Peggy Lee were having a little problem with Aretha, who was young and at the top of the charts. They ragged on Aretha and complained that she couldn't read music and wouldn't wear a black dress like they did. Aretha responded in self-defense by kicking ass and taking names vocally when the four of them did an Ellington medley arranged by Mitzi and

Kenny Welch. She definitely smoked it. The message was clear: The Reverend Ree-Ree had sent out the signal—rise to the occasion. Lord knows, they knew how to do it, and they all did. They got a standing ovation, as did Roberta Flack for her solo version of Billy Strayhorn's "Lush Life," which every other singer there wanted to perform.

The Duke was so ill with pneumonia they had to take him directly to the hospital after taping the show. He knew his time was short. Every December since the fifties he'd send us a big personalized Christmas card. In 1973, he sent it in May. He died the twenty-fourth of that month, but when he left the auditorium that night in 1972, there was a smile on his handsome face. He knew we loved him madly.

Incidentally, I had an assistant whom I asked to take care of Duke during the special, to make him fresh orange juice every morning. Her name was Anne Spielberg. She used to walk around the office asking folks, "Does anybody want to take a look at my kid brother's videotape?" Nobody checked it out. Anne's kid brother Steven only became the most talented and successful director in Hollywood history. Anne herself later wrote and produced Tom Hanks's *Big,* among other achievements.

My life leaped forward. At every turn I burrowed into more projects. Billy Eckstine brought Jesse Jackson by my home to introduce us. I flew back to Chicago and volunteered for his "army," the new Operation PUSH, which Jesse had started after leaving the Southern Christian Leadership Conference in the wake of Martin Luther King's assassination. A seriously committed group of us serving on the board of PUSH—including John Levy, Cannonball Adderley, Roberta Flack, Nat Adderley, Jerry Butler (who acted as chairman), Pete Long, Isaac Hayes, Lena McLin, Donny Hathaway, and Hermene Hartman, among others—founded the Institute for Black American Music. I had never been that political before, but following the mule-drawn wagon carrying Dr. King's casket through the streets of Memphis in a crowd of thousands pushed me right to the edge. I had gone down to the funeral with Marlon Brando, Haskell

Wexler, James Baldwin, Norman Jewison, Tony Franciosa, Hal Ashby, and Cesar Chavez. We all slept on a hotel floor down there and were enormously affected by the whole experience.

On very little sleep—we were holding seminars in the local high schools by day—the other members of the Institute for Black American Music and I put on fantastic variety shows for seven nights at the Chicago Amphitheater featuring Stevie Wonder, the Supremes, the Jackson Five, Marvin Gaye, the entire Motown roster, the cast of *Sesame Street,* and on one stage on the same night, Flip Wilson, Richard Pryor, Dick Gregory, and Bill Cosby. Sammy Davis, Jr., was booed at one of these events; the papers had just run a photo of him hugging Richard Nixon. To be rejected this way was one of the most painful moments in Sammy's life. Few in the audience could have known that in terms of contributing and raising money for civil rights causes, Sammy was second to no one. And few could have known, either, that Sammy could ill afford the $25,000 he put up that night.

Black artists have always been forced to walk the thin line between what is politically acceptable for them to say and what is not. My entire career, indeed my entire life, has been based on trying to break down the walls between people of all colors throughout the world. I've lived that. Yet my newly politicized life drew death threats. The White Citizens Council's national newsletter, *The Thunderbolt,* had a large picture of Ulla, me, and my mixed children Snoopy and Tina on the front page, calling them mongrels. For the first time in my life I had to worry about security. Our phones were tapped—we could never figure out by whom.

I went on a U.S. tour costarring Roberta Flack in 1971 with a thirty-seven-piece all-star orchestra, including Toots Thielemans, Ray Brown, and Donny Hathaway. I tutored Donny on orchestration, starting with Ravel's *Daphnis and Chloe* score. The resulting record, *Extensions of a Man,* was a critical and commercial success for him. Donny got it quick; he was truly a genius. But he couldn't understand why Stevie Wonder, whom I'd known and admired since he was 12, was more popular than him. He said, "I've done everything right. I know how to touch people. What do I have to do to get people to love me like they love Stevie?" He used to travel with $200,000 to $300,000 in cash, and he felt safe enough to call me from almost every city in America, day or night. The last time was from his grandmother's in St. Louis. Months after he made the record, on a Sunday, Donny took off all his clothes and managed to unscrew two-inch-thick floor-to-ceiling glass windows at the Park Lane Hotel in New York, then leap out and land on an awning twenty-three stories down. These calls were desperate pleas for help. This memory pains me deeply; it is only one of many.

In 1974 I did *Body Heat*, my first near-platinum album, which sold 800,000 copies. This time I replaced the large orchestral arrangements with a driving rhythm section, including Herbie Hancock on keyboards with Eric Gale and Wah Wah Watson on guitar, Ralph McDonald on percussion, Richard Tee on Fender piano, and James Gadson on drums. I collaborated with Leon Ware, Tom Bähler, and Joe Green on the new material. I was in heaven. On vocals Minnie Riperton and Al Jarreau debuted on this album, as did Benard Ighner, who wrote and sang "Everything Must Change." I was buried in my professional life, living large at forty-two years old, so full, so busy, feeling so strong, never looking back, never looking around me, forgetting about my buried past. Then I literally blew my mind.

After working nonstop for three days and three nights in my Brentwood home on my next album, *Mellow Madness,* I was sitting in bed one hot August afternoon relaxing with Peggy when a terrible pain shot through my head. It felt as if someone had blown through the back of my head with a shotgun. I tried to sit up and could not, fighting double vision and a feeling of vertigo. The pain was blinding. I collapsed back onto the bed in a coma. Peggy, horrified, called the paramedics, who checked my heart and pronounced me as strong as a horse. It hadn't been a heart attack, they said. As I lay there I thought only about all my kids, and daughter Kidada, five months old, who hadn't called me Daddy yet.

Three days later, my doctor, Elsie Giorgi, told Peggy to get me to the hospital as quickly as she could. Elsie knew what it was, and she said she hoped it wasn't too late. By this time I had almost total amnesia. At Cedars-Sinai Medical Center they told me I had a Beri aneurysm, that the main artery delivering blood to the right side of my brain had ruptured, the equivalent of sixteen strokes, according to Dr. Marshall Grode. The actor Bruce Lee had died of a similar aneurysm at thirty-five, and the actress Patricia Neal suffered brain damage when her artery burst. I needed a brain operation and my chances of surviving it were one out of a hundred. There was also a good chance that I could suffer complications that would leave me paralyzed or blind or brain-damaged or all three. Dr. Giorgi had trained at Bellevue in New York, and had once saved a Bowery wino who'd hit his head on a rock in the snow. The cold kept the brain from swelling. At the suggestion of Dr. Giorgi, the surgeons made two incisions to insert two tubes up through my throat in order to freeze my brain at 32 degrees so that they could operate without the brain popping out like a coiled spring.

The day of the operation they shaved my hair off and put it in a plastic bag on the side of my stretcher just in case they needed to paste it back onto my scalp so I would be presentable for my funeral. They used indelible ink to mark off the area where my skull would be drilled and sawed and opened in several small blocks to reveal my brain. My brother Lloyd came down from Seattle and had to sign the consent form for the operation, because Peggy and I weren't legally married, and he was closest of kin. Lloyd was falling apart. He said, "I don't know what to do, I don't know what to do." I said, "Don't worry, man. Sign the form." He did. Phil Ramone flew out from New York, arriving pasty-faced and looking scared. The day of the operation, Phil, Peggy, Lloyd, and a couple of my other relatives gathered around my bed as the doctors gave me a series of drugs that were supposed to prepare me. It was hazy then, because my brain had been floating in blood for several days, and the drugs were taking effect. I stared at them for as long as I could and then they disappeared.

As the anesthesia took effect, I knew I was dying. I was going down. I felt my memory bank unload. It flies. It burns past and your whole life goes by in twenty seconds. All the people I hadn't taken time to tell how I felt about them flew past my eyes, so fast I couldn't see them. It's like you're on a computer and you hold a key down and the cursor just races across the screen, blurring everything. Everything I'd ever known and felt and would never feel again flowed past my eyeballs, and I could feel myself going down, going to sleep, going toward that tunnel of white and gold light. It was the most blissful moment I've experienced in my entire life. I couldn't believe that leaving this world could be so beautiful; it's hanging in here that's the hard part.

I went further and further down until I barely saw a faint image of my own father sweep past the blur of faces and events and only then did I try to stop myself. I wanted to call out to him and tell him the pain and sorrow I felt for not coming to see him more and for not writing to him. Even as I was dying, the guilt of it washed over me because I loved him so much. I wanted to reach out and touch him.

Then I went down all the way.

When I came to, I remember seeing Lloyd, Phil Ramone, Peggy, and Rev. Jesse Jackson, who was praying over me and giving me last rites, along with a few others around my bed. They told me the operation had been seven and a half hours long. I was groggy as hell and half conscious.

Lloyd said, "You thought I was Daddy."

Later, my neurosurgeons, Dr. Marshall Grode and Dr. Milton Heifetz, who invented the metal clips now inserted in my head, came in and said, "The good news is, you are the one out of a hundred who lived. The bad news is, we found another one on the other side that could be ready to explode at any minute under pressure. We can't let you get too excited about anything, because in two months we have to go back in again."

After the first operation a group of friends in the artistic community, who were told I wasn't going to make it, prepared a memorial for me at the Shrine Auditorium. The operation was in August, the memorial in September. It turned out to be a concert: they were going ahead anyway, so I decided to attend. Dr. Grode and I sat up in a guest box. It felt like I was watching my own funeral. The show was conceived and produced by Peter Long, who'd been working with me at Black Expo and then joined my company, Quincy Jones Productions, and Darlene Chan, who puts together all the concerts for George Wein. Ed Eckstine wrote some of the material. It was a mind-boggling affair. They had just about everybody I'd ever known and cared about: Cannonball Adderley with Freddie Hubbard in the band; Sarah Vaughan; Minnie Riperton; The Main Ingredient, with Cuba Gooding, Sr., on lead vocals; Ray Charles; Billy Eckstine; the Watts Prophets; Marvin Gaye. Roscoe Lee Brown did a recitation, as did Brock Peters, and Sidney Poitier and Richard Pryor. That's some lineup: it was unbelievable. And my neurosurgeon kept telling me that I couldn't afford to get excited. I asked, "How do you do that?" He told me that I should try to concentrate on stopping my heart, which triggers a mechanism that puts you automatically in an alpha state, which is like cool water running through your veins. Stopping your heart this way is not actually possible, but the mere attempt to do so induces the desired state. I've remembered that ever since.

Right after the next operation, too weak to move, I asked Lloyd to come closer. He leaned in and I managed to reach over the wires and hoses they had hooked me to. I fumbled to grab his hand and felt his fingers, and just for a moment, I thought they were the huge fingers I used to grab when I was little. The ones that thumped me, the ones that gripped hammers and saws so tightly. The ones that stroked my face at night while I lay sleeping. Daddy's big and bony fingers. I held them tight and fell asleep.

CHAPTER 26

A sorry emotion

| Peggy Lipton, ex-wife, actress | Quincy's operations were the most horrible moments of my life. His head was swollen to |

the size of a cantaloupe. They put steel plates in his head and wrapped it in bandages. It was awful. He had the first one and survived it and then had the second one a few months later. The second one was just as frightening as the first, but he survived it again. Enduring the emotional and physical impact of one surgery, and knowing it was time to have another, would have taken the average person to the brink of his or her sanity. But Quincy's sheer joy for living was evident in everything he did at this time, and it was a lifesaver for me too. With our baby daughter Kidada six months old and another operation a few weeks away, we decided to marry. I wanted our daughter to be able to say "Daddy" to the man I loved.

He won his life back after those operations, and one of the first things he took on was the score for the movie *Roots*. He loved Alex Haley, who had written the book. Alex used to spend time in our house in Brentwood. He even lived there a little while. Just before *Roots* came out, Alex came to Quincy and said he was going to ask for a $2,500 advance from Doubleday to fix up his yard and get a new stereo. Quincy thought that was funny. He said, "Alex, you don't realize what you've done, do you?" He told him not to embarrass himself by borrowing from Doubleday and gave him a check for $5,000. Alex paid him back every dime. He also paid us back for his temporary lodgings with the most soulfully delicious short ribs and steam-fried shredded cabbage, lovingly cooked and served "navy style" by Alex in huge stainless-steel baking pans. That cabbage dish is still one of Quincy's favorites.

Quincy loved *Roots*. I heard him weep at his Rhodes piano in the home studio as he worked on the score: all this was obviously touching a deep physical nerve as he stayed in that studio night after night. When the TV production company sent over videos of the rough cut from David Greene, the director, with graphic depictions of life in the slave holds—they had lice in their hair and were branded like cattle—the executives were in shock and had it edited out. None of us had ever seen anything like it before. Alex had also sent us diagrams, almost like architectural blueprints, of the slave ships. When we spread them out on Quincy's worktable there was absolute silence: body upon body, row upon row of humanity. We were both deeply sad and inside I knew this was a door opening into unfathomable grief I could never fully share with him. He threw himself into researching a vast amount of African history, percussive songs and traditional songs, and wrote a very powerful score. The beautiful African theme was based on a traditional Nigerian folk song, "Oluwa," that he adapted with Caiphus Semenya, who found it.

Basically the producers replaced him with Gerald Fried after the first episode. They wanted him to write a conventional score. Actually, the network didn't understand what they had in *Roots*. The music budget for eight episodes was only $105,000. At the last minute a series that was supposed to run for eight weeks was aired on eight consecutive nights, right before sweeps week. They didn't believe it was going to be the big hit it became. It was one of the most widely watched programs in television history. After that, they were falling over themselves trying to take credit for it. That's Hollywood for you.

I began to see this pattern time and time again in Quincy's life, where the corporate world was always testing him. He is a perfectionist, and with each rejection he'd come back stronger and stronger, even when he went on these B flat money gigs. We went to Japan twice. I even sang with the band because I wanted to share that infectious energy. He put together a tremendous band and they loved him in Japan completely. But there he was, still on the bus with the band. When he had his successes with Michael Jackson and *The Color Purple*, I remember the feeling of the buildup to it. It was wonderful. He deserved it, but the cost had been high in terms of overcoming obstacles. Quincy was a great musician. Why did he have to kill himself for these people? He was already successful. He'd already proved his talent.

We were together fourteen years. We had a beautiful marriage and most of those years were filled with wonder. He changed my life. I knew the first minute I saw him that I was in love with him. From the moment I looked into his eyes and glimpsed his soul, I knew there was something there. It started with a kiss in the front seat of a funky old Buick station wagon in 1972. Ten years later we were still together. It was the pull of destiny. I was twenty-three and he was thirty-six when we first met, and he answered as many needs and questions about my life as I could expect at that age. He wanted to relieve the pain of my childhood and I sought refuge and comfort in his. He had a misunderstanding that I came from a stable background—I wanted him to believe that. We perpetuated the myth together.

I came from a background where I was hurt. I grew up in New York and was very guarded and had a wall around me. My childhood was filled with secrets. I was a shy girl: I stuttered. When I was fifteen a friend of the family took me to see Eileen Ford, who runs the famous modeling agency. She signed me. I took acting classes and realized that when I acted, my stammer disappeared and an inner peace enveloped me. I got the *Mod Squad* role playing Julie when I was eighteen, and did it for five years.

I had my share of dates before I met Quincy. I dated Elvis Presley, who was very sweet, and Paul McCartney, who was savvy. There were others: Lou Adler and I lived together for two years. But Quincy was my biggest love. I still love him. His kindness is unimaginable. He has a thirst for giving in every way. But there are lots of closed doors he'll never open up. When someone does something bad to him, he forgets it and closes it off. He's closed off parts of his life that way: there are things he can't reveal to anyone.

When we first met he and his brother Lloyd hadn't spoken for a while. I didn't understand why. He tried to explain it to me and through his explanation I could hear that he needed his brother, because whenever he talked about growing up it was just about them, those two. I wanted them to be close again. I urged Quincy to call Lloyd, and we took the girls up to Seattle to visit him. When I saw them together and saw how much they loved each other, I thought, "My God, this had to be," because there was so much ease between them. Lloyd was quieter, he had his own strength, but they were both gentle and refined, and handsome too—there's a handsome gene in that family, I can tell you. Quincy was completely relaxed around Lloyd in a way he wasn't around anyone else.

I admired their relationship. I never had that kind of relationship in my family, where you could stay in the house with the bedroom doors open and hang out and laugh and have a lot of fun. Lloyd got Hodgkin's the year after Quincy had his brain operation, and when Quincy went up to see Lloyd to help him through chemotherapy, they decided to hide Lloyd's illness from their mother. She was living not far from Lloyd's house and decided to come over to see them one night. They were nervous wrecks. They went downstairs in Lloyd's basement, and when I got down there I saw these two grown men hovering over this overgrown pot plant—it was part of Lloyd's cancer therapy—smoking and laughing like four-year-olds. It was so touching and funny.

I gave up my career for my husband and children and I'm not sorry about that. When Quincy and I raised our family, we did it really well. I think we raised two incredible kids. They're beautiful people. I've seen the way other people have raised their children here, and I wanted to do it differently. The schooling of our girls, Kidada and Rashida, was always done with the two of us. I may have made some wrong choices, we all do, but our children are beautiful people, and that comes from both of us. I have a lot of talks with my two girls about him. Kidada lived with him for several years and knows him really, really well, not in terms of his past, but his behavior, holding back because he doesn't want his heart broken any more. She knows there are a lot of closed doors he'll never open up, but she also knows how big his heart is. Rashida was only ten at the time of the divorce and stayed with me until she went off to Harvard. She missed her father deeply even though she saw him often.

Quincy and I grew apart, that's all I can tell you. It wasn't race that brought us together and it wasn't race that tore us apart. We'd been all through that business, where the police stopped us and asked him if he knew my middle name, because they thought I was a prostitute and not his wife. We were stronger than that, and stronger than Hollywood, but we had differences spiritually. I grew up in a Reform Jewish family, and sought a connection with my own spirituality. I'd met my guru, my life teacher, as Quincy and I were breaking up. My experiences came from my escaping my past, my childhood. Then I met my teacher, and my mother, who meant the world to me, was dying. After my mother died a part of me died too. I couldn't open up to him or to anyone else, and I ended our marriage in a way that hurt and devastated everyone. I was bereft and longing for answers.

Between his work schedule, my mother's illness, and our separation, he had a nervous breakdown, and I was as frightened and confused as I had ever been. He went to Tahiti to stay at Marlon Brando's place and while he was there he had a mystical experience, an out-of-body experience. When he came home he needed me, but I couldn't handle it. I had my own problems, and I didn't take any responsibility. I had a lot of guilt about that. I should've said, "Let's go see my spiritual teacher, let's see what's going on," but I didn't. I was in such horrible shape myself: there was nothing I could do for him.

If life had been different, if our destinies had been different, and if we had each dealt with the issues in our own pasts, it would've been different for us, but when he came home from Tahiti and needed me, I just couldn't cope. He feels I didn't want to make it work. But I was out of my mind, not knowing who I was. Guilt is a sorry emotion when it comes after the fact. But I shut out nothing in my life. We're proud of our children. We had a good marriage. We both grew from the relationship. With my memories of being deeply loved, and through my beautiful children, there will always be a place in my heart filled with gratitude for what he has given me. I love him still from afar. We're still friends. We loved more in our fourteen years than most do in a lifetime. I think we're both thankful for that.

CHAPTER 27

Thriller

I first met Michael Jackson when he was twelve at an afternoon party at Sammy Davis' house in LA in 1972 as we all watched an *Ed Sullivan Show* with the Jackson Five, which Sammy had pre-taped on a precursor to home video. Michael is still a genius of pop music, but his greatness is still misunderstood, even to himself. He started as a boy wonder at Motown under Berry Gordy in the sixties. Few people realize what a pitiful place Michael's hometown, Gary, Indiana, was: Michael and his family had built-in incentives to escape. I felt he had the potential to go way beyond the wonderful trademark bubblegum he'd done on Motown with the Jackson Five, such as "Dancing Machine" and "Ben," the love song about the rat. As he said on the *Motown 25* television special: "I love working with my brothers, but . . ." Most child stars never make it beyond kid stardom, but Michael was different. I'll always love him. Today the writers and critics seem determined to try to write him out of history, but it ain't gonna happen. That's why they call it history. Elvis got strange; so did others, later in their careers. Michael Jackson has his place in pop history—at the top, no matter what anybody says about the Eagles surpassing him in domestic sales or how eccentric he's become. When it comes to worldwide sales, Michael is the man to beat.

We first worked together on *The Wiz,* for which I was musical supervisor. I really did not want to work on that movie. With the exception of three of the songs—"Home," "Ease on Down the Road," written by Charlie Smalls, and "Brand New Day," written by Luther Vandross—I was not feeling the songs from the show, despite the Broadway version's enormous success. I did it because Sidney Lumet, who had given me my first U.S. film-scoring break on *The Pawnbroker,* plus five more films, asked me to do it. I felt I owed him more than one; I owed him a lot. Sidney had been married to Lena Horne's daughter Gail for fourteen years. On the fourth night of shooting the biggest scene in the picture, "Emerald City," he was already over budget for the first time in his career. After the final shoot of the evening his wife announced that she wanted a divorce. Not unlike the rest of us "work junkies," he asked if she could wait until the picture was over, but she said, "I've heard that fourteen times." He was a mess. I remember seeing them for the first time, sitting on the floor at a party at Lena's apartment, falling in love. They were a beautiful couple with two lovely daughters that I used to help Sidney diaper. We were all heartbroken. I adored them both.

Michael was the best thing that came out of *The Wiz* for me along with finally getting to work with Nick Ashford and Valerie Simpson. I took great pride in having been one of their friends since the sixties and one of their rare collaborators in the years to follow on several wonderful songs.

After my brain operations I had of course gone right back to work, and the success of my albums *Body Heat* and *Mellow Madness,* which featured four tracks by the Brothers Johnson, who were members of my band at the time, had given me a real lift. *Mellow Madness* was in fact a launching pad for the Brothers, who went on to make four multiplatinum albums, all of which I produced.

By the time I met Michael Jackson, he'd been in the music business fifteen years, and they didn't even have a featured song for him in the movie. Most of the people involved with the film had no idea what Michael Jackson was about. With Lumet's support we shoehorned the song for the scarecrow and crows, "You Can't Win," in there for him. At age nineteen he had the wisdom of a sixty-year-old and the enthusiasm of a child. He was a genuinely shy, handsome kid who hid his amazing intelligence with small smiles and giggles. But beneath that shy exterior was an artist with a burning desire for perfection and an unlimited ambition to be the biggest entertainer in the world, make no mistake. James Brown, Sammy Davis, Jr., Fred Astaire, Gene Kelly—these are the people Michael really admired and studied. He would watch tapes of gazelles and cheetahs and panthers to imitate the natural grace of their movements. He wanted to be the best of everything—to take it all in. He went to the top model in each category to create an act and a persona that would be unequaled. Sammy Davis did exactly the same thing.

It started out with just role models, but somehow later on the line between the reality and the fantasy got blurred. Michael is a total sponge, a chameleon. He has some of the same qualities as the great jazz singers I'd worked with: Ella, Sinatra, Sassy, Aretha, Ray Charles, Dinah. Each of them had that purity, that strong signature sound and that open wound that pushed them to greatness. Singing crushed their pain, healed their hurts, and dissolved their issues. Music was their release from emotional prisons. The press likes to make fun of Michael for his Captain Marvel outfits and odd lifestyle, but I don't know how anybody could expect him to end up like Mr. Joe Next Door, given that he's been in the public eye since he was five years old. How do you ever get used to more than a dozen teenaged girls being at your door, watching and waiting, 24/7? It was the same thing Presley had to deal with. When I asked Michael about the girls, he said, "They've always been there, as long as I can remember." In fact, according to Michael, the song "Billie Jean" was based on an incident in which a young lady allegedly climbed over a wall enclosing Michael's property and lounged at his pool. Later she tried to sue him, claiming he was the father of one of her twins.

The first time he came to my home he said to me, "I'm getting ready to do my first solo record for Epic Records. Do you think you can help me find a producer?" I said, "I've got my plate pretty full right now trying to get this movie's preproduction going, but I'll think about it." As we rehearsed the musical scenes for *The Wiz,* I became more and more impressed. He was always super-prepared. He showed up at 5 A.M. for his scarecrow makeup call and had every detail of what he needed to do memorized and ready for every shooting. He also knew every dance step, every word of dialogue, and all the lyrics of every song by everyone in the entire production. Part of his role was to pull little paper slips with proverbs from famous philosophers out of his straw chest. One afternoon as he rehearsed a scene, he kept mispronouncing the name of the Greek philosopher Socrates, which was in one of his lines. He kept referring to him as "Sow-*cray*-tees." After three days no one had corrected him, so I pulled him aside during a break and whispered, "Michael, before it becomes a habit, I think you should know that the name is pronounced '*Sock*-ra-tees.' "

He said, "Really?"

What a reaction! He was so sweet about it. Those big eyes opened wide, and right then and there I committed: "I'd like to take a shot at producing your new record."

After the movie finished filming, he went back to his label, Epic Records, with his managers, Freddie DeMann and Ron Weisner, and told the honchos there that he wanted me to produce his album. Black and white, they balked. After all, this was 1977 and disco reigned supreme. The word was: "Quincy Jones is too jazzy, and has only produced dance hits with the Brothers Johnson." Those were the same words that Michael's A&R people at Motown had used to describe me years before when Stevie Wonder and Marvin Gaye would call me and say, "Let's do somethin' together." When Michael shared his concern about it I said, "If it's meant for us to work together, God will make it happen. Don't worry about it."

Michael's a devout Jehovah's Witness—he even used to dress up occasionally like a normal person and walk through neighborhoods to spread his gospel—but he wasn't leaving that one up to religion. He marched back into Epic with DeMann and Weisner and said, "I don't care what you think, Quincy is doing my record," and they agreed. We rehearsed the record at my house. He was so shy he'd sit down and sing behind the couch with his back to me while I sat there with my hands over my eyes with the lights off. We tried all kinds of things I'd learned over the years to help him with his artistic growth, like dropping keys just a minor third to give him flexibility and a more mature range in the upper and lower registers, and more than a few tempo changes. I also tried to steer him to songs with more depth, some of them about relationships. Seth Riggs, a leading vocal coach, gave him vigorous warm-up exercises to expand his top and bottom range by at least a fourth, which I desperately needed to get the vocal drama going.

Michael and I got along well. When he was ready to record, I got my killer Q posse together: Rod "Worms" Temperton, one of the best songwriters who ever lived, with the melodic and contrapuntal gifts and instincts of a classical composer; Bruce "Svensk" Swedien, the guru of engineers worldwide, whom I'd known since the fifties when we worked together with Basie and Dinah in Chicago; and the A team of Greg "Mouse" Phillinganes, a virtuoso keyboardist, who'd played hooky from school in Detroit to meet me five years earlier; Jerry Hey, monster trumpeter and arranger, who was introduced to me during a seminar by Cannonball Adderley when Jerry was still a student at the University of Illinois at Champaign; Louis "Thunderthumbs" Johnson, the youngest of the Brothers Johnson, formerly with my band on the road, on fender bass; John "J. R." Robinson, a fellow Berklee alumni and the drummer for Rufus; Paulinho DaCosta from Brazil on percussion; and many others. I've always been blessed to work with some of the best in the business, and these guys were not only like a family of friends but like my own musical mafia: every one was a black-belt master in his own category. We attacked that record. Michael did most of his vocals "live," with no overdubs. The resulting record, *Off the Wall*, sold ten million copies. How's that for jazz? Ironically, all the initial naysayers at Epic, black and white, kept their jobs because of the success of *Off the Wall*, the biggest-selling black record in history at that time.

Just as Michael and I were about to get started on a second album, I met Steven Spielberg, who was doing *E.T.* while I was doing *Thriller*. We had been introduced by Kathleen Carey, an amazingly astute music publishing executive at Warner Brothers, who was dating Steven at the time. It was love at first sight between Steven and me. He had a beguiling way about him, and he was always the same, a very down-to-earth guy by any standard, let alone for a genius. He took me to watch him in action on the *E.T.* set. He and "Leen" introduced me to Steve and Courtney Ross in Malibu, in New York City, and in Easthampton. We all vacationed together in Aspen and the South of France. Steve was the visionary who created Warner Communications from a funeral company, then merged Time and Warner. He taught me most of what I know about the business. Steve was the King of Kings. After a while Spielberg said, "Q, let's intern each other." He gave me a viewfinder and a director's chair, and I gave him a synthesizer. I took him to the studio in Westlake, where we were in the process of recording *Thriller*. At Laird Studios, where he was shooting *E.T.*, he made me put on a mask to protect me from the kerosene smoke. He also told me, "Q, come look in the camera: this is what winds up on the screen." He had been instructed by John Ford to study the master painters for the best insight on lighting for film.

After *E.T.* came out and conquered the world, Steven asked me to do an *E.T.* storybook song with Michael singing. I was already behind with scheduling on *Thriller*. We only had four months to do it, but I said okay, because initially the *E.T.* storybook involved only one song. I asked Marilyn and Alan Bergman and Rod Temperton to write the song, which Michael sang, and Steven loved it. He said, "This is great! Why don't you guys do the whole *E.T.* album." This was quite a challenge given that we had to boil down a two-hour-long visual experience—one of the most successful films in history—to a forty-minute listening experience.

Steven had no idea of the kind of time involved in putting together this kind of record. Plus, Epic was getting antsy for *Thriller* at that point. As in a situation comedy, right at this point in walked Kathy Kennedy, Steven's 28-year-old wunderkind producer, and his film editor, Bruce Cannon, with a huge box loaded with E.T.'s footsteps, sound effects, Johnny Williams' entire score, and all the spoken dialogue from the picture. I got started right away, assuming that the Universal lawyers would work out the details.

We started the project and it was a rocky road. They had this so-so narrative, and we had to rewrite it so a listener who had never seen the movie could clearly understand the story by listening to the record. We didn't even have time to put it on a separate reel; it was just one forty-minute spiral-band reel of continuous dialogue, music, and special effects. There was no digital editing then, which would've saved us time and grief. It was a nightmare. It took us six weeks to put it together, while working on *Thriller* at the same time, and now I had only two months to finish *Thriller*.

In the meantime, Epic had gotten wind of what Michael was doing, and the fit hit the shan. MCA Records at Universal Studios, where Steven was headquartered, didn't even bother to get clearances with Epic for the biggest black artist in the world. Their actions appeared to reflect the attitude that "Michael Jackson is working with Spielberg. He should be happy." They had no respect for Michael whatsoever.

Walter Yetnikoff, the president at Epic Records, came out with both barrels blazing. He said, "The hell with Quincy. The hell with Steven. The hell with Sid Scheinberg and Universal." He dropped off an injunction. He wanted half a million dollars cash or the *E.T.* storybook was not coming out. Somehow someone must have convinced Steven and Kathleen Carey that I was the one who should've straightened it all out. Straightened out what? The people at Universal read the trade papers. They had to know Michael Jackson was one of the biggest recording artists in the world. *Off the Wall* was on its way to selling 10 million records. There was nothing to straighten out. Universal remained complacent and appeared unconcerned. They didn't care. Understandably, Steven was loyal to Universal because of his long relationship with Sid Scheinberg, who gave him his first gigs doing *Night Gallery* with Joan Crawford and then *Jaws.* Steven didn't want to hear about it.

I was getting faxes and conference calls all day during the session and in the middle of the night about the *E.T.* storybook album while trying to work on *Thriller.* It went on for months, corporate lawyers yammering back and forth as only they can. Finally Clarence Avant, the master fixer and my best friend, was brought in. They don't call him the black godfather for nothing. Clarence was asked to go to Yetnikoff and fix it. He knew all the players, including me and Steven. He knew Scheinberg. He came in the day after Thanksgiving for a meeting with all of us at a law firm: Michael's attorney John Branca and his managers Freddie DeMann and Ron Weisner; Myron Roth, a VP at CBS; Zack Horowitz, an attorney at CBS; Alan and Marilyn Bergman; and Rod Temperton and myself. By the end of the day it was worked out. Walter Yetnikoff demanded that a $500,000 advance be paid to CBS which owned Epic. They kept every cent of it. Neither Walter nor CBS paid me or Michael one dime—ever. In the end Universal released half a million records of *E.T.,* a beautiful deluxe package, a box set, which was all the deal allowed. The records became collectors' items immediately and the album won a Grammy. Onstage at the Grammy Awards I absent-mindedly forgot to thank Kathleen Carey and Ed Eckstine; I'd like to do so now. Steven and I fought like two children over the thing and didn't talk to each other for over a year because of the conflict between CBS and Universal.

When it was all over, I took my family back to Aspen the next year for the Christmas holidays and bumped into Steven on the slope at Snow Mass. We stopped and just hugged each other. He said, "I was wrong. We should've never let it get that far." I said, "I was wrong too." I apologized and it was over. He likes to say, "Quincy and I, we've seriously earned our friendship," and he's right. We got a Purple Heart over it, and God sent down a little gift for both of us the next year in the form of *The Color Purple,* which we co-produced together with my other gurus Kathy Kennedy and Frank Marshall. Nobody in the world—especially in LA—thought we would ever pull it off. Working daily side by side with Steven for thirteen months from script to screen was a once-in-a-lifetime roller-coaster experience in filmmaking with a true genius during which we truly bonded as friends and brothers.

The making of *Thriller* in a little more than two months was like riding a rocket. Everything about it was done at hyperspeed. Rod Temperton, who also co-wrote several of the album's songs, and I listened to nearly 600 songs before picking out a dozen we liked. Rod would then submit to me about thirty-three of his own songs on totally complete demos with bass lines, counter lines, and all, recorded on the Temperton high-tech system of bouncing the sound of two cassette recordings between ghetto blasters, and ten to twenty-five alternate titles for each song, with the beginnings of lyric schemes. He was absolutely the best to work with— always totally prepared, not one drop of b.s. We have always kept it very real with each other, exchanging strong opinions and comments without ever "throwing a wobbly"—British slang for "losing it." He's the kind of warrior you want at your side on the battlefield.

Michael was also writing music like a machine. He could really crank it up. In the time I worked with him he wrote three of the songs on *Off the Wall,* four on *Thriller,* and six on *Bad.* At this point on *Thriller* I'd been bugging him for months to write a Michael Jackson version of "My Sharona." One day I went to his house and said, "Smelly, give it up. The train is leaving the station." He said, "Quincy, I got this thing I want you to hear, but it's not finished yet. I don't have any vocals on it."

I called Michael "Smelly" because when he liked a piece of music or a certain beat, instead of calling it funky, he'd call it "smelly jelly." When it was really good, he'd say, "That's some smelly jelly." I said, "Smelly, it's getting late. Let's do it."

I took him to the studio inside his house. He called his engineer and we stacked the vocals on then and there. Michael sang his heart out. The song was "Beat It."

We knew the music was hot. On "Beat It" the level was literally so hot that at one point in the studio Bruce Swedien called us over and the right speaker burst into flames. We'd never seen anything like that in forty years in the business. That was the first time I began to see the wildness that was in Michael's life during the *Thriller* sessions. One time we were working in the Westlake studio and a healthy California girl walked by the front window of the studio, which was a one-way mirror facing the street, and pulled her dress up over her head. She was wearing absolutely nothing underneath. Rod and Bruce and I got an eyeful. It was right on time in the middle of intense deadline pressure. We stood there gawking. We turned around and saw Michael, devoted Jehovah's Witness that he was, hiding behind the console.

We did the final mixes and fixes and overdubs up until nine o'clock in the morning of the deadline for the reference copy. We had three studios going at once. We put final touches on Michael's vocals on "Billie Jean," which he sang through six-foot cardboard tubes. Then Bruce put his magic on the final overdub of Ndugu Chancler's live drums, replacing the drum machine. I took Eddie Van Halen to another small studio with two huge Gibson speakers and two six-packs of beer to do his classic guitar solo, dubbing the bass line on "Beat It" with Greg on mini Moog. Bruce liked to record our rhythm tracks on sixteen-track tape, then go to digital to get that fat, analog rhythm sound that we all loved and called "big legs and tight skirts." He left with the tape to go to Bernie Grundman's studio to master the record: Bernie's the absolute best in the business. In the meantime I took Michael to my place, laid him out on the couch in my den, and covered him with a blanket for a three-hour nap at 9 A.M. By twelve o'clock we had to be back to hear the test pressing that was going out to the world. I couldn't sleep myself; the anticipation was tremendous. We'd all worked ourselves into a near-frenzy. Meanwhile, back at the studio, Larkin Arnold, the head honcho of black music at Epic, was popping champagne, anxiously waiting to hear the final mix.

This was it, the big moment: Rod, Bruce, Michael, his managers Freddie DeMann and Ron Weisner, and myself sat down and listened to the final test pressing of a record that was to be the follow-up to *Off the Wall*. It was a disaster. After all the great songs and the great performances and great mixes and a great tune stack, we had 24-karat sonic doo-doo. There was total silence in the studio. One by one we crept across the hall for some privacy: more silence ensued.

We'd put too much material on the record. To be really competitive on the radio, you need big fat grooves to make a big fat sound. If you squeeze it into thin grooves, you get tinny sound. We had twenty-eight minutes of sound on each side; we knew there was nothing to discuss. Smelly would say, "Oh, no, that's the jelly—that's what makes me want to dance," which would end the conversation every time. With vinyl, you had to be realistic; it had to be under nineteen minutes of music per side. This was now all about physics first, then music. On CDs it doesn't matter, because it's digital. Deep down inside we must have all known this all along as we were working, but chose not to deal with reality in our fatigue and musical euphoria.

We were in trouble and tears were streaming down Michael's face. He said, "What do we do now?" "The Girl Is Mine" single was already out in the marketplace and charting at number 2 with a bullet: the album was late. The record company wanted the masters that afternoon.

We told Larkin Arnold, "In its present state, this record is unreleasable."

We took two days off and in the next eight days we put it dead in the pocket, mixing one tune per day. Rod cut one verse from "The Lady in My Life," and Smelly finally agreed to give up some of the jelly in the long, long, long intro to "Billie Jean." Something clicked after that, and it wasn't just the album. One prominent performer was reported to have said of "The Girl Is Mine," "After all this time, this is all they've got?" Hell, no—that song was our lead-in, our red herring. On the tail of each other "Billie Jean" and "Beat It" hit the charts and inhaled them. Both went to number 1, providing me with the unique experience of having three number 1 hits in a row replacing each other, since Michael's two songs followed Patti Austin and James Ingram's "Baby, Come to Me." Michael was splashed all over the globe visually as well as musically: Michael, the MTV videos, and the music all rode each other to glory. The single "Thriller," which came out a year and a half after the album, was the first fourteen-minute video ever made and was treated like the premiere of a feature film around the world. The truth is, many of the videos that became trademarks of MTV imitate "Beat It," "Thriller," and "Billie Jean"—it's Michael's choreography all over the screen, even today. His videos made a sensation in tandem with the rise of the video as an art form. He helped define the music video in terms of style, dance ensembles, and overall performances. CBS likes to claim the credit, but it was Steve Ross who insisted that MTV air Michael's videos, because of the channel's policy to focus on "just rock 'n' roll," not black artists. Rick James and Motown were ballistic over the boycott of "Super Freak." I love that—third-generation rockers are thoroughly convinced that rock music was born in Idaho.

Like everyone else in the world, I always go into the studio to make a number 1 record, but the ones that really get my attention are the ones that don't do what you thought they were going to do, like go to number 1. You put a million dollars cash in front of a singer or a songwriter, it doesn't correlate to the music; it doesn't speak one word to the creative process. We just strive to give ourselves goose bumps, and if we do, there's a good chance that the audience will feel the same vibe.

The fans couldn't keep clear of Michael after *Thriller* took over the world.

Michael was a different kind of entertainer. Completely dedicated. He practiced his dancing for hours. Every lick, every gesture, every movement was carefully conceived and considered. He lived in a fantasyland because that's what worked for him. At his place in Havenhurst, he used to have a mouthy parrot with a lot of attitude as well as a boa constrictor named Muscles. One day Muscles was missing. They looked all over the property, inside and out, and after two days they finally found him dangling from the parrot's cage, with the parrot's beak sticking out his mouth. He'd swallowed that sucker whole and couldn't back his head out the bars because he hadn't digested the bird yet. In a way, that's a metaphor for Michael's life after *Thriller,* because at a certain point, he couldn't get back out of the cage. It all became overwhelming for him.

You have to remember that in the music business every decade produced a monster, screaming-groupies phenomenon: in the forties it was Frank Sinatra, in the fifties Elvis Presley, in the sixties the Beatles. In the seventies Stevie Wonder and the introduction of the full-range Dolby sound for films, had a big impact. In the eighties Michael took it home, because no matter what anyone thought music was before, he was light-years ahead. *Thriller* sold 50 million copies all over the world, more than any other album in the history of the record business. Let's get real: Michael was the biggest entertainer on the planet Earth. We made history together. This was the first time a young black performer had won the hearts of everyone from eight years old to eighty, all over the world. This was breaking major barriers.

To promote the album, I traveled extensively with Michael, to Japan and all over Europe, helping him with press conferences in major cities with colleague Frank Delio. In Rome, Michael had a huge concert scheduled at the same time that Leonard Bernstein was conducting with his orchestra at the Vatican. One day Lennie called up and suggested we take a private tour of the Sistine Chapel. There were seven or eight of us, including my daughter, Jolie, her husband, and a few of her friends. For months Lennie had been saying he wanted to learn the authentic street way of saying "yo mama." I said, "That's easy. If you're in the middle of a rehearsal and the cellist says, 'Mr. Bernstein, your downbeat on bar forty-one is a little flabby,' you say 'yo mama.' " He kept confusing it with Yo-Yo Ma!

In the Sistine Chapel we were lying on the floor, which is forbidden during normal hours. At the time, the Chapel was closed to the public; half of the ceiling was still being restored. Lennie had on his horn-rimmed glasses. After extensive Harvardese commentary he grabbed me by the neck and pointed up to the ceiling. "Look at that! Michelangelo doesn't know what a woman looks like. He was as gay as I am. Those are just guys with tits."

All of a sudden the monsignor walked in, freaked, and shooed us out in Italian: he didn't recognize Lennie. Bernstein responded with "Yo mama." I said, "That's the right time and the right way to say it, but this is the wrong place."

Two years later Bernstein air-mailed me from London a headline torn from the *International Herald Tribune* from a review of *Back on the Block* that said, "Quincy Jones is black music's Leonard Bernstein." He wrote on the top in red pencil, "Dear Q, I wish I were white music's Quincy Jones. Love, L.B."

Michael and I had many adventures together, but success can be as difficult to handle as its opposite. I believe that you have to look success in the eye. But if you start to guzzle all the praise and adulation, then when they say you're shit, you have to swallow all that too. There's a big trap there, and to deal with it is a major psychological feat. You need a spiritual center to navigate your way through these waters and come out alive. Nobody stays at the top. Nobody. I've been watching this a long time. I've worked with the best, and I've never tried to chase celebrity. We just happened to stumble into each other. I got the benefits of the same goodies Sinatra did, or Basie and Smelly did, without all the hassles. When celebrity hits, you better be ready. Then when it rains, get wet.

Michael changed managers three months after *Thriller* was released. I once said to John Levy, an ex-bass player and a legendary manager and a serial diva magnet, "John, I'm curious. What's the breaking point? When do ordinary singers become divas?"

At that time he said dryly, "At four thousand, nine hundred and ninety-nine dollars a week."

Michael reacted to the externals of our success. It's like a hurricane in a black hole: It sucks you in and stretches you and spits you out. And to this day people forget that, deep down inside, Michael was still "country." I used to live on Stone Canyon Road, one of the most beautiful streets in LA, two blocks from the Bel Air Hotel. Michael came over to a party one day wearing his little Kangol hat and parked his new Rolls about three blocks down the street from my place. Him being from Gary, Indiana, and me being from Chicago, I knew what was on his mind when he went out my exit gate at 2 A.M. and picked up a brick from the edge of my bushes. I said, "Smelly, this ain't Gary or Chicago. This is the safest street in LA." That is so country, I'd tell him kiddingly, and he'd tee-hee. He'd try to play the sophisticate, and I'd wait for the country side to come out, whether he was wearing his raggedy black loafers with the heels pushed down—you can't get more country than that—or sopping "pot likker" off a plate of Chinese takeout.

We did another album together, *Bad,* which sold 25 million copies. At this point Steve Ross and I had joined forces in a multimedia company—always my dream—with Bob Pittman as an executive partner. It was time for me to move on. In addition, key members of Michael's entourage, including his attorney, were whispering in his ear that I'd been getting too much credit. His brother Jackie Jackson told CBS-TV interviewer Les Edwards that I had wanted to take "Billie Jean" off the album. Pleeze! After every hit record Michael and I made, he and his brothers would go into the studio to make a follow-up album of their own. Reportedly his father, Joe, said, "Qwancy ain't no damn producer. I know a producer who coulda made that record for twenty-five thousand."

Michael was like a member of my family, a surrogate son. He spent many hours with my daughter Kidada, who was a precocious child of eight at the time. They adored each other and totally communicated despite the age difference (he was twenty then). Her mother once found a phone bill showing that Kidada made ninety-one long-distance calls to Michael in a single month. She played the telephone like Herbie Hancock plays the keyboards. These days, I'm sorry to say, I don't see Michael as much as I'd like to; both of our lives have changed dramatically. But as long as I live he'll always be a big part of my soul and memories, and my heart and arms will always be open to him. The eighties were as good as it gets. To this day no one has ever done it bigger and broader than Smelly. I thank God for every minute (with as much modesty as you can muster up for 50 million sales).

After *Give Me the Night, The Dude, Off the Wall,* and *Thriller* I had greater financial freedom than I'd ever had in my life, but I was also more visible. I was deluged with tapes. I had a bathtub full of tapes of songs and demos that people sent to me. I served as a pallbearer at the funeral of my home-girl, the singer Minnie Riperton, and as I was carrying the casket, with Stevie Wonder, also a pall-bearer, crying behind me, someone came up to me and said, "When you get a minute, check this out," and slipped a cassette into my suit pocket. Despite all that, we all loved the feeling of making a difference in the industry.

It was in high contrast to the jazz world I'd known and loved, and a lot of my jazz friends misread my presence in the pop arena. Since age thirteen in Seattle I'd played rhythm and blues, swing, big band, Sousa marches, polkas, Debussy, and bebop. I even played for strippers and sang backup vocals. It was always 360 degree gumbo. Every step along the way prepared me for wherever I needed to go musically. There were never any limitations. No genre was ever a stretch, not even an inch. Pianist Billy Taylor, who taught me about publishing, understood my pop presence; the late, great bassist Milt "the Judge" Hinton, who back in '54, when I could barely find two dimes, tore up my check when Milt Gabler of Decca Records made me pay the eighteen musicians on the session out of my own pocket because we were in overtime, understood; drummer Grady Tate, who called me from New York after I had my two brain operations and said with humor and affection, "Q, I heard you might be in trouble and be a vegetable. Don't worry, baby, I'll come out to LA and spread a little manure around you and water your ass every day," he definitely understood. And so did Basie. Basie was the best of them all.

In 1984, when *Thriller* took the world by storm, Basie played a gig at the Palladium in LA. I went with Benny Carter and Ed Eckstine, Billy's son, whom I'd known since he was eight and who was running my companies then. It was near the end of Basie's life. We had no idea that it would be the last time we'd see him. The Count was in a wheelchair: he looked tired but exuberant. After the concert they wheeled him over to me backstage. He reached up and touched my arm. With those huge nostrils typically flared open, his eyes wide, he said, "Man—that shit you and Michael did, me and Duke would never even dream about nothin' that big. You hear me? We wouldn't even dare to *dream* about it!"

I'd known Basie since I was thirteen years old, staring up at him in the spotlights of the Palomar Theater in Seattle. Looking down at him in that wheelchair was like looking down the long path of our thirty-seven-year relationship. Two years earlier, I'd attended a tribute to him at Radio City Music Hall. Count Basie could do more with two notes than any musician I've ever known, and was the master of the in-the-pocket tempo. To get a pat on the back from him was the highest compliment in the world. It meant more to me than fame or fortune. Grammys, you win some, you lose some. Money is spent, earned, and spent again. But there will never, ever, be another Count Basie.

We always took time to see each other. When you go forward in life, you have to leave so much behind. Basie reminded me of everything I'd come from. My dad. Jazz. My past. My dignity. He wasn't a complicated man. He was pure hip, old-time, down-home goodness. He harked back to the days when we played music not to get over: we just wanted to be good. But I couldn't stay there. A few of my jazz friends, they backed away from me as I became more famous. It's only human nature. I wanted our relationships to be like they were before, fun, free, without strain or pretension, yet some wouldn't allow it. Dizzy telephoned my office once when I was in a recording session. When I couldn't call him back right away, Benny Carter later told me, Diz felt scorned and hurt. We made up, but it stung. Still, Diz and I both understood that nothing small should ever be allowed to destroy a lifelong friendship. Basie's love was always unconditional. He was always proud of me. He remembered me as a rugrat with Clark Terry. He was there for me, and vice versa. He was always true to what we believed in, which was all he knew. To him music was love, pure and simple, even if it wasn't his music. He was a King.

Back in LA when I looked down at him, sitting in that wheelchair, I knew he was dying. I could see it in his eyes. I said, "Thank you, Splank," and I hugged him and turned away, escaping to the dressing room.

When I got there I looked in the mirror and saw my own reflection and said, "I'm not going to do this again." I'd told myself that I would never cry over anyone again. I'd done that when Daddy died, when Jeri and I divorced, when Peggy and I split, and when my stepbrother Waymond's son Butchie was killed in a freak swimming accident at age sixteen. It was usually easier to separate myself from my pain, but I couldn't help myself at that moment. I bowed my head and began to sob. I cried for Basie. I cried for myself. I cried for Jeri. For my dad. I cried for everyone and everything I'd ever left behind that I knew I could never have again.

I'd cried just as hard before at Radio City when he asked me to push him onstage in his wheelchair to play his piano introduction to "I Can't Stop Lovin' You." He could barely lift his hands to the keyboard. I'd known then that I was losing him. Lena Horne came into the dressing room. She saw me sitting there crying alone. She put her arms around me and said, "God, I sure hope somebody cries like that for me when I die."

I hope somebody does the same for me too.

CHAPTER 28

House of papers

Kidada Jones, model, former housemate

We live in a house full of papers. Papers everywhere. In the kitchen, on the desk, in the living room, in the hallway, in the bathroom, in the den. Everywhere. There's musical score papers, faxes, reports, trades, letters, requests, responses, crossword puzzles, scripts. This is what my daddy does. His work ethic is amazing. Work is also his response to pain.

I lived with him for fourteen years after my parents separated, from 1986 to 2000. At the time, I went with him, and my sister Rashida went with my mom, and I can tell you that my dad does not deal well with pain. He does not allow it in. He's like Winnie the Pooh. He is the sweetest, kindest person and doesn't have a mean bone in his body. He couldn't hurt someone's feelings if he tried. But his own pain, he buries it with deals, food, ideas, scripts, work, work, work, and whatever papers he can fill it with. Sometimes I get frustrated with it, I can tell you that, but I'm the only one who will speak out and tell the truth. No one else will. Of all his

kids, I'm the one that's most like his mother. Maybe that's why I'm so outspoken. Everyone says it.

For years, I never knew how my dad grew up. He kept it from me.
To protect me, I guess. Because he didn't want me to think bad of his
stepmother and the people he grew up with. When I asked him about his
past he'd say, "Pie"—that's my nickname—"Pie, we never had enough to
eat." Or "Pie, you should be grateful," one of those parent-type remarks.
I knew a little, because he loves to talk about the good old days, but I had
no idea of the depth of it. To be honest, I wasn't that interested until I got
a little older, and even then he didn't volunteer much.

I was eleven when my parents divorced, and there was not one mean
word said between them. I never knew what the hell was going on. It was
like *Life Is Beautiful* where the father makes the kid believe that everything
was fine. That's how it was for me and Rashida. It was never a bad situation, but we had to share him with the world; not only that, we had to
share him with the rest of our family. After all, he's got seven kids by five
different women. For a long time there was so much different energy between us kids. We've all been raised by different mothers and we all came
along at different times in Dad's life. My eldest sister, Jolie, was the product of his high school love. She was twenty-one and on her own when I
was born. My sister Rachel was raised by her mother away from us in
Pennsylvania. Snoopy and Tina are from Dad's marriage to Ulla. They
came into my life when I was eleven. Kenya is six, she's Dad and Nastassja
Kinski's daughter. We all want his love and attention, and there's only so
much he can give back. He's always taken care of us, but I feel like I've
lived a life of constant adjustment, all of us jockeying for position. It cre-
ates a lot of issues.

I'm not blaming anyone for anything. I don't want to repeat my
mother's history and I don't want the luggage of my father's legend. Don't
think that my heart doesn't ache when I talk about my dad. I feel so horrible and bad and guilty he didn't get a better life, because he is such a

wonderful, remarkable human being. I can't be like him, though. When he shuts a door, he shuts it completely. Sometimes I force him to face it because of what I do in my life, and sometimes it's good for him. Like I forced Tupac Shakur on him. Tupac was the love of my life.

He didn't like Tupac at first. Tupac said in an interview in *The Source* magazine, "Interracial couples. Quincy Jones is disgusting. All he does is stick his dick in white bitches and make fucked up kids." That made Daddy mad. My sister wrote back a nasty letter to *The Source* and they printed it. Not only that, two white girls in San Francisco wrote letters to the editor that said, "If you don't like white people, what about when you hung with us?" Anyway, I met Tupac at a club after that and he said, "I want to apologize to you. I didn't mean that about your dad or you. I didn't see you as real human beings. Now that I see you . . ." He was all game. He was trying to get a play, let's face it, but I liked him. I didn't tell my dad about it, because I thought there'd be trouble.

We started dating steadily, and one night Tupac and I were sitting in a booth at Jerry's Deli in LA and these two hands slammed down on Tupac's shoulders from behind. We jumped up, and there was Dad standing there. He said to Tupac, "I need to kick it with you for a minute." This was the first time they'd met, so he took Tupac to a booth and they sat and got real for a long time. They stood up and hugged when it was over and they got along fine from then on. Tupac was excited because him and Snoop Doggy Dogg hoped to do this movie that Dad was producing called *Pimp,* based on the Iceberg Slim book that every other rapper in America also wanted to do. He never got to it, though.

He and I lived together for four months and then he was murdered in Las Vegas in 1998. It was the most horrible thing that ever happened to me.

I knew we should've never gone to Vegas that night. I had a horrible feeling about it. I've gone over it in my mind a million times. It wasn't supposed to happen. We weren't supposed to be there. It was the worst possible thing that could've happened—I still to this day don't know who shot him. I wasn't able to say goodbye. It's not something that should happen to anyone.

We were at the Luxor Hotel and he went to a party. He said, "I'm not taking you. There's been a fight with a Crip and it's not safe. So you stay here." So I waited in our suite for him to come back. I lay down and was going to sleep when I got a call. They said, "Pac's been shot."

I was like, "Okay." He'd been shot five times before that. I said, "Where was he hit? In the leg, an arm? No big deal." When I got to the hospital they handed me a bag of bloody clothes and jewelry and told me, "He had no blood pressure when he came in. He's had two blood transfusions and he is in the ICU hanging by a string."

I got a blanket from the hospital and circled the parking lot for nine hours. I said, "There's no way he's gonna die. There's just no way." I walked around there till the sun came up and I had to keep my head down because I felt like I was going to projectile-vomit all over the place. I wanted to explode, just come out of my skin. I was in complete physical shock.

My mom was in New York and she flew down to Vegas. Here's my white Jewish mom, you know, praying with Pac's family, the ghetto family for real, you know? She's doing praying sessions with this conjure lady from Tupac's family who had called me and Tupac just a week before, telling us, "I see Tupac settling in Vegas."

I said, "There's no way he's settling in Vegas."

And then, a week later, he was definitely settled in Vegas. For good. He died at 4:30 P.M. a few days after that.

For a while afterward, I didn't want to be alive. I was on my back, literally on my back, for months. My father underestimated how that affected me and shaped and molded me as a human being. He came around. Eventually he realized how it affected me, though I had to really show him. It didn't make him happy that I was running around with gangster rappers who were shooting each other; that part he never liked, but he understood rap, and he understood and respected Tupac, and he wasn't angry at Tupac at all. In a way, accepting Tupac was his way of acknowledging me—my pain, and my struggle to find myself—and for that I love him.

You know what my favorite memory of him is? When I was little I had a pet hamster that got stuck in my closet and he had to get it out. He took out the whole wall to get it out. I mean, his dad was a carpenter and his brother Lloyd is a carpenter, but Dad is definitely not. He started by poking a hole in the corner of the closet wall, and then he poked a bigger hole, and then he just took the whole corner of the wall down. He was just so focused on it. It was beautiful. He knew I really wanted that hamster back, and he got it. It was one of the most wonderful moments of my life, because it was just him and me, and he was focused on me, and he was doing this stupid mundane task because he cared about me.

You know what I want for him more than anything else? I want to see him sit at the piano and play music and just create again. That's the only time he has peace. I just wish he'd give himself something. Every project he does is always the one that's going to make everything right. All my life it's been that way. It's like, "We'll have a lot more time to spend together once this last thing is done." So another project happens and the house is full of even more papers. Sometimes when we're in the kitchen, I look at his hands and I think, "That's sixty-eight years of grueling, fulfilling work that has gone into those hands." And it's four o'clock in the morning and he's got to be up at eight to meet somebody and he's sitting reading through more papers.

It hurts me so bad I can't describe it, but I can't fight with him anymore about it. You try to tell him something when he's preoccupied and he'll say, "Put it on paper." And then it's just another paper in this house. Another paper in a house full of papers.

CHAPTER 29

Check your egos at the door

In 1984 I was in New York when I got a call from singer Lionel "Skeet" Richie and promoter Ken Kragen, who told me Harry Belafonte felt we should do something about hundreds of thousands of people in Ethiopia who were starving to death as a result of a famine and a civil war there. Band Aid had been a big success in Europe as a model. I've known Harry since the early fifties as a jazz singer, when he and Sidney Poitier hung out in Birdland and ran a joint called Ribs in the Rough (barbecue and fried chicken) up in Harlem. I agreed to help.

We started out as best we could. We were trying to figure out who should write the song. First they said, "Maybe Stevie Wonder and Lionel Richie could write it." I said, "No. Stevie's the best, but don't bother him—he's in the middle of making a record." I suggested to Lionel that he ask Michael to do it with him. In those days Michael would like nothing better than to sit around and write, so those two took it on.

Two weeks before the session, I started calling Michael's house to listen to what they came up with, and sure enough he and Lionel were there hangin', sitting around talking about Motown and old times. I said, "My dear brothers, we have forty-six stars coming in less than three weeks and we need a damn song." Lionel came up with something first. He played a cassette with the melody on the title lines for Michael. Michael locked himself in his house for a couple of days and finished the rest. The lyrics were written by the two of them.

We needed a demo on the song "like yesterday." After recording the basic instrumental track, we'd have Lionel, Stevie, and Smelly do "guide" vocals to teach the other artists the melody and lyrics in preparation for the main session. We were sitting in my den listening to the demo and Lionel said, "Q, I'm not so sure about that minor part yet." I said, "I think the minor part is perfect, Skeet. It's a great contrast to the chorus. You both brought it home—it's just what we needed." Then we called Michael, who suggested that he and Lionel sing the leads, and everyone else sing background.

Right! That would have really gone over great. I could just see Bruce Springsteen and Tina Turner and Ray Charles and Diana Ross and all the others singing background. Forget it. But Michael was serious. I had to talk him out of it. He asked Lionel to try to convince me. But forty-four other divas when they have to be don't play that shit. They were coming there to do something unselfish collectively for the benefit of starving people in Africa. We did change one line in the demo to avoid any implication of suicide: "There's a chance we're taking, we're taking our own lives" to "There's a choice we're making, we're saving our own lives."

We had forty-six superstars coming: Billy Joel. Diana Ross. Stevie Wonder, Ray Charles, Paul Simon, Bob Dylan. Forty-six fiercely independent nations. If cornered, any one of them could take your skin off layer by layer. If I hadn't worked individually with over half of these singers before, there was no way I would have even considered doing this. Tommy Bähler, a major arranger and an old friend and colleague, got records of each of the artists in order to pinpoint everyone's range. I'm guessing I was chosen for this assignment because three years before I'd produced an album with Donna Summer and asked about a third of the same people to come in and sing a sixteen-bar choir segment in *State of Independence.* They accepted graciously and did it. We all loved it, because a singer, no matter how big or small, loves singing with other singers. Music can bond like nothing else.

We planned the session like the Invasion of Normandy at Lionel and Brenda's house the night before the recording. Humberto Gatica, the engineer, was there, Ken Kragen, Tommy Bähler, and Marty Rogel, executive director of USA for Africa. Collectively we decided to mark the spots on the floor where everyone would be standing. We didn't want to encourage decision making during the session. *Any* decision. Where they would stand, what they would sing, when they sing it—we had to think it through and spell it all out. Over the years I'd learned the hard way that once a group of this size and stature gets involved in making decisions, you're in trouble. Then we went to the studio to check the floor where they'd marked the spots where everyone was going to stand. I had the sign put on the door that said, "Check your egos at the door." With the demo I'd made with Lionel, Michael, and Stevie, I'd sent a letter to all the artists beforehand, using the phrase we had adopted when we created the Institute for Black American Music in Chicago with Jesse Jackson in the early seventies. I think it was Jerry Butler who'd come up with it. I wanted to remind them that this project was bigger than all of us, but the fact is they already felt and understood this very clearly before they walked through the door.

January 28, 1985, the day of the session, we were scheduled to start at the A&M studio at 10 P.M. After the American Music Awards downtown, at 9 P.M. a bunch of limos full of singers and security guards pulled up—followed by a pickup truck. Out of the truck hopped Bruce Springsteen, who parked in a nearby grocery store lot and walked over without a single bodyguard. The artists converged in various forms of apparel, getting out of their tuxes, into their working clothes. They were on the case: everybody was really on a mission, ready to get busy.

Cyndi Lauper's manager tapped me on the shoulder to inform me that "We have a problem; the rockers don't like the song." I suggested that we talk to the rockers: Hall and Oates, Billy Joel, Bruce Springsteen, Steve Perry, Cyndi herself. They all claimed to love the song. "What's the problem?" I wanted to know.

The first potential problem was now out of the way. When we walked into the studio we felt our first brush with divinity that night. We needed to put down a lead vocal on the first chorus as a guide. Sure enough, as planned, Smelly was standing at the mike, earphones on, ready to hit it, at ten o'clock. As we proceeded to put his voice on the first chorus, and then stack it—which means double it, to double it with himself—I knew this was going to be a special evening.

Ken Kragen had arranged for a greenroom in the next studio with amenities for spouses, managers, and friends, so that only the artists were in the main studio. We did the background parts first and the lead vocals last. If we did solos first, they'd say, "I'm done with my solo, I'm outta here." With the clock ticking I just kept plowing ahead. It's not a wise choice with a project of this size to allow too much room for individual paralysis from analysis. If you do, the session can descend into anarchy; you lose focus, and you're in big trouble. I'd have forty-six potential land mines there if we didn't keep it moving. I had all forty-six sing "We Are the World" choral parts. No problem. When we got to the last part of the song, where we were to sing answers to the title melody, they were supposed to sing "Sha la/sha lingay," as Smelly had done it on the demo.

Bob Geldof, the guiding force from Band Aid/Live Aid, said, "No, you can't do that. The Africans might feel that we're making fun of them, that we're mocking their language. They'll think we think they're savages. Forget the sha la, sha lingay."

With the kind of potential tension hovering over a session involving this many creative people, there has to be one moment where as a conductor or producer you must make a very important decision as to where to let them go and just vent. This was a spot where I couldn't lose: I was mostly interested in the choir parts and the solos. But this was the spot to do it, with these answer backgrounds. I could feel it coming, the time to let them release and get it all out. This was the moment.

Sure enough, there was an explosion of opinions. The whole session stopped cold. I told the crew there filming for MTV: "Turn off the cameras. We're gonna throw down here for a minute."

Some of the singers started to split into teams. Sides were chosen. A few swords were drawn. Paces were marked out. By this time Stevie Wonder was steadily making his way toward a ghetto blaster to get to the phone and call Nigeria to get the correct pronunciation in Swahili. Meanwhile the lodge meeting was starting to simmer in the studio with the other artists. By the time he got back, the debate was going full steam. Stevie asked for silence, and after a pause he told them he'd just talked to the Motherland, and that in Swahili the correct lyrics should be "willi moing-gu."

Sure enough, the shit hit the fan.

Ray Charles slapped the side of his pants in his usual "fed-up" fashion. "Say what! Willi what! Willi moing-gu, my ass! It's three o'clock in the goddamn mornin'. Swahili, shit—I can't even sing in English no more." They were *not* having it. Everybody lost it. And while the whole thing was falling apart, a country singer who for the whole evening had been hanging out in a trailer having some laughs with Ray and Willie Nelson while enjoying a few sips of emotion lotion, disappeared, never to be seen again. A whole lot of black people and some white liberals raising money for some hungry Africans, that was one thing; but on top of it to have to sing in Swahili was way beyond the call of duty for any self-respecting good ole boy.

Finally we all agreed to repeat the first title lines of the chorus so that everybody could go home. I didn't want to press our luck, and closing time was beginning to make itself apparent. Now we were down to the moment of truth. The original plan had been to do the solos one at a time, but time would not permit, so we had to go to Plan B and have the assistants set up twenty-one mikes in a U formation. Instead of having the singers do their solos separately in a vocal booth with the proper mike and sound control, we had them perform right out in the open, standing side by side. Taking this kind of chance is like running through hell with gasoline drawers on. Any talking or outside noises, laughing, giggling, even a creak in the floor, could ruin the whole thing. In fact, the jangling of Cyndi Lauper's necklaces on the mike did prompt a retake. Only twenty-one solos out of forty-six people were indicated on the lead sheet, with each soloist's name printed in Old English script in brackets, as in the New Testament.

In the end professionalism reigned supreme. We held over a few of the artists to do little mixes and fixes before we left. The first was one take of ad-lib fills by a group consisting of Stevie Wonder, Diana Ross, and James Ingram. Then God must have tapped me on the shoulder to save the record by suggesting that I ask Bruce Springsteen—for no logical reason at all—to supply solo answers to the choir melody on the title choruses because of the textures and intensity of his truly unique vocal equipment, especially in this register.

The next day when we got down to mixing the record, we found out in the cold light of day that the energy I needed to conclude had dissipated earlier than I had anticipated. The power of the choir had peaked after two choruses and one change of key. Now I was searching for two contrasting elements to rotate the ending of the song. Somewhere in the course of that night, God tapped me on the shoulder again and gave me a solution, which was to call Stevie Wonder back into the studio. Fortunately, I already had Bruce answering the choir: if I replaced the choir with Stevie Wonder, we'd end up with a duet having enough energy to go to Mars. So that's what we did, and the result was a structure that allowed us to alternate choruses between the Bruce and Stevie duet and the choir solo fills in rotation. The rest is history. Stevie was the perfect choice to complement Bruce and carry the song to the end. With the vocal intensity of these two master artists, plus the choir with ad-lib fills by James Ingram and Ray Charles, we now had the power to conclude a production of this magnitude. I have never before or since experienced the joy I felt that night working with this rich, complex human tapestry of love, talent, and grace.

None of us had a clue that the event would ever be that big; it was beyond our wildest dreams. Predictably, afterward there were those who took potshots at us. I think it takes a strange mind—and, for sure, a small mind— to find fault with a project that raised $60 million to feed the hungry and reportedly prodded the U.S. government to spend $800 million more in the same cause. Those forty-six singers came into the studio with only one thing on their minds: to try to make a difference, and they did, and I know God blessed each of them for it. Everyone in the studio that night was at the peak of his or her career individually; most were already doing tens of millions in record sales. Their collective star power was what made this a global event. When a reporter asked me about the naysayers, I responded, "Anybody who wants to throw stones at something like this can get up off his or her butt and get busy." Lord knows, there's plenty more to be done.

With a single call, we persuaded artists in other countries to join the effort. In Canada, "Northern Lights," produced by David Foster, featured everyone from Bryan Adams to Wayne Gretzky; Olivia Newton-John went with us to the satellite station to spread the word to Australia; and a song for the Spanish-language market was recorded again at the A&M Studio with Gloria Estefan, Luis Miguel, and Julio Iglesias, among others. Overall it was one of the most successful and unified outreaches ever in the music world.

The night after we finished *We Are the World,* I arranged a meeting with Steven Spielberg and Tina Turner at Steven's Amblin Pictures office at Universal Studios. I'd first been approached about *The Color Purple* by co-executive producer Peter Guber, who asked me if I was interested in doing the score, and possibly being an associate producer on the film. Knowing how busy he and his partner Jon Peters were, I proposed instead that he trust me to run with the whole project. He said, "Great." I'll always be grateful for his mentoring and for opening this door for me. When he asked me who I'd like to direct, I said I wanted Spielberg. He said ironically, "Maybe down the road."

Steven, Kathleen Kennedy, her husband, Frank Marshall, and I were producing the film based on the wonderfully inspired novel by Alice Walker. We were praying Tina would accept one of the lead roles, the part of Shug. I'd already spoken briefly to Tina about it, and assumed she wanted it, but at the meeting she flipped on me. She said, "I wouldn't do a black picture if I was dying. It took me twenty years to get out of that black shit and I ain't going back. I came out here to talk to Steven about playing Harrison Ford's role in *Indiana Jones.*"

I was so shocked I couldn't open my mouth, but I certainly understood her feelings about not wanting to play an abused woman after seeing *What's Love Got to Do with It.* Steven ended up getting Margaret Avery to play the part of Shug.

Tina's reaction was a metaphor for the entire movie, though. Nobody wanted to make a black movie in Hollywood. Even some of my closest friends didn't believe Steven Spielberg would direct *The Color Purple.* Universal had *Schindler's List* waiting for Steven to direct before he had even heard of *The Color Purple.* Universal was also the studio that had made *The Wiz,* fueling my obsession with proving them wrong when their head of distribution said, "Black pictures and stories don't work." Bad films don't work, black or white. One top-level executive told Clarence Avant, "Quincy must be out of his mind thinking Steven's gonna direct a black picture before *Schindler.*" But he was wrong. Steven not only directed it, he directed it for scale and directed the shit out of it. Kathy Kennedy, Terry Semel, Frank Marshall, and Lucy Fisher are the ones you want on your side when you're serious about bringin' it all the way home.

By then, Steven and I had become as close as brothers. We had bonded with Steve Ross, who was the closest thing to a guru that he and I would ever know, on every level. Steve was the first to create a mega-giant media corporation. He was so far ahead of his time it wasn't funny. He started out by running his father-in-law's funeral homes, and one day when they were trying to figure out how to increase business, he said, "We use our limos for funerals during the day, but nobody gets buried at night, so let's start a limo service. Just be back by eight in the morning." He tripled the business. He parlayed that into parking lots, businesses, computers. He bought Atari; four record companies, Warner, Elektra, Atlantic, and Asylum; three film companies; the toy company Hasbro; started MTV with Bob Pittman and orchestrated the first mega-merger, between Time and Warner, putting record and video distribution under one umbrella, WEA. Years before people saw that cable TV was the medium of the future, Steve Ross was experimenting with QUBE in Columbus, Ohio. And in the same breath he'd advise me to go after the Baby Bells: he saw the potential for fiber optics and coaxial cable. Eventually Steve was the one that brought my multimedia company, Quincy Jones Entertainment, into the Warner fold, though Mo Ostin at Warner Brothers had been the first to offer me a joint venture, in 1980. With Qwest Records he'd started the ball rolling.

Steve was a dealmaker and math genius with the soul of an artist. He loved to bargain. He loved the game. He'd bargain with an African beads vendor just as easily as he would with a multibillion-dollar CEO. He won so consistently at blackjack tables that he was banned in Vegas and Monte Carlo. He didn't care about gambling; he just knew the system and he loved the game. They started the six-deck system in Vegas because of people like Steve. He was an accomplished counter who could memorize six decks, a skill taught to him by his grandfather when Steve was six. Steven and Steve and I and our families spent time together at his houses in Long Island, in LA, in New York City, and in France. Steve taught me more about business than any other man I've ever known, and that says a lot about him because a white American male will share many things with a black man, but it usually stops at the paper with the dead presidents printed on it. Steve was for real. His friendship knew no bounds, professional or personal. I even mentored his son, Mark, when he came out to LA.

Steve Ross loved the idea of *The Color Purple* and the fact that Steven Spielberg and I would work on it together. Spielberg said he'd do it for scale if I did. We did it for $84,000 each—the hottest director in the history of cinema working for scale, from his heart. He did it because he believed in the novel, which had won the Pulitzer Prize and become a huge best-seller. It was just some country black people walking around on the ground; there were no extraterrestrials or close encounters or special effects. Steven could've done any movie he wanted then, but he believed in this story. That's another reason why I'll respect him till the day I die. In a land of bullshitters, he's a stand-up man of true principles.

We talked for hours about the lead role of Celie. Alice Walker recommended an actress working in San Francisco who'd once been on welfare. Whoopi Goldberg was invited to perform at the Amblin studios before an audience that included Michael Jackson, Richard Pryor, and Ashford and Simpson. When she entered the theater from behind the audience and sang "Around the world in eighty mu'fuckin' days" at her audition, she brought the house down. She got the part.

At around this time I had to go to Chicago to testify for a Michael Jackson lawsuit. Some idiot and his lawyers claimed that Michael had stolen his songs. CBS sent the plane and Smelly and Walter Yetnikoff insisted that I go there to testify. It was a bullshit claim and Chicago in frigid January was the last place in the world I wanted to be. The night before the trial, I rolled around in my bed for hours in frustration, my mind on the movie we were still trying to cast. At 9:15 A.M. I turned on the television to a local talk show and when I saw the hostess I said, "That's her. That's Sophia." It was Oprah Winfrey. Her name spelled backwards, Harpo, was the name of Sophia's husband in the film. Oprah got $35,000 to do *The Color Purple,* and because of a favored-nation contract, she didn't even get her name on the poster. Once Oprah got the Oscar nomination, though, Jeffrey Jacobs, the head of her company, Harpo, and the King Brothers, her production company, mounted an unprecedented promotional blitz that started her on the path to where she is now. Success is about preparation, then finding the right opportunity. She'd been preparing for fifteen years as a TV broadcaster in Nashville, Baltimore, and Chicago. Today, she's one of the wealthiest, most centered, and most successful figures in the history of show business. I agree with Sidney Poitier that Oprah is a miracle whose gift and mission are beyond even her own comprehension. One of the gifts I cherish most is a T-shirt that says: "Oprah loves me unconditionally. I can never fuck up."

The movie cost $14 million to make and brought close to $200 million worldwide. It garnered eleven Oscar nominations, including ones for Oprah, Whoopi, and Margaret Avery. But the director's branch at the Academy neglected to nominate Steven Spielberg for *The Color Purple.* Certain segments of the black community were blaming the content of the book on Steven, saying the movie glorified black men mistreating black women. In fact, Steven cleaned the movie up; even if Spike Lee and John Singleton together had directed Alice Walker's book the way she'd written it, they'd have run both of them out of the country. She was not writing about black men in Africa or America; her interest was about sisterhood, period.

The movie was a hit, but the aftershock also partially set up my nervous breakdown. We finished the film in five and a half months, working from June 5 to delivering the final print on November 22. Most pictures usually take eighteen months to make. After principal photography had been completed, I still had to create a score in less than two months; with a creative army of arrangers, collaborators, and copyists, we finally got there. This was when I started taking Halcion, at my doctor's recommendation, to enable me to sleep. Halcion dream-deprives you. I didn't dream for ten months. I didn't slow down. I always kept moving. I told myself I could make it and that everything was okay. Careerwise, I couldn't have asked for any more success. I was at a higher altitude in the music and film worlds than I had ever dreamed possible, but I was about to crash.

CHAPTER 30

Normal

Quincy Jones III, son, record producer, Internet entrepreneur

When I was a kid, I used to suck my fingers, dragging a big blanket, so my mother, being Swedish, she figured Linus, Charlie Brown, Snoopy. She called me Snoopy. My real name is Quincy Delight Jones III. Sometimes I go by QDIII, my professional name, but people who know me call me Snoop.

I'm Pop's only son, but I didn't know him that well when I was a kid. I don't have many early memories of him. They began at age four; he came in and out of my life. My sister Tina has more memories because she was older and moved to America with Peggy and Pops a couple years after the divorce. Me, I stayed in Sweden with Moms. I was four when my parents divorced. I lived in Stockholm, more or less until I was seventeen. My mother's entire settlement was stolen by a "friend," so we landed in Stockholm with nothing and had to stay with her mother at first. In Stockholm, if you don't have money, you live in the suburbs—the farther out, the worse it gets. We lived way out, on the next-to-the-last stop on the subway. When I would tell my friends that my father was Quincy Jones, they never believed me. They'd say, "Yeah, right, if he produced Michael Jackson, why in the hell do you live out here?"

I grew up fast. My moms was kinda wild, a free spirit. When I was real young, I would ride on the back of her bicycle to the city and kick it with her at her hangout. I would find stuff to get into while she was hangin'— roulette, one-armed bandit, whatever. When she was ready to come home, I'd ride home with her. I went to eleven schools before high school. We moved a lot, so it was kind of hard for me to keep up in school as well as to maintain friendships. Moms would always have bad luck pickin' boyfriends and would end up with these psychos who would literally end up trying to kill us. We had to move twice 'cause of that. One time when I was nine or ten, I stuck one of them in the chest with a ski pole to get him off my mother. Then we had to hit him with the car so we could leave, with me and my friend jumpin' in the trunk as Moms was pullin' out. It was crazy. I feel like I raised myself to a large degree because I felt so responsible, I hated to see my mother suffering. Anything I needed, I tried to get on my own.

I did a breaking and entering and got shot at when I was ten. By four-teen I was really hanging out with a bad crowd. Street life exists in Stock-holm just like it does here in the States. They have gangs, skinheads, dopeheads, hustlers, everything you find in any other city. Even the white cats in Stockholm are completely different from here, in that the "Viking" attitude does not admit any fear of brothers. They do not give a fuck. When I was young they used to mess with me in school because Sweden can be racist, especially in the suburbs where there are broke white kids in the mix. I was bleeding every other day. I had to fight. In about sixth grade my moms had this boyfriend who taught me some martial arts and the next day I took what he taught me to school and used it. It worked. That was a turning point in my life, 'cause up until that point, I just took a lot of shit.

Looking back at it all, I regret a lot of the stuff I did and it doesn't represent me as a person today at all. I just didn't know I had other options. I would try to tell my moms about the racial stuff at school and she didn't realize how serious it was and would tell me they were just jealous. I dealt with it the best way I knew how and it kind of got out of control.

My mother had grown up in a rough situation and she had her own things to deal with: she developed a substance abuse problem that lasted twenty-five years, from which she has fully recovered (ten years and counting). But she raised me to eat healthy and be a good person. It was hardly *The Cosby Show*, but her love was enough for me and that was the most important thing.

I had a really hard time learning what's normal and what's not. I didn't understand how families lived. I had very little structure and in retrospect too much freedom that I really took advantage of. Me and my friends would spend afternoons sitting outside grocery stores waiting for the delivery vans to come by. The vans would bring meat and bread at certain times every day. We had them timed down to the minute. When the driver walked into the store to make his deliveries with trays of food, we'd open the back of the truck and clean it out. Sausages, steaks, bread— whatever we needed, we took. Sometimes our freezer would be packed with big boxes of meat, ice cream, bread, all kinds of things. I guess it was my way of showing responsibility at age twelve. I used to tell Moms that my friend's pops worked at the grocery store and that he gave it to us. She knew the score but she used to mess with me by asking for my friend's father's phone number so she could call to thank him.

I used to come and visit my dad maybe two weeks to a month each year in the summertime. And occasionally I would try school here in the States, like summer school. But this was in the early eighties, when Pops was at the peak of his career, and we weren't super close. It was never bad. There was never animosity. He always cared about me, but it was a pro forma caring. Like if you asked him, "What schools did Snoopy go to?" he could probably name one or two schools, but that's it. In his mind, he always thinks, "Yeah, I was there. Look at these pictures," and he pulls out the pictures to show it. But in reality I was only there like two weeks. I never tripped off it. I accepted it. But if I had a son, I would want to know what he's doing every five minutes.

Because of the way I grew up, I never got a chance to bond with anyone, and most of the things I really loved were taken away or removed somehow by circumstance. At the time, I kind of grieved, and then after a while I got used to the process, so I said to myself, "Okay, I'm not going to get attached to anybody." So I never even tried to get close to Pops for fear that maybe it wouldn't work out. I had accepted that because he really didn't know what I was going through. It went right by him because he always had so much going. I remember when I got to be about fourteen, I saw a picture of him in a photo album and I said, "Damn, man. I really don't know him."

When I was almost fourteen, I was on my way to juvenile hall twice but Moms knew someone who worked at the social service agency and got me off. But she'd had enough. She took all my shit, like my skateboard, baseball bat, clothes, and a couple of other things, put them in a big cardboard box, taped it up, and put a letter in there to Pops saying, "You got to take him. I don't have the resources to deal with it." I said, "I don't want to leave," but she was like, "This is it. You've got to go." My last question to her was, "Moms, how are you going to make it?"

She sent me to join Pops on vacation in Switzerland with that box. When I got there, they asked, "Why the box?" I was embarrassed to show him the letter because I didn't know how to break it down. When you're a kid, it's too much for you to think about. So we did the vacation thing— me, Pops, Peggy, Kidada, and Rashida—and when it was over and it was time for them to go back home, he was calling Moms and calling and calling, and nobody answered the phone. So finally he opened up the cardboard box with my stuff in it and saw the letter my mother had written to him buried inside my things. He called my uncle in Sweden, who told him what the deal was. He was upset about the way she had handled it, but he and Peggy said they were moving in LA, and it was like, "We don't have enough space right now because we're redoing our house." They sent me to my uncle in Sweden.

That was very rough for me. Very rough.

I went back to my Mother after a while and I continued to groove, but that's when I started getting into more heavy shit.

I knew where I was heading. The subject of boarding school came up and I said, "Send me to the strictest one because I need it, 'cause I'm about to kill myself out here." I knew what I was doing. I wasn't a stupid kid. I was grown way beyond my years. I saw and did things at the age of twelve that I probably shouldn't have. Pops came through. He had me come back to the States and sent me to Ojai, a boarding school near LA. It was just what I needed: every hour of the day was accounted for, there was nothing for me to get into but studying. I did really well and got a student of the month certificate and a brown belt in kung fu while I was there. But they would have Parents Visiting Day, and nobody came. They'd have little workshops there for your parents and I'd be there by myself, so when the school year ended I said, "Fuck this. I'll just roll back to Sweden and kick it with Moms." He didn't want me to go back, but I was like, "I'm going back. Fuck this." And I did go back. But looking back, it saved my life in a lot of ways. That period of my life was the only time I got continuous schooling for a whole year. All my discipline that I have now, I got from that school.

It bothered him a lot that I went back, because now he was seeing what was happening. He got real worried. He called a lot. He'd send an extra check for me but Moms told me it was in my name for tax reasons only, so I never got it directly. My mother was using drugs and alcohol to feel better from a chronic illness, so she wasn't working and probably wasn't the best money manager. But I want to make this real clear—I don't blame her, because she did something nobody else did. She stuck with me. She raised me the best she could with what she had. If you ask her today, "What schools did Snoopy go to when he was eight, nine, fifteen," she can name every one of them. She can rattle them off. That's something nobody else in this world can do.

Because Pops was still concerned, he came over to Europe on business and wanted me to meet him in Paris. I didn't want to go, but I did. I met him at the Orly airport. He said, "Snoopy, I want to know what the problem is, straight up."

I said, "Okay, I'll tell you what the problem is," and for the first time in my life, I broke it down to him, what I'd been going through, sitting there through Parents Day at boarding school, waiting for someone to show. And he listened. And when I got to the part about him sending me back to Sweden with all my things in that cardboard box when I really needed help, it broke him down. He cried. Right in the Paris airport. I cried too. And I don't cry easily. For the first time, I got to know him a little bit.

He said, "Man, I went through the same shit with my family." He said his stepmother never really cared about him, that he and my Uncle Lloyd were on their own when they were kids, and that his father did the best he could but didn't nurture him. He told me that he hadn't known I wasn't getting the money he was sending, and how he couldn't say anything about it because he knew I loved my mother.

Well, that was the beginning. That was the beginning of me getting to know my Pops. That's when he became real to me.

A few years later he brought me back to the States and helped me set up my life. He and his friend Jerold Kayden from Harvard took me to check out all the colleges back East plus Berkeley and Stanford in California. In retrospect I can really appreciate what he was trying to introduce me to, especially now that I'm about to have kids of my own. He was trying to give me what he didn't have available to him at that age. Ironically I chose the Berklee School of Music like him, and ended up cutting that short and moving to the Bronx to stay with my friend T. LaRoc. I loved rap, and Berklee didn't teach that.

This was back in 1986, when rap wasn't about the money yet. A lot of it I did for free just to get into the studio so I could get in the game. New York was the spot. I learned the gear, the studio techniques, sampling, tracking, the technology, drum machines, from just doin' it. I was also working next door to Rakim & KRS1 at Power Play Studios, not knowing they were putting down history. Nobody believed in rap in those days, so by the time it became mainstream, I was on top of it.

It took me seven years to build up momentum, though. Then in 1993 I was nominated for a "Producer of the Year" Source award along with Dr. Dre and others.

Pops helped a little, but I wanted to do it on my own. So I built the business myself. We have produced Tupac Shakur, Ice Cube, L.L. Cool J., and T-Boz, to name a few. We also do a lot of TV and film scoring. I scored *Menace II Society* and *The Fresh Prince of Bel Air.* I got my first Emmy nomination in 1999 for doing the theme to the Eddie Murphy Show *The PJ's.* I also have a production and publishing company housing several successful writers and producers. Every day that I'm in this industry I appreciate my father's work and integrity more and more.

Me and Pops, we've reached a really good space these last few years. It's like we are best friends. Every time we get together to talk about anything, the family jokes, "It's gonna be a looong night," 'cause we usually stay up until three, four in the morning. Even though I didn't spend a lot of childhood years with him, I am like a carbon copy of him in many respects. It's wild. Looking back I wouldn't change a thing, because everything happens for a reason. My early life gave me a drive that I might not have gotten otherwise. Pops and I are working our way towards the Internet together. He prefers analog recording. I prefer digital. He prefers to use live musicians in the studio. I use live players only once in a while. He's a bebopper. I'm a hip-hopper. Whatever our differences, it's cool to know we have each other's back. It's a good feeling to have.

CHAPTER 31

Breakdown

I'm not sorry about much I've done in this life. I've lived it to the hilt and back. But if there is one thing I cannot forgive myself for, it's for not taking my son home with me from a vacation in Switzerland. I never came close to being a perfect father, but I always, always loved my kids deeply and tried to take them with me everywhere I could. I may be an expert about blanking out what I did wrong in my life, but I never truly forget. I'll never forget the déjà vu moment after leaving my hotel room in Sweden when I saw my son Snoopy, eleven years old, running across the street. His mother brought him down so they could hang with Peggy and Rashida and Kidada and his poppa. He was supposed to spend the night in the hotel with us, but that night Ulla left for a party at a nearby restaurant and bar. Snoopy went to find his mother, and as I looked out the hotel window and saw him running across the street looking for her, my heart fell to my feet. He had holes in his raggedy pants, long hair, a T-shirt, no sweater. He looked like a street rat. It cut me to the bone to see it, because as I looked at him running across the street to find his mother, I saw my own self back in Chicago, running through the streets looking for my own mother, eating dill pickles stuffed down the middle with stale peppermint sticks that crumbled into dust, scrounging around to find something to eat. Lloyd and I sometimes chewed tar instead of gum.

Seeing my son like this tore me up. It was like a sword ripping through my insides. The uncanny similarities to my own life struck me like an out-of-control, drunken driver. I always hoped he'd have some street experience, but I wasn't about to go back there with him. Sweden, which I thought would be a safer practice ground, had changed big time since I'd been there. Snoopy had been called "nigger" since he was four and even had his teeth knocked out.

When his mother had sent him to me with a cardboard box with all his things to Switzerland for Christmas when he was fourteen, I couldn't move on it and I didn't know why. I was haggling with her. She never gave him the money I sent him. At ten, Tina made her own decision to stay with me, but Snoopy, doing his oedipal thang, wanted to stay with his mother. Peggy's mother was sick and dying of cancer at the time. The success of *The Color Purple* had taken over my life. I had a million other things going on. Thanks to Mo Ostin, my label Qwest Records had evolved into the first black-owned multimedia company, joining Steve Ross and Time Warner in a joint venture to create Quincy Jones Entertainment. I had employees to deal with, lawyers, contracts, business managers, medical benefits, office drama, TV projects, movies, scripts, records, new artists. Success after success—yet my marriage was slowly evaporating.

I literally didn't know what to do. There was no blueprint. I couldn't think. I sent Snoopy to his Uncle Thomas in Sweden. Eventually he got back with his mom, but I couldn't forgive myself for not bringing him back with me. Normally, guilt is not a word in my vocabulary, but his situation and my deteriorating marriage tore at me. I couldn't run from it. I couldn't turn it off. Nothing worked, not even the success of *The Color Purple*. The success of my records didn't help me either. No success can take away the kind of pain I was feeling. Losing my marriage to Peggy, after fourteen years, was like having my arteries ripped out. I lost the house on Stone Canyon Road, which I loved, and everything in it; I lost the woman I thought I'd live with for the rest of my life; I lost a lot of money in alimony. I'd been left for dead, and had to start all over again. It was time to do the followup to *Thriller*, so I began preliminary meetings with Michael Jackson about *Bad*, but I wasn't in any shape to follow through then.

I knew I was in trouble when I went to the piano one day and played a low C and a G, a perfect fifth. My mind perceived it as a minor third, C and E-flat. That's when I knew I was caving in. Music was the only thing I could ever trust, and I was not quite sure what it was telling me. The next thing I knew my friend Dr. Larry Norton from Sloan-Kettering was at my door. He'd been helping us with Peggy's mother, Rita. I told him that Rita had died last month.

"I'm here for you," he said. "You're in trouble." He'd seen it in my eyes, he told me, at an annual music event for the T.J. Martell Foundation, which raises money for leukemia research. "Whatever you're doing, stop doing it and go somewhere near nature, with no timetable. Your problem is both mental and physical—you have adrenal syndrome. You're going to experience memory lapses, an inability to concentrate, sleeplessness, and anhedonia, a profound lack of joy."

Twenty-five years earlier, I'd been invited to join the Barclays on a pleasure trip from Paris to Tahiti. At the time something had told me to save it for later. Little did I know it would be for a nervous breakdown. In retrospect, nothing could have prepared me for what was about to happen.

When my old friend Marlon Brando got the news and called, he suggested I go to a cluster of islands he'd owned in Tahiti since filming *Mutiny on the Bounty*.

He said, "I'll get my people to set it up for you over there."

I quietly departed Hollywood on June 1, 1986. Alone.

I stayed in Tahiti for thirty-one days. Cynthia Garbutt was Marlon's main lady there. She introduced me to Tarita, the mother of his children. His teen-aged daughter Cheyenne took me by the hand and selflessly and unself-consciously mothered me. Her Chinese boyfriend had a boat they'd christened *Thriller.* They took me to the Gauguin museum, and to her boyfriend's country house. From there I took a small plane to Marlon's place, where his personal chef, Larry Cowan, came to get me. He told me, "Don't worry, Quincy, I've put you on the coconut radio. Everyone knows you're out here and we're going to take care of you." Everyone from the island, artists all, flocked around me. They welcomed me into their lives. I stayed in the Motu Hut at Hotel Bora Bora. They took me on long walks; they fed me what they ate, raw papaya right off the tree served in banyan leaves, raw fish straight out of the ocean served in coconut shells. That was all I ate. I stayed inside alone as much as possible. I did yoga for ninety minutes every day and drank four coconutfuls of water. The Tahitians devoted themselves to making me better. I got used to the jungle life. In my state, though—still on Halcion—everything makes you paranoid, even in paradise. It made all my experiences surrealistic: I was up one day and down the next.

Mo Ostin's son Michael and his wife, Joyce, longtime dear friends who lived next door to me on Stone Canyon Drive in LA., came to visit and support me, and kept me from going totally nuts. Also helpful was a special gentleman simply named Bobby of Huahini, the son of a black man from Georgia and a Hawaiian prostitute. He had delivered a baby by his friend Dorothy and buried the placenta in the yard outside his house. He was a great painter and performer, a singer and a poet. Together we went to Porpoise Beach, where a group of forty porpoises appeared in daily formation, as if they were saluting the mountains. We visited a village where a shallow stream of running water held dozens of totally tame moray eels who came for feeding every day. I sat under the stars and the moon, looking for answers for myself. I also read a great deal, mostly by flashlight, because the generators went off at 7:30 every night.

Alice Walker had given me *The Rays of Dawn* by Dr. Thurman Fleet. I also read *The Essene Gospel of Peace,* translated by Edmond Bordeaux Szekely; *Power Through Constructive Thinking* by Emmet Fox; M. Scott Peck's *The Road Less Traveled;* Dan Millman's *The Ways of the Peaceful Warrior;* and the Bible, books that I reached for in a desperate moment for help. For the first time I also really understood the Lord's Prayer: if you want forgiveness, you have to give forgiveness. I took moral inventories to cleanse the soul; I realized that the Twelve Steps are not all about addictions. I slept a lot, but still, I had no joy. I was utterly drained, vacant, empty, like my soul had left my body. Even my love of food was gone. A sweet, beautiful girl named Vaea, a gifted painter who'd been brought to Tahiti by Roger Vadim, came to me one day, looked into my eyes and said in French, "Let's make love."

"I can't." The words choked in my mouth.

She looked deeper and said, "Your kundalini is gone."

I said I didn't know what she was talking about. I will always remember her by a beautiful large painting she gave me of a duck with wings and a human face, which I still have on my wall.

She said kundalini is a metaphysical term for the core of your sexual energy. A painter named Rosine, sent to Hotel Bora Bora by her husband, George Masson, came on a motorcycle with a container of white paste from the bark of the local trees and wordlessly put it all over my body and covered it with leaves. This was old stuff—African stuff. Then they put leaves on top of that and covered me with a salve made from breadfruit root paste and cocoa oil. They sat me down on a short tree stump in a big tin tub full of hot water mixed with bark and herbs and boiled for six hours. My feet were on the ground outside the tub. Then they draped towels on my head that had been dampened in hot water, so it was like a steam bath. I inhaled the eucalyptus concoction and felt like I was fifteen.

Still there were problems. Back in Papayete, on the island, they had a party for me, and it was a disaster. I couldn't deal with crowds at all. I was totally paranoid. When a local man took me to a roped-off area of the ocean, he told me to wear rubber flippers and to watch out for sea urchins. Swimming alone underwater with a snorkel and goggles, I saw seven huge sharks and six large turtles. When a stingray came at me and stopped three feet in front of me, I thought, "If I survive this, I'll survive anything." I felt like Drew Barrymore meeting *E.T.* for the first time. In truth, he just wanted to play. I was delirious in so many ways, partially because of the Halcion.

I began to take long walks by myself then, something I hadn't done since I was a kid. Being there, alone, on Father's Day, thinking you might have to check into a sanitarium and spend your whole life feeling like Gauguin, was sobering. It came to me then that I'd spent too many years trying to make sure I wasn't missing anything, always meeting someone new, always trying to fill up that black hole in my soul with something that existed here and now rather than to draw from the past and live from the inside out. I realized that from the time I was a little boy to that moment, I was always running, but every time I ran I kept crashing into myself coming from the opposite direction, and *he* didn't know where he was going either. I ran because there was nothing behind me to hold me up. I ran because I thought that was all there was to do. I thought that to stay in one place meant to die.

I should have stayed longer than thirty-one days, but I came back because I had to find out why I wasn't doing better, despite my spiritual rebirth, in Tahiti and in 2 Bunch Palms in the California desert. All I could think about was my kids, how my success had been at their expense in so many ways. I came home wanting to know where my kids were, how they were, and what I'd missed. I wasn't completely cured. Crowds were still impossible for me. I still couldn't face my best friend Clarence, still couldn't face my kids for long stretches. I wore shades all the time because without my sunglasses you could see in my eyes that I wasn't all there.

Back in Los Angeles I called Dr. Norton to tell him it was over: I needed help to find a sanitarium. He asked me what I was taking, and when I told him Halcion, he told me to stop immediately and put me on Valium for sixty days to ease me off. He said they used to use Halcion in Korea on prisoners of war for interrogation purposes. Once I stopped taking it, after two days I started to dream again, literally, and found that my energy came surging back. I felt reborn. I was whole again.

CHAPTER 32

Back on the block

Melle Mel, rap music
pioneer

What another man saw in a race of people,
To see him give his life for the price of equal,
The highest wisdoms, the richest kingdom,
The song of songs we heard David sing them . . .

In 1974, when I was thirteen, there was a DJ in the South Bronx named Kool Herc. He would set up a microphone next to his turntable and spin records at house parties. He didn't let anyone touch his mike, but he'd say hip things like "It's a party. Everybody groove now . . ." as he spun records.

I liked that, so me and my brother, whose nickname was Kid Creole, we went home and started embellishing on what Kool Herc said. Then we went to parties where a DJ named Flash spun records, because Flash also set up a mike, but he'd let any knucklehead use it. We spoke rhyming poems, phrases, just to motivate the crowd.

No one called it rap then. It had no name.

We got better at it and grew popular very quickly. Me, Flash, Kid Creole, and another kid nicknamed Cowboy got together and formed a group. We did our first house party in 1976. That night, a friend named Cocoa Mo came by. Cocoa Mo was leaving for the Army and Cowboy was on the microphone. When he saw Cocoa Mo dancing he said, "Hip, hop, hibbit to the hip-hop," like they do in the Army when they march. Somebody laughed and said, "Y'all motherfuckers need to get a job. You can't make no money doing that hip-hop shit." That's when we started calling it hip-hop. We never called it rap. The press called it rap later on.

It grew so fast it was unbelievable. It was just a thing we did. We didn't realize we were starting a billion-dollar industry. At the time I was a teenager, looking at the rest of my life, knowing that I wasn't spending any time in high school, getting into trouble, burglarizing houses. I knew something had to give. This gave me an out.

We got a kid named Eddie Morris, who called himself Mr. Ness, to join us, and later another rapper named Raheem, and we ultimately became GrandMaster Flash and the Furious Five. We didn't think we were starting an art form. We were happy to get paid. We were playing parties and clubs all through the Bronx, New York City, New Jersey, Connecticut. I thought we'd stay on that level, like a traveling road show. I didn't understand radio or TV exposure or even record promotion.

Then a record called *Rappers' Delight* hit.

We laughed at it when we first heard it. The group was called the Sugar Hill Gang, and they weren't even from the Bronx. Two of them were from Jersey. Every rapper hated it. You could tell it was patchwork. Other than using Cowboy's phrase, "hip, hop, hibbit," they didn't execute well, and every real rapper could tell. We said, "It'll never work," but it caught fire worldwide. It was all over the motherfuckin' radio, man. It made *Billboard*'s Top Twenty list. We stopped laughing at it then.

We got on the wave and got signed by the same label as the Sugar Hill Gang. We put out big records: *The Birthday Party, Freedom, Genius of Love.*

They all scored big, but *The Message* was the biggest. It changed the scope of what rap was. *The Message* was the first rap song that wasn't about partying and meeting girls. It was about the hard life, the stress of being alive in the city. We started playing big places, the Ritz, the Peppermint Lounge, and doing shows with U2, Stray Cats, Cameo, and Zap. Bikers, porn stars, cops, ex-cops would come to see us play. It was a scene. We sold records hand over fist—hundreds of thousands, maybe millions—but we never saw royalties because we were never charted by the industry. We worked with a series of advances. The label would advance us money to do a record and we always got statements that showed us in the hole. We always owed them money.

We fought about it and drugs became a problem among us and we broke apart. Flash wanted to take the label to court to get our money. I knew we wouldn't win. Flash came up with a lawyer. I had gotten into trouble before, and I understood the dynamics of how it works. We were at Flash's house and I was talking to the lawyer on the phone. I asked him, "How long will it take for us to get our money?"

He said, "It'll take years."

I gave Flash the phone and went to New Jersey and cut another record with the label while Flash fought it out. I needed the money. I took half the group with me. Flash took the other half. We put out a couple more hits, *White Lines* and *Frankie Goes to Hollywood*, before the group disbanded completely. We got together in the eighties to do a radio show in New York for a while, and then I did a record with Chaka Khan called *I Feel for You*, which won a Grammy in 1984. After that, my life fell apart.

I fell into drugs, hard. I thought drugs came with the territory. It's like you test your greatness against the odds, to see which man falls and rises at the end. Everybody I knew, all the stars, were getting high on coke and crack. It was easy. Meanwhile, the opportunities slipped away. Rap music became huge. Record companies made millions, but no one would return my calls.

Five years passed. I went to prison. I did hard time. I smoked crack.

I was on a pay phone in the Bronx in 1989, high on crack or trying to get high, and a guy came up to me and said, "Melle Mel, Quincy Jones is looking for you."

I didn't think I'd heard him right. I said, "What?"

He said, "Quincy Jones is out in LA looking for you."

I'd met Quincy five years before, right after I won a Grammy with Chaka Khan. He'd asked me to work with him on this Bugs Bunny and the Dude animated feature he was doing. We were creating characters and I was writing raps for it. I had lunch at his house then. I said to myself, "Here's my big chance. I'm gonna get back in the business."

I called him. He said, "Melle, how you doing?"

Standing there at a pay phone on Tiffany Street at night in the Fort Apache section of the South Bronx, I had the biggest revelation of my life: How the fuck am I doing? I'm standing here trying to kill myself with crack and talking on a pay phone, that's how the fuck I'm doing. It hit me right then and there.

I said, "I'm doing all right, Q."

He said, "I been hearing about you."

I said, "Whatever you heard, I'm doing all right."

He said, "You're on a pay phone. You're an artist. How you gonna make things happen that way? Why don't you come out here and see me."

He got me a plane ticket and flew me out to his house and sat me down in his living room. Even though he'd heard I was in jail and was a crack addict, it said a lot to me that he would fly me out to his house in Bel Air and sit me in his living room with all his Grammys and jewelry and not worry about me stealing his shit. How many people from Bel Air would do that?

He got some food out of the refrigerator and made us something to eat. We sat and ate and talked for a long time. I'd known him from his work with Michael Jackson, but he didn't talk about that. He talked about

Charlie Parker and the jazz guys he'd grown up with, and how society refused to accept them when they did bebop, so they ended up doing drugs
and dying. He said he felt the same way about rap. He said, "All great music comes from the street someplace. There's no difference between a gutter in Vienna in 1850 and a gutter in Harlem today. No one with your
talent should be on the street talking on a pay phone. I've seen it a hundred times in my life. You're a philosopher, Melle. I want you to work on
a record with me." He said he had an idea for a record called *Back on the
Block* that he wanted me to work on.

Just like that I was back in the business. He brought me and Big
Daddy Kane and Kool Moe Dee and a West Coast rapper named Ice-T
into the studio and played a track for us. It was about the blending of jazz,
rhythm and blues, gospel, African music, and hip-hop. When he played it
for us, we said, "What do we do with this shit?"

He said, "Stretch yourself. Think about the Dude as a symbol, the
older cat who comes back to the neighborhood to share his wisdom about
our cultural heritage. It's about mind solution, not mind pollution, about
keeping it real with the street and true to yourself." He never mentioned
the word "profanity." We decided not to go there on our own. He had
George Benson, Ella Fitzgerald, Sarah Vaughan, Miles Davis, Dizzy Gillespie, all these jazz artists, working on the record. None of us knew each
other. We were like foreigners talking different languages. George Benson
was like, "Who the fuck are these people?" and we were like, "Who the
fuck is he?" But we all dug each other when we played, and the music was
out of sight. The next day we recorded everything in about two hours. It
was like an epiphany, it came together tremendously. Quincy knows how
to pull it out of different people. It's the love he has for artists and his understanding of music that does it. It's tribal. He understands everybody's
talking drum. He's the only guy in the world who can do that, who can
reach all the way back to Frank Sinatra and Ella Fitzgerald and connect

them to the rappers. He brought the rapper L.L. Cool J. to meet Frank Sinatra. Who else in the business can do that?

Back on the Block won a Grammy for me and helped put me back on my feet. I got my life together now. I've been clean for twelve years, no cigarettes, drugs, nothing. I'm touring Europe. I've got the group together again. In Japan and Europe they know every record I've ever done, including the bootleg records. I'm a little like the jazz cats Quincy talks about who had to go to Europe to get recognition. I can't do rap to exploit kids. I never did it for money. I did it to illuminate the ghetto, not glamorize death. Most rap artists today hang on to their bullshit, tough-guy image like it's money—and it is. A lot of these muthafuckas are selling theater, it's a front. Some are college graduates. There's a girl rapper now who acts like a goddamn whore, saying she used to be a porn star. She wasn't no muthafuckin' porn star. If she was, I would know it—I got a collection in my house—but she glamorizes the shit and rides it to the bank and the record companies love it because it makes money. And our little daughters hear this shit. It's our fault. All of our faults. Because we support it.

I never did rap to make kids shoot Tech nines and gang-bang and abuse women. I did it for opportunity. I did it to humanize my neighborhood, the part of America that's in my heart, the part that the world never sees. I love Quincy for his understanding of that. He told me once, "Music is a measuring stick of society. There's nothing cute about being poor, selling dope, and ending up in jail. You've been there, Melle. You know."

I do know.

Ya dig?

CHAPTER 33

From bebop to hip-hop

I'm a bebopper to my core, and always will be. I love and create all kinds of music, but bebop helped to define my soul and my musical destiny. More than music, bebop was a stance, a mind-set, a lifestyle, a way for people—black men in particular—to express themselves artistically and intellectually, but hold on to the cool that made it all possible. It was more than a style—it was a wavelength, a network of common interests with adherents worldwide. The bebop world signaled such a change just with the song titles. Instead of "Has Anybody Seen My Gal?" you had Charlie Parker coming up with "Ornithology," and Thelonious Monk writing "Epistrophy."

From an early age my friends and I tried to set ourselves apart, though we barely understood it at the time. The group of musicians I came up with in Seattle was full of curious people. When we were thirteen, fourteen, we were reading the Kama Sutra and *The Rubaiyat of Omar Khayyam* and *The Prophet* by Kahlil Gibran and *Dianetics* by L. Ron Hubbard as well as *The Life and Teachings of Masters of the Far East.* Several of these books were given to me by a trumpeter friend, Neil Friel. We even looked into Reichian therapy and built our own orgone accumulator out of tinfoil from cigarette packages—we were all the way out there!

Black music has always had to invent its own society, a subculture to help the disenfranchised survive, psychologically, spiritually, and creatively. We come up with our own slang, body language, sensibility, ideology, and lifestyle to go with the music. Not since bebop has a music so taken over a whole culture the way hip-hop has—it's everywhere. Like the rest of the new genres, hip-hop came straight from the street, and in the tradition of African life-force music—in contrast to the virtuosity of Western concert music—it's as powerful a form in its way as any of its predecessors. As Chuck D. put it, hip-hop is the CNN of the street.

I see hip-hop communication as a continuation of the old school: Lester Young and Count Basie and everyone in the subculture were using the words "homeboy" and "rap" back in the forties. Bebop was all about not just instrumentation but also scat, vocalese, and attitude. Hip-hop can sometimes come out at the raw end of the spectrum, and some of it has been polluted by the hustle—the big cars and the obsession with the Benjamins and worst of all by the violence of brothers killing brothers, most of it perpetuated not by the rappers themselves but by the gangs who've appropriated the music in the name of "keeping it real." Our country's greatest cultural contributions, whether you're talking about jazz and gospel, an Irish jig or black tap dancing, the Broadway musical, barbershop, doo-wop, bebop, or rhythm and blues, reflect our gumbo nature. Now even the most hard-core rap is playing in shopping malls in Dallas not to mention Estonia, Paris, and Tokyo, and on the African continent itself. The first time Jackie and Clarence Avant and I were guests in the castle of Princess Gloria von Thurn und Taxis in Germany, we heard her twelve-year-old son Albert listening to Snoop Doggy Dogg and Dr. Dre! It's our freshest gumbo with an African motor and flava, and the whole world's feeling it.

Beats and rhymes go all the way back to Africa, to black folklore.

There's a strong oral tradition in American black music: call and response; Imbongi, the praise shouters; the storytellers who share the mantle with the griots, the oral historians. This mix of elements—what people now label rap—first came on my radar screen in the 1960s, with performers like the Last Poets and Gil Scott-Heron. In 1975 on an album called *Mellow Madness* I featured a lovers' rap called "Beautiful Black Girl" by a "toasting" group known as the Watts Prophets, made up of Otis O'Sullivan, Richard Dedeaux, and Dee Dee MacNeil, who were an LA equivalent of the Last Poets and Gil Scott-Heron. They used poetic call-and-response chants, which I framed with funky African percussion. The whole music industry woke up to the commercial potential of the music in 1979 when Joe and Sylvia Robinson's label sold over 11 million copies of the Sugar Hill Gang's *Rappers' Delight*. Then I won seven Grammys in 1980 for *The Dude*, with James Ingram and Patti Austin singing the title song. Ten years later in my experiment in musical cross-pollination, *Back on the Block*, I returned to the memories I had of a "dude" on the corner of every ghetto in America. This was the Main Man, and everybody emulated him. In 1989 people in the mainstream music business told me I was in arrested development—rap was over, they all said.

My kids have been a big influence. As I was drawn to bebop as a kid, my son Snoopy took to hip-hop. In Sweden as a teenager, he'd incorporated break dancing from the South Bronx and the California-originated poppin' 'n' lockin' into a very successful group called Bezerk. He and Jolie and Rashida are carrying on the family's musical legacy. By 1985 Snoopy had moved in with me and had his own private "war zone" in the guest room downstairs. Over the next year or so I toured a great deal to promote *We Are the World*, and *The Color Purple*, and he came with me, including attending a wonderful concert at the Kennedy Center, where Stevie Wonder helped celebrate the first Martin Luther King day. I wanted to set up his birthday party in 1986 as a surprise so that he could meet all his idols in the rap world. At that point the music wasn't as big commercially; it was more underground, like bebop had been when I was coming up. But bebop, in contrast, never went mainstream.

First we were invited down to the early Fred Sanford-style Def Jam offices in the Village to meet Russell Simmons. We were just in time to hear the first airplay of "My Adidas" by Run-D.M.C., which turned out to be a pivotal moment in the history of rap. Russell was saying amid the cheers that greeted the exposure for the song, "Guys, why don't you change it to Nikes so that I can get you a real good deal." Adidas gave up only two pairs of shoes apiece as a promotion. The company didn't know then that it was the rappers, not just the jocks, who were really driving street sales. But the name Adidas had a hipper meter than Nikes. Seven months later Adidas sales had shot up some 30 percent and they came back and offered Russell a $5 million deal. At the same time Def Jam had just released a video of "Walking in the Rain" with Oran "Juice" Jones. This was the genesis of the rap movement: L.L. Cool J. was all of fifteen. The very first thing he ever said to me was, "Mr. Jones, what do the musicians and singers think about us?" That was the first time it hit me that rap really was a third entity, between songs and instrumental music. It was all so new then.

Afterward we wound up at Canastel's on Park Avenue South with Russell, his partner Lyor Cohen, L.L. Cool J., Run-D.M.C., Roxanne, the Beastie Boys, Kurtis Blow, Whodini, Andre Harrell and T LaRoc, and the Fat Boys, among other heavies. Ed Eckstine and Grady Tate were there too. Snoopy was a rap junkie and his excitement at meeting these guys reminded me exactly of the way I felt when Oscar Pettiford first brought me to New York and I met Dizzy and Miles and Art Tatum and Charlie Parker and Charlie Mingus thirty-five years earlier. When Snoopy cut his birthday cake all the rappers chanted their anthem, "Together Forever." After having insisted that rappers only drink beer, Russell Simmons and the posse decided to make an exception for champagne, given that it was a birthday celebration: at the end of the evening $6,500 worth had been consumed.

By then it was clear—at least to some of us—that rap had made its mark in our culture. It was our newest baby and it was here to stay.

There were plenty of doubters about the music's staying power. When we made *Bad* in 1987, I wanted to put an anticrack song on one side with Run-D.M.C. and Michael. The group showed up at Westlake Studios several times, ready to jam, but Smelly was skeptical of rap as an option for a couple of the album's cuts and he wasn't the only one. Snoopy never budged from his rock-steady conviction that rap would rule for quite some time.

In 1989 I decided to do *Back on the Block*, which included a huge range of talent, from George Benson and Ella, Bobby McFerrin and Ray Charles, Sassy and Take Six and Dizzy and Miles, to Melle Mel and Kool Moe Dee and Big Daddy Kane and Ice-T. At age eleven my grandson Sunny, after hearing the record, asked me, "Grandpa, who's Miles Davis that Daddy Kane was talking about?" I told him to go find out, and he did: he became a major fan, and eventually a major singer-songwriter, band leader, and producer-engineer, fusing jazz and funk with trip-hop and hip-hop—the works! His father is the producer Stewart Levine, who's done everything from *Grazin' in the Grass* to *Right Up Where We Belong* to *Holding Back the Years.*

The kids coming up needed to be introduced to jazz; most important, they needed to understand that all of our music springs from the same roots. The power of African music derives from polyrhythms, the call-and-response form, and the "significant tone" of the African source, because it emanates from nature itself—the sounds of birds and crickets, thunder, and the pulse of the animals. There doesn't need to be a disconnect between the various forms of expression. I've always been turned on by a simmering musical stew, and in *Back on the Block* I achieved this, in both a cross-cultural and a cross-generational sense. We had twelve-year-old Tevin Campbell singing a Zulu melody in that language with Caiphus Semenya and Letta Mbulu from South Africa, Joe Zawinul on jazz synthesizer, and the Andre and Sandra Crouch Choir doing gospel alongside Ice-T and Melle Mel and other rappers talking about everything from body bags and

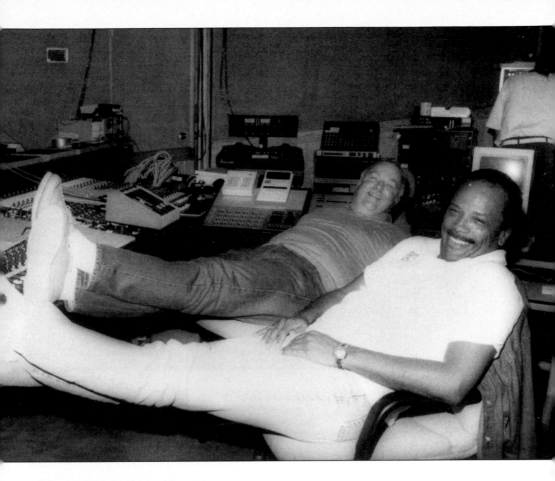

(Above and left)
Two key members
of the killer Q posse:
ace songwriter Rod
Temperton, and master
engineer Bruce Swedien.

Backstage at Radio City Music Hall in New York City
with one of my idols, Count Basie.

Ray Charles is one of my oldest friends. We met up in Seattle when I was
fourteen and Ray was sixteen. This photo was taken at the American Academy
of Achievement in Minneapolis, 1984.

The artists who made the chart-topper "We Are the World" in 1984, a monumental collective effort that raised $60 million to feed the hungry.

One happy guy with an armful of Grammys for *The Dude.*

With Aunt Mabel Delaney, the only mother I've ever really known. We're at Ole Miss, where I took the art director Mike Riva on *The Color Purple* to do research.

On the set of *The Color Purple* in 1985 with producer Kathleen Kennedy, director Steven Spielberg, and author Alice Walker.

Clarence Avant, my best friend, also known as "the black Godfather," "Sweet Potato," and "Bump."

With my son Snoopy and the Champ of Champs, Muhammad Ali.

Winning the Jean Hersholt Humanitarian Award from the
Academy of Motion Picture Arts and Sciences in 1985.

Snoopy with a cadre of rappers. Back row: Jam Master Jay from Run-DMC, DJ Hurricane, Cool Rockski from the Fat Boys, Charles Stetler—manager of the Fat Boys, Prince Markie Dee of the Fat Boys (hidden), Adam Yauch of the Beastie Boys, rapper unknown from Whodini, T La Rock. Middle row: Jalil from Whodini, Buffy the Human Beat Box from the Fat Boys, Snoopy, Grandmaster Dee from Whodini. Front row: Lyor Cohen, Ecstacy from Whodini.

(Left) Rapper Melle Mel in the studio during the recording of *Back on the Block*, 1989.

(Below) Accepting the Legion d'Honneur in France. Steve Ross flew in for the evening.

Sammy Davis, Jr.'s sixtieth anniversary show in 1990, the last time he appeared on television: with Mike Tyson, Frank Sinatra, Goldie Hawn, Michael Jackson, Sammy's wife, Altovese, Anita Baker, Stevie Wonder, Ella Fitzgerald, Lola Falana, Diahann Carroll, Eddie Murphy, Shirley MacLaine, Dean Martin, me, Dionne Warwick, Whitney Houston, Debbie Allen, Nell Carter, Bill Cosby, Gregory Peck, Jesse Jackson, Gregory Hines, Clint Eastwood, Tony Danza, Richard Pryor, Magic Johnson, and Bob Hope. A George Schlatter production.

Conducting Miles at Montreux, Switzerland, in 1991,
playing Gil Evans' arrangements—one of his last appearances.

My sister Margie's fiftieth birthday party in Anchorage, Alaska. Clockwise from top: Waymond, Barbara, Janet, Lloyd, me, Margie, Theresa, and Richard.

At Bill Clinton's first inaugural celebration, which I executive produced: with Stedman Graham, Oprah Winfrey, and Jack Nicholson.

My brother Lloyd
hugging his wife, Gloria.

At the White House
with Oprah. We were
attending a state dinner
for the Emperor
of Japan.

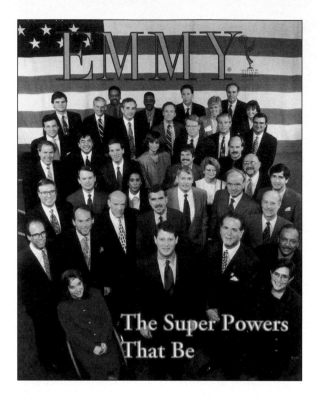

Pictured on the cover of the Academy of Television Arts and Sciences magazine in 1994, with Dick Cavett, Michael Eisner, Jeffrey Katzenberg, Barry Diller, Rupert Murdoch, Al Gore, Gerald Levin, John Malone, Robert Iger, Geraldine Laybourne, Larry Ellison, Robert Johnson, Steve Case, Alan Kay, and Bernard Shaw, among others.

A meeting with "my older brother," the current U.S. Secretary of State, Colin Powell. My younger brother, Superior Court Judge Richard Jones, is at right.

With the former President.

As a guest of Nelson Mandela in South Africa during
the Transafrica Democracy Now Tour.

Me, Nastassja, and our daughter, Kenya.

Kicking back with Lisette in Martha's Vineyard in 1997.

The posse at Snoopy and Koa's wedding, from left to right: Kidada, Rashida, Tina, me, Snoopy, Jolie, and Rachel holding her daughter Jessica. In front are Koa and Kenya.

being strung out to the spirit of the ancestors coming through for every-body at the end. When you come back to your block, you've come full cir-cle, back to the community that sustains no matter how far you stray.

By 1992 I was ready to reach for another dream, extending my mul-timedia company under the Time Warner umbrella to publishing. My friend and mentor Steve Ross understood what 98 percent of corporate America didn't get—the influence of black culture. Two years earlier, in 1990, I'd been on the beach in Sardinia with Steve discussing the prospects for our initial venture when he'd said, "Are you ready to do it?" In 1990 Bob Pittman wasn't thrilled with where he'd gone after the sale of MTV. We'd been talking, so when Steve had asked me whom I'd like to work with, and I mentioned Bob's name, his mind whirred like a computer and in a New York minute he said, "Let's do it." Steve and Bob were both true visionaries. They'd worked together at Warner Brothers a decade ear-lier. When Bob Pittman proposed a $39 million business plan for what be-came MTV, the Warner board threw him out. Steve took him aside and said, "Here's fifty million, go do it." By the time the pioneering network was sold to Viacom four years later in 1985, it was worth $780 million as a result of the Atari catastrophe, which had resulted in a $2 billion loss. The value today is close to $20 billion. Steve and Bob were truly men who could see around the corner.

So Bob Pittman became a key figure in Quincy Jones Entertainment or Q JE, my fifty-fifty joint venture with Time Warner, which is still the model for every other black-owned entertainment businesses who've seri-ously joined forces with a major media company. Now Babyface and his wife, Tracey, have a deal with Fox, and Russell Simmons with MCA, among others. Bob was my main man in the office of the president—we were in the same frequency range.

One of the first things we discussed was a talk show for the Reverend Jesse Jackson, a natural for the role. I called Bob in New York from Los Angeles at nine in the morning, and he said, "I'll meet you at the airport—

tonight." After meeting at ten that evening at the Bonaventure Hotel in LA, we'd made a deal by eleven the same night. Jesse was a quick study, but the show didn't evolve quickly enough to survive. He went on to a successful career at CNN; and I knew I had in Bob Pittman a partner who was resolute and determined, a visionary able to turn on a dime.

Bob's television connections were also very helpful to me in the early days of the partnership with Time Warner when we bought WNOL, a Fox affiliate in New Orleans, which was brilliantly managed by Madelyn Bonnot. The station had some great community programming, including a children's show called *Great Expectations* that taught that it was hip to be smart—a pat on the back for the kids who were doing it right. After acquiring TV rights to the NFL, Fox wanted to own a station with wider exposure in this market and found a loophole in the fine print of our contract. After they pulled out I had barely blinked before Tom Murphy of ABC said, "Come join us." At breakfast the next morning, Dennis Fitzsimmons, president of the Tribune broadcasting group, who wanted to start a minority-owned television company, said he'd made a separate deal with Tom at ABC. Tribune also agreed to buy out Time Warner's 50 percent stake in our company. So we were back in business. In 1994 I formed a consortium with Willie Davis, Don Cornelius, Geraldo Rivera, and Sonia Gonsalves Salzman; I served as CEO of the group, Qwest Broadcasting. Together with the Tribune group we went on to buy WATL in Atlanta, a Top Ten station expertly run by Dan Berkery, again from Fox.

My company Qwest Records was also partnered with Time Warner in 1980. Our debut project, George Benson's *Give Me the Night*, was followed by my own *Back on the Block*, which won seven Grammys, including Best LP of the Year. In 1991 our soundtrack album for the movie *Boyz in the Hood* was extremely successful, and was followed by the soundtracks for *Malcolm X* and *The Color Purple*. Tevin Campbell's album *I'm Ready* went double platinum.

When I hear the words "That's never been done," I feel like a lion being thrown some meat. These words pique my interest immediately. In my view the people who achieve greatness in their chosen fields have a core skill upon which they expand. In Steve's case it was his astounding ability with figures and his photographic memory. He could juggle an extraordinary number of diverse elements and people at one time and keep it all fluent. And neither he nor Bob Pittman messed around. The vision was followed up by speed-of-lightning execution. They didn't hesitate or fumble. Steve taught me to try to hold on to 25 or 30 percent of anything you sell, and that the last two points in closing any deal are a deadline and a consequence. He also advised, "Mean what you say," "Make it win-win," and "Always try to return phone calls." Now you'd have to throw in faxes, e-mails, and the rest.

Right after the Time Warner merger, Steve was feeling pressure to show some "synergy" at work between the various divisions of the new company. I had an idea for a magazine about hip-hop, but didn't know that business. He advised me to consult with the top people on the masthead team at Time, Inc.

I got the idea for a magazine about hip-hop in all its forms—music, fashion, style—after putting together *Back on the Block*. Originally I asked Russell Simmons to be a partner, but he passed. I want to go on record to say that I was never, ever even remotely interested in buying *The Source*, because I felt there would always be a proprietary attitude there, and I wanted to expand the reach of such a magazine and start fresh. The editors at *Time*, particularly Gil Rogin, saw the potential of an "urban *Rolling Stone* for the 90s," as did his colleague Chris Meigher III. Greg Sandow, the music editor for *Entertainment Weekly*, also contributed a long, supportive memo to the masthead team, Gil and Dick Stolley and Jason McManus. Jane Pratt was also very helpful. After a "wet test," or test issue, suggested by Gerry Levin, who saw the potential immediately, *Vibe* hit the newsstands in 1993, with CEO Keith Clinkscales driving the vision, along with John Rollins as publisher and Jonathan Van Meter as the first editor in chief. Van Meter had wanted to call the magazine *Volume*, but there were copyright problems.

Scott Poulson-Bryant was the one who came up with the name *Vibe*. On an early issue we had a real problem with a cover that had featured the Beastie Boys, whose most recent album had been delayed, and then didn't perform up to expectations commercially. We were only beginning to find out then how vital covers are to magazines' success. The next one, which Jon Van Meter had already shot, featured Madonna and Dennis Rodman. I said, "Over my dead body, because it makes it look as though we're pandering, that we're not sure *Vibe* can be a black magazine and make it." We'd misfired on the Beasties, so I was adamant, though technically Van Meter did not report to me and I had backed off on editorial matters after my initial involvement. It wasn't about Madonna or Dennis: it was about our not having been around long enough to establish a personality as an urban magazine. Van Meter was furious: he was gone after that. Still, he did a great job editorially and was very important in shaping the publication.

When I called Madonna as a friend to explain that it wasn't at all personal, she took it personal and got an attitude about it. She said, "Quincy, you and I could change the world together if we wanted to. See you around, pal." Unfortunately, I don't think we've spoken since. Her publicist Liz Rosenberg then called Liz Smith, and before you knew it there was an item in Liz's column reporting that "Quincy killed the cover because it showed a mixed couple." Right. Me, of all people—pleeze!

At one point we were sitting face to face with Bob Miller, then the head of Time Life, and his associate Seymour Boutros-Ghali, the brother of the former UN head, in the company's California offices. They said *Vibe* was losing money and that we needed to cut costs drastically. They said that if we didn't cut overhead, the publication would be shut down. This business is like a battleship, we were told—no matter what you do, it can't be turned around. Wrong. Not only did it turn around; after that office closed, Bob Miller took his severance and bought half the magazine! It was a success; the marketplace was ready. Bob Miller Publishing eventually bought *Vibe* back from Time Warner, after also snapping up *Spin* for $42 million.

By this time our numbers showed the Powers That Be that hip-hop had arrived in the heart of America as a commercial force to be reckoned with. The two publications now represent 13 percent of the music market, spanning from so-called urban music to alternative rock. *Vibe* exerts considerable influence in the hip-hop marketplace and urban world.

With the *Vibe* launch, the promotion for my new album, *Jook Joint*, and other projects and commitments, I was pushing the edge of the envelope, as usual. I had become co-producer of the Montreux Jazz Festival at the request of its founder, Claude Nobs. In 1991 we produced a historic concert in Montreux with Miles, re-creating some of the incredible music he had made with the arranger Gil Evans on *Sketches of Spain* and *Porgy and Bess.* Conducting Gil's orchestrations for Miles was one of the most gratifying experiences in my career. Claude and I had been in Miles's apartment in New York negotiating the contract with several lawyers while the man himself was upstairs working on a rap project with Flavor Flav and a rap producer. Eventually Miles eased down and inched further and further to the center of the room. Before we knew it, he had gotten exactly the deal he wanted, for video and TV rights, and control of his image on the poster. "This is gonna be real expensive," he told us. I said, "But Dewey, all we need is a large orchestra." To my great amusement, he insisted, "Q, *you* understand—this shit is hard to play." It was the first time Miles had played this music since he had recorded it in the late fifties; up to that point he had adamantly refused to look back, ever. In general, his musical philosophy did not encompass retrospection. He died three months later.

It was also at the 1991 Montreux festival that my friend Herman Leonard, the master photographer, acted as Cupid in my love affair with actress Nastassja Kinski, with whom I had an extraordinarily beautiful and vibrant daughter, Kenya, who has me totally wrapped around her finger. Though Nastassja's and my relationship as a couple was not destined to last, she is a great friend, and she and Kenya still live next door to me in California, so that I can be there for them and for her two other loving children, Ali and Sonja. I think I'm finally getting to be a good daddy.

At this point hip-hop was my window on the future and one of my forums for activism. In the summer of 1995 I had the notion of gathering together some important voices to mix, mingle, and discuss the state of hip-hop. The *Vibe* summit took place at New York's Peninsula Hotel after being switched from the Marriott at the last minute to elude the press. I confiscated all videotapes and film to protect Colin Powell, who wound up staying for five hours instead of two. I didn't want anyone using photos or footage to damage him if he decided to run for the presidency, which he was contemplating at the time. Some of the younger rappers didn't even know who he was. When addressing some of the more confrontational comments from the floor, Powell maintained his South Bronx demeanor and authoritative cool throughout. I had been concerned about the potentially volatile diversity of a group who'd never been in the same room together. The Fruit of Islam provided security, and the gathering opened with a letter of greeting from Maya Angelou, which I read from the podium.

Panel members included Clarence Avant, Malcolm X's eldest daughter, Attalah Shabazz—who spoke at length about the dangers of "dumbing down"—Ed Lewis from *Essence*, Allen Shaw from MIT, and Alan Kay, the guru from Silicon Valley, with Fab 5 Freddy as moderator. In the audience were Minister Conrad Muhammad, John Singleton, members of A Tribe Called Qwest, Ahmet Ertegun, Dr. Dre, Suge Knight, Alan Light, John Rollins and Keith Clinkscales from *Vibe*, MC Lyte, Harry Allan and Chuck D. from Public Enemy, Puffy Combs, Andre Harrell, Kris Kross, Jermaine Dupri, and Biggie Smalls. Clarence Avant and Colin Powell, among others, told the gathering that the anger unleashed by hip-hop had to be dealt with and steered in more positive direction, more brain solution than brain pollution. Speaker after speaker talked about power as a form of responsibility, about talent as a power that shouldn't be used to destroy, about being guided by the inner conscience, even if anger is the initial motivator for your actions. It was clear that the rappers needed to organize their own coalition in order to control their own destiny. Some of the young rap community—one of whom, Jake Robles, a Def Jam exec, was shot and killed a week later in Atlanta—kept intoning that entertainment is entertainment. But to me, the bebop to hip-hop connection is about feeding yourself with knowledge—being hip is about being aware. The section of the symposium devoted to business and technology and the emerging power of the Internet was therefore the hippest thing we had going, if you had the awareness to see it that way.

The symposium's bittersweet aftermath was more commercial success for rap and hip-hop—and more violence. The East-West rivalry turned into a psychodrama of major proportions. I had just begun to connect with Tupac Shakur, who was dating my daughter Kidada, before he was gunned down in Las Vegas. Though we got off to a rocky start, as I came to know and feel him I saw his enormous potential and sensitivity as an artist and as a human being. I'll never forget that when he made an appointment to meet me at the Bel Air Hotel, he arrived promptly at ten, then left a message with the maître d' that he'd be back in a suit and tie. He wanted to greet me respectfully, not just as an artist and entrepreneur but as the father of the woman he loved. This is the side of Tupac that the media and his fans never saw, because of the mythology of the gangsta pose. A collection of his poetry that has become a best-seller in the wake of his death, *The Rose That Grew from Concrete,* reveals a tragic fear of being seen as "soft" because of his avocation for writing, which he thought exposed his vulnerability. In addition, Amaru Records released a CD of his closet poetry, on which Tupac's mother Afeni asked me to recite "Starry Night," Tupac's poem dedicated to Vincent van Gogh. The CD was produced by my son, with my daughter Rashida singing.

Just a short while after Tupac was shot, I was attending Sharon Stone's birthday celebration. Leaving later than I had intended to, I called Kidada, who was in charge of organizing a party for *Vibe* and Qwest

Records, to say that I'd be a bit late. She said, "Daddy, don't come, some-one just got killed." It was Notorious B.I.G. Four minutes after leaving the party, he was ambushed and shot in his own limo. It was all devastatingly traumatic for Kidada, who was still raw from Tupac's death. We all stayed up until nine that morning with her and Tupac's posse, trying to overcome the shock. To this day I am appalled by the fact that not a single arrest has been made in either case.

There's been so much loss of young talent in the hip-hop world: I can't get used to the idea of so many young people half my age passing away. I'll never forget going to the hospital with L.L. Cool J. to visit Easy E, who was dying of AIDS at the age of thirty-two. The life-support machines, the morphine drip, the induced paralysis—tomorrow was just too late.

You stay as hard as you need to be, but the kids need more. Ameri-can kids need leadership and wisdom. Rappers have no choice but to be more responsible, but in order to do that they have to live longer than twenty-five years. It's the first thirty years that are the hardest! And there is no point in being surprised or getting an attitude if thirteen-year-old blond-haired, blue-eyed kids are throwing the N-word back in your face. Attempts to flatten that word have failed decade after decade, from Lenny Bruce to Redd Foxx to Richard Pryor.

What I tell the young musicians is how important it is to be in control of your musical destiny. There are some standout examples in the younger generation who understand this: Russell Simmons, Dr. Dre, QDIII, Sean "P.Diddy" Combs, Glen Ballard, Babyface, Wyclef Jean, Chuck D., L.L. Cool J, Will Smith, Timbaland, Shekespere, Queen Latifah, Damon and Darien Dash, Mervyn Warren, Teddy Riley, and John Clayton. When I was coming up in the entertainment business, there were no Oprahs or Michael Jordans or Bob Johnsons or Tiger Woodses in our culture, billion-aires and media icons. My models were Picasso and Stravinsky—protean talents who had control of how their work was presented and how their legacy continued. After meeting Stravinsky in France while studying with

Nadia Boulanger, she shared with me a story about him being commissioned by the city fathers of Venice to write a fifteen-minute piece about the city. He went there for two weeks, looking around and absorbing the atmosphere for inspiration. Then he told them, "Gentlemen, that'll be $250,000. The music is cheap—it's the name that's expensive."

Picasso owned twelve lithograph plants. Raymond Moretti, the jazz painter from Nice, experimented with him on an electronic easel that could've transmitted each one of the master's strokes in color to every university in the world. He was way ahead of his time. He and Stravinsky had their destinies in their hands. Each time I didn't understand or control mine, I paid the price.

Another model, a true pioneer and personal hero, is John Johnson of Johnson Publications, who built a real empire and remains a guiding light for us all.

In the music business, I admired and learned from the savvy of Clarence Avant, David Geffen, Berry Gordy at Motown, Herb Alpert, Jerry Moss and Gil Friesen at A&M, Chris Blackwell at Island, Gamble and Huff in Philadelphia, Al Bell at Volt and Stax, and Ewart Abner at VeeJay, an early distributor of the Beatles in America. There were other brothers who made it too: from the fifties, a guy named Don Robey, who had Duke and Peacock Records in Texas. Not to mention the infamous Jones Boys, who'd gotten my attention back when I was a child in Chicago when my father worked for them. These were people who took the bull by the horns—they were the original Dudes.

My philosophy as a businessman has always come from the same roots as my personal credo: take talented people on their own terms, and treat them fairly and with respect, no matter who they are or where they come from. Creatively, I am inspired not only by musicians but also by writers like Ralph Ellison, who called me "a fearless explorer of the territory" in a signed copy of his book *Into the Territory*. It was one of the highest compliments I could receive. Refusing to accept limitations imposed from the outside—whether it's from critics or fellow musicians who think you've "sold out"—has been the only way I've been able to live as an artist and as the director of a multimedia company. I was honored to be associated with Sinatra, Ella, Sarah, Ray Charles, *Roots, Thriller,* Oprah, the "We Are the World" crew, because I never acknowledged the lines in the sand that separate races or musical genres or nationalities or demographic groups since I began in the music business as a teenager.

In terms of my business, the influence of rap and hip-hop has gone beyond the world of music. After an eight-minute pitch to Brandon Tartikoff and Warren Littlefield at NBC with Kevin Wendle and Warner Brothers black-music head Benny Medina, I was asked to speak to 500 advertisers the next morning about *The Fresh Prince of Bel Air,* to assure them that a sitcom starring a rapper wasn't risky. After the presentation of the Heritage Award on *Soul Train* on my birthday in 1990, we'd had a meeting at my home in LA, where Will Smith, a rapper with no previous acting experience, was asked to read a few pages of dialogue for about twenty NBC executives. After fifteen minutes' worth, he was hired.

I was attracted to the idea for the show after talking with Benny Medina, whose life formed the core of the story. Jack Elliott, who used to conduct for Jacqueline Francoise when I worked for the Barclays in Paris, had taken parentless Benny out of the ghetto and installed him in an apartment over the garage of his Beverly Hills home, which was shared with his son Alan. Later, along with executive producers Andy and Susan Borowitz, the decision was made to shift the situation so that the hosts were black bourgeois relatives, which makes it even more interesting in terms of the clash of cultures and gives it more juice and fish-out-of-water humor. I had to assure the network's sponsors that rappers weren't dangerous. Imagine Will Smith and Jazzy Jeff being dangerous! Pleeze! Will is one of the smartest and most centered young people I've met. The first day of shooting, Will didn't know where the camera was—but he learned fast, and grew like a weed. Directed by Debbie Allen, the show was scripted, cast, and on the air in a lightning-fast ten weeks. It proved to be a solid hit, running for 150 shows over six years on the air. The success of *Fresh Prince* in the mainstream is further proof that hip-hop has become the rock 'n' roll of our era. L.L. Cool J. was another multitalented rapper we inducted into TV, on our sit-com *In the House*, which ran for three years. He also has a very centered mind and is a consummate pro. His grandma raised him right.

America has come a long way in acknowledging that the vitality of black culture is a true national—and international—asset. And make no mistake about it, America understands everything about the Benjamins. If you achieve the sales, everything else falls into place. Participating in the ownership and control over the means of production, sales, marketing, and distribution is another matter.

These days music is literally global in sweep. The genie's out of the bottle, never to return, with MP3, Napster/Scour, and Freenet and Gnutella rendering all previous lines of demarcation meaningless. There's a revolution in progress, leveling everything in its path. Copyrights, masters, negatives, books, records, and films: it's all the same to a binary number, or a carbon atom and hydrogen qubit. Legislation, global police monitoring by knocking on two million doors—I don't think so. All I know is, you can't afford to make the customers your enemy. They no longer want to purchase a CD with ten or twelve songs on it to get the two they really want. They are also hip enough to know about artists' earnings and no longer want to pay the price for all the people in the middle of the distribution chain. These technological changes have provided an un-expected and highly efficient platform for rebellion for the current gener-ation. We better get together and figure it out—and quickly!

You've gotta dive in with open arms. Snoopy was born for the infor-mation age, and he's had his own company now for almost a decade, QD III Sound Lab, and we're working together to form a joint-venture com-pany for projects that will spin out from music into video and the Internet: you've got to cover all formats. We are also exploring a video collector's series, like an urban version of Time Life or MTV or the Discovery Channel, utilizing a large collection of content that crosses genres and spans fifty years, from bebop to hip-hop.

As far as I'm concerned, retirement is like sitting around waiting to die. Staying in touch with the world is about anticipating change—cultural, spiritual, and technological—and embracing it. You have to feel the need to be needed. I've been lucky enough to roll with the technology all these years: since 1953 the changes have been extraordinary, as I have personally witnessed the playing of the first Fender bass, the first stereo recording, the first audio cassette, the first dime-thin video disc at Philips, the first modular Moog synthesizer with Paul Beaver, and the first DVD. I saw the first video laser disc demo in Einhoven, Holland in 1962, and the first demo of a DVD in Japan with Warren Lieberfarb, who developed it with Toshiba. So far I've seen it all, from 78 rpm discs to DAT.

The young producers and musicians coming up always ask me how I got going in so many different enterprises. Even though my father wanted me to be an architect, for me, everything starts with my first love, the music. Arranging, orchestrating, mastering a core skill, conducting, and selecting musicians and singers, choosing the studio and the engineer, prepared me to be a businessman. I never knew what producing was per se: I just threw myself into everything involved with making the song or the album work. After a while the A&R guy would come in and say, "Take one."

Working with singers like Frank Sinatra and Ray Charles prepared me well—these are rough dudes if they even sniff that you don't know what you're doing. I've always learned by watching and apprenticing myself to the ones that I admire, no matter what the discipline. I saw a lot of people get into trouble when they didn't really pay attention. Your powers of observation are critical. When I first got to New York, it was clear to me from walking the streets that in this country there are two choices: capitalism or poverty. There aren't many gray areas there. During the time I was existing on writing arrangements for Dinah, James Moody, and the Basie band, I looked up and saw that Morris Levy had found a way to split the publishing rights between himself and a partner. Billy Taylor, God bless him, took me under his wing and filled me in on the essentials of the music publishing business and steered me to a print music man named Charlie Hansen. In 1954, I got involved with my own publishing company, Silhouette Music. As co-owners, Charlie and I split everything 50/50.

So then when Morris Levy would say, "What're we gonna do about the publishing on the second Basie album?" I could say, "We're not gonna do anything about it. I have my own publishing company." Morris came back with "Now you're getting smart, kid." So I figured I was on to something. Morris discovered music publishing when ASCAP and BMI wanted to do a performance agreement with him at Birdland: Every time someone played at his club, he had to pay a certain amount of money for the rights to the music being played. That was his education in the business. He said, "Publishing is where it's at. All I want is to own 20,000 copyrights that pay two dollars a quarter from record sales—that's $160,000 a year." It's an incredible business.

At one point I was writing $150 arrangements for Lurlene Hunter with one of my arranging teachers, Marion Evans, for RCA Victor. At dinner after the session the producer, Al Nevins, who played with the Three Suns, said, "Guys, I want to talk to you about an idea. I want to get offices at 1650, down the street from the Brill Building, and get all the young writers no one pays attention to right now—Carole King and Neil Sedaka and Cynthia Weil and Barry Mann and Ellie Greenwich and Jeff Barry. We'll pay them seventy dollars a week and train them to read music and everything else. We'll build a great company like that." Marion and I were so tuned out, we didn't have time even to consider it: we were too busy writing $150 arrangements. Every time Al said, "Do you follow my thinking?" we'd laugh. Unfortunately we didn't follow his thinking, so he went instead to Don Kirshner, and they started a company called Al-don Music at 1650 Broadway. They got all the writers, with the arranger Charlie Albertine supervising them instead of us. Eventually it became Screen Gems Music and is worth a fortune today. We blew it big time because we just didn't get it. You have to learn how to figure it out: you learn from missed opportunities.

And you learn from your mistakes. It took me seven years to get out of the debt that I accumulated during the failed tour of Europe with my big band from *Free and Easy*. It's always a question of survival—you learn because you have to. When I was stranded in Europe, I had to hock the rights to my catalogue with Charlie Hansen to bail out the band, and I had to buy it back later for $105,000, which was more than seven times more than I'd borrowed on it. One of the songs I bought back was "Soul Bossa Nova," which I composed in twenty minutes in 1962. It became the theme to *Austin Powers* thirty-eight years later and has made a fortune. It's like real estate—you must believe in the music first, then you gamble and hold on. It's important to own the copyright or the masters or the negatives. In music it's the copyrights: if you don't own them, you're in the music, not the music business. I'm also still earning significant royalties as the rappers sample a lot of my earlier music: my publishing companies, run by Judith Bright—who could run the Pentagon if she had to—gets about thirty-five requests a week. One of Tupac's biggest hits, "How Do You Want It," is a sample of "Body Heat," from 1974.

Having a career and developing business sense is a cumulative process. When you're doing it, you're messing up. One step after another: winning one, then not getting it right. After a little while, at a certain age, "messing up" changes to getting valuable "experience." The more opportunities you have to win, lose, or draw—that's experience. You don't learn as much just from winning alone, or from playing it safe.

I put in twenty-five, twenty-eight years of my life as an artist before I really thought about business. I wanted to cultivate a core talent, which in my case since the age of thirteen was composing and orchestrating and arranging. In some funny way there's a subconscious connection between your creative side and your business side. To me business is about solving puzzles and juggling components. For that I draw from my background as an arranger, where little solutions can contribute to the whole. Over the past forty years I have also come to depend on the process of my subconscious, which is why I always leave a pad of paper near my bedside. Everything I relate to—even cooking in the kitchen—I refer to in terms of orchestration. As a flavor, for instance, lemon blows everything else away; the equivalent in the symphony orchestra is the piccolo. The book *Jamming* by John Kao of San Francisco explains this concept better than I ever could.

Drawing out each individual's talents is a skill I can relate to orchestration. Ellington's band was like that. He would take the personality of each player and find a special place where each could contribute to the whole of the Duke Ellington sound. Harry Carney didn't play the bottom notes like most baritone saxophone players in other bands. Sometimes he played over the tenor—a very distinctive sound. Then there was Cootie Williams with his plunger trumpet, Ray Nance on trumpet and violin, and Johnny Hodges' slinky and sultry alto sax. The composite sound was hypnotic.

One vision is about recognizing income streams and market changes and emerging trends and tastes. You develop it over time. When we were young, we used to think that making our music commercial was as simple as just dumbing down. There were four of us: Cannonball Adderley, Miles, Herbie Hancock, and me. We didn't think our music lacked that lengthy reach, just because we were playing bebop. We were rebels: we wanted to be real, but we also wanted everyone to love our music. Any artist who says, I'm gonna write and play what I want, and I don't care if anybody likes it, is full of shit. I've had it both ways: nothing, and everything. You have to understand the business and the creative aspects alike, because if some manager comes in and says, you do the music, I'll do the business, they will take your butt out. Ignorance in the name of art is never justified.

With some of what's happened to me, people say, "Oh, Quincy's such a tough businessman." Sometimes I wish I were, but it's not true: I've always needed business managers and lawyers to protect me. The way I do business is totally emotional, which is not how you do it. When I first started my own company, I published sixteen-year-old Marvin Hamlisch's first song, "Sunshine, Lollipops and Rainbows," with Lesley Gore. Years later, after winning a Pulitzer Prize for *A Chorus Line,* Marvin asked for the copyright back, and I gave it to him. After owning Horace Silver's "The Preacher" or "Doodlin'" and other great songs for thirty years, I gave them back to him; the same with "Whisper Not" by Benny Golson. This is not good business, but after all, I'm a composer, and these people are, above all, my friends. You have to walk the talk. Jazz conditioned me not to be a rigid thinker, to have my mind constantly open. You need to improvise on life. So when people say I've turned my back on jazz, that is as far from the truth as you could ever imagine. It shapes how you deal with people, how you love people. It's about freedom, imagination, and being able to shift on a dime. It's a totally nonrigid, democratic perspective on the world. All this shapes me as a businessman, and influences how I deal with other people as well as with myself.

The risks I've taken have always involved stretching, jumping into water just a little bit too deep for me. They've always forced me to grow. Over the course of my career a change has always been as good as a rest. Now I'm stepping into one of the most difficult genres, the Broadway musical. I orchestrated and appeared in the *Free and Easy* tour forty years ago, but this new project involves working on the libretto and original songs with Leslie Bricusse, on the choreography with Savion Glover and the creators of *Stomp,* as well as working with a set designer, a lighting designer, and a costume designer as part of a team led by a brilliant director with a brilliant cast. It's all based on the life and times of my friend Sammy Davis, Jr. There's no place to hide. As Julie Taymor's husband, the composer Elliot Goldenthal, put it: "Quincy, Broadway is a very comfortable place to embarrass yourself."

I'm also working on a multimedia project on the history and evolution of black music. I'd like to dedicate the rest of my life to kids and education. Some of this will be through the work of the Listen Up! Foundation, led by Lisette Derouaux with Shawn Amos as executive director. Our school system doesn't work, and Americans don't understand their own music. Unfortunately, the rest of the world knows it better than we do. If properly focused, rap could single-handedly revolutionize our educational system. For black kids in particular, this knowledge could be crucial for self-esteem. It enables you to hold on to your heritage. All the African-American musicians who've gone into our musical past to see where we come from have become better musicians in the process—Maurice White of Earth, Wind and Fire, Stevie Wonder, Aretha Franklin, Donny Hathaway, Marvin Gaye, Michael Jackson, Herbie Hancock, and Ray Charles, to name a few.

I've been driven all my life by a spirit of adventure and a criminal level of optimism. I believed in my dreams because they were my only option. The people who make it to the top—whether they're musicians or great chefs or corporate honchos—are addicted to their calling. You have to honor the gift God has given you. The people who get the call are the ones who'd be doing whatever it is they love even if they weren't being paid. The junkies love what they do: they revel in it. They exude not only expertise but also joie de vivre. I'll always cherish the memories of celebrating the Bicentennial of the French Revolution in 1989 in Paris with Steve Ross as the court in Delaware simultaneously gave the first of two approvals for the Time Warner merger. Steve had taken a whole floor at the Ritz, and his guests included Alex Haley, Beverly Sills, Michel Legrand, Jerold Kayden from Harvard, my executive vice-president, Louise Velasquez, and Anouk Aimée as well as myself and my brother Lloyd and his wife, Gloria. There were fireworks all over the city and 250,000 students hanging from lampposts in Bastille Square, where I conducted the National Orchestre de Jazz. Ten days later, after the second court decision regarding the merger came down, Steve was on a plane from New York out to my place in LA for a surprise birthday party I threw for Verna Harrah, where he danced his heart out until four in the morning. This was a real soul mate, full of life and vision and fun and generosity. I can say the same about Verna.

What Nadia Boulanger told me about art applies to all of life: the music can never be more or less than the creators are as human beings. She also told me that the more specific and peripheral boundaries you choose for your work the more freedom you have. It goes back to music, as always. The bottom line is that it all starts with the song or the story.

I drew these boundaries for myself early on. Nobody cared if I stayed out all night. I fantasized about someone saying, "Why weren't you home?" Nobody ever did. I remember vividly walking to school as if Lloyd and I were tiptoeing on razor blades: damn, we made it. Now all we had to do was get back home.

What it all comes down to is that being chronically underestimated can be a gift. I'm a blessed survivor, a fact I try to honor and thank God for every day I breathe.

CHAPTER 34

The refund line in heaven

Lloyd Jones

One of the things you realize when you're dying is that you've wasted a lot of time. Everything comes into focus real quick. I was contemplating retirement when they found a cancerous tumor in my kidney. I stopped working right away. I didn't tell a soul at my job about it. Somebody there asked me, "How will you identify yourself after you retire?" Shit. I can identify myself a hundred different ways. I'm a man. An engineer. A carpenter. A husband. A brother. A father. I'm a bicyclist. A skater. A skier. Shit. I'm a lot of things. But one thing I'm not is a quitter.

They found the cancer in my kidney in November 1997 and they wanted to remove it. About a week before the operation, ABC taped a big special in LA honoring Quincy's first fifty years in show business and Quincy asked me to come down. Everybody in the world was there; Oprah, Ray Charles, Stomp, everyone. They sat me and my wife, Gloria, up front and marched Quincy onstage in front of a packed auditorium in Pasadena with millions of viewers watching or however many, and I was sitting there just so . . . I can't think of a time in my life where I went through such a wide range of emotions, knowing I had cancer, knowing I'd beat Hodgkin's disease twenty years before, and yet being so proud of Quincy, because I know how far he's come. More than anybody in the world, I know how far he's traveled.

After the show I went to his house and I wanted to tell him about the cancer, but the phone was ringing and his kids were there, so I said, "I'll wait till tomorrow." The next day he was taking Christmas card pictures with his kids, and I said, "I can't tell him now." So I waited a little longer. Then the phone rang again and somebody else was calling to congratulate him, and then another person called, then somebody came by. This went on all day. Finally, just before leaving to go home, I had to go downstairs and lay it on him.

He was sitting in his bedroom when I told him, and he got that scared look on his face. He said, "When's the operation?" and I told him it was that next Friday, so he came up that Friday and spent the weekend with me in Seattle. He plied me with books on how to beat cancer. He talked to me all night about staying positive and leaving all our shit behind us, especially with Sarah. He said, "That stuff with Sarah will kill you, Lloyd." She's ninety-one now. Quincy and I used to joke that she'd outlive us. It ain't a joke no more.

Sarah just kept living. She never went away. She disappeared to the East Coast for almost twenty years—to Boston, New York—who knows where else, and came back to Seattle around 1966. I'm not sure exactly where she went during those years, because it's hard to know what's real and what's not when she talks to you. She can write letters to congressmen, the President, Rev. Billy Graham, Jesse Jackson, Andy Young, Gregory Peck, the City Council, and they're so well typed and worded, she'll always get a response. The letters can be about anything: prayers in the schools, the stock market, the treatment of chickens in egg-processing plants, whatever's on her mind. She even caught the mayor of Seattle reading a *Play-*

boy and blackmailed him to come to her house and have tea every Saturday at two o'clock. She fought with my stepmother Elvera for years. She never divorced from my father, so she sued Elvera for his social security and got it. She felt she'd been robbed of us, and she never forgave Elvera for that, even though what happened wasn't Elvera's fault at all. It's just life. Life happens.

There's so much we never knew about her, me and Quincy. That's the hard part. Because you love her, but you don't know her, and she doesn't know you. We found out when we were grown that Sarah had another child before we were born. We used to call him "cousin George." Can you imagine after forty-five years finding out that "cousin George" isn't your cousin, but your half brother? Can you imagine what that was like for him? That's the kind of thing we always had to deal with. Always a new surprise. Always something. Never any peace.

When Sarah got back to Seattle in 1966 she found an apartment in a senior citizens housing development in the Queen Anne section. She liked to walk the neighborhood and preach at people. She spent a lot of time with church groups, giving concerts, sponsoring kids. She once typed out the entire New Testament and gave it to Quincy. My wife and I would go by her place two or three times a week, wash her dishes, change her sheets, put Christmas lights up on the holidays, and she'd criticize me and say I should read the Bible. Holidays were always hell. Gloria and I never had the heart or courage to leave her alone on holidays. Quincy sent her money—he always supported Sarah financially—but otherwise, he bailed on it. He'd call me and say, "How's Sarah?" and as soon as I'd start to tell him, he'd get off the line. It was like peeling back his own skin to talk about her. He'd say "Do whatever you think is best, Lloyd," and he'd send money.

But that's all over now.

I haven't even told my mother about my cancer. She's ninety-four. She's slipping. She doesn't recognize me that much anymore. She's had enough pain. Quincy is the only one that knows. Quincy and my wife and son.

After they took my kidney out, the doctors thought they had the cancer all encapsulated and everyone was optimistic. Quincy stayed with me a couple of days and then went back to LA and wanted me to go to Fiji with him for the Christmas holidays, but I said, "Naw. I wanna stay in Seattle with my wife." I retired that following January, and then in February I went back for a checkup and they told me they'd found cancer again and it had metastasized. It got serious then.

Quincy used everything he knew, and every bit of power he had. Based on advice from Dr. Keith Black, he flew me around in a private jet to the best doctors on the planet: Sloan-Kettering in New York, UCLA in LA. They all said the same thing. The cancer had metastasized. It was growing like a weed. He got his friend Dr. Dean Ornish to come up and see me. He even sent Dean Ornish's cook and dietician from San Francisco to my house. His companion Lisette would knock on my door carrying a Puma bag of organic herbs and medicine. He had Tom Laughlin call me and talk with me about his book *Cancer in the Mind*. It was my bible, I put it in a loose-leaf book and stared at each page an hour at a time. Dean Ornish and Tom Laughlin are both into self-healing. It was like a breath of fresh air, dealing with them, but they got to me too late.

I'm not okay with this. I'm not okay at all, but there's nothing anyone can do for me. It's got to come from inside me. Quincy keeps calling people all over the planet, but this ain't one of those things where he can pick up the phone and get the problem fixed. He called the doctor in Seattle last month to ask about me and the guy said, "Which Lloyd Jones? I got four Lloyd Joneses here." Quincy was so mad about it he talked about it for days. That doctor was pitiful, man. Some of them were wonderful. One guy, Dr. Kirtland, he came to my house personally, he really cared. He said I made a difference in his life. But a lot of these doctors, they don't give a damn about you. These doctors had me taking test after test, CAT scans, X rays, body scans, taking my blood, filling me up with pills, prednisone, x, y, and z. I was eating thirty-five pills a day at one point. They told me at the hospital, "You can stay here if you want." I said, "The hell with that. Give me some pain medication and send me home."

So I sit here on my back-porch deck now and I listen to these positive-thinking tapes and read Dr. Andrew Weil's books and magazine articles that Quincy and Jolie send me, and I watch the sunset and talk with my wife. I tell myself, "I am well. I am a strong, thinking positive person and wellness is within me," and every night I try to sleep. Nights are the hardest.

Quincy comes up from LA sometimes and sits on my deck with me and massages my shoulders until I fall asleep. One night he sat next to my bed and held my hand and chanted with me till I fell asleep. He has Maria, his cook, up here from LA cooking for me because I'm losing weight and have no appetite. He sits here and analyzes my spit. I'm monitoring my lungs, and if I don't spit a lot of green stuff in my phlegm and it's clear, it means the infections are clearing up. He dozes in a chair and when I spit he stirs awake and says, "How was that last one?" We laugh about it, the absurdity of two grown men staring at a dirty Kleenex on a back porch in the Mount Baker section of Seattle, analyzing my spit to see what color it is. But we've been in worse places. It's the greatest thing in the world to have him here. All the doctors he called, all the people he pulled in to help, I'm so grateful, but having him here with me means more than anything in the world. He's always loved me for me, and I've always loved him for him.

He was with me for a few weeks like that, popping in for a day or two to hang, then going back to LA to work, but finally he bailed two days ago. He went to Europe.

I understand it. It's his way of coping. He knows what's happening to me and he can't handle it. He's always been that way. His circuitry can only handle so much. He calls me every day from Europe, and it's gotten so I worry about him now. It's funny. When we were growing up, I was the snot-nosed kid dragging behind him, but as the years passed it was me who was the anchor and he was the one who flew the world. We went in different directions. I got married. I got a beautiful wife. A beautiful son. I live in a simple house. I worked at the same place for twenty-five years. But if I hadn't seen him get out and do what he's done, I would've never done shit with myself.

He called me the other day from one of his hiding places in Europe and he sounded so bad, I said, "What can I do for you, Quincy?"

He said, "The only thing you can do for me is to get well."

I promised him, and I promised my wife and son, that I would try my best, and I'm trying my best. My wife was so strong for me, hiding her tears.

I have a blanket that I wrap around me when I hunker down, and a teddy bear, which is something I never had as a kid, and I don't answer the phone unless it's Quincy. I know it's hurting a lot of people who want to see me, but I've already got enough shit around here to remind me that I'm sick: the coughing, the weakness, the medicine, the pain. The last thing I need is people coming into my house all sad-eyed and talking to me about hospices with tears in their eyes. They're dealing with their own mortality and their guilt through me. Fuck that. Tell me a dirty joke. I promised my wife I would try. I owe it to her and to myself to try. That's all I live for.

Every sunset seems magical to me now. Every tiny bit of air I breathe is just so exquisite. The smell of my wife's hair brings tears to my eyes. I sit in this wonderful deck chair and eat brownies made with pot so I can get my appetite back. They tried to bring a hospital bed in my house and I ran them outta here. I told them, "Take that shit back. I'm out here on my deck getting deep with a squirrel." I watch this squirrel in my back-yard. This little sucker, he sits in a tree that blocks my view of Washington Lake—a tree which I've tried to kill about a million times by hammering copper nails into it—and he gnaws at nuts and stares at me. And I stare at him. Sometimes I swear the sucker and I are having a conversation. Sometimes I look at the sky and watch the clouds move. I looked up there the other day and saw a cloud in the shape of Snoopy the cartoon character. When Quincy called that day, he asked me what I was doing and I said, "I'm eating herb brownies and I saw Snoopy in the clouds."

He laughed his ass off. He said, "You feeling better?"

I told him I was doing the best I could under the circumstances.

We talked for a while and he said, "Lloyd, I'm sorry I can't get up there until Friday. I feel guilty about it."

I got mad with him. I said, "I don't ever want you to feel guilt about me, with everything you've done for me. Never. If I hadn't seen you do what you did, I would've never done anything with myself. Look where I've been. When you conducted the Academy Awards, remember I sat in the orchestra pit right next to Shelly Manne and Larry Bunker? Remember when we met Jacques Chirac, the President of France, when he was mayor of Paris? Remember when Lena Horne threw me and Sarah out of her dressing room after Sarah told Lena she was wearing too much makeup and that her dress was too tight? And the time Dinah Washington cooked me chitterlings, and we partied at the Bicentennial on the Champs-Elysées with Alex Haley and Courtney and Steve Ross? Remember Mardi Gras, when I rode on the float with you when you were Grand Master? A million people would give an eyetooth to do what I've done. None of that would've happened if it weren't for you. You're not to have any guilt—none—'cause I'm gonna be in the refund line when I get to heaven, Quincy. I've still got change coming to me, and if you don't fuck up too much, you might get a little change back too. Are you listening?"

He said he was. I hope he was. I hope he listened to me.

Lloyd Jones died on July 13, 1998.

CHAPTER 35

Acceptance

They gave Lloyd six weeks. He beat it back for six months. Then he died. He just died.

That's it. A man lives his life. Comes from nothing. Makes something of himself. For twenty-five years, he was a pioneer black electrical engineer at KOMO-TV, an ABC affiliate, one of the top three stations in the city of Seattle. He had no one to help him when he started in life. He was happily married to a beautiful woman for thirty-three years. He raised a good son. Lived a straight life. Ten years earlier he had overcome Hodgkin's disease, as his son Marlon had overcome his sickle-cell anemia trait. He was only sixty-two and looked forty. He had not one soul who hated him in this life. Everyone who knew him loved and respected him. And he still died.

I couldn't take it. I knew he was slipping away; that's why I rushed to Europe with my precious companion Lisette to stay with my friends Rod and Kathy Temperton at their apartment in the South of France. I had no reason whatsoever to go except to get away. Lloyd was on my mind every minute, and I knew he would be leaving me, very soon. I dreamed about him. He was with me every single second. When I got the call at a restaurant in the French countryside at 10:35 P.M. on July 13, 1998, to tell me my brother was gone, I knew it before it happened. Even so I'd been praying this call would never come. The devastation was paralyzing: it was all unreal.

I rushed back from Cannes to bury him. It was the hardest thing I have ever done. A discreet funeral was planned at Freddie Mae's funeral parlor. Freddie Mae Gautier has always been a part of our family, and she moved my mother from her apartment into a beautiful nursing home. Jolie wanted me to make a speech. I thank God for my daughter Jolie: Born when I barely had two nickels to rub together, she's always been there when things got rough for me. In truth as a young girl she was probably the wildest of all my children, a fact I can easily forget when I witness her prudence and maternal devotion to her sons Sunny and Donovan. Our relationship has always been very special to me because she is my firstborn: her Libra nature is a good balance to my excessive tendencies. Through all our family crises, she has always been the one with the stabilizing influence, even when her siblings weren't mature enough to appreciate that fact. Now she graciously stepped in and made all the arrangements for her uncle's funeral. I went down into Lloyd's basement office to try to collect my thoughts and write my speech on his computer.

In Lloyd's basement that hot July day, my brain was spinning: I felt like I was literally losing my mind. I'd lost a lot of people by that time: Alex Haley, Sassy, Ella, Hal Ashby, Frank Sinatra, Steve Ross, Miles Davis, Dizzy Gillespie, Sammy Davis, Henry Mancini. The list is endless. Miles's nephew Vernon called me at 4 A.M. the day of his funeral in New York and said, "We're not doing so good. We could use some help." Herbie Hancock and I did our best. So did Max Roach, Bill Cosby, and Jeff Wald at the service. All Miles's ladies came to say goodbye, including Frances, Josie, and Cecily Tyson. In December 1992, when Steve Ross died, everyone from Time Warner was there. It was raining and freezing. The funeral was at the beautiful Guild Hall in Easthampton that Steve loved, but no one knew whether to cry or laugh. I tried to speak but there was too much to say about this man; my mouth would not respond. Barbra Streisand sang "Papa, Can You Hear Me?" to his casket. In 1993 the producer George Duke and I did our best to keep Sarah Vaughan alive by planning a Brazilian LP; it was her favorite kind of music. She wanted to sing Ivan Lins's "Dinorah." George and I played songs on cassette while she lay in a hospital bed at Cedars dying of cancer. Sarah's old friend June Eckstine, as well as her daughter Paris and her mother Ida, watched helplessly. She called me as she left the hospital to go home to the end and told me, "Don't worry, I won't disappoint you. I can sing lying down." She never finished. We buried the lead sheets and cassettes with her at the request of her mother and daughter. It is important to me that her last recording was "Setembro" from *Back on the Block,* which she'd always wanted to sing with Chaka Khan.

Marvin Gaye's funeral ran for hours. It was a free-for-all jam with no plan whatsoever. Someone would get up to the podium and talk for half an hour; then nothin' would happen, then somebody else would get up and ramble on for another twenty minutes. It was a mess. And Frank Sinatra, God bless him. We spent afternoons at the Sinatra house with him and his family almost till the end, sitting by his bed as Alzheimer's took its toll. One day he impatiently demanded coffee with cream and sugar. When the nurse came in with the coffee on a tray, he took one look at it and said, "What are you bringing me that for? You know coffee makes me nervous." She backed out of the room. After she left he looked at me and said softly, "Q, I'm a pain in the ass, right?" I laughed and said, "Right. Yes—you are. You always have been, but I still love you, you blue-eyed muthatrucka." He and Barbara laughed.

But Lloyd was different—Lloyd was beyond my reality. He was my heart and soul. I sat in his basement and looked around. He'd shown me three tall file cabinets filled with everything I've ever done. My first recording, my first scores, my high school yearbook, my first clippings, my junior high graduation pictures, notes, paperwork, videotapes, old 78s, and a huge, 800-page computer printout with every recording session I've ever done, many of which I'd forgotten about, many of which I'm not even mentioned in. He'd collected everything I've ever done and never had time to collect, everything that a normal mother would've held on to; things that no secretary in the world would know how to collect—things that only a brother would know about; things that only a brother would want. It was his big brother's shrine, which was hard to deal with. I couldn't stop thinking about his own dreams, how he passionately longed to see the finished version of our friend Dennis Washington's new boat, the *Attessa*, which we'd visited months before in Vancouver when construction had just begun.

Sitting there in his basement, I gazed at all of the things that Lloyd had collected for me over fifty years, all amassed and filed with the greatest care, and it filled my heart with so much pain I felt like I was drowning. He was so unselfish. I couldn't run from this pain. He had always been there for me. He had never changed. The gifts I lavished on him, he never asked for. He never deserted me on my down days, or tripped out on my celebrity shit. He loved me for *me*, with a deep, quiet love that only a brother can have. As a birthday present he redid my entire address book: 5,000 names, organized and neatly categorized by name, instrument, date of birth, names of children, occupation, something my staff of twenty-five people couldn't manage. He included a short note: "I hope this makes your life a little easier. Happy Birthday! Love, Lloyd."

I fired him from his job as our mother's caretaker—it was too much at that point. Our friend, Dr. Dean Ornish, told him that that's how he'd gotten sick in the first place—taking it all in the chest, my mother and Elvera. "Send me her checkbooks," I told Lloyd. "You're fired." He never did tell her he was sick, and when she was eventually told of his death by his wife, Gloria, along with Jolie and me, she was too far gone to know or to deal with it. Or maybe she did know, because she had a stroke and slipped into death peacefully at age ninety-five, six months after Lloyd passed.

All he ever wanted was for her to nurture and validate him, to feel proud of him. That's all he ever wanted. That's all that any child wants. It's something he never got. There's no feeling like that desire to hear your mother say—just once—"Well done, son, I love you." That feeling never leaves you, even when you're grown. He would have given anything in the world to hear that.

Yet you learn to accept the past, and to forgive things and people in it. Deep inside, Lloyd and I both knew that Sarah was having a rougher ride than all of us put together. Just weeks before she died, Sarah made a phone call to my daughter Kidada. Of all my children, Kidada is the most like my mother: smart, talented, witty, outspoken, with a tongue that can strike with the impact of a poison dart. Underneath it all she is as sweet and sensitive as can be. She lived with me for fourteen years; I know her better than anyone else in the world. All her life, I've had to claw through all that Sarah in her to get to my little girl.

Sarah told Kidada she had something to send to her. Kidada asked what it was.

Sarah told her it was $40,000. It was what she had left of all the money I'd given her over the past few years; money I'd sent for housing, food, clothing, whatever Lloyd and Gloria said she'd needed it for. She told Kidada she wanted her to have it. Every dime of it. Kidada told her she didn't want it. Sarah said, *Give it to your father, then. Because he has all these kids and he's paying everyone all his money. And I want him to have something for himself, because all these years he's been sending me all this money. I never wanted his money.*

It was the closest she could come to saying how she loved me. And you know what? So be it. That's good enough for me. For her sake and my own, I only wish I had known then what I know now.

CHAPTER 36

Immortality

Rashida Jones, recording artist, actress

He's sixty-eight years old and he still thinks he's fifteen. He took a heart test at UCLA and the doctor told him he had the heart of a twenty-two-year-old. That's how he's been acting all along, but that's all he needed to hear. He's such a complex-minded person and he digests so much information, I can't understand how he accesses and processes so much in his brain. He can tell you the exact names of all the musicians he recorded with in 1960, for example, down to the alto sax player—he'll even tell you who was married to whom at the time. He has boundless optimism. He's always talking about a future full of flying cars that don't pollute and fiber optics and coaxial cables and laser beams that will cure cancer. He looks forward. He has the trust and enthusiasm and purity of a young man, even though he has every reason not to be any of these things. Thank God he won't grow up.

We like to talk about music now more than anything. We talk about everything else—there was never a point in my life where I couldn't access him—but these days it's music because of where I'm at. I didn't want to become a musician. It just happened. When I was five, I had this nightly ritual. We had a big bathroom in our house with a vanity sink, a tub, and a rug, and he would put headphones on and sit in the bathroom and write music on big score paper all night. There was no piano in there, just him and some headphones and a blank page, and he'd write on the floor, just scribble across the page like you and I write a letter. I'd sneak out of bed and curl up on the floor and watch him write till I fell asleep. Then he'd pick me up and carry me to my bed and lay me down and say, "I love you, Doonkie," and kiss me and caress my hair and watch me sleep.

I think my love of music is an outgrowth of my love for him, because I didn't consciously want to become a musician. I grew up wanting to be the first female, Jewish, black President of the United States. I was the good girl—the youngest. I was an easy childbirth for my mom. They used the LeBoyer method where the baby comes out and is placed on the mother's stomach while the umbilical cord is cut and then the father bathes the child. I was a very calm baby. I was ambidextrous and learned reading quickly. I advanced a grade and was really into schoolwork. My sister Kidada had dyslexia and required a lot of my parents' attention. She was more vocal and took up more space. My parents were very loving with me but had no need to worry about me. I was very independent and undemanding, and they let me be. Music and performing were always my ways of keeping myself company.

I started taking piano lessons when I was five, and I would play two-part Bach inventions before I knew how to read music. I'd hear my teacher play it and I'd play it myself from memory. I have a photographic memory like my dad, but in some ways it's a disability. Because I have a strong ear and pick up all things musical quickly, I never learned to sight-read well. My father has always taught me, though, that a strong ear is not enough; you've got to get a command of the theory. I'm still working on that.

I was in almost every performance at school. Dad was supportive and often came to my concerts and musicals, and plays. He never pushed me. If I had wanted to be a truck driver, he would have said, "I love you no matter what, baby, but did you ever consider business school?" All he wants for me is my happiness and security. Still, he unconditionally supports and loves me through whatever I choose to do. I would watch him beam while telling a friend about my performance in the school play. He's just a proud daddy.

When it was time for me to visit colleges, he dropped everything and took me to every single school, me, him, and a friend named Jerold Kayden, a Harvard professor. We went to Brown, Yale, Columbia, Barnard, Wesleyan, Princeton, Stanford, and Harvard. Daddy was completely into it, asking questions, talking to the professors, checking out the dorms. When I saw him eating in the college cafeterias, I knew he was serious, because he hates shitty food. He'll starve rather than eat shitty food. He'll spend fifteen minutes chopping up chicken Marbella, and he'll serve it to himself in very small pieces, and he'll spend another fifteen minutes choosing the right wine that gives the Marbella the proper taste. But there he was in the cafeteria gobbling hamburgers and nasty, muddy gravy with mashed potatoes, saying, "Oh, Harvard is the bomb, baby. What do you think?" I went to Harvard.

When I graduated from college in '97, he called me and said, "Would it bother you if I got an honorary degree the day you graduated?" I told him don't be silly. They gave it to him and he gave the commencement speech, but the fact is, he left his honorary degree someplace later that day and somebody had to go back and get it for him. I was his first child to graduate from college. He brought the whole family out, all my sisters and my brother, my mom, his brothers Lloyd and Richard, and Nastassja Kinski, the mother of my little sister Kenya, who was five then. Kenya's getting the best part of him now. Every drop. He spends a lot of time with her because he now knows what she needs from her father. He has so much love in his heart but with his other kids he didn't quite get the application. He always said love for him was a roof over his head and food in his mouth. And that's all he knew. He was always so busy expanding his boundaries that he just couldn't be as available to us. But it's a great testament to him and to the ex-wives that he has seven kids and we're not all fucked up. We all work. We have jobs. We live. We all love each other. We're normal people who have lived atypical lives.

When we flew back to California after I graduated, Dad and I talked about orchestration. That's what he loves to talk about more than anything else. He talks about the quality of intervals. For example, octaves, fifths, and fourths are masculine; thirds, sixths, and tritones are feminine. We analyze Aaron Copland's *Billy the Kid*, and talk about his musicalization of Americana, or what instrumentation depicts a rugged man traveling out West. Suspensions, resolutions, voice leading, transpositions, everything. One time we re-arranged part of Aretha Franklin's "Somewhere" from *West Side Story*, which is one of his favorite productions. We did it as an exercise for an audition I had. We went through several keys and piano arrangements, changing the voicings.

He pulled out a piece of paper and showed me another way of voicing the strings using cluster chords. He said, "See, we can do it this way, with big, open chords in contrary motion, leading into the part where she sings, 'We'll find a new way of living.'" He gave it to me to look at, and I transposed it as practice. After fifty years, he is still transfixed by music. For me music is continuous and constantly changing, and it's a fundamental connection I have with my father.

The next day he came to me with a different voicing; he was in his element, scribbling out notes on score paper. He said, "I came up with another one while I was asleep," and he sketched out a different voicing. "Nadia Boulanger once told me and Bobby Tucker that there is no right way with music," he said. "Nothing is ever wrong if it's going someplace. Music is about ever-changing." This is what I love so much about him: his thirst for more, his ability to see one thing from every side, and his unrelenting passion.

I watched him as he was writing and I thought to myself, "That's him. That's the essence of him. That's his immortality."

CHAPTER 37

Epilogue: getting the call

Life is like a dream, the Spanish poet and philosopher Federico Garcia
Lorca said. Mine's been in Technicolor, with full Dolby sound through
THX amplification before they knew what these systems were. Even as a
small boy I could never afford the luxury of being carefree: I worried about
why my mother had gone, and how Lloyd and I would get by in Elvera's
house, and whether or not Daddy would still be there when we woke up
each morning. I hustled because I had to, but also because I'd seen the
lights, the ones in the jook joints Daddy had declared off-limits, places full
of loving women and sounds that rocked the floorboards, with lowdown
music, and smoky red and blue lights. Music was the touchstone because it
instilled in me a belief in myself, which is the rarest of gifts, like a hard and
brilliant diamond held in the deepest recesses of the heart. When I saw the
California blues combos of six or eight pieces that came to Seattle, or the
eighteen-piece black big bands, I saw a group of men acting as a family: I
heard innovations creeping through even in the most danceable commercial sounds. I experienced Toscanini for the first time at age fifteen at the

Seattle Civic Center and saw the potential for the divine focus and collective action that forms a symphony. Most exciting of all were Norman Granz's "Jazz at the Philharmonic" concerts, which were as thrilling to us as the music of the Stones or the Beatles to a later generation.

This was music that stoked my belief that I could shape my world; that I could find a place in which to grow up.

In a way the rest of my life has been about trying to honor my gift, and the gifts of the many extraordinary people I've encountered along the way. Some part of me will always be that raggedy-ass little kid getting Clark Terry and Ray Charles out of bed at six in the morning to give me trumpet and arranging lessons. Some part of me will always wonder if I've done enough to make myself ready to get the call. They say there are no second acts in American lives: well, I've had nine or ten. As my friend of fifty years, Marlon Brando, put it to me in a note in the summer of 1992: "For Q: We had tears, pain, love, and laughter. Not enough, but at least we've still got time to rock a while. You taught me much, and dammit, man, I love you. Whatever happens, we'll always have memories enough for the rest of the season. Leroy" [Marlon's nickname].

The call came from Joseph Powe and Charlie Taylor and Bumps Blackwell in Seattle and from Larry Berk and Bob Share at the Berklee School of Music in Boston. It came from my sweet Aunt Mabel, offering a welcome in Chicago as I made my way east to a new life. It came from Oscar Pettiford and Lionel Hampton and James Moody and Dinah Washington and Dizzy Gillespie, trusting me at age twenty-three to put together a touring band for our State Department. It came from John Hammond and Irving Green and Roy Furman and Clarence Avant and Jackie Avant, offering friendship, a helping hand, a job and a start as a businessman when I needed both the money and insight into the world of the marketplace. It came from Count Basie and Frank Sinatra on "Fly Me to the Moon." It came from Pete Long and Julian Bond and Jesse Jackson, who helped me expand my social consciousness and showed me the ways to give back to where you came from. It came from Mo and Evelyn Ostin and from Steve and Courtney Ross and Bob Pittman and later from Richard Parsons when I was ready to unite my creative enterprise with world-class marketing, distribution, and entrepreneurial energy. It came from so many people offering entrée to new worlds: Arne Sucksdorf, Sidney Lumet, Benny Carter, Henry Mancini, Richard Brooks, and Steven Spielberg, walking me into the wonder world of film; Oscar Pettiford, Dizzy Gillespie, and Nadia Boulanger in areas of music I never knew existed; Colin Powell when I needed help in showing young people that if you can see it, you can be it. I'll never forget being with him and his wife Alma at their home on the last day of his tenure as head of the Joint Chiefs of Staff, and seeing a tear on his cheek as he recited from memory poetry written by black nurses who cared for and were in love with the terminally wounded black vets during the Vietnam War. It came from Bono and Take Six and Savion Glover and from the cast of *Stomp,* to say "We'll be there for you"—and they always were. So were Will Smith and his guru James Lassiter.

It came from Hillary Clinton when it was time to plan the White House celebration to greet the new millennium. I'd executive-produced the 1993 inauguration, "An American Reunion," and the Clintons and the Gores have always been real friends. President Clinton even came through for me in 1997, with an on-screen introduction for the ill-fated late-night *Vibe* TV, and later offering me a lift on Air Force One to the World Economic Forum in Davos, Switzerland. Being selected to help lead America into the new century at the 2000 D.C. celebration, along with Steven Spielberg and George Stevens, was a serious honor. I cherished the opportunity and I'll remember it for as long as I live—a party for 500,000 people, plus millions of others around the world via CBS and the Discovery Channel. The next day, after following Will Smith and Jada Pinkett as guests in the Lincoln bedroom, the reality of being in this place on the first day of the new millennium hit me when I saw a handwritten document framed in bronze on a big table. It contained four pages under glass, inscribed with a quill pen: it was the Gettysburg Address. I couldn't help but wonder what Lincoln was really thinking and feeling as he scrawled these immortal words by candlelight.

To greet the new millennium, we wanted to let the ideas flow, free of Y2K fears. I wanted to imagine a future that is multiracial and multigenerational and full of champagne and fireworks for everyone. There's nothing I like better than an extravaganza, whether it's a production of the Academy Awards, in a recording studio with dozens of divas and superstars, or at my house for a family holiday dinner or a special birthday party. I also have a soft spot in my heart for a candlelit dinner with wine for two beside an open fire.

Last year I received the Crystal Award from Klaus Schwab at the World Economic Forum in Switzerland, the Lena Horne Award from Bill Cosby, and the National Humanities Medal from President Clinton, and I was promoted to Commander of the French Legion of Honor by Jacques Chirac. When I go out I want to go in style, the way I tried to live. I want all my friends to have a great dinner party produced by Jerry Inzerillo and Victor Drai, with food by Nobu and Leah Chase and Wolfgang Puck and Freddy Giradet, with the finest of wines and my favorite music. Maybe they'll play Aretha Franklin's version of "Somewhere," or "How Do You Keep the Music Playing," with James Ingram and Patti Austin, or "Setembro" or "Kind of Blue" by Miles and Cannonball and Coltrane, or anything by Take Six or Sinatra or my oldest friend, Ray Charles, or by my mate Rod Temperton. And yeah, what about a rap from my homie and favorite o.g., Melle Mel? I'll write the testimonials in advance and seal them in a vault. I have so many people to thank—like at the Oscars—that the party could go on for days, like an old-fashioned New Orleans-style "let the good times roll" service.

But I'm not ready yet because there's far too much to do. I'm sixty-eight and I'm writing my first musical, with Leslie Bricusse, about the life and times of my childhood friend Sammy Davis, Jr. I want to write and compose a show based on the evolution of black music with Franco Dragone and Guy LaLiberté and the Cirque du Soleil. I want to make films about the life of the poet Alexander Pushkin, who was of Ethiopian descent, and of Ralph Ellison's last book, *Juneteenth*, with Morgan Freeman. There are meetings to go to: about realizing my dreams; about continuing to support Bono in putting pressures on the G8 countries regarding Third World debt relief—we even went to see the Pope together with Bob Geldof at the summer Vatican at Castel Gondolfo to enlist his aid in our cause, and as of 1999 almost $80 billion has been forgiven by the World Bank and the IMF; about providing for kids who need hope and a chance in a world where 1.3 billion people have to decide whether to put that $1.50 a day toward food, education, or health; about being on the board of NET Aid working with Cisco Systems and the United Nations on the war against HIV and AIDS in Africa; and about the Listen Up! Foundation, reaching from South Central to South Africa, where we're working with Habitat for Humanity to build much-needed new housing and standing ready to support John Chambers' high-tech training academy, along with Canadian Minister of Industry Brian Toblin, as we attempt to create a potential Silicon Valley in Africa. So many people have extended the hand of friendship, of shared creativity, of pure and unadulterated love to me in the course of my life: thank God and these generous souls for making it feel so natural to give back unconditionally.

The best and only useful aspect of fame and celebrity is having a platform to help others. In April 2000, Gerry Levin of AOL-Time Warner invited me and my son to Harvard as guests of Professor Henry "Skip" Gates, where Gerry announced the endowment of the Quincy Jones Professorship of African-American Music. It's the first time that an American corporation has endowed a chair in African-American studies—and it's the first chair expressly dedicated to the study of African-American music.

It is time for me to pay my respects to the ones who've led the way—not just Armstrong and Ray Charles and the Duke and the Count, but to Buddy Catlett and Grady Tate and Bobby Tucker and Clark Terry and

Ray Brown and Milt Jackson, and to Miles and Frank and Hamp, the ones who taught me how to groove and how to laugh and how to hang and how to live like a man. I have been privileged to work with so many of the "A Team." Jerome Richardson—whom I loved and worked with since the age of thirteen—died in the summer of the first year of the new century, as this book was nearing completion. I am honored that his "witness" account is part of this narrative.

None of this would have been possible without the countless contributions of my brother Lloyd, whose chapters in this book enable me to have him with me forever. I treasure my continuing relationship with his wife, Gloria, and son, Marlon. And it is time for me to say that not a day of my life goes by that I don't miss Daddy and Lloyd and Waymond—who passed earlier this year. I understand at this stage that my mother, Sarah, did all she knew how to do before she died in early 1999. My strength was her gift. I've been told that maybe vitamin B could have spared her the pain: in today's world, she could have really been something. All she ever wanted was her kids, and we never knew how to be children for her. Likewise it is time for me to extend the hand of forgiveness in memory of my stepmother, Elvera, who died shortly after my mother.

It takes a large life to be blessed with such a long list. My gratitude to so many would fill a valley so deep and wide, I can't begin to measure it. So I won't try. I am blessed to be working with a Garfield high school buddy and friend of fifty years, Jerry Allison, on the building of my dream house. Some night when it's finished and the sky is calm and full, I'll sit down at my piano surrounded by my kids and family and let God's whispers guide my soul and fingers, as I've always done. Searching for just the right notes and seeking the right love have been my lifelong quests. I am especially grateful to have been blessed with a most warm and loving relationship with Lisette Derouaux, her mother, Odette, her father, Laurent, and their wonderful family: "*un petit peu pour les enfants.*"

It is time to say how much I deeply love and cherish all my children—my sweet Jolie, Rachel, Tina, Snoopy, Rashida, Kidada, and Kenya, and my grandchildren Donovan, Sunny D., Eric, and Jessica— with more pride and joy than I'll ever be able to express. The only deep regret I have in the entirety of my life is that I didn't know sooner how much I didn't understand about their needs and how to nurture them. They are the best teachers any father could ever dream of having, especially since they are all finding inner peace.

All my children have outrageous senses of humor, huge warm hearts, humungous appetites for food and for life, and diversified and special talents. First baby lady love, Jolie "Smolie," is successfully pursuing her dream as a great singer, and her animated children's project, *Twinklefoot*, will no doubt be as successful as "Take It Back," her recycling project sponsored by MTV and supported by Senator Joseph Lieberman. Rachel works so hard at following her bliss: a Tuskegee graduate, she's now a master veterinarian. She found a wonderful husband, Tony Jones, who's not only a great human being—he didn't even have to change his last name. Snoopy and I look forward to working with Tina in extending her career onto the Internet. Nobody loves, nurtures, and relates to kids like Tina-Bina. I call her "Ms. Midget Magnet.com." Snoopy has grown beyond my wildest dreams: finally after all these years, with our minds, souls, and goals aligned, we think and even walk alike. It is a joy to have bonded with this highly principled and self-motivated person whom I would respect even if he weren't my son. I am comforted by my beloved daughter-in-law Koa's presence in his life and pleased that she is helping him match my tummy "temple of happiness." I'd like to be like Snoopy when I grow up.

Kidada I know better than anyone in the world: she is one of my favorite and most memorable housemates. Her nickname, "Pie," came from the way I used to wedge her into the sand in Hawaii when she was four years old. As the "Odd Couple," our roles switched every week. I appreciate her innate ability to see around the corner creatively: she keeps me on it. As hard as she works on her tough "hootchie" image, I've always been able to see through to the tender, generous, vulnerable, lovable core. Rashida, "Doonkie," who from birth always knew how to follow her bliss, is thriving as an actress after flying through Harvard, and could grow and prosper as a singer, a record producer, or anything she wants to be. I cherish the memories of our three-in-the-morning phone calls, trading musical riffs across the wires. I also cherish the way our "Piscean" souls connect. When Kenya, "Popsicle," was born, her horoscope said that she'd be someone who would change the world for the better: she's already got a good start. At age eight she's been halfway around the world twice. Her first spoken words shocked me to my socks. Her first written words best describe her presence and her essence: "Kenya sees the sun."

All my kids have helped me grow as a person and a poppa. If I've managed to earn a place in their hearts, I'll have a free ride into the future.

It is time to say that I wish the best for Jeri, Carol, Ulla, Peggy, and Nastassja, the mothers of my precious children. I tried never to mess with married women. The women that I loved, I loved completely and without reservation as to time, place, color, or circumstance.

It is time to thank and to express my heartfelt pride for my family who survived the 410 22nd Avenue holocaust with me. They had every excuse to have blown it, but they took the high road instead: Richard, a Superior Court judge; Catherine, a member of the Bremerton A-team; Margie, who was with Alaskan Airlines for twenty years, her husband Chris, a stockbroker and the unofficial ambassador to Alaska, and their wonderful family; Theresa, my sweet Willie Lee—you've lived enough life for twenty people, and have always been a rock in times of crisis; and precious Janet, who makes me wish I lived closer to Portland—I've always been uplifted by your sense of humor. And a prayer and special thank you to Freddie Mae Gautier, always a cherished member of the clan.

It is time to say that one of the greatest thrills of my life is having shared the planet and the friendship of Graca and Nelson Mandela, Adelaide and Dali Tambo, Caiphus and Letta Semenya, Lindewe Mbuza, and Archbishop Desmond Tutu. Being part of the American delegation at Mandela's inauguration in South Africa was an unparalleled experience.

It is time to say that I always tried my best never to dissappoint those who placed their trust in me. Inevitably there will be hardship: that goes with the territory. But you don't have to let suffering define your experience of life, and you don't have to pass it along to others just because it hurts. You learn and grow from it—you teach your pain to sing. You let the light wash out the darkness.

It is time to say that despite all the Grammys and the special awards and testimonials that maturity bestows, it will always be the values you carry within yourself—of work, love, and integrity—that carry the greatest worth, because these are what get you through with your dreams intact, your heart held firm, and your spirit ready for another day. Then when you get the call you can't anticipate but which will always come, you can look back and say, I lived it 360 degrees, like my predecessors who cared and led me here, teaching me to approach creativity with humility and respond to success with grace. They had style and dignity and pride. They lived and loved as fiercely as they played: that's all I ever wanted. That's all I ever dreamed.

Acknowledgments

Writing this book has forced me to look back in a way I never have or could before, and that hasn't been so easy, especially for a master of diversion. In a strange way it's like looking back at someone else's life. No matter who you are, you leave your tracks: these are some of mine. So many people have stood me on their shoulders that it's hard to know where to begin. In a way this entire book is one big act of loving gratitude. Most importantly I have to thank the Creator, who uses us as instruments of His divine grace, and who blessed me with some talent, universally broad taste in wine, women, and song, a lot of imagination, a sense of humor, some common sense and out-of-control vision, and a huge capacity to feel and be interested in almost everything. The Lord has truly watched over me, putting me in the right place at crucial points in my life. As we worked on the book, one of my co-writers, Pat, compared me to a bebop version of "Forrest Gump," bumping into Ray Charles and Billie Holiday as a kid, having the last Christmas dinner of the century with the First Family at the home of Vernon and Anne Jordan, waking up in the Lincoln bedroom of the White House on the first day of the new millennium. So I accept the title of "Ghetto Gump."

My first set of thanks has to be to those who helped make this book a symphony of voices with their "witness" chapters: my childhood friend Lucy Jackson; my beloved brothers, Lloyd and Richard; my best friend Clarence Avant; fellow musicians, teachers, and unconditional friends Clark Terry, Ray Charles, Jerome Richardson, Bobby Tucker, Buddy Catlett, and Melle Mel; my ex-wives Jeri Caldwell-Jones and Peggy Lipton; my children Quincy Jones III, Kidada, and Rashida. Each of these chapters could have been a separate book on its own. All my children—Jolie, Rachel, Tina, Snoopy, Rashida, Kidada, and Kenya—are the most precious people on the planet. And as I've said on many occasions, without their love, patience, and tolerance I wouldn't be where I am today as an artist or a human being.

I'd also like to extend my love to all the family, whose warmth and support has been so crucial over the years: Mabel Dulaney, Charlotte Crawford, Margie and Chris, Hope Lauren, Pohaku, and Chris Jay, Jr., Leslie Jones, Karen and Eldridge Reccasner, Chelon Jones, Dana and Steve Looney, Theresa and Robin Frank, Billy and Dolores, Michael and Phillip and Linda Beckham and Phillip Beckham, Jr., Catherine Council and Mike and Renee and Steve and Joe and James and Teresa Anne, Janet and Nicole and Ardiena Christmas, Darice Griffin and her children, Martin and Aislynn, Bea and Earl Smith and Earl Jr., Jackie, Mary Agnes, Estalita, James, Cathy, and Donald, Audrey Miller and Lori and Maureen and Stephanie, Tracie and Helmut and Marc Mayer, Freddie Mae Gautier, Koa and Tony Jones, and my new half-brother, cousin George Ferris, as well as all my godchildren: Marlon Jones, Emily Estefan, Patti Austin, Bo Pittman, Sandy Pittman, Nicole Ross, Nicole Richie, Quincy Bähler, Anika and Sydney Poitier, Samantha Rollins, Mario Burrell, and Lukas William Ornish. God bless all the deep roots and fruits of my loving family.

A number of people from the publishing and writing communities were crucial in bringing this project to fruition: the late Swifty Lazar, who got the ball rolling; my agent at William Morris, Joni Evans; my editor and referee at Doubleday, Gerald "Bix" Howard; and an earlier collaborator who had the talent to create a blueprint for this book. Patricia Mulcahy was there both at the beginning as an editor and at the end as a warm, sensitive, and focused collaborator. I'd also like to extend thanks to Steve Rubin and Suzanne Herz at Doubleday for their enthusiastic support. I have to acknowledge my close friend, the late Alex Haley, who insisted on being the writer for my story up until his last days. I would also like to thank my loving daughter, Jolie Jones, my sister-in-law, Gloria Jones, and my "baby sister," Oprah Winfrey, for their unstinting support and help in keeping this manuscript and my life in perspective. And I can't forget "Squirt"—you know who you are—for selflessly assisting me with the original proposal. I couldn't have done it without all of you. I'd also like to thank my surrogate family, Jaime and Toni Camil and their family, for graciously putting me up and putting up with me in their home while I was working on this project.

Nor could I have managed this book without the support of my loving and loyal staff. At home I'd like to thank Ana Jaco, Maria Bonilla, Martha Bonilla, Yaasmyn Fula, Ronnie Williams, Glenn Fuentes, Joe Rivera, Anthony Randle, Michael Davis, George Frank, Sandra Coria, Reymundo Arellano, Chickie Armour, Nancy Mehajian, Meredith, Renee VandeSande, and Yanci Lopez. At the executive offices: Debborah Foreman—my right hand and Rock of Ages—and Michele Whitney-Morrison. At Quincy Jones Music Publishing: Judith "the Mighty Myrtle" Bright, who could run the Pentagon if she had to, Karen Lamberton, Charles McCullough, and Kimani Callender. At the Quincy Jones Media Group: Joel Simon, Jill Tanner, and Zenaida Torres. At Qwest: Josie Aiello, Ernestine Anderson, Maya Angelou, Patti Austin, Tevin Campbell, Dori Cayin, Ray Charles, the John and Hamilton Clayton Orchestra, Andre and Sandra Crouch, Michael Fredo, Siedah Garrett, Savion Glover, Herbie Hancock, Hiroshima, Lena Horne, James Ingram, Milt Jackson, the late Carmen McRae, New Order, St. Gian, Tate Vega, Keith Washington, Ernie Watts, Mark Weiner, the Winans, the Youth Asylum, Andy and Tommy Hilfiger, Carol Davis, Barry Hankerson, Andre Fischer, Lorraine Spurge, Larry Davis, Don Eason, Fabian Duvernay, Denise Williams, Marcia Johnson, Stacy Turner, Steve Stevenson, Evette Fergerson, Darnell Gamble, Victor Guardia, Cynthia Montes, Pat Shanks, and Stacy Barnes. At the Listen Up! Foundation: co-founder Courtney Ross Holst, V.P. Lisette Derouaux, Shawn Amos, Clarence Avant, Marilyn Bergman, Judith Bright, Amy Brown, Willie Brown, Kathy Buskin, Anne Marie Burke, Bob Butt, Juanita Bryant, Naomi Campbell, Dr. Iva Carruthers, Dale Chihuly, Joyce Deep, Robert De Niro, Joel Dreyfuss, Clint Eastwood, Gloria Estefan, Toni Fay, Jane Fonda, B. Keith Fulton, Sharon Gelman, Leslie Kirschenbaum, Michelle Kydd, Louise Miti, Joe Morello, Diane Moss, Dr. Dean Ornish, Richard Parsons, Jim Pitofsky, Arnold Robinson, Anthony Robbins, Michele Romero, Attalah Shabazz, Russell Simmons, Marge Tabakian, Rosemary Tomich, Kiko Washington, Cornel West, and Oprah Winfrey. At the Global Health Organization: Dr. Gary Blick. At "Squash It!" at Harvard: Dr. Jay Winston. At America's Promise: Colin Powell. At AMER-I-CAN: Jim Brown. At Univision: Jerry and Marge Perenchio. At the Davis Company: Marvin and Barbara Davis and family. At the Ross Institute: Courtney Ross Holst and Anders Holst. At *Vibe* and *Spin:* Bob Miller, everyone at Freeman and Spogli, Gil Rogin, John Rollins, Alan Light, Emil Wilbekin, Kenard Gibbs, Keith Clinkscales, George Pitts, Danyel Smith, Scott Poulson-Bryant, Dana Sacher, Jeanine Triolo, Karla Radford, Anne Welch, Rob Kenner, Matt Pressman, Len Burnett, Fred Jackson, Jeffrey Byrnes, Mimi Valdes, Ryan Jones, Robin Gibson, Kathleen Guthrie, Onnalee Outman, Brendan Amyot, Chan Shu, Bonz Malone, Kevin Powell, and Gary Koepke. At NUE TV: Dennis Brownlee, Alfred Liggins, Richard Roberts at Goldman, Sachs, Robert Townsend, Leo Hindery, and David Falk. At XM Radio: Hugh Pinero, Lee Abrams, and David Logan. At the Tribune Broadcasting Company: John Madigan and Dennis Fitzsimmons. At Qwest Broadcasting: Dan Berkery, Madelyn Bono, Don Cornelius, Willie Davis, Geraldo Rivera, and Sonia Salzman. For the cast and crew of *The Fresh Prince of Bel Air:* Warren Littlefield and the late Brandon Tartikoff, for trust and a jump-start; Andy and Susan Borowitz, Benny Medina and Jeff Pollack, Winifred Hervey, Debbie Allen, Gary Miller, Cheryl Gard, Werner Walian, Mara Lopez, Jeff Melman, Ellen Gittlesohn, Shelley Jensen, Will Smith, James Avery, Tatyana Ali, Janet Hubert-Whitten, Daphne Maxwell Reid, Alfonso Ribeiro, Karyn Parsons, Joseph Marcell, Ross Elliot Bagley, QDIII. For the cast and crew of *MAD TV:* David Salzman, Jerry Gottlieb, Rita Katsotis, Dick Blasucci, Steven Haft, Scott Sites, David Grossman, Bruce Leddy, John Tracy, Amanda Bearse, W. Fax Bahr and Adam Small, Lauren Dombrowski, Devon Shepard, Scott King, Michael Hitchcock, Bryan Adams, Bruce McCoy, Jennifer Joyce, J. J. Philbin, Michael Koman, Xavier Cook, Steven Cragg, Nicole Sullivan, Debra Wilson, Phil LaMarr, Artie Lange, David Herman, Mary Sheer, Bryan Callen, Orlando Jones, Michael McDonald, Mo Collins, Will Sasso, Alex Bornstein, Pat Kilbane, Aries Spears, Chris Hogan, Lisa Kushell, Andrew Bowen, Nelson Ascencio, and Christian Duguay. For the cast and crew of *In the House:* Winifred Hervey, Bob Burris, Michael Ware, Gary Harwick, Werner Walian, Sean O'Brien, Debbie Allen, L.L. Cool J, Maia Campbell, Jeffrey Wood, Lisa Arrindell Anderson, Alfonso Ribeiro, Kim Wayans, James Widdoes, Gil Junger, Asaad Kelada, John Tracy, and QDIII. At Africana.com: Kwame Anthony Appiah, Henry Louis Gates, Jr., Harry Lasker, Wole Soyinka, Marty Payson, Elizabeth Cardiff, Karen C.C. Dalton, Terry Lasker, Peter T. Glenshaw, Jack McKeown, Frank Pearl. For the crew building my dream house: Jerry Allison, Sarah Cardoza, Tom Fo, George Pepper, Joey Goldfarb, Trisha Wilson, and George Aldridge. For the recording engineers: Tommy Vicari, Humberto Gatica, Phil Macy, Phil Schier, Francis Buckley, Brad Sundberg, Mick Gazauski, Bones Howe, Gerhard Lehner, Al Schmidt, Phil Ramone, and Bruce Swedien.

I'd like to thank my inestimable colleagues Bernie Beiser, Lydia Plotkin, Amy McGrane, Don Passman, Gregg Harrison, Helen Stotler, Irwin Barnett, Elliott Brown, Jay Rakow, Gary Sommerstein, Bob Finklestein, the late Milton Rudin, and Arnold Robinson of Rogers and Cowan. And of course I have to express my gratitude to my doctors, without whom we wouldn't be here to tell the tale: Keith Black, Elsie Giorgi, Marshall Grode, Milton Heifetz, Richard Gold, Morrie Lazarus, Robert Landau, Joe Sugarman, Larry Norton, Bill Wright, Dean Ornish, Richard Lee, David Kipper, Arnie Klein, Gary Gitnick, Russell Jackson, Stanley Vogel, and Mark Helm and the ladies in his office: Suzanne, Rebecca, and Karen. Thanks to gifted sculptress Artis Lane for convincing me to let her capture me while I still "had it."

To my esteemed colleagues at the AOL-Time Warner family, thanks for your encouragement, support, and great team spirit over the years: Merv Adelson, Kent Alterman, Keith Altman, Dave Altshul, David Auerbach, Les Bider, Ed Blier, Richard Bressler, Kathy Buskin, Steve Case, Gordon Crawford, Tony Dowdello, Fred Dressler, Toni Fay, Richard Fox, Eric Frankel, Derek Johnson, Jamie Kellner, Jim Kelly, Bruce Kirton, Gary LeMel, Gerry Levin, Don Logan, Barry Meyer, Linda Moran, Jim Paratore, Richard Parsons, Norm Pearlstine, and Nancy Friday, Bob Pitman, Phil Quartararo, Sandy Reisenbach, Dan Romanelli, Bob Shea, Beverly Sills, Russ Thyret, Ted Turner, and at *Essence*, Ed Lewis and Clarence Smith. At HBO, Chris Albrecht and Colin Callender. I would also like to extend my regards to my former partner, David Salzman, and to his wife, Sonia, and children, Daniel, Adam, and Andrea, whom I will always adore.

When I started this project, they told me I couldn't fit all the events and blessed encounters of sixty-eight years into one book: they were right. We tried over and over again, but on the page it somehow diluted the dignity of my many cherished friendships. Please forgive me, each and every beloved friend I may not have mentioned here. With each passing day I value my lifelong associations more deeply. With God's grace, there will be further volumes in which to express my love and deep appreciation of every one of you.

Though the writing of the book has brought me cathartic joy, it has also brought great pain, including bottomless regret at having lost so many of my musical heroes and comrades-in-arms over the years. I'll name them now to bear witness to the tremendous contributions they made not only to my life, but also to the culture of this country, and of the world:

Tommy Adams	Big Maybelle
Cannonball Adderly	Sharon Blackman
Nat Adderly	Bumps Blackwell
Willard Alexander	Eubie Blake
Steve Allen	Art Blakey
John Alonzo	Brook Benton
Harold Arlen	Ashley Boone
Louis Armstrong	Richard Boone
Harry Arnold	Nadia Boulanger
Hal Ashby	Cheyenne Brando
Arthur Ashe	Simon Brehm
Gordon Austin	Lloyd Bridges
Mrs. Ayres	Richard Brooks
Pearl Bailey	Clifford Brown
Nicole Barclay	Ron Brown
Pascal Barclay	Milt Buckner
Bunny Bardoch	Johnny Burke
George Barnes	Dave Burns
Ellis Bartee	Jaki Byard
Count Basie	Don Byas
Mario Bausa	Billy Byers
Paul Beaver	Sammy Cahn
Michael Bennett	Cab Calloway
Brook Benton	Bunny Campbell
Skeeter Best	Vince Cannon

Piero Cariaggi

Harry Carney

Betty Carter

Paul Chambers

Kenny Clarke

James Cleveland

Arnett Cobb

Richard Cohen

Al Cohn

Nat King Cole

Earl Coleman

Honi Coles

Peter Collinson

John Coltrane

Willis Conover

Parker Cook

Sam Cooke

Ennis Cosby

Don Costa

Xavier Cougat

Jimmy "Old Gal" Crawford

Frankie Crocker

Maurice Cullaz

Tadd Dameron

Bobby Darin

Eddie Lockjaw Davis

Miles Davis

Sammy Davis, Jr.

Walter Davis

Elaine and Willem
    DeKooning

Vinicius De Moraes

Jacques Demy

Oscar Dennard

Dorothy Donegan

Kenny Dorham

Jimmy Dorsey

Tommy Dorsey

George Duvivier

Easy E

Billy Eckstine

Harry "Sweets" Edison

Roy Eldridge

Duke Ellington

Mercer Ellington

Mama Cass Elliot

Don Elliott

Nesuhi Ertegun

Gil Evans

Percy Faith

Peter Faith

Addison Farmer

Art Farmer

Jane Feather

Leonard Feather

Victor Feldman

Ella Fitzgerald

Pops Foster

Charlie Fowlkes

Redd Foxx

Gerald Frank

Floyd Franklin

Neil Friel

Eric Gale

Erroll Garner

Milt Garred

Marvin Gaye

Joe Gershenson

Stan Getz

Astrud Gilberto

Dizzy Gillespie

Bernie Glow

Roberto Goizueta

Babs Gonzalves

Dexter Gordon

Joe Gordon

Conrad Gozzo

Cary Grant

Earl Grant

Stéphane Grappelli

Johnny Green

Milt Green

William Green

Freddy Greenwell

Wardell Grey

Gigi Gryce

Sydney Guilaroff

Lars Gullin

Manos Hajidakis

Alex Haley

Jack Haley, Jr.

Jimmy Hamilton

John Hammond

Gladys Hampton

Charles Hansen

Laurence Harvey

Donny Hathaway

Coleman Hawkins

Erskine Hawkins

Tubby Hayes

Dick Hazard

Jimi Hendrix

Sam Herman

Woody Herman

Al Hibbler

Billy Higgins

Milt Hinton

Johnny Hodges

Billie Holiday

Major Holley

Marvin Holtzman

John Lee Hooker

Traft Hubert

John Hubley

Lurlene Hunter

Michael Hutchence

Milt Jackson

Quentin Jackson

Eddie Jefferson

Antonio Carlos Jobim

Egil Johansen

Billy Johnson

Budd Johnson

Debbie Johnson

Gus Johnson

Lenny Johnson

Osie Johnson

Roy Johnson

Eddie Jones

Jimmy Jones

Jo Jones (Kansas City)

Jonah Jones

Philly Joe Jones

Thad Jones

Louis Jordan

Connie Kay

Wynton Kelly

Carolyn and John Kennedy,
  Jr.

John Fitzgerald Kennedy

Robert Kennedy

Porter Kilbert

Martin Luther King, Jr.

Winfield King

Rahsaan Roland Kirk

Manny Klein

Howard Koch

Irwin Kostal

Stanley Kramer

Gene Krupa

Herb Lance

Joe Layton

Bruce Lee

Jack Lemmon

John Lennon

Lou Levy

John Lewis

Mel Lewis

Arthur Liman

Carl-Eric Lindgren

Harold Lipton

Melba Liston

Pete Long

Harry Lookofsky

Joe Lorris

Jacques Lowe

William Makel

Louis Malle

Henry Mancini

Shelly Manne

Stan Margolies

Walter Matthau

Les McCann

Linda McCartney

Van McCoy

Gary McFarland

Howard McGhee

Steve McQueen

Carmen McRae

Greg McRitchie

Butch Miller

Charles Mingus

Charlie Minor

Billy Mitchell

Thelonious Monk

Matt Monroe

Monk Montgomery

Wes Montgomery

Hal Mooney

Lee Morgan

Akio Morita

Gerry Mulligan

Moon Mullins

Jimmy Mundy

Tats Nagashima

Phineas Newborn

Anthony Newley

Alfred Newman

Harold Nicholas

Harry Nicolausson

Jack Noren

Jimmy Nottingham

Carroll O'Connor

Chico O'Farrell

Jacqueline Onassis

Seymour Osterwall

Chan Parker

Charlie Parker

Sonny Parker

Jaco Pastorius

Cecil Payne

Nick Perito

Tony Perkins

Ake Persson

Oscar Pettiford

John Phillips

Astor Piazzola

Jacqueline Picasso

Nat Pierce

Al Pierre

Major Pigford

Bobby Plater

King Pleasure

Pony Poindexter

Jeff Porcaro

Dennis Potter

Adam Clayton Powell, Jr.

Bud Powell

Chano Pozo

Milt Price

Vincent Price

Russell Procope

Arthur Prysock

Tito Puente

Paul Quinichette

Anthony Quinn

Don Redman

Elise Regina

Frank Rehak

Buddy Rich

Marty Rich

Johnny Richards

Jerome Richardson

Nelson Riddle

Minnie Riperton

Harold Robbins

Jerome Robbins

Jake Robles

Frank Rosolino

Steve Ross

Jimmy Rowles

Ernie Royal

Marshall Royal

Bob Russell

Preston Sandiford

Walter Scharf

Bobby Scott

Hazel Scott

Ronnie Scott

Joe Seneca

Betty Shabazz

Tupac Shakur

Charlie Shavers

Arnold Shaw

Sahib Shihab

Leo Shuken

Lester Sill

Sterling Silliphant

George T. Simon

Andy Simpkins

Zoot Sims

Frank Sinatra

Moneta Sleet

Lucien Smith

Mary Smith

Willie "the Lion" Smith

Sherman Sneed

Les Spann

Marshall Stearns

Sonny Stitt

Billy Strayhorn

Jules Styne

Arne Sucksdorff

Isaac Sutton

Tommy Tedesco

Richard Tee

Sonny Terry

Leon Thomas

Sonny Til

Mel Tormé

George Tremblay

Stanley Turrentine

Sarah Vaughan

Gianni Versace

Boris Vian

Heitor Villa-Lobos

Leroy Vinnegar

Joe Viola

Frank Waldron

George Wallington

Frank Walton

Dinah Washington

Tiffany Washington

John Wasserman

Julius Watkins

Roscoe Weathers

Chick Webb

Ben Webster

Warren Weibe

Bob Wells

Frank Wells

Josh White

Ernie Wilkins

Cootie Williams

Irene Williams

Joe Williams

Mary Lou Williams

Chuck Willis

Stanley Wilson

Kai Winding

Britt Woodman

Sam Woodyard

Marvin Worth

Malcolm X

Tokugen Yamamoto

Cecil Young

There's no music to orchestrate here, only solo voices rising up to form a collective tapestry—the voice of a people and the voices of the many, like the cast of the current Broadway show *Blast,* whose work moved me to tears. I salute the young artists and producers and shapers of the destiny who'll be solidifying their own contributions in years to come. The world they live in is very different from the one I was born into in 1933 on Chicago's South Side, but I long to help them realize that to know where you're going, you have to understand where you've come from: reach back to the riches of your heritage, and carry it forward with you as you face the future. With that knowledge, there are no obstacles—spiritual, cultural, or artistic—that can't be overcome. It's been said that the pain you hear in John Coltrane's saxophone is no different from the field hollers from times of slavery, and from Africa and Cuba and Brazil. The sacred space between pain and joy is the ultimate source for my musical expression and for my life's work: Just listen.

Discography

Key: PD-Producer, CD-Conductor, CP-Composer, AR-Arranger,
MS-Music Supervisor, TRPT-Trumpet, VO-Vocal, P-Piano

Adderley, Cannonball
Julian "Cannonball" Adderley; 1955, EmArcy: MG-36043 (CD; CP; AR)

Alpert, Herb
You Smile, the Song Begins; 1974, A & M: 3620 (AR)

Anderson, Ernestine
"After the Lights Go Down"/"Hurry, Hurry"; 1962, Mercury: 71960 (PD)

Anthony, Ray
Standards; 1954, Capitol: T663 (AR)

Armstrong, Louis
Louis; 1964, Mercury: MG-61081 (AR)

Arnold, Harry

Harry Arnold + Big Band + Quincy Jones = Jazz!; 1958, Metronome: MLP-15010 (CD; CP; AR)

Austin, Patti

Every Home Should Have One; 1981, Qwest: QWS-3591 (PD; AR)

Patti Austin; 1984, Qwest: 1-23974 (PD)

Baker, LaVern

"Game of Love"/"Jim Dandy Got Married," "Learning to Love"/"Substitute," "Humpty Dumpty Heart"/"Love Me Right"; 1957, Atlantic: 1136, 1150, 1176 (45s) (CD; AR)

Barclay, Eddie

Et Voilà; 1957, Barclay: 82.138 (AR)

Twilight Time; 1960, Barclay: SR-60167 (CP; AR)

Bennett, Tony

The Movie Song Album; 1966, Columbia: CS-9272 (CD; CP; AR)

Benson, George

Give Me the Night; 1980, Qwest: HS-3453 (PD; AR)

Benton, Brook, a.k.a. Benjamin Peay

"Can I Help It"/"The Kentuckian"; 1955, Okeh: (45 RPM) (AR)

There Goes That Song Again; 1961, Mercury: MG-20673 (CD; AR)

Big Maybelle

"Whole Lot-ta Shakin' Goin' On"/"The Other Night," "Such a Cutie"/"Ocean of Tears"; 1955, Okeh: (78 RPM, EPs) 7060/7066 (CD; AR)

Brothers Johnson

Look Out for #1; 1976, A & M: SP-4567 (CD; CP; AR)

Right on Time; 1977, A & M: SP-4644 (CD; CP; AR)

Blam; 1978, A & M: SP-4685 (PD; AR; CP)

Light Up the Night; 1980, A & M: SP-3716 (PD; AR; VO)

Brown, Clifford/ Farmer, Art
Stockholm Sweetnin'; 1953, Metronome: MLP-15020 (CD; CP; AR)

Brown, Clifford/ A. Farmer, Sw. A-Str
Stockholm Sweetnin'; 1953, Metronome: MEP18 & 19 (10") (CD; CP; AR)

Brown, Ray
Harold Robbins Presents Music from The Adventurers; 1970, Symbolic: SYS-9000 (PD; AR)

Cardinals
"Sunshine," "Near You"/"One Love"; 1956, Atlantic: (78 RPM EPs, 1126) (AR)

Carol, Lily Ann
"Oh No!"/"So Used to You," "Ooh Poppa Doo"/"Everybody"; 1956, Mercury: (45 RPM)/70958X45 (CD; AR)

Carroll, David
Happy Feet; 1964, Mercury: SR-60846 (PD)

Carroll, Diahann
Diahann Carroll Sings Harold Arlen's Songs; 1956, Victor: LPM-1467 (CD; AR)

Carter, Betty
Meet Betty Carter and Ray Bryant; 1955, Epic: LN-3202 (CD; AR)

Charles, Ray
The Great Ray Charles; 1956, Atlantic: SD-1259 (CP; AR)

The Genius of Ray Charles; 1959, Atlantic: 1312 (AR)

Genius + Soul = Jazz; 1960, Impulse: A-2 (AR)

A Message from the People; 1972, Tangerine: ABCX-755/TRC (CD; AR)

Cleveland, Jimmy

Introducing Jimmy Cleveland and His All-Stars; 1955, EmArcy: MG-36066 (CD; CP; AR)

Clovers

"Shakin'," "I-I-I Love You," "So Young," "Pretty, Pretty Eyes," "Baby, Darling";
1957, Atlantic: EP (AR)

Count Basie

Basie—One More Time; 1958, Roulette: SR-52024 (CP; AR)

Basie-Eckstine, Inc.; 1959, Roulette: SR-52029 (AR)

String Along with Basie; 1959, Roulette: R-52051 (CP; AR)

Li'l Ol' Groovemaker . . . . . Basie!; 1963, Verve: V6-8549 (CD; CP; AR)

This Time by Basie: Hits of the '50s and '60s; 1963, Reprise: R-6070 (CD; AR)

Davis, Sammy/Count Basie

Our Shining Hour; 1964, Verve: V6-8605 (CD; AR)

Davis, (Wild) Bill Trio

"Belle of the Ball," "Syncopated Clock," "Serenade to Benny"; 1955, Okeh (CP; AR)

Double Six of Paris

The Double Six Meet Quincy Jones; 1960, Columbia (Foreign): FPX188 (CD; CP; AR)

Eckstine, Billy

Mr. B. in Paris with the Bobby Tucker Orchestra; 1957, Barclay (PD; CD; CO-AR)

Billy Eckstine and Quincy Jones at Basin Street East; 1961, Mercury: SR-60674 (PD; AR)

Don't Worry 'Bout Me; 1962, Mercury: MG-20736 (PD)

The Golden Hits of Billy Eckstine; 1963, Mercury: SR-60796 (PD)

The Modern Sounds of Mr. B.; 1964, Mercury: SR-60916 (PD)

Elliott, Don

A Musical Offering by Don Elliott; 1955, ABC-Paramount: ABC-106 (CD; AR)

Farmer, Art

A. Farmer Septet Plays Arrangements of G. Gryce and Q. Jones; 1953, Prestige: P-7031 (CP; AR; P)

Work of Art; 1953, Prestige: PrLP-162 (10") (CP; AR; P)

Last Night When We Were Young; 1957, ABC Paramount: ABC-200 (CD; AR)

Farnon, Robert

The Sensuous Strings of Robert Farnon; Philips: PHM-200-038 (PD)

Captain from Castile; 1964, Philips: PHM-200-098 (PD)

Fitzgerald, Ella

Ella and Basie; 1963, Verve: MGV-4061 (CD; AR)

Franklin, Aretha

Hey Now Hey (The Other Side of the Sky); 1972, Atlantic: SD-7265 (PD; CD; AR)

"Master of Eyes"; 1973, Atlantic: 2941 (PD; CD; AR)

Gibbs, Terry

Terry Gibbs Plays Jewish Melodies in Jazztime; 1963, Mercury: MG-20812 (PD)

Gillespie, Dizzy

Afro; 1954, Norgran: MG N-1003 (TRPT)

Diz Big Band; 1954, Verve: MGV-8178 (EP) (TRPT)

Dizzy Gillespie: World Statesman; 1956, Norgran: MG N-1084 (CP; AR; TRPT)

Dizzy in Greece; 1956, Verve: MGV-8017 (CP; AR; TRPT)

Dizzy on the French Riviera; 1962, Philips: PHM-200-048 (PD)

New Wave; 1962, Philips: PHM-200-070 (PD)

Gordon, Joe

Introducing Joe Gordon; 1954, EmArcy: MG-26046 (10") (CP; AR)

Gore, Lesley

I'll Cry If I Want To; 1963, Mercury: MG-20805 (PD)

Boys, Boys, Boys; 1964, Mercury: MG-20901 (PD)

Girl Talk; 1964, Mercury: MG-20943 (PD)

California Nights; 1967, Mercury: MG-61120 (PD)

Love Me by Name; 1976, A & M: SP-4564 (PD; CD; AR; KB; VO)

Gryce, Gigi

"Jazz Time Paris" Vol. 10; 1953, Vogue: LD173 (AR; CP; TRPT; P)

Hamlisch, Marvin

"If You Hadn't Left Me (Crying)"/"One"; 1976, A & M: 1775-S (45 RPM) (PD; CD; AR)

Hampton, Lionel

"Kingfish"/"Don't Flee the Scene Salty"; 1951, M.G.M.: 11227 (78 RPM) (CP; AR; TRPT)

Hathaway, Donny

Come Back, Charleston Blues (Soundtrack); 1972, Atco: SD-7010 (CP; MS)

Hendricks, Jon

"Flyin' Home"/"Happy Feet," "Cloud Burst"; 1955, Decca: EP (AR)

Hodeir, Andre

Jazz et Jazz; 1963, Philips: PHS 600-073 (TRPT)

Horn, Shirley

Shirley Horn with Horn; 1963, Mercury: MG-20835 (PD; CD; AR)

"For Love of Ivy"; 1968, ABC: 11108 (45 RPM) (PD; CP; CD)

"If You Want Love (Main Theme from Film *A Dandy in Aspic)*"/"The Spell You Spin"; 1968, Bell: B-727 (45 RPM) (CD; CP; AR)

Horne, Lena

The Lady and Her Music—Live on Broadway; 1981, Qwest: 2QW-3597 (PD)

Hunter, Lurlene

Lonesome Gal; 1955, RCA Victor: LPM-1151 (AR; CD)

Ingram, James

It's Your Night; 1983, Qwest: 1-23970 (PD; CP; AR; P; VO)

Never Felt So Good; 1986, Qwest: 1-25424 (PD)

Jackie and Roy

Bits and Pieces; 1957, ABC Paramount: ABC-163 (CD; AR)

Jackson, Michael

Off the Wall; 1979, Epic: FE-35745 (PD; AR)

E.T. The Extra-Terrestrial (Soundtrack); 1982, MCA: MCA-70000 (PD)

Thriller; 1982, Epic: QE-38112 (PD; CP; AR)

Bad; 1987, Epic: OE-40600 (PD; AR)

Jackson, Milt

Plenty, Plenty Soul; 1957, Atlantic: 1269 (CP; AR)

The Ballad Artistry of Milt Jackson; 1959, Atlantic: SD-1342 (CD; CP; AR)

Jacquet, Illinois

Illinois Jacquet Flies Again; 1959, Roulette: 97272 (CP; AR)

Jacquet, Russell

"They Tried"/"Port of Rico"; 1953, Network (AR; VO; TRPT)

Jo, Damita

This One's for Me; 1964, Mercury: MG-20818 (PD; CD)

Johnson, J. J.

Man and Boy (Soundtrack); 1971, Sussex: SXSB-7011 (PD; MS)

Jones Boys

The Jones Boys; 1956, Period: SPL-1210 (CP; AR; FLH)

Jones, Quincy

Lullaby of Birdland; 1955, RCA Victor: LPM-1146 (CD; AR)

The Giants of Jazz; 1955, Columbia: CL-1970 (CD; CP; AR)

This Is How I Feel About Jazz; 1956, ABC Paramount: ABC-149 (CP; AR)

Go West, Man; 1957, ABC-Paramount: ABC-186 (PD)

The Birth of a Band; 1959, Mercury: MG-20444 (CP; AR)

The Great Wide World of Quincy Jones; 1959, Mercury: SR-60221 (CD)

I Dig Dancers; 1960, Mercury: SR-60612 (CD; CP; AR)

Around the World; 1961, Mercury: PPS-6014 (CD; CP; AR)

Newport '61; 1961, Mercury: SR-60653 (CD; CP; AR)

The Boy in the Tree (Soundtrack); 1961, Mercury-Sweden: EP-60338 (EP) (CD; CP; AR)

The Great Wide World of Quincy Jones—Live (in Zurich)!; 1961, Mercury: 195J-32 (CD; AR)

The Quintessence; 1961, Impulse: A-11 (CD; CP; AR)

Big Band Bossa Nova; 1962, Mercury: MG-20751 (CD; CP; AR; PD)

Quincy Jones Plays the Hip Hits; 1963, Mercury: SR-60799 (CD; AR)

Golden Boy; 1964, Mercury: MG-20938 (CD; CP; AR)

I Had a Ball; 1964, Mercury: MG-21022 (PD; AR)

Quincy Jones Explores the Music of Henry Mancini; 1964, Mercury: MG-20863 (CD; AR)

The Pawnbroker (Soundtrack); 1964, Mercury: SR-61011 (PD; CD; CP; AR)

Mirage (Soundtrack); 1965, Mercury: MG-21025 (CD; CP; AR)

Quincy Plays for Pussycats; 1965, Mercury: MG-21050 (CD; AR)

Quincy's Got a Brand-New Bag; 1965, Mercury: MG-21063 (PD; CD; AR)

The Slender Thread (Soundtrack); 1966, Mercury: MG-21070 (CD; CP)

Walk, Don't Run (Soundtrack); 1966, Mainstream: S-6080 (CD; CP)

Enter Laughing (Soundtrack); 1967, Liberty: LOM-16004 (CD; CP)

In Cold Blood (Soundtrack); 1967, Colgems: COM-107 (CD; CP)

In the Heat of the Night (Soundtrack); 1967, United Artist: UAL-4160 (CD; CP)

The Deadly Affair (Soundtrack); 1967, Verve: V-8679-ST (CD; CP)

For Love of Ivy (Soundtrack); 1968, ABC: ABCS-OC-7 (CD; CP)

Bob & Carol & Ted & Alice (Soundtrack); 1969, Bell: 1200 (PD; CD; AR; CP)

John and Mary (Soundtrack); 1969, A & M: SP-4230 (PD; CP; CD)

MacKenna's Gold (Soundtrack); 1969, RCA Victor: LSP-4096 (PD; CD; CP; AR)

The Italian Job (Soundtrack); 1969, Paramount: PAS-5007 (CD; CP)

The Lost Man (Soundtrack); 1969, Uni: 73060 (PD; CP)

Walking in Space; 1969, A & M: SP-3023 (CD; AR)

Cactus Flower (Soundtrack); 1970, Bell: 1201 (PD; CD; CP; AR)

Gula Matari; 1970, A & M: SP-3030 (CP; AR; CD)

They Call Me Mister Tibbs! (Soundtrack); 1970, United Artist: UAS-5241 (PD; CD; CP)

Dollars (Soundtrack); 1971, Reprise: MS-2051 (PD; CD; CP; AR)

Smackwater Jack; 1971, A & M: SP-3037 (PD; CD; CP; AR; VO)

The Hot Rock (Soundtrack); 1972, Prophesy: SD-6055 (PD; CD; CP; AR)

You've Got It Bad, Girl; 1972, A & M: SP-3041 (PD; CD; CP; AR; VO)

Body Heat; 1974, A & M: SP-3617 (PD; CD; CP; AR; VO)

Mellow Madness; 1975, A & M: SP-4526 (PD; CD; CP; AR; KB; TRPT; VO)

I Heard That; 1976, A & M: SP-3705 (PD; CD; CP; AR; KB; VO; TR; PT)

Roots; 1977, A & M: SP-4626 (PD; CP; AR; CD)

Sounds . . . and Stuff Like That; 1978, A & M: SP-4685 (PD; CP; AR)

The Wiz (Soundtrack); 1978, MCA: MCA2-14000 (PD; CD; CP; AR; AD; MS; KB)

Live at the Budokan; 1981, A & M: AMP-28045 (PD; CD; CP; AR; KB)

The Dude; 1981, A & M: SP-3721 (PD; CP; AR; VO)

The Birth of a Band—Vol. 2; 1984, Mercury: 195J-30 (CP; AR)

The Color Purple (Soundtrack); 1985, Qwest: 25389–1 (PD; CD; CP; AR)

Back on the Block; 1989, Qwest: 26020–1 (PD; CD; CP; AR; VO)

Q's Jook Joint; 1995, Qwest: 45875 (PD; CD; CP; AR)

Q, Live in Paris Circa 1960; 1996, Qwest: 46190; (PD; CD; CP; AR)

From Q with Love; 1999; Qwest: 46490; (PD; CD; CP; AR)

The Quincy Jones–Sammy Nestico Orchestra: Basie and Beyond; 2000, Qwest: 47792 (PD; CD; CP; AR)

Q: The Music of Quincy Jones; 2001, Rhino: R2-74363 (PD; CD; CP; AR; TRPT; VO; P)

Jones, Quincy / Farmer, Art

Quincy Jones and Swedish-American All-Stars; 1953, Prestige: PrLP-172 (10") (CD; CP; AR)

Jordan, Louis

Somebody Up There Digs Me (Greatest Hits); 1956, Mercury: MG-20242 (PD; AR)

King Pleasure

"Don't Get Scared"/"Funk Junction," "I'm Gone"/"You're Crying"; 1954, Prestige: 913/908 (78 RPM), EPs (CD; CP; AR)

Krupa, Gene / Feat. R. Eldridge, A. O'Day

Drummer Man; 1956, Verve: MGV-2008 (AR)

Laws, Hubert

Hubert Laws—Quincy Jones—Chick Corea; 1985, CBS Masterworks: M-39858 (CD)

Lee, Peggy

Blues Cross Country; 1961, Capitol: ST-1671 (CD; CP; AR)

If You Go; 1961, Capitol: T-1630 (CD; AR)

Little Richard

It's Real; 1961, Mercury: MG-20656 (CD; CP; AR)

Lookofsky, Harry

Miracle in Strings; 1954, Epic: EG-7081 (EP) (CP; AR)

The Hash Brown Sounds; 1962, Philips: PHM-200-018 (PD)

Mardigan, Art

The Jazz School; 1954, Wing: MGW-60002 (CP; AR)

Mays, Willie / The Treniers

"Say Hey (The Willie Mays Song)"; 1954, Okeh: 9066 (78 RPM) (CD; AR)

McRae, Carmen

Carmen / Carmen McRae; 1972, Temponic: TB-29562 (CD; AR)

Merrill, Helen

Helen Merrill with Clifford Brown; 1954, EmArcy: MG-36006 (AR)

You've Got a Date with the Blues; 1959, Metrojazz: E-1010 (CD)

Moody, James

James Moody's Mood for Blues; 1954, Prestige: PrLP-198 (CP; AR)

Moody's Mood; 1954, Prestige: PrLP-192 (10") (CP; AR)

Wail, Moody, Wail; 1955, Prestige: LP-7036 (CP; AR)

Newman, Joe

Happy Cats; 1957, Coral: 57121 (AR)

Joe Newman Quintet at Count Basie's; 1961, Mercury: SR-60696 (PD)

Pettiford, Oscar

The New Oscar Pettiford Sextet; 1951, Debut: DLP-8 (CP; AR)

Basically Duke; 1954, Bethlehem: BCP-1019 (10") (AR)

Oscar Pettiford; 1954, Bethlehem: BCP-1003 (10") (CP; AR)

The Finest of Oscar Pettiford; 1955, Bethlehem: BCP-6007 (CP; AR)

Quinichette, Paul

Moods; 1954, EmArcy: MG-36003 (CP; AR)

Renaud, Henri

"Meet Quincy Jones," "Dillon," "Wallington Special"; 1954, Vogue: EP (AR)

Richmond, June

"Sleep"/"Everybody's Doin' It," "Devil and Deep Blue Sea"/ "Between the Devil and the Deep Blue Sea"; 1957, Barclay: EP-70105 (EP) (CD; AR)

Ross, Annie

"Jackie"/"The Song Is You"; 1953, Metronome: B-647 (78 RPM) (P)

Rufus and Chaka

Masterjam; 1979, MCA: MCA-5103 (PD; CP)

Sachs, Aaron

Aaron Sachs Quintette; 1954, Bethlehem: BCP-1008 (10") (CD; CP; AR)

Salvador, Henri

"Blouse du Dentiste"/"Moi J'Prefere La Marche à Pied," "Trompette D'Occasion"/"Tous Les Saints"; 1958, Barclay: 70141 (EP) (CD; AR)

Sandmen, The / Feat. Brook Benton

"Ooh, Fool Enough to Love You," "Bring Me Love"; 1955, Okeh (AR)

Scott, Bobby

Joyful Noises; 1962, Mercury: MG-20701 (PD)

When the Feeling Hits You; 1962, Mercury: SR-60767 (PD)

Simon, Paul

There Goes Rhymin' Simon; 1973, CBS: 32280 (AR)

Sinatra, Frank

It Might as Well Be Swing; 1964, Reprise: FS-1012 (CD; AR)

L.A. Is My Lady; 1984, Qwest: 25145-1 (PD; CD; CP; AR)

Sinatra, Frank / C. Basie / Q. Jones

Sinatra at the Sands; 1966, Reprise: 1019 (CD; AR)

Starr, Ringo

Sentimental Journey; 1970, Apple: SW-3365 (AR)

Stitt, Sonny

Sonny Stitt Plays Arrangements from the Pen of Quincy Jones; 1955, Roost: LP-2204 (CD; CP; AR)

Summer, Donna

Donna Summer; 1982, Geffen: GHS-2005 (PD; CP; AR; VO)

Taylor, Billy

My Fair Lady Loves Jazz; 1957, ABC Paramount: ABC-177 (CD; AR)

Terry, Clark

Clark Terry; 1955, EmArcy: MG-36007 (CP; AR)

Clark Terry in the P.M.; 1955, EmArcy: EP-1-6108 (EP) (CP; AR)

Three Sounds

The Three Sounds Play Jazz on Broadway; 1962, Mercury: MG-20776 (PD)

Some Like It Modern; 1963, Mercury: SR-60839 (PD)

Live at the Living Room; 1964, Mercury: MG-20921 (PD)

Treniers, The / Feat. Willie Mays

"Go! Go! Go!"; 1954, Okeh: 9127 (CD; AR)

USA for Africa

"We Are the World" (12" Single); 1985, Columbia: US2-05179 (PD; CD; AR)

Various Artists

Save the Children; 1973, Motown: M800-R2 (CD; AR)

The Official Music of the 23rd Olympiad in Los Angeles; 1984, Columbia: BJS-39322 (PD; CP; AR)

Vaughan, Sarah

Vaughan and Violins; 1958, Mercury: MG-20370 (CD; CP; AR)

You're Mine, You; 1962, Roulette: R-52082 (CD; AR)

Sassy Swings the Tivoli; 1963, Mercury: SR-60831 (CD)

Vaughan with Voices; 1963, Mercury: MG-20882 (PD)

Viva! Vaughan; 1964, Mercury: MG-20941 (PD)

Sarah Vaughan Sings the Mancini Songbook; 1965, Mercury: MG-21009 (PD)

Wallington, George

George Wallington Showcase; 1954, Blue Note: BLP-5045 (10") (CP; AR)

Washington, Dinah

For Those in Love; 1955, Mercury: MG-36011 (CD; AR)

The Swingin' Miss D; 1956, EmArcy: MG-36104 (CP; AR)

I Wanna Be Loved; 1961, Mercury: MG-20729 (CD; CP; AR)

Tears and Laughter; 1961, Mercury: SR-60661 (PD; CD)

This Is My Story (Vol. 1 & 2); 1962, Mercury: SR-60765/60769 (CD)

The Queen and Quincy; 1965, Mercury: SR-60928 (CD)

Watkins, Julius

French Horns for My Lady; 1960, Philips: PHM-200-001 (PD; AR)

Watts, Ernie

Chariots of Fire; 1981, Qwest: QWS-3637 (PD; CP; AR)

White, Josh

At Town Hall; 1961, Mercury: MG-20672 (PD)

Williams, Andy

Under Paris Skies; 1960, Cadence: CLP-3047 (CD; AR)

Willis, Chuck

"Come on Home," "I Can Tell," "Give Me a Break," "Search My Heart," "Ring-Ding-Doo"; 1955, Okeh: 4-7062 (45 RPM, EP) (CD; AR)

Yuro, Timi

The Amazing Timi Yuro; 1964, Wing: MG-20963 (PD)

Filmography

Film scores

1961 — *The Boy in the Tree* (Sweden)
Prod. and Dir. by Arne Sucksdorff; starring Tomas Bolme, Birgitta
Pettersson

1965 — *The Pawnbroker* (Allied Artists)
[Academy Award Nomination for Best Actor]
Dir. by Sidney Lumet; produced by Ely A. Landau, Philip Langner,
Roger Lewis, Herbert R. Steinman; starring Rod Steiger,
Geraldine Fitzgerald, Brock Peters, Juano Hernandez, Raymond
St. Jacques

1965 — *Mirage* (Universal Pictures)
Dir. by Edward Dmytryk; produced by Harry Keller; starring Gregory
Peck, Jack Weston, Walter Matthau, Diane Baker
(Title Song: "Mirage," music by Quincy Jones, lyrics by Bob Russell)

1965 — *The Slender Thread* (Paramount Pictures)
Dir. by Sydney Pollack (his first film); produced by Stephen Alexander;
starring Sidney Poitier, Anne Bancroft, Telly Savalas

1966 —— *Walk, Don't Run* (Columbia Pictures)

Dir. by Charles Walters; produced by Sol C. Siegel; starring Cary Grant, Samantha Egger, Jim Hutton

(Main Theme Song: "Happy Feet," and Songs: "Stay with Me" and "Copycat," music by Quincy Jones, lyrics by Peggy Lee)

1967 —— *The Deadly Affair* (Columbia Pictures)

Dir. and prod. by Sidney Lumet; starring James Mason, Simone Signoret, Maximilian Schell, Lynn Redgrave

(Main Theme Song: "Who Needs Forever," music by Quincy Jones, lyrics by Howard Greenfield; performed by Astrud Gilberto)

1967 —— *Enter Laughing* (Columbia Pictures)

Dir. by Carl Reiner; produced by Carl Reiner and Joseph Stein; starring Jose Ferrer, Shelley Winters, Rob Reiner, Elaine May

(Title Song: "Enter Laughing," music by Quincy Jones, lyrics by Mack David; performed by Mel Carter)

† 1967 —— *Banning* (Universal Pictures)

[Academy Award Nomination for Best Song]

Dir. by Ron Winston; produced by Richard Berg; starring Robert Wagner, Jill St. John, Gene Hackman, Anjanette Comer

(Main Theme Song: "The Eyes of Love [Carol's Theme]," music by Quincy Jones, lyrics by Bob Russell; performed by Gil Bernal)

* 1967 —— *In the Heat of the Night* (United Artists)

[Received 5 Academy Awards for Best Picture, Best Actor, Best Adapted Screenplay, Film Editing, Sound; Nominated for Best Director, Sound Effects]

Dir. by Norman Jewison; produced by Walter Mirisch; starring Sidney Poitier, Rod Steiger, Scott Wilson

(Title Song: "In the Heat of the Night," performed by Ray Charles, and Songs: "It Sure Is Groovy," performed by Gil Bernal; "Bow Legged Polly," performed by Glen Campbell; "Foul Owl," performed by Boomer & Travis: music by Quincy Jones, lyrics by Alan and Marilyn Bergman)

---

†–Denotes Academy Award nomination. Please reference awards/nominations list

*–Denotes Grammy Award/nomination. Please reference awards/nominations list

† 1967 — *In Cold Blood* (Columbia Pictures)

[4 Academy Award Nominations, including Best Original Score, Best Director, Cinematography, Best Adapted Screenplay]

Dir. and prod. by Richard Brooks; starring Robert Blake, Scott Wilson, John Forsythe

1968 — *The Split* (MGM/United Artists)

Dir. by Gordon Flemyng; produced by Robert Chartoff and Irwin Winkler; starring Jim Brown, Diahann Carroll, Gene Hackman, Ernest Borgnine, Julie Harris, Warren Oates, Jack Klugman, Donald Sutherland, James Whitmore

1968 — *The Hell with Heroes* (Universal Pictures)

Dir. by Joseph Sargent; produced by Stanley Chase; starring Rod Taylor, Claudia Cardinale

† 1968 — *For Love of Ivy* (Cinerama)

[Academy Award Nomination for Title Song]

Dir. by Daniel Mann; produced by Edgar Scherick and Jay Weston; starring Sidney Poitier, Abbey Lincoln, Beau Bridges, Carroll O'Connor

(Title Song: "For Love of Ivy," music by Quincy Jones, lyrics by Bob Russell; performed by Shirley Horn; "You Put It on Me" and "B. B. Jones," music by Quincy Jones, lyrics by Maya Angelou; performed by B. B. King)

1968 — *A Dandy in Aspic* (Columbia Pictures)

Dir. by Laurence Harvey/Anthony Mann; produced by Anthony Mann; starring Laurence Harvey, Mia Farrow, Tom Courtenay, Peter Cook, Harry Andrews, Per Oscarsson

(Main Theme Song: "If You Want Love," music by Quincy Jones, lyrics by Ernie Sheldon; performed by Shirley Horn; Song: "The Spell You Spin, The Web You Weave," music by Quincy Jones and Dave Grusin, lyrics by Bob Russell; performed by Shirley Horn)

*² 1969 — *MacKenna's Gold* (Columbia Pictures)

Dir. by J. Lee Thompson; produced by Carl Foreman and Dimitri Tiomkin;

---

†–Denotes Academy Award nomination. Please reference awards/nominations list

†–Denotes Academy Award nominations. Please reference awards/nominations list

*²–Denotes Grammy Award/nomination. Please reference awards/nominations list

starring Gregory Peck, Omar Sharif, Edward G. Robinson, Eli Wallach, Telly Savalas, Julie Newmar, Burgess Meredith

(Main Theme Song: "Ole Turkey Buzzard," music by Quincy Jones, lyrics by Freddie Douglas, aka Carl Foreman, Spanish lyrics by Pupi Hurtado; performed in English and Spanish by José Feliciano)

1969 — *The Italian Job* (Paramount Pictures)

Dir. by Peter Collinson; produced by Michael Deeley and Robert Porter; starring Michael Caine, Noël Coward, Benny Hill

(Main Theme Song: "On Days Like These"; performed by Matt Monro; and Songs "Get a Bloomin' Move On" and "It's Caper Time," music by Quincy Jones, lyrics by Don Black; performed by The Self-Preservation Society)

* 1969 — *The Lost Man* (Universal Pictures)

Dir. by Robert Alan Arthur; produced by Edward Muhl and Melville Tucker; starring Sidney Poitier, Joanna Shimkus, Paul Winfield

(Song: "He Says He Loves Me," words and music written by Quincy Jones, Dick Cooper, Diane Hildebrand, Ernie Shelby; performed by Ernestine Anderson and The Pree Sisters) [Author's Note: My goddaughter's mom and dad fell in love during the making of this picture.]

1969 — *Bob & Carol & Ted & Alice* (Columbia Pictures)

Dir. by Paul Mazursky; produced by Larry Tucker; starring Natalie Wood, Robert Culp, Elliott Gould, Dyan Cannon

(Adaptation of "Handel's Hallelujah Chorus" and "Handel's Messiah, Part 3"; with vocals by Sarah Vaughan; Arrangement of Song: "What the World Needs Now," music by Burt Bacharach, lyrics by Hal David; performed by Merilee Rush)

‡ 1969 — *Cactus Flower* (Columbia Pictures)

Dir. by Gene Saks; produced by M. J. Frankovich; starring Goldie Hawn (received Academy Award), Ingrid Bergman, Walter Matthau, Jack Weston

(Main Theme Song: "The Time for Love Is Anytime," music by Quincy Jones, lyrics by Cynthia Weil; performed by Sarah Vaughan)

---

*–Denotes Grammy award/nomination. Please reference awards/nominations list

‡–Denotes Golden Globe nomination. Please reference awards/nominations list

1969 — *John and Mary* (Twentieth Century Fox)
Dir. by Peter Yates; produced by Ben Kadish; starring Dustin Hoffman, Mia Farrow, Tyne Daly
(Composed score, Song: "Lost in Space," words and music by Jeff Bridges)

1970 — *Last of the Mobile Hot-Shots* (Warner Bros.)
Dir. and prod. by Sidney Lumet; starring James Coburn, Lynn Redgrave, Robert Hooks
(Based on the Tennessee Williams play *The Seven Descents of Myrtle*)

1970 — *The Out-of-Towners* (Paramount Pictures)
Dir. by Arthur Hiller; produced by Paul Nathan; starring Jack Lemmon, Sandy Dennis, Billy Dee Williams

* 1970 — *They Call Me Mister Tibbs!* (United Artists)
Dir. by Gordon Douglas; produced by Herbert Hirschman; starring Sidney Poitier, Martin Landau, Ed Asner, Juano Hernandez

1971 — *The Anderson Tapes* (Columbia Pictures)
Dir. by Sidney Lumet; produced by Robert Wortman; starring Sean Connery, Dyan Cannon, Alan King

1971 — *Brother John* (Columbia Pictures)
Dir. by James Goldstone; produced by Joel Glickman; starring Sidney Poitier, Will Geer, Paul Winfield, Beverly Todd
("Children of Summer," music by Quincy Jones, lyrics by Ernie Sheldon; performed by Clydie King)

*³ 1971 — *$* (Columbia Pictures)
Dir. by Richard Brooks; produced by M. J. Frankovich; starring Warren Beatty, Goldie Hawn
("Money Is" and "Do It to It," music and lyrics by Quincy Jones; performed by Little Richard)

1972 — *The New Centurions* (Columbia Pictures)
Dir. by Richard Fleischer; produced by Robert Charthoff and Irwin Winkler; starring George C. Scott, Stacy Keach, Jane Alexander, Scott Wilson, Rosalind Cash

---

*–Denotes Grammy award/nomination. Please reference awards/nominations list

*³–Denotes Grammy award/nomination. Please reference awards/nominations list

1972 — *The Hot Rock* (Twentieth Century Fox)
Dir. by Peter Yates; produced by Hal Landers and Bobby Roberts;
starring Robert Redford, George Segal, Zero Mostel
(Score featuring musicians: Clark Terry, Jerome Richardson, Frank
Rosolino, Gerry Mulligan, Grady Tate, Ray Brown, Tommy Tedesco and
Victor Feldman)

‡ 1972 — *The Getaway* (First Artists/Warner Bros.)
Dir. by Sam Peckinpah; produced by Mitchell Brower and David Foster;
starring Steve McQueen, Ali MacGraw

1972 — *Come Back Charleston Blue* (Warner Bros.)
Dir. by Mark Warren; produced by Samuel Goldwyn, Jr.; starring Godfrey
Cambridge, Raymond St. Jacques
(Music Supervisor for Donny Hathaway's first score; Title Song: "Come
Back Charleston Blue," music by Donny Hathaway, lyrics by Quincy Jones,
Al Cleveland; performed by Donny Hathaway and Valerie Simpson)

1972 — *Man and Boy* (Levitt-Pickman)
Dir. by E. W. Swackhamer; produced by Marvin Miller; starring Bill
Cosby, Gloria Foster
(Music Supervisor for J. J. Johnson's first score; Main Theme Song:
"Better Days," music by J. J. Johnson, lyrics by Bill Withers; performed by
Bill Withers)

† *2 1978 — *The Wiz* (Universal Pictures)
[5 Academy Award Nominations: Best Adapted Score, Art Direction,
Cinematography, Costume Design, Set Decoration]
Dir. by Sidney Lumet; produced by Rob Cohen; starring Diana Ross,
Michael Jackson, Nipsey Russell, Ted Ross, Richard Pryor, Lena Horne
(Songs from the Broadway Show *The Wiz,* words and music by Charlie
Smalls; additional songs for the film: "Is This What Feeling Gets" and
"Can I Go On?," music by Quincy Jones, lyrics by Nick Ashford, Valerie
Simpson; performed by Diana Ross; "A Brand New Day" words and

---

‡–Denotes Golden Globe nomination. Please reference awards/nominations list

*2–Denotes Grammy award/nomination. Please reference awards/nominations list

†–Denotes Academy Award nomination. Please reference awards/nominations list

music by Luther Vandross; "Green, Red and Gold—Emerald City
sequence," music by Quincy Jones, lyrics by Charlie Small; performed by
principals and entire cast)

‡ †³   1985   —   *The Color Purple* (Warner Bros.)

Dir. by Steven Spielberg; produced by Quincy Jones, Kathleen Kennedy,
Frank Marshall, and Steven Spielberg; starring Danny Glover, Whoopi
Goldberg, Oprah Winfrey, Margaret Avery, Willard Pugh, Adolph Ceasar
[First film as coproducer with Steven Spielberg, Kathleen Kennedy, Frank
Marshall. Film received 11 Academy Award Nominations: Best Picture, Best
Actress, 2 Best Supporting Actress, Best Adapted Screenplay, Art Direction,
Cinematography, Best Score, Costume Design, Makeup, Original Song]
(Song: "Miss Celie's Blues (Sister)," music by Quincy Jones and Rod
Temperton, lyrics by Quincy Jones, Rod Temperton, Lionel Richie;
performed by Tata Vega)

1990   —   *Listen Up: The Lives of Quincy Jones* (Warner Bros.)

Dir. by Ellen Weissbrod; prod. by Courtney Sale Ross; starring Ray
Charles, Frank Sinatra (last feature film appearance), Miles Davis, Ella
Fitzgerald, Oprah Winfrey, Steven Spielberg, Michael Jackson, Barbra
Streisand, among others

Television scores and themes

1966   —   *Hey, Landlord* series (NBC)

Prod. by Lee Rich; Writers: Garry Marshall, James Brooks, Ed
Weinberger, Jerry Belson; starring Will Hutchins and Sandy Baron
(Composed theme and scored series)

1967   —   *Split Second to an Epitaph* (NBC—Movie of the Week)

Dir. by Leonard Horn; Produced by Frank Price and Paul Mason;
starring Raymond Burr, Don Mitchell, Barbara Anderson, Geraldine
Brooks, Don Galloway

---

‡–Denotes Golden Globe nomination. Please reference awards/nominations list

†³–Denotes Academy Award nomination. Please reference awards/nominations list

(Composed score. Note: This movie of the week was the pilot for the
Ironside series.)

1967 — *Ironside* series (NBC)

Dir. by James Goldstone; Prod. by Collier Young; starring Raymond Burr,
Don Mitchell, Barbara Anderson, Geraldine Brooks, Don Galloway
(Composed theme, scored series, actor in one episode)

1968 — *Jigsaw* (Movie of the Week)

Dir. by James Goldstone; Prod. by Ranald MacDougall; starring Harry
Guardino, Bradford Dillman
(Composed score)

1968 — *The Counterfeit Killer* (Movie of the Week)

Dir. by Joseph Lejtes; starring Jack Lord, Shirley Knight, Jack Weston
(Composed score)

‡‡ 1969 — *The Bill Cosby Show* series (NBC)

Dir. by Luther James, Coby Ruskin; Prod. by Marvin Miller; starring
Bill Cosby
Aired 56 episodes
(Composed theme song "Hikky Burr," cowritten with Bill Cosby, scored series)

1971 — *The NBC Mystery Movie* series (NBC)
(Composed theme)

1972 — *The New Bill Cosby Show* (CBS)

Prod. by George Schlatter; Dir. by Donald McKayle, Marc Warren
1 hour variety show starring Bill Cosby and Lola Falana, Groucho Marx,
Peter Sellers, Lily Tomlin, Richard Pryor, Harry Belafonte, Sidney Poitier,
Ray Charles, among others
Aired 27 episodes
(Musical director, Conductor, Skit Actor, Composed theme song "Chump
Change" co-written with Bill Cosby)

1972 — *Killer by Night* (CBS—Movie of the Week)

Dir. by Bernard McEveety; Prod. by Fred Engel; starring Robert Wagner,
Diane Baker
(Composed score)

---

‡‡–Denotes Emmy award/nomination. Please reference awards/nominations list

1972 — *Sanford and Son* series (NBC)

Dir. by Norman Abbott, Peter Baldwin, and others; Prod. by Bud Yorkin, Norman Lear; starring Redd Foxx, Demond Wilson

(Composed theme song)

1973 — *Duke Ellington . . . We Love You Madly* tribute (CBS)

Dir. by Stan Harris; Various guests included Duke Ellington, Count Basie, Billy Eckstine, Aretha Franklin, Sarah Vaughan and Peggy Lee, Ray Charles, Sammy Davis, Jr., Chicago, Roberta Flack, The James Cleveland Choir, Joe Williams, Paula Kelly (Note: Coproducer with Bud Yorkin; First position as Coexecutive Producer of a television show with Bud Yorkin and Norman Lear; Conductor, Performer)

‡‡ * 1977 — *Roots* miniseries—Episode 1 (ABC)

[Emmy Award for Outstanding Achievement in Music Composition for a Series, Or a Single Program of a Series]

Dir. by David Greene; Prod. by Stan Margulies, David L. Wolper; Cowinner Gerald Fried for dramatic underscore; Written by Alex Haley; starring LeVar Burton, Louis Gossett, Jr., Leslie Uggams, Ben Vereen ("African Theme: Oluwa (Many Rains Ago)," musical adaptation and lyrics by Quincy Jones and Caiphus Semenya; performed by Letta M'bulu; additional score composed with Gerald Fried)

1986 — *The Oprah Winfrey Show* (ABC)

Hosted by Oprah Winfrey

(Cocomposed original theme song "Harpoprah" with Rod Temperton)

Animated films

1969 — *Of Men and Demons* (Paramount Pictures/Hubley Studios)

[Academy Award Nomination]

Dir. and Prod. by John Hubley; Faith Hubley

Animated by Art Babbit, Tissa David

(Composed score)

---

‡‡–Denotes Emmy award/nomination. Please reference awards/nominations list

*–Denotes Grammy award/nomination. Please reference awards/nominations list

1970 —   *Eggs* (Paramount Pictures/Hubley Studios)
         [American Film Festival, Red Ribbon]
         Dir. and Prod. by John Hubley; Faith Hubley
         Animated by Tissa David
         (Composed score)

1972 —   *Dig* (Paramount Pictures/Hubley Studios)
         [CINE Golden Eagle]
         Dir. and Prod. by John Hubley; Faith Hubley
         Animated by Tissa David, John Gentilella
         (Composed score, Cowrote songs with John and Faith Hubley)

1999 —   *Fantasia 2000—Rhapsody in Blue Segment* (Walt Disney Pictures)
         Dir. by Eric Goldberg, Executive Producer Roy Edward Disney, Segment
         Producer Patricia Hicks
         Animated by Al Hirschfeld
         (Segment Host)

Music videos

QUINCY JONES ARTIST VIDEOS

1985 —   *USA for Africa*
         (Quincy Jones served as Producer and Conductor)
            "We Are the World"—performed by various artists

1990 —   *Back on the Block*
            "Don't Go for That"—performed by Siedah Garrett
            "I'll Be Good to You"—performed by Ray Charles
            "The Places You Find Love"—performed by Chaka Khan and Siedah
            Garrett
            "Secret Garden"—performed by El DeBarge, James Ingram, Al b.
            Sure, Barry White, and Siedah Garrett
            "Tomorrow"—performed by and introducing Tevin Campbell

1995 —   *Q's Jook Joint*
            "You Put a Move on My Heart"—performed by and introducing
            Tamia

"Slow Jams"—performed by Babyface, Tamia, Portrait, and Barry White

1997 — *From Q, With Love*

"I'm Yours"—performed by El DeBarge and Siedah Garrett

QUINCY JONES CAMEO APPEARANCES

1979 — "Ease On Down the Road"—with Diana Ross and Michael Jackson

1997 — *No Way Out*—Puffy Combs

"Around the World"

1997 — *Wu-Tang Forever*—Wu-Tang Clan

"Triumph"

Television appearances

1963 — *Blues for Trumpet and Koto* (Japan—Movie of the Week)

Guest appearance with Anthony George. Title song composed by Marvin Hamlisch

1965 — *The Rat Pack—St. Louis Concert*

Conducted Count Basie Orchestra for concert featuring performances by Frank Sinatra, Sammy Davis Jr., Dean Martin, and The Step Brothers; hosted by Johnny Carson

1967 — *Ironside* series (NBC)

Guest appearance—"Eat, Drink and Be Buried" episode

1990 — *Saturday Night Live* (NBC)

Guest host and musical guest

(Author's note: Show filmed and aired the same night as Nelson Mandela's release from South Africa's Robbin Island prison)

1990 — *Fresh Prince of Bel Air* series (NBC/Quincy Jones Entertainment)

Guest appearance with Little Richard—"Someday Your Prince Will Be in Effect" episode

1995 — *Mad TV* (Fox/Quincy Jones • David Salzman Entertainment)

Guest appearance

1996 — *New York Undercover* (Fox)

Guest appearance—"Kill the Noise" episode

Awards and honors

Grammy awards

National Academy of Recording Arts and Sciences

1963 — **Best Instrumental Arrangement:** "I Can't Stop Loving You" [Count Basie] (Reprise)

1969 — **Best Instrumental Jazz Performance, Large Group or Soloist with Large Group:** "Walking in Space" (A & M)

1971 — **Best Pop Instrumental Performance:** *Smackwater Jack* [album] (A & M)

1973 — **Best Instrumental Arrangement:** "Summer in the City" (A & M)

1978 — **Best Instrumental Arrangement:** "Main Title" Overture Part One; track from *The Wiz Original Soundtrack*—Quincy Jones [cowinner: Robert Freedman] (MCA)

1980 — **Best Instrumental Arrangement:** "Dinorah, Dinorah" (George Benson) [cowinner: Jerry Hey] (Warner Bros.)

1981 — **Best R&B Performance by Duo or Group with Vocal:** "The Dude"—Quincy Jones (A & M)

Best Cast Show Album: *Lena Horne: The Lady and Her Music—Live on*

Broadway—Producer Quincy Jones [various composers and lyricists] (Qwest/Warner Bros.)

Best Arrangement on an Instrumental Recording: "Velas" (A & M) Track from *The Dude*—Quincy Jones, arranger [Johnny Mandel, synthesizer and string arranger]

Best Instrumental Arrangement Accompanying Vocal: "Ai No Corrida" (A & M) Track from *The Dude* [cowinner: Jerry Hey, instrument arranger]

Producer of the Year: Best Producer 1981—Quincy Jones

1983 — **Record of the Year:** "Beat It" (Michael Jackson) (Epic/CBS)— Producer Quincy Jones [cowinner: Michael Jackson]

Album of the Year: *Thriller* (Michael Jackson) (Epic/CBS)—Producer Quincy Jones [cowinner: Michael Jackson]

Best Recording for Children: *E.T. The Extra-Terrestrial* album (MCA) Producer, Quincy Jones [cowinner: Michael Jackson, Narrator/Vocals]

Producer of the Year: Best Producer of 1983—Quincy Jones [cowinner: Michael Jackson]

1984 — **Best Arrangement of an Instrumental:** "Grace (Gymnastics Theme)"—Quincy Jones [cowinner: Jerry Lubbock] *The Official Music of the 23rd Olympiad in Los Angeles* (Columbia)

1985 — **Record of the Year:** "We Are the World"—USA for Africa (Columbia/CBS)

Best Pop Performance by a Duo or Group with Vocal: "We Are the World" (single)—USA for Africa (Columbia/CBS)

Best Music Video, Short Form: *"We Are the World"—The Video Event*— USA for Africa [cowinner: Tom Trbovich, video director]

1988 — **Trustees Award:** Special award presented to Quincy Jones—arranger, composer, producer, conductor

1990 — **Album of the Year:** *Back on the Block* (Qwest) Producer Quincy Jones

Best Rap Performance by a Duo or a Group: "Back on the Block" from *Back on the Block* (Qwest) [cowinners: Ice-T, Melle Mel, Big Daddy Kane, Kool Moe Dee, Quincy D. III]

Best Jazz Fusion Performance: "Birdland" from *Back on the Block*

Best Arrangement on an Instrumental: "Birdland" from *Back on the Block*

Best Instrumental Arrangement Accompanying Vocal(s): "The Places You Find Love" from *Back on the Block*

Producer of the Year (nonclassical): Best Producer of 1990—Quincy Jones

Grammy Living Legend Award

1993 — **Best Large Jazz Ensemble Performance:** *Miles and Quincy Live at Montreux* (Warner Bros.)

1996 — **MusiCares Person of the Year:** Special Humanitarian Award

Grammy nominations

National Academy of Recording Arts and Sciences

1960 — **Best Arrangement:** "Let the Good Times Roll" [Ray Charles] (Mercury)

Best Jazz Performance, Large Group: *The Great Wide World of Quincy Jones* (Mercury)

1961 — **Best Performance by an Orchestra for Dancing:** *I Dig Dancers* (Mercury)

1962 — **Best Performance by an Orchestra for Dancing:** *Big Band Bossa Nova* (Mercury)

Best Instrumental Arrangement: *Quintessence* (Impulse)

Best Original Jazz Composition: *Quintessence* (Impulse)

1963 — **Best Instrumental Arrangement:** "I Can't Stop Loving You" [Count Basie] (Reprise)

Best Instrumental Jazz Performance, Large Group: *Quincy Jones Plays the Hip Hits* (Mercury)

Best Performance by an Orchestra for Dancing: *Quincy Jones Plays the Hip Hits* (Mercury)

1964 — **Best Instrumental Arrangement:** "Golden Boy"—String Version (Mercury)

Best Instrumental Performance, Non-Jazz: "Golden Boy"—String Version (Mercury)

Best Instrumental Jazz Performance, Large Group or Soloist

with Large Group: *Quincy Jones Explores the Music of Henry Mancini* (Mercury)

Best Original Jazz Composition: "The Witching Hour"; track from *Golden Boy* (Mercury)

1967 — **Best Original Score Written for a Motion Picture or Television Show:** *In the Heat of the Night* (United Artists)

1969 — **Best Instrumental Jazz Performance, Large Group or Soloist with Large Group:** *Walking in Space* (A & M)

Best Original Score for a Motion Picture or Television Show: *MacKenna's Gold* (RCA)

Best Instrumental Theme: *MacKenna's Gold—Main Title* (RCA)

Best Original Score for a Motion Picture or a Television Show: *The Lost Man* (Universal)

Best Instrumental Arrangement: *Walking in Space* (A & M)

1970 — **Best Instrumental Arrangement:** *Gula Matari* (A & M)

Best Instrumental Composition: *Gula Matari* (A & M)

Best Jazz Performance, Large Group or Soloist with Large Group: *Gula Matari* (A & M)

Best Contemporary Instrumental Performance: "Soul Flower"; track from *They Call Me Mister Tibbs!* soundtrack (United Artists)

1971 — **Best Pop Instrumental Performance:** *Smackwater Jack* [album] (A & M)

1972 — **Best Original Score Written for a Motion Picture:** *$* Soundtrack (Reprise)

Best Instrumental Arrangement: "Money Runner"; track from *$* Soundtrack (Reprise)

Best Pop Instrumental by Arranger, Composer, Orchestra: "Money Runner"; track from *$* Soundtrack (Reprise)

1973 — **Best Instrumental Arrangement:** "Summer in the City" (A & M)

Best Pop Instrumental Performance: *You've Got It Bad, Girl* (A & M)

1974 — **Best Pop Instrumental Performance:** "Along Came Betty"; track from *Body Heat* (A & M)

Best Pop Vocal Performance by a Duo or Group or Chorus: *Body Heat* (A & M)

1976 — **Best Instrumental Composition:** "Midnight Soul Patrol"; single from *I Heard That* (A & M)

1977 — **Best Arrangement for Voices:** "Oh Lord, Come by Here"; track from the *Roots* soundtrack (A & M)

Best Inspirational Performance: "Oh Lord, Come by Here" [James Cleveland]; track from the *Roots* Soundtrack (A & M)

Best Instrumental Composition: "Roots Medley (Motherland, *Roots* Mural Theme)" (A & M)

1978 — **Best Instrumental Arrangement:** "Main Title" Overture Part One; track from *The Wiz Original Soundtrack*—Quincy Jones [cowinner: Robert Freedman] (MCA)

Best Instrumental Composition: "End of the Yellow Brick Road" [Nick Ashford and Valerie Simpson]; single from *The Wiz* (A & M)

Best Arrangement for Voices: "Stuff Like That;" single from *Sounds . . . and Stuff Like That* (A & M)

Producer of the Year

1979 — **Best Disco Recording:** "Don't Stop 'Til You Get Enough" [Michael Jackson]; single from *Off the Wall* (Epic)

Producer of the Year

1980 — **Best Instrumental Arrangement:** "Dinorah, Dinorah" (George Benson) [cowinner: Jerry Hey] (Warner Bros.)

Producer of the Year

1981 — **Best R&B Performance by Duo or Group with Vocal:** "The Dude"—Quincy Jones (A & M)

Best Cast Show Album: *Lena Horne: The Lady and Her Music—Live on Broadway*—Quincy Jones, producer [various composers and lyricists] (Qwest/Warner Bros.)

Best Arrangement on an Instrumental Recording: "Velas" (A & M) Track from *The Dude*—Quincy Jones, arranger [Johnny Mandel, synthesizer and string arranger]

Best Instrumental Arrangement Accompanying Vocal: "Ai No Corrida" (A & M) Track from *The Dude* [cowinner: Jerry Hey, instrument arranger]

Producer of the Year: Best Producer 1981—Quincy Jones

Album of the Year: *The Dude* (A & M)

Best Pop Instrumental Performance: "Velas"; track from *The Dude* (A & M)

1982 — **Producer of the Year**

1983 — **Record of the Year:** "Beat It" (Michael Jackson) (Epic/CBS)—
Producer Quincy Jones [cowinner: Michael Jackson]

Album of the Year: *Thriller* (Michael Jackson) (Epic/CBS)—Producer
Quincy Jones [cowinner: Michael Jackson]

Best Recording for Children: *E.T. The Extra-Terrestrial* album (MCA)
Producer, Quincy Jones [cowinner: Michael Jackson, Narrator/Vocals]

Producer of the Year: Best Producer of 1983—Quincy Jones
[cowinner: Michael Jackson]

Best R&B Instrumental Performance: "Billie Jean"—(Instrumental
version) [Michael Jackson]; track from *Thriller* (Epic)

Best New R&B Song: "P.Y.T. (Pretty Young Thing)" [Michael Jackson];
track from *Thriller* (Epic)

Producer of the Year

1984 — **Best Arrangement of an Instrumental:** "Grace (Gymnastics
Theme)"—Quincy Jones [cowinner: Jerry Lubbock] *The Official Music of
the 23rd Olympiad in Los Angeles* (Columbia)

Best R&B Song: "Yah Mo B There" [James Ingram and Michael
McDonald] (Qwest/Warner Bros.)

1985 — **Album of the Year:** *We Are the World (USA for Africa/The Album)* [various
artists] (Columbia)

Record of the Year: "We Are the World"—USA for Africa (Columbia/CBS)

Best Pop Performance by a Duo or Group with Vocal: "We Are
the World"—single USA for Africa (Columbia/CBS)

Best Music Video, Short Form: *"We Are the World"—The Video Event*
USA for Africa [cowinner: Tom Trbovich, video director]

1987 — **Album of the Year:** *Bad* [Michael Jackson] (Epic)

Producer of the Year

1988 — **Record of the Year:** "Man in the Mirror" [Michael Jackson]; single
from *Bad* (Epic)

1990 — **Best Pop Instrumental Performance:** "Setembro (Brazilian Wedding
Song)" [Quincy Jones and various artists]; track from *Back on the Block*
(Qwest/Warner Bros.)

1990 — **Album of the Year:** *Back on the Block* (Qwest) Producer Quincy Jones

Best Rap Performance by a Duo or a Group: "Back on the Block"

from *Back on the Block* (Qwest) [cowinners: Ice-T, Melle Mel, Big Daddy Kane, Kool Moe Dee, Quincy D. III]

Best Jazz Fusion Performance: "Birdland" from *Back on the Block*

Best Arrangement on an Instrumental: "Birdland" from *Back on the Block*

Best Instrumental Arrangement Accompanying Vocal(s): "The Places You Find Love" from *Back on the Block*

Producer of the Year (nonclassical): Best Producer 1990—Quincy Jones

1993 — **Best Music Video, Long Form:** *Miles and Quincy Live at Montreux* [Miles Davis and Quincy Jones] (Reprise)

Best Large Jazz Ensemble Performance: *Miles and Quincy Live at Montreux* (Warner Bros.)

1996 — **Best Instrumental Arrangement with Accompanying Vocal(s):** "Do Nothin' Till You Hear from Me" [Phil Collins]; track from *Q's Jook Joint* (Qwest/Warner Bros.)

Grammy participation certificates

National Academy of Recording Arts and Sciences

(Grammy Winning Recordings Where Quincy Jones Served as Producer/Arranger/Conductor/Composer/Vocalist/Artist)

1960 — **Best R&B Performance:** "Let the Good Times Roll" [Ray Charles] track from *The Genius of Ray Charles* (Atlantic)/*Arranger/Conductor*

1963 — **Best Performance by an Orchestra for Dancing:** *This Time by Basie! Hits of the '50s and '60s* [Count Basie] (Reprise)/*Conductor/Arranger*

1965 — **Song of the Year:** "The Shadow of Your Smile (Love Theme from *The Sandpiper)*" [Composers: Johnny Mandel and Paul Francis Webster] (Mercury)/*Producer*

Best Original Score Written for a Motion Picture or TV Show: *The Sandpiper* [Robert Armbruster/Conductor; Johnny Mandel/Composer] (Mercury)/*Producer*

1973 — **Best R&B Vocal Performance, Female:** "Master of Eyes" (Single)
[Aretha Franklin] (Atlantic)/ *Coproducer with Aretha Franklin*
Best R&B Instrumental Performance: "Q" [Brothers Johnson] track
from *Right on Time* (A & M)/ *Producer*

1979 — **Best R&B Performance, Male:** "Don't Stop 'Til You Get Enough"
(Single) [Michael Jackson] track from *Off the Wall* (Epic)/ *Producer*

1980 — **Best R&B Vocal Performance, Male:** *Give Me the Night* (Album)
[George Benson] (Qwest/Warner Bros.)/ *Producer/Arranger*
Best R&B Instrumental Performance: "Off Broadway" [George
Benson] track from *Give Me the Night* (Qwest/Warner Bros.)/ *Producer*
Best Jazz Vocal Performance, Male: "Moody's Mood" [George
Benson] track from *Give Me the Night* (Qwest/Warner Bros.)/ *Producer/Arranger*

1981 — **Best Pop Vocal Performance, Female:** *Lena Horne: The Lady and Her
Music—Live on Broadway* (Album) [Lena Horne] (Qwest/Warner Bros.)/ *Producer*
Best R&B Vocal Performance, Male: "One Hundred Ways" track
from *The Dude* [James Ingram] (A & M)/ *Producer/Artist*

1982 — **Best Pop Instrumental Performance:** "Chariots of Fire" (Theme/Dance
Version) [Ernie Watts] track from *Chariots of Fire* (Qwest/Warner Bros.)/ *Producer*

1983 — **Best Pop Vocal Performance, Male:** *Thriller* (Album) [Michael
Jackson] (Epic/CBS)/ *Producer*
Best Rock Vocal Performance, Male: "Beat It" (Single) [Michael
Jackson] track from *Thriller* (Epic/CBS)/ *Producer/Arranger*
Best R&B Vocal Performance, Male: "Billie Jean" (Single) [Michael
Jackson] track from *Thriller* (Epic/CBS)/ *Producer*
Best New R&B Song: "Billie Jean" [Songwriter: Michael Jackson] track
from *Thriller* (Epic/CBS)/ *Producer*
Best Engineered Recording (nonclassical): *Thriller* (Michael
Jackson/Album) [Engineer: Bruce Swedien] (Epic/CBS)/ *Producer*

1984 — **Best R&B Performance by a Duo or Group with Vocal:** "Yah Mo
Be There" (Single) [James Ingram and Michael McDonald] track from
It's Your Night (Qwest/Warner Bros.)/ *Producer/Cocomposer/Arranger*
Best Video Album: *Making Michael Jackson's Thriller* [Michael Jackson]
(Vestron Music Video)/ *Producer*

1985 — **Song of the Year:** "We Are the World" [Songwriters: Michael Jackson and
Lionel Richie] track from *We Are the World* (Columbia/CBS)/ *Producer/Conductor*

1987 — **Best Engineered Recording (nonclassical):** *Bad* (Michael Jackson/Album) [Engineer: Bruce Swedien and Humberto Gatica] (Epic)/*Producer*

1990 — **Best R&B Performance by a Duo or Group with Vocal:** "I'll Be Good to You" (Single) [Ray Charles and Chaka Khan] track from *Back on the Block* (Qwest/Warner Bros.)/*Producer/Arranger/Artist*

Best Engineered Recording (nonclassical): *Back on the Block* (Quincy Jones/Album) [Engineer: Bruce Swedien] (Qwest/Warner Bros.)/*Producer/Artist*

1992 — **Best Contemporary Soul Gospel Album:** *Handel's Messiah—A Soulful Celebration* (Album) [Various Artists]; Mervyn Warren, Producer (Reprise)/*Conductor*

American music award

1986 — **Special Recognition,** *We Are the World*

MTV video award

1984 — **Special Recognition** (First Annual MTV Video Awards Ceremony)

Academy awards

Academy of Motion Picture Arts and Sciences

(Note: In 1971, Quincy Jones conducted the orchestra for the 43rd Annual Academy Awards Telecast. In 1996, Quincy Jones served as Executive Producer and coproducer with David Salzman of the 68th Annual Academy Awards Telecast)

1995 — **Jean Hersholt Humanitarian Award**
Awarded to an individual in the motion picture industry whose humanitarian efforts have brought credit to the industry; presented by Oprah Winfrey during the 67th Annual Academy Awards Telecast.

Academy award nominations

Academy of Motion Picture Arts and Sciences

1967 — **Best Original Music Score,** from the film *In Cold Blood*
Best Original Song, "The Eyes of Love" from the film *Banning*
(Music by Quincy Jones, lyrics by Bob Russell, performed by Gil Bernal)

1968 — **Best Original Song,** "For Love of Ivy" from the film *For Love of Ivy* (Music by Quincy Jones, lyrics by Bob Russell, performed by Shirley Horn)

1978 — **Best Adaptation Score,** from the film *The Wiz*

1985 — **Best Original Song,** "Miss Celie's Blues (Sister)" from the film *The Color Purple* (Music by Quincy Jones and Rod Temperton, lyrics by Quincy Jones, Rod Temperton, Lionel Richie, performed by Tata Vega)
Best Original Score, from the film *The Color Purple*
Best Picture (producer), *The Color Purple*

Golden Globe nominations

Hollywood Foreign Press Association

1970 — **Best Original Song, Motion Picture,** "The Time for Love Is Anytime" from the film *Cactus Flower*

1973 — **Best Original Score, Motion Picture,** *The Getaway*

1986 — **Best Original Score, Motion Picture,** *The Color Purple*

Emmy awards

Academy of Television Arts and Sciences

1977 — **Outstanding Achievement in Music Composition for a Series, or a Single Program of a Series,** *Roots—Episode I* (ABC) (cowinner, Gerald Fried)

Emmy nominations

Academy of Television Arts and Sciences

1970 — **Outstanding Achievement in Music Composition,** *The Bill Cosby Show* (NBC)

1977 — **Outstanding Achievement in Music Composition for a Series, or a Single Program of a Series,** *Roots—Episode I* (ABC)

1995 — **Outstanding Informational Series,** *The History of Rock 'n' Roll: Punk* (WBN)

1996 — **Outstanding Variety, Music, or Comedy Special,** *The 68th Annual Academy Awards* (ABC)

Image Awards

National Association for the Advancement of Colored People

1972 — **Big Band Album of the Year,** *Smackwater Jack*

1974 — **Best Jazz Artist,** *You've Got It Bad, Girl*

1975 — **Best Jazz Artist,** *Body Heat*

1980 — **Best Musical Score, Motion Picture,** *The Wiz*

1981 — **Best Jazz Album,** *The Dude*

1981 — **Album of the Year,** *Off the Wall*

1983 — **Producer of the Decade**

1986 — **Best Motion Picture,** *The Color Purple*

1990 — **Best Album,** *Back on the Block*

1990 — **Hall of Fame Award**

1996 — **Outstanding Jazz Artist,** *Q's Jook Joint*

1996 — **Entertainer of the Year**

1997 — **Outstanding Jazz Artist,** *Q Live in Paris—Circa 1960*

2000 — **Outstanding Jazz Artist,** *From Q, with Love*

Ebony Music Awards

Johnson Publications

1976 — **Ebony Music Award—Best Composer, Jazz,** *I Heard That*

1976 — **Ebony Music Award—Musician of the Year, Jazz,** *I Heard That*

1976 — **Ebony Music Award—Big Band Leader, Jazz,** *I Heard That*

1976 — **Ebony Music Award—Arranger of the Year, Jazz,** *I Heard That*

1978 — **Ebony American Black Achievement Award for Music,** *Sounds . . . and Stuff Like That*

1982 — **Ebony American Black Achievement Award for Music,** *Thriller*

1985 — **Ebony American Black Achievement Award for Music,** *We Are the World*

1990 — **Ebony American Black Achievement Lifetime Achievement Award**

Recording industry awards

1964 — **Edison Music Award,** MPVI—Edison Foundation (International music award from the Netherlands, equivalent to Grammy Awards)

1970 — **Edison Music Award,** MPVI—Edison Foundation

1972 — **Edison Music Award,** MPVI—Edison Foundation

1978 — **Edison Music Award,** MPVI—Edison Foundation

1979 — **Edison Music Award,** MPVI—Edison Foundation

1979 — **Most Popular Arranger/Producer/Composer,** Black College Radio Convention

1982 — **Golden Note Award,** American Society of Composers, Authors, and Publishers

1988 — **Luminary Award,** American Society of Young Musicians

1989 — **Lifetime Achievement Award,** National Academy of Songwriters

1990 — **Heritage Award for Lifetime Achievement,** *Soul Train* Music Awards

1990 — **Nesuhi Ertegun—Cartier Man of the Year,** MIDEM (International Music Market Conference Held Annually in Cannes, France)

1994 — **Golden Score Award,** American Society of Music Arrangers and
Composers

1997 — **Vanguard Award for Lifetime Achievement,** National Academy of
Songwriters

1999 — **Henry Mancini Lifetime Achievement Award,** American Society of
Composers, Authors, and Publishers

Film/television industry awards

1993 — **Trumpet "Living Legend" Award,** Turner Broadcasting Systems (For
Outstanding Career Achievement)

1999 — **Oscar Micheaux Award,** Producers Guild of America (For
Outstanding Career Achievement as a Film and Television Producer)

Newspaper/magazine awards

1960 — **"Best New Arranger of the Year,"** International Critics' Poll, *Down
Beat* Magazine

1960 — **"Best New Big Band of the Year,"** International Critics' Poll, *Down
Beat* Magazine

1960 — **Reader's Choice Award, Jazz Arranger/Composer of the Year,** *Jet*
Magazine-Johnson Publications

1971 — **"Arranger of the Year,"** Readers' Poll, *Down Beat* Magazine

1972 — **"Arranger of the Year,"** Readers' Poll, *Down Beat* Magazine

1972 — **Trendsetters Award,** *Billboard* Magazine

1973 — **"Arranger of the Year,"** Readers' Poll, *Down Beat* Magazine

1974 — **"Arranger of the Year,"** Readers' Poll, *Down Beat* Magazine

1980 — **Producer of the Year,** *Billboard* Magazine

1982 — **Trendsetters Award,** *Billboard* Magazine

1983 — **Producer of the Year,** *Billboard* Magazine

1983 — **Jazz Composer/Songwriter of the Year,** *Playboy* Music Award

1984 — **Jazz Composer/Songwriter of the Year,** *Playboy* Music Award

1985 — **Jazz Composer/Songwriter of the Year,** *Playboy* Music Award

1986 — **Jazz Composer/Songwriter of the Year,** *Playboy* Music Award

1986 — **Record Producer of the Year,** *Playboy* Music Award

1990 — **Entrepreneur of the Year,** *USA Today*/Financial News Network

1994 — **Essence Lifetime Achievement Award,** *Essence* Magazine

1996 — **Entertainer of the Year,** *Weekly Variety*

1999 — **Influential Jazz Artist of the Century,** *Time* Magazine (Shared
Honor with Louis Armstrong, Duke Ellington, Charlie Parker, Miles
Davis, and Wynton Marsalis)

Humanitarian awards

(In 1991, Quincy Jones and Courtney Ross Founded *The Quincy Jones
Listen Up Foundation* to Address and Confront the State of Emergency
That Currently Threatens the Future of the World's Youth; and to
Recognize and Encourage Youth Who Are Achievers and
Support Them in Their Pursuits)

1971 — **Distinguished Service Award,** The Brotherhood Crusade (In
Recognition of Commitment to Addressing the Socioeconomic Needs
and Concerns of America's Urban Communities)

1982 — **Spirit of Life—"Man of the Year,"** City of Hope (In Recognition of
Ongoing Support on Behalf of Cancer Research)

1984 — **American Academy of Achievement Golden Plate** (In Recognition
of Personal and Professional Accomplishments Which Established Him
as a Role Model for America's Youth)

1986 — **Humanitarian of the Year,** T. J. Martell Foundation (In Recognition of
Ongoing Support on Behalf of Leukemia, Cancer, and AIDS Research)

1986 — **Norma Zarky Humanitarian Crystal Award,** Women in Film (In
Recognition for Ongoing Charitable Contributions and Efforts to
Improve the Human Condition)

1986 — **Whitney Young, Jr., Award,** National Urban League (In Recognition for Commitment to Enabling African Americans to Secure Economic Self-Reliance, Parity, Power, and Civil Rights)

1991 — **Angel Award,** Center for Population Options (In Recognition of Commitment to Encouraging Normal, Positive, and Healthy Attitudes Toward Sexual Relationships Between Young Adults)

1992 — **Spirit of Liberty Award,** People for the American Way (In Recognition of Work to Promote and Defend the Values of the American Way of Life: Fairness, Equality, Tolerance, Opportunity, and Individual Liberty)

1993 — **Entertainment and Community Achievement Award,** NAACP Legal Defense Fund (In Recognition of Commitment to Ensuring the Legal Civil Rights of All Individuals)

1994 — **Distinguished Service Award,** Northside Center for Child Development (In Recognition of Commitment to Addressing the Socioeconomic Concerns of Urban Families)

1994 — **Equal Opportunity Award,** National Urban League (In Recognition for Commitment to Enabling African Americans to Secure Economic Self-Reliance and Equal Opportunity)

1995 — **Horatio Alger Award,** Horatio Alger Association (In Recognition of Accomplishments and Achievements Succeeded in the Face of Adversity and for Encouragement of Young People to Pursue Their Dreams with Determination and Perseverance)

1996 — **Time Warner Ambassador of Goodwill,** Time Warner Inc. (Designated Ambassador of Goodwill by Time Warner Chairman and CEO Gerald Levin)

1996 — **International Committee Award,** Intercambios Culturales (In Recognition of Work to Promote Arts Education in Third World Nations)

1996 — **1996 Honoree,** Young Audiences of America (In Recognition of Being an Advocate of Arts Education for All Children)

1996 — **Humanitarian Award,** The H.E.L.P. Group (In Recognition of Commitment to Helping Young People Fulfill Their Potential to Lead Positive, Productive, and Rewarding Lives)

1996 — **Thurgood Marshall Lifetime Achievement Award,** NAACP Legal Defense Fund (In Recognition of Lifetime Career Achievements and Commitment to Ensuring the Legal Civil Rights of All Individuals)

1996 — **Pioneer in Black Achievement Lifetime Achievement Award,**
The Brotherhood Crusade (In Recognition of Lifetime Career
Achievements and Commitment to Addressing the Socioeconomic Needs
and Concerns of America's Urban Communities)

1998 — **Spirit Award,** Children's Defense Fund (In Recognition of
Commitment to Addressing the Needs and Concerns of Children)

1999 — **Ellis Island Medal of Honor,** National Ethnic Coalition of
Organizations (In Recognition of Exemplifying Outstanding Qualities in
Both Personal and Professional Life, While Continuing to Represent the
Richness of His Heritage)

1999 — **Media Spotlight Award for Lifetime Achievement,** Amnesty
International (In Recognition for Commitment to Promoting Human
Rights and Social Consciousness Throughout the World)

1999 — **Seasons of Hope Award,** AMFAR (In Recognition for Ongoing
Commitment to AIDS Research)

2000 — **Lena Horne Legend Award,** Citizens Committee for New York
(For Outstanding Career Achievement and Commitment to
Improving the Quality of Life in New York City and Its
Neighborhoods)

Arts and humanities awards

1990 — **Honors Award,** Los Angeles Arts Council (For Outstanding Career
Achievement in the Arts)

1994 — **President's Committee on the Arts & Humanities** (Presidential
Appointment to Address the Needs and Concerns Regarding
the Nation's Commitment to Promoting the Arts and
Humanities)

2001 — **Ted Arison Award,** National Foundation for Advancement in the Arts
(In Recognition for Commitment to Promoting Arts Education)

2001 — **Inducted into the American Academy of Arts and Sciences**
(International Learned Society Composed of the World's Leading
Scientists, Scholars, Artists, Businesspeople, and Public Leaders)

City/state/country/world awards

(For Outstanding Career Achievement and Contributions to the
World's Culture)

1973 — **Citation of Excellence,** Texas House of Representatives

1973 — **Citation of Excellence,** Canadian National Exhibition

1974 — **Special Recognition,** California State Assembly

1976 — **In Special Recognition of 20th Anniversary in Music,** City of
Philadelphia, PA

1980 — **Hollywood Walk of Fame,** Hollywood, CA

1982 — **Key to the City,** Indianapolis, IN

1985 — **Centennial Hall of Honor,** State of Washington

1990 — **"Living Treasure,"** Governor's Arts Awards, State of California

1990 — **Officier de la Legion d'Honneur,** Republic of France

1990 — **Album of the Year—Jazz Fusion,** *Back on the Block,* Japan Grand Prix

1991 — **Alexander Pushkin Award,** Union of Soviet Socialist Republics

1991 — **Lifetime Achievement Award,** Rosedór de Montreux, France

1994 — **Polar Music Prize,** Royal Swedish Academy of Music (Considered the
Nobel Peace Prize of Music; Award Presented by Sweden's King Gustav)

1995 — **Rudolph Valentino Award,** Republic of Italy

1996 — **Distinguished Arts & Letters Award,** French Ministry of Culture
(Award presented by United States Ambassador to France Pamela Harrison)

1999 — **Trophee des Arts,** French Institute Alliance Francaise

2000 — **Crystal Award,** World Economic Forum—Davos, Switzerland
(Award presented by World Economic Forum Founder, Professor Klaus
Schwab)

2000 — **Key to the City of Paris,** Paris, France

2000 — **National Medal of the Humanities,** National Endowment of the
Humanities, United States of America (Award Presented by President
William Clinton)

2001 — **Commandeur de la Legion d'Honneur,** Republic of France (Only
American-Born Musician to Hold Honor; Award Presented by French
President Jacques Chirac)

2001 — **Marian Anderson Award,** City of Philadelphia

| Honorary doctorates/academic awards |

1983 — **Honorary Doctor of Arts,** Berklee College of Music

1985 — **Honorary Doctor of Arts and Letters,** Howard University

1990 — **Honorary Doctor of Philosophy,** Seattle University

1991 — **Honorary Doctor of Arts,** Wesleyan University

1991 — **Scopus Award,** Hebrew University

1992 — **Honorary Doctor of Arts,** Loyola University

1992 — **Honorary Doctor of Arts and Letters,** Brandeis University

1993 — **Honorary Doctor of Philosophy,** Clark University—Atlanta

1994 — **Legend in Leadership Award,** Emory University, Atlanta

1995 — **Honorary Doctor of Letters,** Claremont University Graduate School

1995 — **The UCLA Chancellor's Medal,** University of California—Los Angeles

1996 — **Honorary Doctor of Fine Arts,** University of Connecticut

1996 — **Magnum Opus Award for Lifetime Achievement,** USC School of Music

1996 — **Lifetime Achievement Award,** The Thelonious Monk Institute of Jazz

1996 — **Harvard Foundation Medal for Intercultural & Race Relations,** Harvard University

1997 — **Honorary Doctor of Fine Arts,** Harvard University

1997 — **Honorary Doctor of Fine Arts,** American Film Institute

1998 — **Honorary Doctor of Music,** University of Southern California

1999 — **Honorary Doctor of Fine Arts,** Tuskegee University

1999 — **Honorary Doctor of Fine Arts,** New York University

1999 — **Honorary Doctor of Fine Arts,** University of Miami

1999 — **Frederick D. Patterson Award,** United Negro College Fund

1999 — **Candle of Light Award,** Morehouse College

2000 — **Quincy Jones Professorship of African American Music,** Harvard University ($3 Million Endowment Established by AOL Time Warner, Inc.)

2000 — **W.E.B. DuBois Medal,** Harvard University

2001 — **American Academy of Sciences,** Cambridge, MA

Index

Photo Credits

Pages i, iv, v: Chuck Stewart.

INSERT 1

Page 4, top: Charles W. Taylor. *Page 7, top:* Bobby Tucker. *Page 9, top:* © Herman Leonard. *Page 9, bottom:* Chuck Stewart. *Page 9, center:* Courtesy of the Orkester Journalen Archives. *Page 11, top:* AP/Wide World Photos. *Page 11, bottom:* Jean-Pierre Leloir. *Page 12, bottom:* © Milt Hinton. *Page 14, top:* Chuck Stewart. *Page 15, top:* NARAS, © 1963. *Page 16:* Condé Nast.

INSERT 2

Page 2, center: Peter Borsari. *Page 3, top:* Courtesy of *Down Beat* magazine. *Page 3, bottom:* Sam Emerson. *Page 4, 2nd row center:* A&M Records. *Page 4, 2nd row left:* A&M Records. *Page 4, 2nd row right:* A&M Records. *Page 4, 3rd row center:* Quincy Jones Productions/Qwest Records. *Page 4, 3rd row left:* Courtesy of Epic Records. *Page 4, 3rd row right:* Quincy Jones Productions/Qwest Records. *Page 4, top left:* A&M Records. *Page 5, bottom right:* Warner Brothers. *Page 5, center left:* MGM/United Artists. *Page 5, center right:* Warner Brothers. *Page 5, top left: The Pawnbroker,* © 2001 by Paramount

Pictures. All Rights Reserved. Courtesy of Paramount Pictures. *Page 5, top right: In Cold Blood,* © 1967, renewed 1995, Pax Enterprises, Inc. All Rights Reserved. Courtesy of Columbia Pictures. *Page 5, center right:* "ROOTS," © 1977 Wolper Pictures. All Rights Reserved. *Page 5, bottom right: The Color Purple,* © 1985 Warner Bros., Inc. All Rights Reserved. *Page 5, bottom left: In the Heat of the Night,* clip and still courtesy of MGM, © 1967 The Mirisch Corporation of Delaware. All Rights Reserved. *Page 8, center:* NARAS, © 1983.

INSERT 3

Page 2, bottom: American Academy of Achievement, © 1984. Used with permission. *Page 2, top:* Carol Friedman. *Page 3, bottom:* Sam Emerson. *Page 3, top:* Harry Benson. *Page 4, bottom:* Gordon Parks. *Page 4, top:* Jason Miccolo Johnson. *Page 5, top:* Roz Levin. *Page 6:* Academy of Motion Picture Arts and Sciences. *Page 7, bottom right:* Yves Coatsaliou. *Page 8:* George Schlatter Productions. *Page 9:* © Herman Leonard. *Page 10, top:* Robert Boyer. *Page 11, bottom:* Matt Mendelsohn. *Page 12, bottom:* Bronson Photography. *Page 12, top:* Charles William Bush. Courtesy Academy of Television, Arts & Sciences. *Page 13, top:* Office of William Jefferson Clinton. *Page 15:* Albane Navizet. *Page 16:* Patrick Demarchelier.